COUNTRY BOY

COUNTRY BOY

THE ROOTS OF JOHNNY CASH

◆◆◆

Colin Edward Woodward

THE UNIVERSITY OF ARKANSAS PRESS
FAYETTEVILLE | 2022

Copyright © 2022 by The University of Arkansas Press.
All rights reserved. No part of this book should be used or reproduced in any manner without prior permission in writing from the University of Arkansas Press or as expressly permitted by law.

ISBN: 978-1-68226-208-5
eISBN: 978-1-61075-777-5

26 25 24 23 22 5 4 3 2 1

Manufactured in the United States of America

Designed by April Leidig

∞ The paper used in this publication meets the minimum requirements of the American National Standard for Permanence of Paper for Printed Library Materials Z39.48-1984.

Library of Congress Cataloging-in-Publication Data
Names: Woodward, Colin Edward, 1975– author.
Title: Country boy: the roots of Johnny Cash / Colin Woodward.
Description: Fayetteville: The University of Arkansas Press, 2022. | Includes bibliographical references and index. | Summary: "In Country Boy, Colin Woodward combines biography, social and political history, and music criticism to tell the story of Johnny Cash's time in his native Arkansas. Woodward explores how some of Cash's best songs are based on his experiences growing up in northeastern Arkansas, and he recounts that Cash often returned to his home state, where he played some of his most memorable and personal concerts" —Provided by publisher.
Identifiers: LCCN 2021055563 (print) | LCCN 2021055564 (ebook) | ISBN 9781682262085 (paperback) | ISBN 9781610757775 (ebook)
Subjects: LCSH: Cash, Johnny—Childhood and youth. | Cash, Johnny—Family. | Cash, Johnny—Travel—Arkansas. | Country musicians—United States—Biography. | Arkansas—History.
Classification: LCC ML420.C265 W65 2022 (print) | LCC ML420.C265 (ebook) | DDC 782.421642092 [B]—dc23
LC record available at https://lccn.loc.gov/2021055563
LC ebook record available at https://lccn.loc.gov/2021055564

Dedicated to
Shane Woodward (1973–2019), music lover

---

and Johnny Cash fans everywhere

CONTENTS

ACKNOWLEDGMENTS

JUST ABOUT EVERYONE loves Johnny Cash, so it is no surprise that I have encountered many fans willing to help me on my journey. First, I want to thank the folks in Little Rock. The UA-Little Rock Center for Arkansas History and Culture employed me for more than three years as an archivist. There, I discovered Cash treasures that I knew had to be shared with the world. Had I not worked there, this project never would have happened. The Center sponsored trips to Kingland, Dyess, and Cummins prison farm while I was living in Little Rock. And in 2017, UALR awarded me a G. Thomas Eisele Fellowship, which allowed me to do research in the archives for a week and attend the inaugural Johnny Cash Heritage Festival in Dyess.

In Little Rock, I also had the good fortune to receive funding from the Butler Center for Arkansas Studies. Big John Miller at the Butler Center showed me rare Cash footage courtesy of his friend Ken King. Drummer Stan James—one of the nicest people I've ever met—found great articles in Arkansas newspapers for a Cash exhibit we worked on back in 2014. Those articles were enormously helpful in my book research. Wayne Cash of Maumelle provided a direct link to Johnny Cash and also shared a terrific set of family and genealogical papers with me. I also want to thank Guy Lancaster and Lindsey Millar, both of whom have asked me to write about Cash for their publications. Stan Sadler and I have never met, but Stan has generously let me use his photographs of Cash in Cleveland County more than once. At the UALR Department of History, Jim Ross and Barclay Key provided moral support through talks on Drive-By Truckers and checking out local music. Hopefully, we will have a reunion at an Adam Faucett show at the White Water before long.

I would have been foolish to dive into all things Cash without the help of Ruth Hawkins, formerly of Arkansas State University. Ruth read a portion of the manuscript and provided invaluable feedback concerning the restoration of the Cash family house in Dyess through the efforts of the Heritage Sites Program at ASU.

David Scott Cunningham at the University of Arkansas Press made this book happen. I appreciate his guidance and patience as I struggled to get the book finished amid job changes and the worst pandemic in American history. I also want to thank everyone else at the press for their help as well as the outside readers and their valuable feedback.

Mark Stielper invited me to his home several years ago for a podcast about Cash, and we have been in touch ever since. I have benefited greatly from his friendship, guidance, and frank talk about the Man in Black. Patrick Carr was another one of my podcasting victims. Despite my lack of credentials when I spoke to him, he shared some things about Cash that I needed to understand.

Court Carney, who knows more about music than anyone I have ever met, read an entire draft of the manuscript. I took him up on his suggestion that I focus more on Cash's music, and the book is much better for it. Mark Thompson asked some important questions early on about where I was going with Cash. Mike Foley took time out of his busy schedule—including writing his own book on Cash—to read the manuscript and offer insight. I hope we can talk some Cash over coffee in France one day.

Since beginning this project ten years ago, my family has grown. I was married before I started writing about Cash, but having two daughters since then has helped me understand the country music obsession with family. The love of Sydney, Ella, and Nola has kept me rooted.

I've dedicated this book to my brother. As was true of Cash, I know what it's like to lose a brother too soon. It wasn't Dyess, but growing up, we shared a room together in a small town in a five-room house. A lot of the music I love is because of him. RIP, Shane.

COUNTRY BOY

INTRODUCTION

A Country Boy from Arkansas

No one has ever sounded quite like Johnny Cash. But there's no place quite like Arkansas either.

Johnny Cash was a country music star, an early rocker, a hillbilly concept-album maker, a folkie, and an inspiration to rock minimalists and punks. He was also a gospel singer, Americana icon, and natural storyteller. Musicians don't like being labeled. "You'll just have to call me as you see me," Cash was fond of saying. As is true of the Beatles or Bob Dylan, Cash was in his own category. Even when he didn't write his songs, which was most of the time, he had a way of turning other artists' compositions into his own. Anyone who has heard "Ring of Fire," "Cocaine Blues," or "(Ghost) Riders in the Sky" can attest to this. Cash's version of those songs—originally penned with other singers in mind—are definitive.

Johnny Cash toured the country and the world, made movies and television shows, and cut hundreds of his own songs, not to mention hundreds by other artists. But in his mind, he never really left Arkansas. Cash moved to Tennessee later in life, and he died there. But the first eighteen years of his life, all spent in Arkansas, inspired and shaped his music for the rest of his life. Johnny Cash was a true country boy.

"I think every one of them must have come in on the midnight train from nowhere," Bill Williams, Sam Phillips's publicist in Memphis, said of Cash and the rest of the men at Sun. "I mean, it was like they came from outer space."[1] Everyone, of course, comes from somewhere. Cash was born in Kingsland, a small town in Cleveland County, Arkansas, in 1932. His was a poor and struggling family. He took his first breaths at the height of the Great Depression, the worst economic crisis in the country's history. It was a hard time for America and an even harder time for Arkansas, one of its most underdeveloped and impoverished states.

Yet out of struggle and poverty came great art. Arkansas is a place seemingly devoid of artifice and pretense. It is tempting to say that Cash had what many musicians prize: authenticity (a subject discussed at length in this book's Memphis chapter). Later, however, Cash's career would get shrouded in legends and myth—some of his own making. Jesse Butler has defined Cash's authenticity by saying, "Being an authentic person does not involve shedding an external persona as if it were a false mask, but rather involves actively vesting one's persona with value as it takes shape throughout life, much in the same way that cash money takes on value through its use. . . . Cash is a remarkable example of how this can happen."[2] Whatever Cash's personal faults—and despite his own mythmaking, which goes against the idea of authenticity—his music is what matters most and has doubtless maintained his integrity. Cash's music was at its best when it felt most authentic. And regardless of how good it was at any one time, what kept Cash rooted, what kept him authentic, was his commitment to family, faith, history, and place.

Perhaps a better term for what defined Cash would be "sincerity." From his surroundings, Cash developed a gift for honest, straightforward songwriting and an empathy for common people and society's castoffs. As an adult, he wrote about the people and places of his youth in such classics as "Big River," "Five Feet High and Rising," and "Pickin' Time." His songs were born and shaped in a particular place, and his music drew on the musical elements of Delta blues, Ozark folk, country, and the gospel tunes of the Baptist and Methodist churches. From these varied sources came the blueprint for Cash's warehouse of music.

Cash's roots in so many genres gave him a unique ability to balance the light and the dark in his music and his own persona. His songs can be incredibly bleak and mournful. They can also be funny, lighthearted, and among the most uplifting and energizing songs in American music. As Robert Hilburn has noted, Cash believed in the power of music to "lift one's spirits."[3] Cash's songs were born of a long and varied musical education, one that began in Arkansas.

The Geography of Arkansas

Johnny Cash's home state has a unique story. It is a place understudied and underappreciated as a force in American history. Arkansas was carved out of the frontier, becoming the twenty-fifth state on June 15, 1836. The state is located in the center of the continental United States but exists entirely below the Mason-Dixon Line. It is a southern place, no doubt. But it borders six other states, giving it elements of the Deep South, Midwest, and Southwest. Arkansas has no ocean or great lakes.[4] It is instead a land of rivers, from the Mississippi (the nation's longest) to the smaller but still large White and Ouachita rivers. Sixth longest in the United States, the Arkansas River cuts through the heart of the state, flowing east through Little Rock and into the Mississippi. The Arkansas was a highway for transporting cotton to market and remains a major source of river traffic. The Red River, the eighth longest in the country, slices through the southwestern part of the state. It too has played an important role in the state's history, being the focus of major operations during the Civil War and a place for large cotton planters of the antebellum and postwar era.

Arkansas is not only a land of rivers, it has several large and distinct regions. Traveling west toward Little Rock from Memphis, one moves through the flat, seemingly treeless Delta. At the age of three, Johnny moved with his family to the Delta town of Dyess in Mississippi County. The Cash house was not far from the Mississippi, which later inspired classic songs. Arkansas still grows lots of cotton (1.5 million bales in 2019) but its farmers have diversified.[5] Today one can view the rice fields along Interstate 40, which runs east–west through fertile farmland.

The Delta has a colorful, troubled, and important history. It had some of the wealthiest plantations and American towns before the Civil War. The defeat of the Confederacy ended Arkansas's generation of prosperity. Later, the Delta, with its large Black population and cotton culture, served as the cradle for blues music. When Americans think of the Delta, they might think of Mississippi or Louisiana. But Arkansas has also featured strongly in Delta music history. Helena, for example, south of Memphis and not far from legendary Clarksdale, Mississippi, was home to Sonny Boy Williamson, Levon Helm, and Conway Twitty. The Mississippi carried not only people and products north to south but also music.

As important as the Delta was in shaping Cash and his music, Johnny also drew upon southern mountain culture. He eventually married June Carter, who grew up in mountainous western Virginia and was the daughter of Mother Maybelle Carter, a founding member of the Carter Family, which was pivotal in the creation of country music. The Carter Family had an enormous impact on Cash's musical development, and eventually his marriage to June symbolized both the greatest country coupling in history and the joining of the Carter Family's Appalachia-flavored country with the postwar, post–Hank Williams brand of amphetamine-fueled rockabilly that Cash epitomized. But it wasn't just Appalachia that informed Cash's music. He also had an affinity for Arkansas's own mountain culture. Johnny never lived in the mountains, but as a young Boy Scout, he spent several weeks at a summer camp in the Ozarks. He remembered the experience fondly for the rest of his life.

Along with its rich Delta and Ozark heritage, Arkansas contains many elements of the Wild West. Traveling west from Little Rock toward Fort Smith, one moves through the old Indian Territory, the gateway to the western plains. The area around Fort Smith—a frontier well into the twentieth century—was a refuge for outlaws and home to no-nonsense lawman Judge Isaac Parker, the Hanging Judge of Fort Smith. Today, Fort Smith houses the United States Marshals Museum.

Heading toward Hope and Washington in southwestern Arkansas, the landscape begins to feel like neighboring Texas. It was in southwestern Arkansas that the state's pro-Confederate government fled after the fall of Little Rock in September 1863. The Confederacy died in the spring of 1865, but the state was never truly conquered. Guerrilla bands roamed Arkansas after the Federals took Little Rock in September 1863. Horrific violence and blood feuds continued long after the war.

Arkansas was very much a part of the Wild West, with bandits and killers such as Jesse James making headlines in the state. In the 1930s, Bonnie and Clyde, Al Capone, and Lucky Luciano spent many hours in Arkansas, especially Hot Springs, an old gambling town located roughly an hour south of Little Rock. Further to the southwest you can find Hope, Bill Clinton's birthplace (though he grew up in Hot Springs) and a short drive from the Texas border.

Though not technically one of the so-called Outlaws who changed country music in the 1970s, Cash embodied the attitude that defied Nashville conventions. The Outlaws included such luminaries as Waylon Jennings, Willie Nelson, and Kris Kristofferson—all of them from Texas (though Kristofferson was a military brat). Unlike Waylon or Willie, Cash never wore a cowboy hat (at least not on stage). But his music was infused with Western mythology, and he even starred in Western movies and television shows. Cash was friends with the Outlaw performers and, along with Waylon, Willie, and Kris, was a proud member of the successful 1980s and early-'90s supergroup the Highwaymen. The Outlaws carried on the work that Cash had begun.

Cash not only inspired Outlaw country, he has come to epitomize Americana and roots music. *Country Boy* examines one of America's greatest roots musicians, and to do that, my book mines Cash's vast musical catalog and examines the documentary record. Almost every published work on Johnny Cash has been written by nonhistorians and mostly nonacademics. Some writing on Cash has been scholarly. Much of it has not. Unfortunately for historians, Cash has become the stuff of legend. His life and career has been the subject of many popular works, from print to film to television. Everything from comic books to movies have sought to capture the man, and these works have not always been true to the historical record.

To call Cash a legend is accurate, but it also does a disservice to the man. Rosanne Cash, for one, has grown tired of the mythic version of her father. She has rejected the "icon-ization and the mythmaking about my dad, because that very thing was so destructive to him. And the projections just keep piling up. It's not just the prisoners. It's the downtrodden, wherever they live, and the people who were seeming to turn it into a religion and making him less than human."[6] Cash was certainly a giant in the realm of American music. But one should also reconstruct his life and career according to the historical facts. At one level, Cash seems to be from a time and place lost to us. At the same time, he was human. A man of flaws, complications, and occasional contradictions. But he was also the subject of historical forces at odds with one another. The 1950s, after all, were a time of rigid conformity that simultaneously gave birth to rebellious rock and roll and the civil rights movement. The 1960s were a time of bloody war and a massive peace movement. The 1970s were a decade of hedonism as well as a great religious revival. If Johnny Cash were a contradiction, he lived in conflicted times. Cash could not escape history.

Any serious Cash scholar should start with Cristopher Wren's 1971 biography, *Winners Got Scars Too.*[7] While Cash didn't write the book, Wren was close to his subject, and he wrote in a journalistic style that virtually makes it a primary source. Robert Hilburn's *Johnny Cash: The Life* is the most comprehensive and readable biography of Cash. Hilburn casts doubt on such well-known Cash stories as the singer's claim that he crawled into a cave in Tennessee in the fall of 1967 in order to kill himself. Hilburn's book benefits from the author's firsthand knowledge of Cash, including his coverage of the famous 1968 Folsom prison concert. Yet while Hilburn's book is well researched, it does not contain footnotes. Thus, the many stories in it are left uncited.

The most meticulous chronicler of Cash's life and career to date is journalist, filmmaker, and professor Michael Streissguth, who has written extensively on Cash's life, his Folsom prison concert, and "The List" that Cash passed down to his daughter Rosanne.[8] Other books have taken a less biographical look at Cash, such as Leigh Edwards's *Johnny Cash and the Paradox of American Identity* and John Huss and David Werther's *Johnny Cash and Philosophy*.[9] Edwards's book claims that Cash "embodied paradoxical or contradictory images" that are unique to the American character.[10] Edwards sees in Cash a man who blended rebellion and patriotism, sinful rock and roll and conservative religiosity—in short, contradiction. But Cash was no different than most people in this regard. We are all riddled with contradictions. Cash's fame, however, amplified the tensions within his own personality. By his own admission, Cash struggled with personal demons, as people do. He could be contradictory, but in many ways he was consistent. He was a hard worker who made some of his best music during his lowest times. He searched relentlessly for a new sound, a new story to tell—a different way to reach his listeners and better his art.

For Cash, Arkansas kept him grounded. He might eventually have considered Tennessee home, but Arkansas was where his roots were. The Arkansas soil literally fed Cash as he grew to manhood, and it gave him the inspiration for some of his best songs. If any part of Cash's life had a purity and consistency to it, it was his feelings toward his home state. Cash had a love–hate relationship with Nashville, his adopted home. Johnny, though, had great fondness for Arkansas, and his home state always embraced him. While no stranger to big cities, Cash at heart was the "Country Boy" he sang about on his first album. And fewer places are more "country" than Arkansas.

In the past few years, people in the United States have revived talk of "American exceptionalism." Usually these discussions center on the United States as a place of high ideals, an experiment in self-rule and democratic beliefs, not to mention vast natural resources, material wealth, and a high standard of living. Whatever "exceptionalism" might mean to some, it is clear that two things in particular have driven American history: race and space. This book examines Johnny Cash's views on race—more specifically in regard to African and Native Americans. More important than race, however, is the story of place in Cash's life.

The United States is a big country. Only two nations on earth are larger in terms of geographic size (Canada and Russia) or population (China and India). Other than Canada, which is sparsely populated, the US is alone among large developed nations. Abraham Lincoln put it well in 1838. "We find ourselves in the peaceful possession, of the fairest portion of the earth, as regards extent of territory, fertility of soil, and salubrity of climate," he told an audience of young men in Illinois. With such an advantage of geography, the young Lincoln wrote, "we find ourselves under the government of a system of political institutions, conducing more essentially to the ends of civil and religious liberty, than any of which the history of former times tells us."[11] More recently, Patterson Hood of the alt-country band Drive-By Truckers has talked about the importance of place in the American saga. "I've always responded to music with a great sense of place," Hood said, and he has written songs that have "used geography as an anchor to hold down some big ideas or stories."[12] As was true of Cash, Hood has leaned on a sense of place in order to stay rooted.

We all take nourishment from the soil. And nothing put Cash more in contact with the soil than his many long hours in the cotton fields of Dyess. Many threads ran through his songs and his life. In addition to place, *Country Boy* examines how family, faith, and history bound Cash's experiences and his art together.

Cash and Family

Cash wrote many songs, but when he wrote about family it had the ring of truth. Even the fictitious "A Boy Named Sue," penned by Shel Silverstein, could have been about Cash's relationship with his own bestial father. Family was the first thing Cash remembered. According to him, he had his first recollections during the long and icy trip from Kingsland to Dyess in 1935. Whatever Cash's (or our own) first memory, family is the central element of human society, and it is vital to country music. Cash could not escape where he grew up, or his family. Later in life, he sought to "walk the line" in more ways than one by balancing his commitment to his career and his family. When these came into conflict, his career all too often won out.

"Performed by families and often about family," Rosanne Cash has written, "traditional country music spares nothing and no one in its gaze."[13] Family groups, indeed, have been a staple of country music, from the Carter Family to the Secret Sisters. In Cash's family, music was in the blood. Johnny Cash's daughter Rosanne has achieved fame. His younger brother Tommy also became a well-known country musician. Very often, country singers have passed down their talent to their offspring. Hank Williams begat Hank Williams Jr., who begat Hank 3. Shooter Jennings, Bobby Bare Jr., and Justin Townes Earle are the sons of country royalty. The Secret Sisters (Lydia and Laura Rodgers of Muscle Shoals, Alabama) made a name for themselves singing traditional country songs before moving on to write their own country and pop material.

Family has been the subject of countless classic country tunes, from Charlie Rich's "Papa Was a Good Man" to Willie Nelson's "Mammas Don't Let Your Babies Grow Up to Be Cowboys" to "Family Tradition" by Hank Williams Jr. Rosanne Cash has said family has "faded in country."[14] But when we consider more recent country and alt-country, perhaps not. Bobby Bare Jr., for example, appeared with his father on stage at the Grand Ole Opry at a young age, and he has followed his father's path, albeit in a more rock and roll vein. The group Drive-By Truckers have made family the subject of some of the band's best music, from "Heathens" to "Daddy's Cup" and "Daddy Learned to Fly." On the Truckers' 2003 album *Decoration Day*, Jason Isbell's "Outfit" provides a rundown of a father's advice to his son: "Don't call what you're wearing an outfit" and "Call home on your sister's birthday."

Johnny Cash's best music often put family at its center. One of his signature songs, "A Boy Named Sue," concerns the violent, albeit humorous, relationship between a man and his absent father. An earlier tune, "Five Feet High and Rising," begins with the line, "How high's the water, mama?" and goes on to tell the story of a father putting the family on a "homemade boat" as flood waters rose, so that everyone could get to higher ground. The song doesn't mention Arkansas, but it was based on Cash's experiences during the 1937 Mississippi River flood that swept over Dyess. Cash's family survived. It still does.

In musical circles, bands often become a "family." An extended part of Cash's family was his band, which first consisted of the Tennessee Two and later the Tennessee Three. Within a few years, Cash's band literally became part of his family. June Carter Cash, after all, was first a member of the Johnny Cash touring show before becoming Johnny's wife. At the height of Cash's fame, he had an affair with Anita, June's sister.[15] Anita later married Cash's guitarist Bob Wootton. Marty Stuart, who joined Cash's show when Stuart was in his early twenties, married Cash's daughter Cindy. The combination of family and show business made for great music and great drama that sometimes approached soap opera.

Cash and Faith

Johnny Cash was a Christian his entire life, though he often fell from the purer faith. His hometown was strong with Baptist and Methodist churches, but initially Dyess had no churches at all. For his entire life, Cash was tolerant of different faiths. His first wife was a Catholic, whose father—a priest—married them in 1954. Ecumenical by nature, Cash was a seeker, using religion in his quest to find a deeper personal truth. But he was not self-righteous. After years of shocking self-abuse and self-destructive behavior, in the 1970s Cash underwent a spiritual deepening amid the country's—and country music's—turn inward, which entailed a closer embrace of evangelical Christianity. A member of the Gospel Music Hall of Fame, Cash recorded many religious and spiritual songs in his career. Fans have responded far more enthusiastically to his secular rather than his spiritual music, but no one can deny how profoundly Christianity affected Cash's life. The great book about Cash and his religious life has yet to be written. In these pages, I take Cash's religious music seriously, especially as it was being written in transitional moments in his life and career. My take on Cash's religious life is by no means comprehensive, but one cannot discuss Cash without addressing his devotion to (and complicated attitude toward) religion.

Cash and History

Johnny Cash chronicled the American past in song. He was what some would call a history buff. He was comfortable in an Old South or Wild West setting. As an actor, he was a man who could walk the streets of Detective Columbo's 1970s Los Angeles and play both Davy Crockett and John Brown in TV movies. Far more important than his occasional acting turns were the numerous songs he recorded about cowboys, the West, and historic events, from the Civil War and George Custer to tragic Native American war hero Ira Hayes. History was never more important for Cash than in the 1960s, when he recorded a string of concept albums that chronicled American history and legend. Cash loved myths, and he often used his storytelling skills to create his own—the mythic Johnny Cash who supposedly took a hundred pills a day at the height of his drug addiction, crawled into a Tennessee cave to die in the late 1960s, and boasted of Native American ancestry. Cash made history even as he focused on the American past. Not many songwriters, for example, have thought much about James A. Garfield. But Johnny included "Mr. Garfield" on 1965's *Johnny Cash Sings the Ballads of the True West* double album. Cash had a deep love for American history—fashionable or not.

◆ ◆ ◆

Country Boy reclaims Johnny Cash for Arkansas but also tells a larger musical story: one of family, friends, band members, and the fans that make, promote, sustain, and complicate a successful musician's life and career. My book does not dwell much on Cash's drinking, drugging, and trashing of hotel rooms. His self-destructive exploits have been explored in detail in other books and on film. Instead, *Country Boy* provides snapshots of Cash's life, beginning with his family roots in Virginia in the 1600s, continuing into Georgia, then Arkansas and Nashville.

Johnny and his family struggled in Kingsland and Dyess before moving to the Nashville area. By the time Johnny was a music star, his immediate family had left Arkansas behind. Even so, at every important stage of Cash's career, Arkansas played a pivotal role. He played many of his first live shows in his home state. In 1968, Cash's comeback year, he campaigned—more than he would for any other politician—for Republican governor Winthrop Rockefeller. Cash admired Rockefeller's progressive stance on the Arkansas prisons, which were the worst in the nation when Rockefeller took over. Arkansas became a stage for Cash's larger campaign to promote human rights and reform the criminal justice system.

In 1976, Cash served as an unofficial ambassador for the United States bicentennial. That March, he returned to his birthplace in Cleveland County for a homecoming concert. Cash brought his family along with him, and he thought the event one of the best days of his life. Even at one of the low points of his career, the 1980s, Cash returned to Arkansas for a roast, where it was said, "Here in Arkansas, you speak our language."[16] Cash's artistic fortunes improved in the 1990s with his American Recordings. In 1994, just before his second comeback, he played a concert in Kingsland to support the opening of a new post office. For someone of his stature, Cash was remarkably humble, and Arkansas kept him grounded.

Arkansas continues to honor Cash. The state has literally been ground zero for the preservation of Cash's legacy. In 2011, Arkansas State University began restoring the Cash childhood home in Dyess. The restoration is complete, and visitors can now experience the house close to how Johnny did himself. It is the Tupelo of Arkansas. And as is true of Elvis's first residence, Cash's childhood home is a simple New Deal–era dwelling: a small farmhouse that stands alone in the flat Delta. Unlike Elvis's later home at Graceland, it has no jungle room. No television sets. No gold records. It doesn't even have an upstairs. In the yard, you can see miles of prime cotton land. It may not seem like much, but in the Delta, it doesn't take long to see an amazing sunrise or sunset. The Cash house is a monument to the rustic beginnings of the world's biggest country musician.

Country Boy presents a major figure of American music at several important crossroads in his life. It also examines Cash at a historical crossroads: where the man of myth becomes a figure grounded in the documentary record. I use music, film, photographs, newspapers, and Cash's own writings to tell a story about an Arkansan, veteran, husband, and father who drew on his experiences, the people around him, and his knowledge of history and Americana to make great music.

We are all the product of a particular time and place. Cash grew up in a small southern town during the Great Depression, but he came of age in a time when the region was becoming an integral part of modern, industrial American life. Cash might have been born in an obscure place, but he would go from country boy to city slicker fairly quickly. He never fully detached from his country roots, but he became a world traveler, a man as comfortable (or perhaps more fittingly, uncomfortable, given Cash's naturally restless state) in Europe or New York City as he was in rural America.

Cash was a different person in certain stages of his life, which were defined by his attachment to a particular place. Arkansas, Tennessee, California, and even Jamaica all feature prominently in the Cash story.

As is true of hard-touring musicians, Cash was everywhere and nowhere. A man with multiple houses, but whose true home was the road. It was even more important for him, then, that the fixed earth of Arkansas was a place he could return to whenever he wanted, to renew ties with friends and family. To go fishing or hunting. To forget his fame and stresses, to be the country boy he always was at heart.

1

Kingsland

Kingsland, located in Cleveland County, Arkansas, has always been a small town, never numbering more than six hundred people. Johnny Cash's birthplace is about ten miles south of Rison, a larger town and the county seat. As of 2019, there were 347 inhabitants in Kingsland, two hundred fewer than when Cash was born there. One can drive through Kingsland quickly.

Despite the fact that Cash is Kingsland's most famous resident, when I visited in August 2013 there was no "Johnny Cash Lane" or "Man in Black Street." Those looking for anything related to Cash—and there wasn't much—had to rely on the locals for guidance. Kingsland had two signs to mark the town as his birthplace. The oldest was a rough, hand-painted sign just off Highway 79 as you drive south from Rison. The other was a newer iron structure, closer to town, which showed Cash in silhouette with a guitar. Cash fanatics also can find a marker dedicated to him in March 1976, the same month Cash visited Cleveland County to perform a concert at Rison's high school football field. At the time, Cash was an unofficial ambassador for the United States' bicentennial, and the show was the first he ever played in Cleveland County.

Kingsland is no longer the cotton hub it once was, but it epitomizes a small southern town. Churches outnumber walk-in businesses. Visitors might see chickens roaming freely on a Kingslander's lawn. The place gave birth to Johnny Cash, but in terms of what it offers visitors and country music fans, it is about as far removed from Nashville glitz as one could imagine. Given Kingsland's small-town status, when Cash created his persona, he might have overcompensated with cowboy hats or rhinestone suits. Instead, he stayed true to his humble roots. He eventually became known as "the Man in Black" for the way he clothed his six-foot-two,

two-hundred-plus-pound frame. He was a man who shunned artifice, who wrote and played songs that seemed intent on murdering clichés.

Those interested in Johnny Cash can find no shortage of biographies about him. But Cash historians generally have devoted few pages to the early part of his life. They usually pass over his Kingsland days—admittedly short—in order to get to Dyess, where he lived for his next fifteen years and became obsessed with music. Kingsland, however, deserves a more prominent place in the Johnny Cash story.

Cash later settled in Tennessee, after years in California. He had deep roots in Arkansas, though, not only through his family history but also because his songs were grounded in the people, places, and literal soil of his native state. Cash was a patron saint of various American music forms: rock and roll, gospel, Outlaw country, and what later became known as "roots music." The best example of his earliest roots music can be found on his 1959 album *Songs of Our Soil.* One of the album's tracks, "Five Feet High and Rising," immortalized the 1937 flood in Mississippi County, Arkansas. Kingsland, however, had a deep effect on Cash's life, too. When he visited his birthplace in 1994, he said it was to "touch my roots again."[1]

Ironically, one of the most American of singers was born in a town named Kingsland. Perhaps no town is less the domain of kings than Cash's birthplace, which the singer himself once referred to as a "wide place in the road."[2] Kingsland's name was about as close as the Cash family or any other residents came to royalty. Kingsland is in southeastern Arkansas, roughly seventy miles directly south of Little Rock. It has always been a small, dusty, working-class place that has depended on timber, cotton, and other crops. Cash's time there was short, but it was a fitting beginning for a man who became one of the greatest poets of small-town America—in a home state known for its rural character.

From Scotland to Arkansas

The Cash family made its way to Arkansas via Scotland, Virginia, and Georgia. The patron of the Cash family in America, William Cash, was born in 1653 in Glenrothes, a humble place located in east-central Scotland.[3] In his twenties he settled, as so many men from the British Isles did, in Virginia.[4] William lived in Westmoreland County in Virginia's Northern Neck. Still rural today, Westmoreland was plantation country, home to

Johnny Cash was born in Kingsland, Cleveland County, Arkansas, on February 26, 1932. Kingsland was founded as a railroad town in the late 1800s, and it was where Cash's parents struggled to make a living in the 1920s. When this picture was taken in 2013, the population was noted as being 449 people, but it has dwindled since. Cash left Kingsland with his family when he was three years old for Mississippi County in northeastern Arkansas, though he returned to Cleveland County frequently over the years. *Author photo.*

some of the most prominent members of the so-called Virginia gentry. The county was the birthplace of George Washington, James Monroe, and Robert E. Lee. William Cash, too, was of the planter class. When he died in 1708, his plantation was divided among his wife and children.[5]

In 1703, William Cash's son, Robert Howard Cash, was born in Westmoreland County. Robert, who died in 1772, fathered Stephen Cash in 1730. In 1757, Stephen's wife Jemima gave birth to John Cash, who fought in the Revolutionary War. By the time John was born, the Cash family had moved to Amherst County in southwestern Virginia, a considerable distance from the Northern Neck.

The Revolutionary War erupted just a few weeks after John's eighteenth birthday. Of ripe age for military service, John ended up serving with his fellow Americans against the British. Cash was involved in the Cherokee Expedition, also known as Christie's Campaign (named after Colonel William Christian, who led the patriot forces). The fighting in which John Cash took part began in August 1776, when Cherokees attacked American troops in Virginia, Georgia, and the Carolinas. Private John Cash was among the men who served along the Holston River, which runs from southwest Virginia into Tennessee. The campaign lasted until December 1776.[6]

After the war, John moved from Amherst County to neighboring Bedford County, Virginia. He lived there until 1802, when he and his wife Lucy moved again, this time much farther south to Elbert County, Georgia. On June 7, 1832, the United States passed a pension bill that granted partial pay to men who had served six months or more in the American Revolution and full pay for serving two years or more. Most Revolutionary veterans were dead by then, but John Cash, living in Georgia, applied for a pension. Unfortunately for him, that same year his service records were destroyed in a fire. With the help of a lawyer, Cash signed an affidavit concerning his wartime service,[7] and he received his pension shortly before his death in 1836. His wife Lucy lived until 1848.

The next important Cash in our story was Moses, born in 1784—the year after the American Revolution ended—in Amherst County, Virginia. One of seven children, Moses was born amid a baby boom, a post-Revolutionary War population explosion even more dramatic than that of the 1940s and 1950s. In the decades after America's independence, its population doubled every twenty years—historically its greatest rate of expansion.

In 1802, Moses moved with his family to Georgia, where he rose to the ranks of the middling slaveholders. One twentieth-century source notes that Moses Cash was of "considerable means, owning a large number of slaves, land, and stock."[8] Cash's holdings, however, were more modest than such a description suggests. According to the 1820 census, he owned one slave; twenty years later, he owned five.[9] Moses was far from being a planter, but he was doing better than most small farmers in Georgia. Most southerners—at any time—owned no slaves. Most slaveholders owned a total of one. The average number of slaves owned by a master was five.[10] And yet Moses was living the southern version of the American dream: the passage of time brought him greater wealth, and that meant growing crops, owning land, and buying slaves.

Moses's son, Moses Reuben Cash—usually referred to as Reuben—is the man who brought the Cash family to Arkansas. Reuben was born in 1814 in Elbert County, Georgia. In 1836, he married Phelitia (spelled various ways in written accounts) White Taylor, an Elbert County native in her teens. The couple had their first child, Mary, the year after they wed. In 1838, another child was born, whom they named Nancy. Ten more children followed, all of whom survived childhood. Given the rates of infant mortality, infectious disease, and primitive medicine in the mid-nineteenth century South, it is miraculous that all of Reuben's children lived to adulthood.[11]

Moses Cash died in Elbert County in 1845. His will divided his land among his three sons: James G., Reuben, and Seaborn J. Cash.[12] As equitable as Moses Cash's will may have been, it was hardly a windfall for his sons. In 1858, Reuben Cash and his family left Georgia for Arkansas.[13] The exact reasons for Reuben's move are unclear. The most likely motive for his trek west was that Arkansas had opportunities to own land for men willing to travel to a state very much still a frontier.

The timing of his move possibly was related to a national economic crisis. In 1857 the United States suffered a financial downturn, then known as a "panic." The South did not suffer the worst of the crisis, but in Reuben's home state of Georgia the panic sparked serious debate over banking practices.[14] In the wake of the 1857 panic, the struggling Reuben might have thought Arkansas a more promising place to raise a family. Despite the panic, the 1850s was a boom time for the South. Arkansas had good land for farming, and much of it was cheap. Settlers could get land for $1.25 an acre in the area that later became Cleveland County.[15] To put that in perspective, a common laborer in the late antebellum era might earn a dollar a day. A man could amass a fortune quickly if he were hardworking, shrewd, lucky, and—if need be—ruthless. Many men had no problem resorting to the rough, often violent code of the antebellum South to make their fortune. But even less avaricious types could make a life for themselves by quietly working a good piece of land.

A White Man's Country

The Cash family settled in Bradley County, just south of present-day Cleveland County. More specifically, they settled in the Mount Elba region, established in the 1830s. Mount Elba is today located east of Kingsland on the eastern bank of the Saline River, which flows south into the Ouachita. Migrants to Bradley County were, of course, not the first inhabitants of that land. By the 1830s, however, Native Americans in the states and territories of the United States faced internal and external threats. Arkansans, as was true of Americans generally, wanted theirs to be a "white man's country," where African Americans were kept enslaved and Indian tribes removed or exterminated.

Arkansas was at the center of the forced migration of Native Americans from the East Coast to the frontier. The infamous "Trail of Tears" passed through central Arkansas, including modern-day Little Rock. Not until the 1960s would whites begin reassessing how they and their ancestors had treated Native Americans. Johnny Cash championed the cause of Native Americans on his 1964 album, *Bitter Tears,* well before other prominent musicians took Indian culture seriously.[16]

In the territorial period, southern Arkansas was the domain of the Quapaws, though the area also included Tunicas, Caddos, and Osage.[17] The Quapaws were one of the three major tribes in what later became Arkansas, living in much of the eastern part of the state. In 1824, a treaty was signed that opened the land in southern Arkansas to white settlers. The removal of Native Americans left much land for farming and cotton production. Native Americans, nevertheless, had left their stamp on the territory. The first roads used by whites in Kingsland followed the foot paths that Native Americans had worn into the soil.[18]

Mount Elba, where Reuben Cash settled, was not a mountain at all, but rather a rise in an area east of the Saline River. The place was a transportation nexus. Inhabitants took advantage of a road that connected Pine Bluff to the north and Camden to the south. A ferry also helped promote travel and commerce. Mount Elba prospered due to the river traffic, which thrived on the trade in cotton and other goods. In the 1850s, the Masons of Mount Elba built a college for women.

Antebellum Arkansas wasn't just about cotton. Before the Civil War, a sawmill was the largest single employer in the Mount Elba area. The timber industry was vital to southern Arkansas in the late nineteenth and early twentieth centuries. In the antebellum era and beyond, however, "King Cotton" reigned in Bradley County. Planters, usually those who owned twenty or more slaves, made up only 3 percent of the population of the county.[19] But 20 percent of households owned slaves—a figure close to the southern average. The largest planter in the Mount Elba region was Judge Joseph Monroe Meriwether, who owned forty-four slaves in 1860.[20] His plantation was the site of fighting during the Civil War.[21]

Reuben Cash and his family were making their first cotton crop as a decade of great prosperity came to a close. By 1860, the South was the fourth wealthiest "country" in the world (the others being the northern United States, Great Britain, and Australia).[22] In the 1850s, the South built more railroads than the North did, and it seemed the cotton boom would continue indefinitely. As mentioned, Reuben Cash was no planter. He appears in the 1850 census records for Elbert County, Georgia, but only as having owned 140 acres, $317 in livestock, and no slaves.[23] In the 1860 federal census for Arkansas, he is listed as "Reubin Cash" and having $2,000 in real estate and $800 in personal wealth.[24]

Reuben Cash bettered himself financially over the 1850s. For him, the move to Arkansas had been a good idea. Unfortunately for Reuben and the white South, despite the economic good times, in 1861 the nation came apart politically.

The Civil War

When the secession crisis unfolded, Arkansas was a relatively new state, having joined the Union in 1836. As was true of other southern states, slavery thrived there, especially in the cotton-rich Delta regions, not only along the Mississippi but inland along the Arkansas and Red Rivers. By the standards of the time, Arkansas was a prosperous if nonindustrial place.

Rather than continue to ride the wave of opportunity within the Union, the Arkansas political establishment risked all by opting to leave the United States. A mere quarter-century had passed between Arkansas's achieving statehood and voting to secede. Of the eleven states that joined the Confederacy, Arkansas, with 435,000 people—a quarter of them slaves—was the second smallest. And yet, in 1860, far more people lived in Arkansas than in California, Minnesota, or New Hampshire. With a thriving slave economy and plentiful land for cotton farming, Arkansas was not the poor or underdeveloped place it would later be considered.

What became clear as the war dragged on was that Arkansas was a bitterly divided state. It was one of the last to secede, not doing so until after the firing on Fort Sumter. Unionists were strong in Arkansas, and even the influential planter class was forced to contend with not just them but also Yankee armies, unruly slaves waiting (if not fighting) for their freedom, and resident whites who resented the Confederate government even if they didn't support the Union.

The Civil War is the bloodiest and most destructive war in United States history. To wage it, the South mobilized an unprecedented number of its male population. The Confederacy sent 80 percent of its white males of fighting age into the military—a figure far higher than the North.[25] The Cash family did its part. In 1970, Ray Cash told biographer Christopher Wren that his great-grandfather Moses (aka Moses Reuben) "fought for Georgia in the Civil War."[26] No evidence exists, however, that Reuben Cash "wore the gray," let alone in Georgia, but the story had currency among the Cash family. In his first autobiography, Johnny Cash mentioned Reuben moving from Georgia to Arkansas during the Civil War to escape wartime destruction. Cash wrote, "The old Cash family homestead can still be seen there, though it is in ruins, as it has been since the Civil War. Following the burning of Atlanta and the pillage and sacking of the plantations in that area, Reuben Cash put his family in an ox-drawn wagon, and in 1866 he homesteaded in Arkansas."[27]

It is a dramatic story that seeks to explain the Cash family's genesis in Arkansas. Unfortunately, it is not factual. Several Cash biographers, however, have taken the singer at his word in describing his family's Civil War history.[28] Reuben Cash's plantation was not burned by Sherman's troops for the simple reason that he had no plantation to burn. Another problem with Cash's story about his great-grandfather is that Sherman's troops did not burn any plantations in Elbert County. The place was not a scene of Union operations. Elbert County is in the northeastern part of the state and was not along the route by which Sherman marched to the sea.[29]

Reuben Cash was no longer living in Georgia by the time the war broke out, a war in which he apparently did not fight. His name does not appear in the records for Confederate soldiers from Georgia or Arkansas.[30] The most practical reason for why he never served in a formal unit was that he was too old for the Rebel military. Born in 1814, Reuben would have been much older than a typical Confederate private. When the war began, the average Rebel soldier was in his twenties, unmarried, and had little or no property (let alone slaves or plantations).[31] Had he fought, Reuben would have been an atypical soldier. It is possible he ignored his obligations to his family and—with patriotism surging in his veins—signed up anyway. But the older men who joined the military early in the war were usually those with officer's credentials. With little money and no formal education, Reuben had no such prospects for advancement in the Confederate army.

It is possible, but not likely, that Reuben was drafted during the war. The Confederacy passed three drafts. The first two did not cover men of Reuben's age. The third, issued in 1864, made men between the ages of seventeen and fifty eligible for conscription; Reuben Cash would have been close to the upper limit. Yet men over the age of forty-five were not required to leave their state in order to serve.[32] Although Reuben may have served in such a unit, by then it was unlikely that Confederates in southern Arkansas would have been able to enforce the draft provisions in the Mount Elba area, which had already been overrun by Yankees. Might he have served anyway? Yes, but the documentary record does not support this possibility.

One can only speculate as to what Reuben Cash did during the war. If he fought at all, Reuben likely did so in Arkansas, not Georgia. But it is doubtful that in 1861 he would have chosen to leave his family, including a pregnant wife (who birthed a daughter in 1862), to embark on a journey to Georgia just a few years after having left there, when he more readily could have volunteered for an Arkansas unit. Georgia, furthermore, wasn't a major theater of combat until late in the war. In 1861, it didn't need men in their forties from Arkansas.

Many Arkansans served east of the Mississippi, but it was not easy for them to travel across the river at any point during the war. Lee's Army of Northern Virginia had only one Arkansas regiment in it, the Third Arkansas. Arkansans fought fiercely in Tennessee, Georgia, and other areas in the West. But most of those who did so were not men in their late forties with large families to support. It would have been difficult, indeed superhuman, for the forty-seven-year-old Reuben to have completed a passage across the Mississippi, fought for four years, and then have returned home. Even odder is the fact that such a feat never found its way into the family's written records or Reuben's obituary. What is more believable is that Reuben stayed in Arkansas for the war's duration. There, as a non-slaveholder too old for the draft, Reuben was one of the many men who fought on the home front, where he had to struggle to keep his family together amid war and deprivation.

The Civil War devastated the South, and Arkansas was no exception. Major battles were fought at Pea Ridge and Prairie Grove in 1862 and Helena in 1863. With the fall of Little Rock on September 19, 1863, US forces turned their attention to southern Arkansas.[33] By this time, Confederate politicians had fled to Washington in the southwestern portion of their state, where they set up a new seat of government. In the spring of 1864, Union and Confederate forces fought a series of battles in what became known as the Camden Expedition, part of the larger Red River Campaign.

Mount Elba was one of the many communities ravaged by battles fought in Arkansas in 1864. As Union forces moved into the area, masters abandoned cotton lands. In Mount Elba, Federal troops under General Powell Clayton burned the female college and the Masonic Lodge. Rebel forces were defeated when they tried to hold a vital bridge across the Saline River. Confederates won some bloody battles in southern Arkansas that spring but could not achieve a decisive victory.

It is possible that Reuben Cash took part in one of the battles or skirmishes in southern Arkansas in the latter parts of the war. The conventional war in Arkansas essentially came to an end in the spring of 1864, but that did not end the bloodshed. As Daniel Sutherland has noted, "the defining element for Arkansas in 1864 became the surge of violence and banditry." Indeed, the state was home to some of the worst bushwhacking and guerrilla combat of the war, which occasionally surpassed the internecine violence in Missouri and other states.[34]

Although Reuben Cash survived the war, the conflict had a deep effect on him and his family. Nancy Elizabeth Cash, born in 1838, was Reuben's second child. She apparently was engaged to a soldier who died during the war. She never married, living with her parents until her death in 1880. Mary Frances Cash was luckier. Her husband, Dr. George England, joined the Second Arkansas Cavalry at Mount Elba. He was, like his wife, a native of Georgia, who settled in Arkansas in the late 1850s. George fought in the April 1864 battles at Poison Spring in Ouachita County and at Marks' Mills in Bradley County. He also served with Gen. Sterling Price's men in Missouri in late 1864. He eventually surrendered with other Rebels in Shreveport, Louisiana. Upon returning home, he became a farmer, not practicing medicine until 1877.[35]

Reuben Cash's daughters Virginia Ann (born in 1841) and Pheletia (born in 1843) were also fortunate. Virginia's husband, David Crockett Tomme, served in some of the most vicious battles of the war, including

Murfreesboro, Chickamauga, Atlanta, and Franklin. David rose to the rank of sergeant by the war's end and returned to Bradley County. Pheletia, the family's fifth-born child, was married to Nathan Gunn, who fought as a cavalryman during the war, taking part in some of the major fights in Arkansas such as Prairie Grove and Poison Spring.[36]

Yet the Cash family, like so many others in the South, also endured tragedy and loss during the war. In 1861, Reuben's brother, twenty-two-year-old Private Seaborn J. Cash of the Thirty-Eighth Georgia Infantry Regiment, died in Savannah of typhoid fever. Before joining the army, he had been living with his sister, Permelia Cash Craft—a widow who lived on her husband's Elbert County plantation—working as a carpenter.[37]

Reuben's eldest son, John S. Cash, was another of the war's many casualties. Born in 1840, he enlisted with his brothers-in-law in February 1862, serving in Company D (later Company B) of the Second Arkansas Cavalry. He died in the fall of 1862 in Mississippi, most likely during the Corinth Campaign, which concluded that October. Barely old enough to vote when he died, John was among the war's estimated 750,000 men who perished from bullets, shrapnel, and disease.[38] His remains were never located, which was not uncommon during the war.[39] He left behind a seventeen-year-old bride and a daughter, Mary, born the August before he died.[40]

Reuben's second-eldest son, James Wesley Cash, also fought for the Confederacy. Born in 1845, James did not serve until later in the war. He likely volunteered in 1863 or 1864. According to an obituary published in the *Cleveland County Herald*, Cash was wounded at one point but soon rejoined his unit. The obituary claimed he "did valiant service to the end of the war." James also found time during the war to marry Laura J. Tomme. James Wesley survived the conflict, but like many of the Cash men of the nineteenth century, he did not live to an old age. He died in 1898, a man in his early fifties. He was remembered as a "good man, a good citizen, and a kind neighbor. He was a hard-working, painstaking man who was always in fair circumstances."[41] Not all the Cash men, however, would find circumstances so fair.

The Postwar World

The South's economy was devastated by the war and emancipation, and like so many other southerners, Reuben Cash was financially much worse off after the war than before it. The 1870 census lists him as having only

$800 in real estate and $500 in personal wealth, less than half of his 1860 worth.[42] Reuben was not a wealthy man, but he raised a large family—large even by the standards of the mid-nineteenth century—and most of his children survived the war. When he died in 1880, Reuben was remembered as "highly esteemed as a christian [*sic*] and gentleman, honest and upright in all his dealings."[43] He died with 170 acres of land to bequeath to his children. He also left them the humble sum of one dollar each.[44] Reuben likely hoped that even if he had not made his children rich, he had imparted to them the importance of living a Christian life.

Johnny Cash's lineage included preachers and churchgoing Christians. Cleveland County was and is typical of the Bible Belt. It is fitting that the Johnny Cash historical marker in Kingsland is close to a church. Despite being one of Arkansas's least-populated counties, Cleveland County has a rich religious history. The Camp Springs Methodist Church was established in 1852 and stood until a tornado destroyed it in 2012.[45] The First Southern Baptist Church was built in Kingsland in 1885 and is still in operation on West Second Street as simply the First Baptist Church. The Kingsland United Methodist Church was also founded in the 1880s. The Assembly of God Church and the Kingsland Missionary Baptist Church came later. In the 1920s, a Church of God in Christ was established for Kingsland's African American population.[46]

Perhaps the most religious of the early Cashes in Arkansas was Rev. William Henry Cash. Born to Reuben and Phelitia in Elbert County, Georgia, in 1852, he was known as a traveling preacher or "circuit rider." Johnny later noted that his grandfather never took "a penny for his preaching—though as my daddy told it, the yard and the barn and the stables were full of animals people had given him, and there was always enough to feed his twelve children."[47] The "stables full of animals" story is probably a typical Cash invention, or at best an exaggeration. But William Henry Cash, indeed, could not find a living as a preacher. The 1880 and 1900 censuses (most 1890 census records were destroyed in a fire) list his occupation as a farmer.[48] His commitment to the church nevertheless followed him to the end of his days. One story: in 1912, at the age of sixty, he was carried into his church on a chair, preached from where he sat, and was then taken home, where he died soon afterward.[49]

William Henry Cash married Rebecca Overton, who bore him twelve children, eight of whom lived to adulthood. Unlike her husband, she was a native of southern Arkansas, where she was born in 1855. The oldest of William and Rebecca's children was Susan, born in 1875 just after Rebecca's twentieth birthday. The youngest was Ray, the father of Johnny Cash. George Carpozi Jr.'s 1970 book *The Johnny Cash Story* notes that Rebecca was "full-blooded Cherokee," but this is untrue.[50] For one, Cherokees were not native to Rebecca's birthplace. A surviving picture of the family shows a woman who is obviously not a full-blooded Native American. Nor would William Henry Cash, an apparently respected farmer and minister in a rural southern community, have taken a Native American wife in a period in which white–Indian relations were at a nadir. Yet for years Johnny Cash wrongly asserted that he had significant Native American ancestry.[51] Cash admitted his mistake later in life, but for a long time, he had convinced himself (or at least acted like he had) that he was Native American. With Johnny, it was always difficult to tell where truth ended and performance began. As I discuss later, the "Cash as Native American myth" died a slow death, not killed until Johnny himself put it to rest.

In 1873, Bradley County was renamed Dorsey County after a Radical Republican senator, Stephen Dorsey. The new county was created by slicing off parts of Bradley, Dallas, Jefferson, and Lincoln Counties. In 1874, however, the state's Republican Party collapsed, effectively ending two-party politics in Arkansas for a century. The end of Reconstruction signaled Arkansas's entry into the ranks of the "Solid South," where fiscal conservatism and white supremacy ruled the day. African Americans and anyone else who voted Republican or challenged the status quo were marginalized through threatened or actual violence. To honor the Democratic resurgence in the South, in 1885 Dorsey County was named after Grover Cleveland, the first Democratic president following the Civil War. The county was divided into eight townships, one of which later became Kingsland.

The Birth of Kingsland

Kingsland began as a railroad town. The place got its name after the arrival of the Texas & St. Louis Southwestern Railway. Later renamed the St. Louis Southwestern Railway, the route was better known as the "Cotton Belt" line. In 1883, the town, formerly called Prairie, was renamed by the postmaster, Austin L. Gresham; in July 1884, the town was incorporated. A highway commissioner wanted to give the place an Indian name, Cohassett, after a chief who used the area as a hunting ground. Arkansas, however, already had two Cohassetts, which, long before zip codes, would have made accurate mail delivery more difficult.[52]

The Cotton Belt railroad was a lifeline for Arkansas farmers in an age when cotton was still king. The Civil War did not kill cotton production or the plantation system in Arkansas, so railroads were central to the post–Civil War cotton trade. Before the interstate highway system was built, railway travel was an important part of American life. Country singers love trains, but Johnny Cash was particularly obsessed with railroads. Cash's favorite aunt was Mabel Cash McKinney, whose husband Edgar worked for the railroad.[53] Cash recalled that when he was three, Uncle Edgar gave him a ride on the train.[54] This obviously made an impression on young Johnny, as songs about trains are central to the Cash catalog, from "Hey Porter" and "Folsom Prison Blues" to "Wreck of the Old 97," "Orange Blossom Special," and "Wabash Cannonball," just to name a few. Trains represented many things for Cash: the joys of travel, freedom, escape, power, romance, progress, the allure of the Wild West and the frontier. It meant taking oneself to a new place and seeing new people—indeed, beginning a new life. Cash recorded train songs long after country musicians had moved on to cars, pickup trucks, and eighteen-wheelers.

Cash was born long after the golden age of the American locomotive had passed. He was, nevertheless, a sentimental person, who knew how well trains worked in songs with his boom-chicka-boom sound. His love for the locomotive appealed to American's constant longing for a mythic and better past, full of heroes and men from forgotten places. The "Ride This Train" segment was his favorite part of his television show. In March 1976, he and his wife rode the Cotton Belt into Rison for his concert at the high school football field, a trip that inspired him to write "Ridin' on the Cotton Belt," which appeared on his 1977 album *The Last Gunfighter Ballad*. A railway still runs through Kingsland, but it has not been the Cotton Belt since 1996, when it was absorbed by the Southern Pacific Railroad. Any romance the Kingsland train might have had has long passed.

Yet in the late nineteenth century, the railroads promised big things for towns like Kingsland. By 1890, its population had grown to six hundred, the largest in the town's history. Kingsland was home to three hotels, a furniture store, a lumber mill, four mercantile stores, three drug stores, and a grocery. The town had newspapers at various times, but they have long since disappeared. Today citizens read the *Cleveland County Herald*, which opened in 1888 and is still operating in Rison.[55] The most important industries in Kingsland were cotton and timber. After the Civil War, Arkansas grew more cotton than before. Harvests in the 1890s were good. In October 1897, the *Herald* reported that Kingsland had processed "more cotton than ever handled before in a whole season and the half is not yet told. She pays a higher price than any other town in South Arkansas."[56] That same year, Kingsland could boast 150 children attending public school, a fact made possible by cotton revenue. A farmer could get 8.25 cents a pound for his cotton in 1902, a price higher than what farmers got during some years of the Great Depression. In the early 1900s, Kingsland also added a brick factory and a newspaper, the *Arkansas Journal*.

By 1902, however, the population of Kingsland had dropped to 364. The town—and Arkansas at large—was still unrefined and worthy of the frontier. A photograph of downtown Kingsland in the first decade of the twentieth century shows a pig on the street sniffing for food.[57] Yet twentieth-century technology was coming to Kingsland. The Fordyce Light and Power Company (later Arkansas Power and Light) provided the town's first electricity in 1907. The automobile was another welcome and major innovation; Kingsland's first Ford appeared in 1904.[58] A decade later, Arkansas Highway 3 was built through Kingsland. By the early 1930s, the *Cleveland County Herald* predicted that "in another decade automobiles will travel at a rate of 150 miles an hour on an ordinary highway."[59] The *Herald* might have been overly optimistic, but Kingsland clearly had come a long way from the early 1900s, when the town passed an ordinance that fined anyone who went faster than twenty-five miles per hour on a horse or in a vehicle.[60]

The Ballad of Ray Cash

Despite the arrival of the automobile, a new car was beyond the means of most Arkansans, including Ray Cash. The 1910s were a troubled time for Ray and the rest of the country. Ray was a "typical country boy," an uneducated common laborer who rolled his own cigarettes.[61] He was born May 13, 1897 and dropped out of school when he fourteen, around the time his father, Rev. William Henry Cash, died. Four years later, Ray's mother died. As Ray came of age and needed work, timber mills began shutting down in Cleveland County, leaving hundreds without jobs.

In 1914, war broke out in Europe, unleashing human slaughter on a massive scale. Luckily for the United States, it did not enter the war until April 1917 and would not have troops engaged until the next year. Yet by the time America entered the Great War, Ray Cash had already enlisted. Undoubtedly he chose the military for the same reason his son Johnny would: to get a regular paycheck without working in the cotton fields. With Europe in flames, Ray decided the military was a good option for him.

The military gave Ray a job and a taste of adventure and the larger world. His enlisted experiences began as a soldier in the Arkansas National Guard, federalized in 1916 to fight Pancho Villa's forces along the US–Mexico border. Ray's unit was the Second Arkansas Infantry, first stationed at Fort Logan Roots—then located on Big Rock overlooking the Arkansas River in present-day North Little Rock. Ray eventually was sent with other Arkansans to the Southwest, where his unit acted as a border patrol trying to track down the elusive Villa, whose men had killed Americans along the border. The United States never captured General Villa, who died in an ambush in 1923 at the hands of other Mexicans.

The fighting along the Mexican border was slight compared to the muddy slaughter in the trenches of France and Belgium, but it served as a warmup for America's entry into the World War. Ray stayed in the military and eventually joined the hundreds of thousands of men deployed to France. Ray had avoided bloodshed along the Mexican border, and he proved similarly lucky in France. His participation in World War I officially began in August 1917. Ray's Second Arkansas Infantry was transformed into the 142nd Field Artillery, a unit in which Ray played a support role for Battery E. To reach France, he rode with thousands of other men on a captured German ship, *Leviathan*, formerly the German passenger ship *Vaterland* but seized by the United States in 1917. One of its American crew members was a young sailor named Humphrey Bogart.[62]

Ray arrived in the French port of Brest, where it seemed to rain constantly.[63] Little improved for him from that point forward. By his own admission, Ray was not a good soldier. He later claimed to have lost a train he was supposed to be guarding. According to him, he had left his post to go to St. Lazare to visit a girlfriend. Upon his return, the train carrying needed supplies was gone. Cash admitted his mistake to his superior officer, who cursed him for his incompetence. Ray faced the added embarrassment of having no money and needing to ask this same officer for fare to return to his barracks.[64]

Ray Cash was no hero, but despite his bungling in France, he was honorably discharged from the army on June 25, 1919. His discharge came a few weeks after making his way back home from Saint-Nazaire on the *Amphion*. Garth Campbell, in his biography of Johnny Cash, notes that when it came to World War I, "Ray never revealed the truth about the ugly scenes of death and destruction he had witnessed."[65] But Johnny Cash's father never actually saw combat, and his wartime service was less than exemplary. Ray could be a hard worker, but he was no soldier, let alone a glory hound or leader of men.

Ray was likely glad to be home, but the thought of returning to Kingsland also might have made him anxious. He had no job, wife, parents, or children awaiting him. He had also no high school diploma and no business training. The army had provided him with employment, allowing him to travel overseas and walk the streets of Paris. Since he had not seen combat, he did not return physically or emotionally shattered the way so many thousands of Americans did. But Ray had few options back in Arkansas. He spent the 1920s roaming from job to job and dwelling to dwelling in and outside Cleveland County, never venturing far from where he grew up.

One job involved working in timber. Cleveland County's timber industry thrived on the area's large pine and hardwood trees. Before the timber trade began slashing its way through southern Arkansas, the region was one of majestic trees, some between four and six feet in diameter and over a hundred feet tall.[66] Ray Cash recalled the eight men needed to take down a cow oak (a type of white oak) that was eight feet thick.[67] On his charming *Children's Album* from 1975, Johnny Cash included a song he had written called "(The) Timber Man." The song does not refer to his father, but it was a tune that aptly summarized Ray's experiences in Kingsland so many years before.

At one point, Ray was on a crew cutting lumber to construct a bridge over the Saline River. During the job, Ray stayed with the Rivers family. There he met sixteen-year-old Carrie Rivers. On August 18, 1920, he and Carrie were wedded. It was a marriage that lasted the rest of their lives. Lucky in love, Ray was less so in finding regular employment. He struggled throughout the 1920s, but his and Carrie's family grew every few years. The couple's first child, Roy, was born in September 1921. Another, Margaret Louise, followed in March 1924. The next, Jack Dempsey—named after the champion boxer—was born in January 1929, the last of the Cash children to arrive before the Great Depression hit.

Ray often worked for his older brother Dave, a prominent landowner, sheriff, and judge in Rison. Dave Cash's education stopped with the fifth grade, but he was successful in the timber trade, buying pine and hardwood that had once belonged to the Meriwether family, owners of Mount Elba's most prosperous plantation before the Civil War.[68] Dave Kelly Cash was like a character from one of William Faulkner's Snopes novels, which chronicle a Mississippi family's ruthless pursuit of wealth and prestige. Dave had a reputation as a hard man, capable of horrifying and cruel behavior. According to Kathy Cash, Ray's granddaughter, Dave once forced the much younger Ray to view the burned body of a Black man, the victim of a lynching in which Dave apparently had taken part.[69] Long after they left Kingsland, neither Ray nor Carrie had good things to say about Dave. When he died in 1959, his obituary notice in a Pine Bluff newspaper is noticeable for its lack of superlatives.[70]

Dave Cash had his troubles, though. In 1924, his wife, Mary Leona Foster Cash, died after an illness. She was remembered as a "woman of ability and made friends easily."[71] Her death left Dave with five children to support, one a three-month-old infant. Dave Cash's two later marriages ended in divorce.[72]

In the 1920s, the modern world—with the automobile, radio, and new ideas about women, sexuality, and human evolution—came to America. Kingsland, however, was more receptive to some ideas than others. Technological innovations were more welcome than theories that challenged the existing social order, based as it was on racial segregation and evangelical Christianity. By the mid-1920s, E. R. Buster, who owned several businesses, had put gas pumps in front of his general store. In 1926, the Kingsland Oil Company was established, one of the many petroleum-related businesses capitalizing on southern Arkansas's oil boom—part of a rush for oil wealth that consumed many Americans in the "Roaring Twenties." In 1926, some Kingslanders listened to the Jack Dempsey–Gene Tunney fight on the radio. The radio also brought popular music to millions of households. It proved one of the most important luxuries in the Cash family, inspiring young Johnny to become a musician.

The 1920s was an era of great prosperity for the United States, but that new wealth rarely reached its farmers. They had benefited from the war in Europe and elsewhere. Hungry armies needed American food, and farmers were happy to supply it. High food prices also made for high land prices. But with the end of war, demand for American commodities declined. Yet US farmers continued to produce at record levels, pushing down prices for things such as cotton, pork, grain, and cattle. American cotton farmers in the 1920s faced greater competition, the use of synthetic fabric, and less cumbersome fashions that used less material. Cotton prices declined every year in the 1920s, which further hurt farmers.[73] Arkansas, being heavily rural and agrarian, was hit hard by this recession. Then the recession became a depression.

The Great Depression

The October 1929 stock market crash set off the worst economic crisis in US history. With no safety net, many people lost everything. As the poorest and least-developed part of the country, the South was made even poorer. Farmers and others who made a living in agricultural communities were hit hard. Ray Cash remembered that by the early 1930s, cotton "went down to almost nothing. A year before the Depression, cotton would bring $100, $125 a bale. In 1931 and 1932—they were the hardest years—I only got $25 for a five-hundred-pound bale. In Kingsland between crops, I'd get out and get any kind of job I could find to get through the winter. I always tried to work locally." "Locally," however, meant Ray had to cover long distances on foot. He remembered walking three miles to a job in a journey that must have taken about an hour. Yet Ray was happy he found work at all and that he could return to his wife and children every day. At one point, he said he was getting between fifteen and twenty cents an hour, resulting in $1.50 or $2 per day. "But," he said, "I was home with my family at night."[74]

Few escaped the depression's ruinous effects. The Cleveland County Bank in Kingsland closed and never reopened. Not until 1979 did the town have another bank.[75] In 1931, teachers and bus drivers in Cleveland County had their salaries cut by 20 percent. One of those teachers was Clara Marie Cash, the daughter of Dave Kelly Cash. Marie never married, and though she didn't have children of her own, she was a dedicated teacher and guidance counselor for most of her adult life. She also worked at the Jerome

Relocation Center during World War II, one of the two major internment camps for Japanese Americans in Arkansas. Marie became the Cash family's most accomplished genealogist. Of the two years she spent on the family history she would write, "I have never enjoyed anything more in my life."[76] Later, her cousin Johnny also took a great interest in genealogy.

Despite the economic depression, Ray and Carrie Cash continued to have children. Their fourth, Johnny, was born "dirt poor" in a "three room shack" in Kingsland on February 26, 1932, at a place known as the Crossroads, a few miles north of Kingsland center.[77] It was an era in which women often had children at home. Carrie, however, was not alone. A midwife by the name of Mary Easterling helped Carrie give birth to Johnny. Unfortunately, the flimsy house where Cash was born disappeared long ago.

In George Capozi's 1970 biography of Cash, he notes Johnny was born on a "cold, snowy day," but the weather report for Cleveland County on that day notes warm, clear, springlike weather for central Arkansas and indeed much of the country.[78] A cold, snowy Cash birthday might add to the Man in Black's legend, but it only reinforces the fact that so much about Johnny's life is shrouded in haze—even his very name. Cash was later known as Johnny Cash, but early in his life he went by J. R. In the late 1960s, Cash noted somewhat proudly that the R didn't stand for anything.[79] The name John, however, was in place from the beginning. A March 1932 announcement in the *Cleveland County Herald* noted the birth of an "11 pound boy, February 26. He has been named John R."[80]

Why John? There were Johns in the Cash and Rivers family. John's maternal grandfather was John Lewis Rivers. Ray also had an older brother named John Reuben Cash. When John Carter Cash, Johnny's only son, asked relatives about the origin of his father's name, he encountered a "mild controversy." Apparently, Johnny's mother wanted to name her son John Rivers Cash, while Ray wanted to name him John Ray Cash. As a compromise, the couple gave Johnny Cash a middle initial of R.[81] Whatever the origins of his name, well into his high school years, Johnny was mostly referred to as J. R.; it was common for boys of that time to go by their initials. Only when his music career took off in the 1950s did he go by the name Johnny Cash.

Cash is the best-known person ever born in Kingsland. In March 1932, however, the world was not concerned much about the birth of a new baby to the Cash family. Instead, the *Cleveland County Herald* discussed the kidnapping of the Lindbergh baby in New Jersey, a case that had made headlines for weeks. It was not until May of that year that the toddler's body was found, not far from the Lindbergh home.[82] Also in the news was Prohibition, which the *Herald* wrongly believed would survive for a long time; in fact it would be undone the next year.[83] Kingsland nevertheless was the kind of community where the churches would have preached against alcohol consumption, regardless of whether Prohibition was in force. As was America as a whole, the Cash family was divided on the issue of drinking. Ray Cash was no stranger to alcohol, while Carrie Rivers abstained. Johnny Cash wasn't a teetotaler, but it would be pills, not alcohol, that most plagued him later in life.

After Ray Cash failed to share in the prosperity the 1920s brought to America and southern Arkansas, the depression only made things worse for him. In early 1932, when Johnny Cash was born, Ray was struggling to keep his family going. The Cashes moved often in Cleveland County. When Johnny was living there, his family spent considerable time not only in the Crossroads area but also in a place known as Saline Siding, which took its name from the Saline River (a tributary of the Ouachita) and "siding," a railroad term for a loop off the main line of railway where cars were loaded and unloaded.

Ray's jobs during the depression included sharecropping and traveling to Mississippi to dismantle a factory. During one particularly unpleasant day of work, Dave Cash asked him to kill fifty head of cattle. Dave offered Ray a hundred bullets, but he only needed fifty. Ray was a good shot, but the slaughter was horrifying. "My nigras will take them off," Dave matter-of-factly told him, after which the cattle were devoured by pigs. Ray was no soft touch, but the experience sickened him and gave him nightmares.[84]

Ray was not the only person desperate for work in the early 1930s. His brother Russell, born in 1891, also struggled. Russell worked as a farmer and a lumber man, a trolley conductor in Pine Bluff, and a road grader. Some winters he worked at a box factory in Pine Bluff. He also spent time as a carpenter. Russell had some talent as a piano player and fiddler. His son, David, remembered he could "get more music out of a comb and a cigarette paper than I can get out of a radio."[85] But Russell never pursued music seriously.

Russell showed that the Cash family had some music in its blood. But so did the Rivers clan. Johnny Cash's mother Carrie made sure her children grew up with music, mostly hymns (songs about God, the Bible, and religious subjects) and spirituals (much like hymns but more associated with southern Black churches). As was the case with Ray, Carrie was a first-generation Arkansan. Her father, John Lewis Rivers, born in 1866, was the son of William and Lydia Rivers of Chesterfield County, South Carolina.

Carrie's grandfather had served in Company B of the Twenty-Sixth South Carolina Infantry during the Civil War. The regiment was organized in Charleston and later saw action in the battles of Jackson, Mississippi, and Petersburg, Virginia. What remained of the regiment by April 1865 surrendered with the rest of Lee's army at Appomattox Court House.

Carrie's father married Roseanna Lee Hurst. The couple wedded before settling in Arkansas, where they built a house on the present-day location of Crossroads Cemetery. The Rivers house had only five rooms, but the high ceilings helped cool it in the blistering summers, while a mudcat (stick-and-mud) chimney heated it in winter. Unlike Ray Cash's family, Carrie's was smaller. Her parents only had four children, three daughters and a son.[86] Carrie enjoyed greater stability as a young woman than Ray did.

Johnny Cash had few memories of his Rivers relatives. He said he did not remember visiting them until he was ten years old, the same year the Cash family got their first car. Ray apparently refused to drive the Pontiac more than thirty-five miles per hour for the 250-mile trip from Dyess to Kingsland. Johnny remembered having "a good time playing with my cousins." He said when he was six, he was in love with his cousin Glenda Rivers. With typical humor, Cash added, "she got married and I got over it." His grandfather showed him how to pull water from a well, and his grandmother "made wonderful biscuits" and liked to dip snuff.[87]

In March 1933, Franklin D. Roosevelt took office, the first Democrat elected to the presidency since the World War. In his first hundred days, Roosevelt put forth his "New Deal," a host of government programs aimed at alleviating the depression. One of the new government agencies was the Federal Emergency Relief Administration, which publicized the creation of a new community in Dyess, Mississippi County, Arkansas. A few hundred families would be provided with a new house, land, and livestock, which the family could pay for in installments.

Ray Cash was one of the applicants. The government was not willing to accept families on a first-come, first-serve basis. Instead, heads of households such as Ray were reviewed for their good character and skill as farmers. Only a few families from Cleveland County were chosen for Dyess. Ray's application initially was denied, then later approved. Cash biographer Michael Streissguth thinks that Dave Cash—Ray's politically influential brother—might have pressured someone to approve Ray's application.[88] Whatever the reason for Ray's good luck, in March 1935 the Cash family hopped on a truck for a two-day trip to Dyess.

Johnny Cash didn't remember life in Kingsland, but the town played a formative role in his life. Cash was a great spokesman for Middle America and the rural South. He drew on his country's folklore and history to become one of America's most accomplished artists. He lived only three years in Kingsland, but the town personified what Cash sang about in his later music: small, working-class towns, where men earned their bread through cutting lumber, picking cotton, and making the railroads move. Similarly, the Cash family included farmers, preachers, and common laborers. Kingsland was also a place where the ghosts of the Civil War and Native American culture lived on. These ghosts would follow Cash northward—and indeed, for the rest of his life.

Johnny Cash's family history in southern Arkansas was an interesting one, spanning the period from just before the Civil War to the Great Depression. Cash, unfortunately, was not a great genealogist. Much of the information concerning his family has been inaccurate—at other times, plain wrong. But what is indisputable is that Cash had strong roots in Arkansas and the South. His parents were true Arkansans, and his family was thoroughly southern, coming as it did from Virginia, Georgia, and South Carolina. The Cash and Rivers families could boast of men who had fought in the Confederate army and worked farms, and were devoted churchgoers—all the ingredients of a solid Arkansas pedigree.

Although short, the Kingsland chapter of Johnny Cash's early life was nevertheless important, both to him and the history of Arkansas.

2

Dyess

It took two days for Johnny Cash and his family to reach Dyess, and their March 1935 journey was baptized in music. Cash remembered his mother playing her guitar as they went, "beating time on the old Sears, Roebuck guitar" while she sang "What Would You Give in Exchange for Your Soul."[1] Johnny later remembered seeing icicles hanging from the truck as the family rattled north.[2] Is it possible the three-year-old Cash had such vivid memories of the journey, even of the songs his mother sang? The trip to Dyess was certainly a major event in his life, but most people can't recall events at three years old when they are in their sixties. Regardless, Johnny Cash knew how to tell a story. And while life in Dyess would be filled with great tragedy, its saving grace was the musical journey Cash embarked on as a young man.

Travel conditions to Dyess might have been far from ideal, but the Cashes arrived safely at their new home, one Johnny would live in for the next fifteen years. In that period, Johnny Cash became a musician. The songs and sounds he heard turned him into a human jukebox.

By 1935, the Great Depression had dragged on for over five years. At the depths of the crisis, the unemployment rate in Arkansas reached an astonishing 39 percent.[3] A half-century later, California novelist John Fante published *1933 Was a Bad Year*.[4] No one needed to tell Ray Cash that. Unlike many Americans, Ray and his family had not indulged in the hedonism and economic good times of the 1920s. Kingsland had been about as far removed from *The Great Gatsby* as anyone could have found in America. The stock market crash brought an end to the Roaring Twenties and worsened an already difficult situation for the Cashes.

Roosevelt's election had brought hope to millions. His New Deal promised to help Americans everywhere, especially in the South, which remained the most tight-fisted and economically underdeveloped region of the nation. Nevertheless, the depression had led many Americans to conclude that they alone were responsible for their financial misfortune, though most were victims of national and international market forces beyond their control. The idea of rugged individualism—pulling oneself up by one's bootstraps, the virtues of "belt tightening," and the allure of the American Dream—had impressed on the minds of millions that their success, or lack thereof, was of their own making. The economic fallout of the 1930s therefore, led many to conclude, "I'm a failure."

Ray Cash, in contrast, had failed for much of the 1920s. He was a man not above picking cotton, slaughtering cattle, or traveling to another state to make a few bucks. He had lost little at the outset of the depression because he had little to lose. Many Americans saw their fortunes disappear, but Ray actually had an opportunity to "go up" in Dyess, and he took it. Ray was no liberal, but the government was ready to help him, and he knew a good opportunity when one came his way. During FDR's presidency, he and his family prospered with the help of an ambitious and unusual government project: the Dyess Colony, a government-sponsored town in Mississippi County, fifty miles north of Memphis. There, young Johnny Cash stayed until he left for the Air Force in 1950.

When the Cash family arrived, the worst of the Great Depression, at least in terms of unemployment, was over. Joblessness peaked nationally at 24.75 percent in 1933. By 1935, it averaged about 20 percent. Yet in that year, FDR's attempts to balance the federal budget backfired economically, causing the "Roosevelt Recession." The unemployment rate stayed high until the nation began gearing up for war at the end of 1941.[5] The year 1942 was the first full year since 1930 that the United States had an unemployment rate below 10 percent.

Despite the desperation gripping the country in the 1930s, Dyess was a land of opportunity for the Cash family. The town was the brainchild of William Reynolds Dyess, head of Arkansas's Emergency Relief Administration (the ERA, which eventually became the WPA, the Works Progress Administration). Dyess was a native of Osceola, roughly a twenty-minute drive from the place that would bear his name. He was a planter and businessman and a major player in Arkansas politics. He had a friend in the governor, Junius Marion Futtrell. The governor, who served from 1933 to 1937, came from a planter background. He was no bleeding heart. He once dismissed leftists as "white trash and shiftless niggers."[6]

Futtrell had the support of such titans of agriculture as Mississippi County superplanter R. E. Lee Wilson. But he also had a feel for the common man. Futtrell backed the yeoman experiment at Dyess.

The New Deal in Dyess

The Dyess Colony was unique in the larger history of Arkansas, but it was one of twelve government-sponsored communities built in Arkansas during the Great Depression.[7] Similar communities were created in neighboring states. Elvis's hometown of Tupelo, Mississippi, for example, benefited from government-sponsored Tupelo Homesteads. Another related project was the Tennessee Valley Authority, a federal program that electrified rural areas. In contrast to other government-sponsored communities, Dyess was exceptional in that it was "the only purely agricultural rehabilitation colony project . . . this side of Alaska." Unlike other colony projects or government towns, Dyess had individual farm plots.[8] That meant men didn't just live there—they could work their own land, raise crops, and pay their way.

The Dyess Colony kept the Cash family out of dire poverty and free from sharecropping. Johnny Cash said he grew up "under socialism."[9] As was true of the New Deal generally, however, the Dyess Colony was not a radical experiment in collectivism. The government wanted to help farmers, but nothing was free. The most socialist aspect of the community was the general store in the center of town, which was a cooperative. Otherwise, the town was privately run. Dyess residents' most common interaction with the federal government occurred when they got their mail.

The government did get the colony going, though. Dyess was a creature of the Federal Emergency Relief Administration. Initially, the board of directors of Dyess Colony Incorporated (DCI) was paid by the WPA, which employed many artists and writers during the depression and helped revive and redesign many urban and rural landscapes. Dyess residents, as was the case with Americans generally, did not want handouts. Dyess was a for-profit venture, and its citizens were hardly socialists. As one historian has written, the colony was "organized similarly to a large Southern plantation, with the Resident Manager, and his staff, acting as landlord and overseer."[10] The plantation model died hard in Arkansas.

Dyess was new, and it had competition. Mississippi County was home to the largest cotton-producing operation in the South, one owned by Robert Edward Lee Wilson. Wilson's very name suggests the continuity between the Old and New South in northeastern Arkansas. Wilson's holdings, however, far surpassed the dreams of even the grandees of the antebellum era. His plantations were so sprawling that the town of Wilson was named after him. He owned other towns, too, which churned out thousands of bales of cotton on his tens of thousands of acres. His labor force was a small army of sharecroppers, tenant farmers, managers, and overseers. The extent of Wilson's holdings granted him enormous influence in Mississippi County.

Wilson exploited the large pool of cheap labor in northeastern Arkansas. At the height of the depression, roughly 63 percent of Arkansans tilling the land were tenant farmers. Tenants, as Nancy Isenberg has written, "were in debt to landlords, had little cash, no education; hookworm and pellagra still haunted them."[11] Despite his previous success in exploiting a large, poor labor pool, in 1933, Wilson and his company needed large loans from the federal government to stave off disaster. Wilson died that same year. His successors were able to keep his empire afloat, but Wilson's financial troubles and subsequent death at the height of the depression showed that things were changing in Mississippi County.[12]

Dyess—the David to Wilson's Goliath—was created from timberlands once owned by Drainage District No. 9. The district was created in 1909, and by 1926 it operated 131,000 acres of improved farmland.[13] During the depression, men running levee operations sold massive amounts of land to the government to pay taxes owed. The Drainage District's money problems allowed officials to purchase the land that became Dyess. The town's builders anticipated that it would cost $3,245,401 to build the colony[14]—a considerable sum at any time, but especially during the cash-strapped 1930s. Nevertheless, in 1934, work began.

The Days before Dyess

The environment played a major role in the history of Dyess and Mississippi County. A present-day visitor to Dyess is struck by its large farms and open fields. In winter, it feels desolate. The restored Cash home, completed in

2014, has few trees on the property. The area around it is stark, flat, and treeless. Such was not the case in 1935. Patrick Carr has described Cash's hometown as "flat as Holland and as green as the Congo."[15] But the Congo parts had to be cleared before it could look like Holland. In fact, before the Dyess settlers arrived, the town's landscape was described as a "swampy jungle, covered with trees, bushes, mud, and water."[16] As the ERA wrote, "Fresh timber grew up and a dense underbrush wove the trees together."[17] Farmers don't like trees. And Dyess would soon undergo a major environmental transformation once settlers began plowing up fields, draining swamps, slashing brush, and removing stumps. Johnny Cash's childhood fear of forest fires seems odd if one did not understand the earlier ecological history of Dyess.[18]

As was true of Kingsland—and so many parts of America—Dyess had once been home to a significant Native American population. Hundreds of years before, the region that became northeastern Arkansas was one of the most densely populated Indian settlements in North America. Natives cleared much land in order to plant corn. While this was good for hungry people, farmland is not kind to the natural environment.

Johnny's obsession with Native American culture had its roots in Dyess. His favorite story growing up was *Lone Bull's Mistake*, a 1918 novel about a proud Native American warrior who disobeys a tribal order not to hunt on certain land, does anyway, and brings disaster upon his people.[19] The author of the tale was James Schultz, a man from upstate New York who "went native." His first wife was Native American, and he spent his last days on a reservation in Wyoming before being buried on a Blackfeet reservation in Montana. While it's uncertain how much Cash knew about the story's author, Schultz's life would have appealed to him. *Lone Bull's Mistake* certainly did.

As was true of Kingsland, in Dyess, Cash did not grow up around Native Americans, but long-departed tribes made a deep imprint on the area's history. Cash learned about Native Americans the way most boys did—from books, radio, and film—and did so in a time when racial stereotypes were common. Cash, however, never denigrated or oversimplified Native American life. The fact that he also thought he had Native American blood helped with this. Thus he empathized with the many tribes—and people of the land, like him—that struggled against government forces. Cash was a lifelong proponent of underdogs, and for him, Native Americans were one of the most ill-treated groups in the country.

That said, Cash grew up in a time when white supremacy was the dominant political force in the South. Children in Dyess were learning United States history that emphasized a triumphant American narrative, one in which white male heroes made a great nation through cunning and sheer force. It was the story of Washington, Jefferson, Lincoln, and Teddy Roosevelt. Even so, the naked truth of the Great Depression certainly complicated the triumphalist narrative. Cash loved his country, but he knew it had problems. As an adult, he had faith in America, but he balanced his belief in a nation that could triumph over adversity with a compassion for those who struggled or were left behind by history. It was one of the many political balancing acts Cash maintained throughout his career. His music and worldview blended shades of dark and light. Cash might have been born and raised in the "Sun Belt," but it didn't stop him later from wearing a suit of black.

Cash's Arkansas was a place with a fascinating post-Columbian history. In the period before Fernando de Soto's 1541 arrival in present-day Arkansas, the area was devastated by a drought that lasted a hundred years.[20] As farming declined and tribes drifted away, lands became overgrown. Forests sprouted on abandoned fields. By the time white settlers moved to northeastern Arkansas, the Delta had become heavily wooded and swampy, with abundant game animals. It was also home to water moccasins, copperheads, and rattlesnakes.[21]

With the arrival of land-hungry white settlers, the Delta began taking on the more treeless appearance it has today. Masters, slaves, and non-slaveholding whites dramatically changed the landscape. These prolific tree killers made small farms and plantations on which to grow cotton. Later farmers made a living growing soybeans and rice. Before the twentieth century, the low-lying, marshy land of Mississippi County made it an unhealthy place to live. By the 1930s, however, residents enjoyed a much more hospitable environment than even a generation previous. Before then, swamps came with malaria-carrying mosquitoes. Not until the early twentieth century did doctors understand that malaria was caused only by mosquitoes, not drinking bad water.[22] The first report on the Dyess project noted, "Health conditions existing in this locality are very good. The rate of mortality compares favorably with that of the mountains."[23] Malaria and other diseases did not bedevil Dyess residents the way they had earlier Delta residents. The creation of Dyess coincided with the rise of modern medicine, with the result that Johnny Cash and his family suffered no major illnesses in the decades they lived in Arkansas.

Dyess was an example of how humans could dramatically remake the landscape. But so could nature. In 1811, a major earthquake occurred in northeastern Arkansas, a quake so severe it was felt in Richmond and Savannah. The quake literally tore the earth open, creating what are known as the "Sunken Lands." The depressions left behind created additional problems for farmers in an already flood-prone region.[24]

Long before the Cash family arrived in Dyess, the region was known to experience severe drought and flood. Major floods occurred in 1882 and 1912. In 1930 and 1931, a few years before Dyess was built, the area was in a drought. Cotton prices, furthermore, had fallen to 5 cents a pound. Nevertheless, according to one man, Mississippi County possibly had "the richest land in the United States."[25] Dyess residents, as historian Jeannie Whayne has written, were in a "desperate search for the American dream in one of the last pieces of frontier."[26] Unlike Kingsland, Dyess was not designed as a railroad town, and it was hardly an ideal place of settlement, given its undeveloped nature and unstable soil. Land prices rose in Mississippi County after World War I. Even so, the 1920s were a tough time for farmers in Arkansas. Planters might have made fortunes, but agriculture was suffering well before the Great Depression.

Twentieth-Century American Colonists

Work at Dyess began in May 1934, but crews did not start major construction until the most oppressive month of the year: July. Yet they worked quickly, erecting as many as three houses a day. From mid-August to mid-September, fourteen hundred men helped build the colony.[27] Houses were constructed according to a general plan, but they varied in the location of rooms, porches, doors, and windows to "avoid monotony."[28] The sites for each house consisted of twenty acres of land, but crews only cleared "approximately two" acres per plot.[29] Families would have to cut and clear the rest themselves.

Today, on a good day of weather, the trip from Kingsland to Dyess would take only a few hours by car. Even by truck, the Cash family's journey took two days. Ray Cash was pleased at the prospect of having his own farm. But he was under no delusions as he headed to Mississippi County: hard work lay ahead. The government sponsored Dyess, but there would be no handouts. Even the bumpy ride to Dyess was not free. The cost of the truck transportation was put toward the Cash family's balance, which already included the cost of a house, twenty acres of land, and livestock.[30]

The Cash family arrived to a house freshly painted white, with the cans still on the floor when they entered, indicating the workers' haste. These cans had been used for the exterior only. Inside walls were kept bare. Houses were built quickly in Dyess. One crew could build a five-room home in a mere sixteen hours.[31]

Settlers had the option of buying a three-room house for $600, a four-room for $800, or a five-room for a thousand, which would take the average colonist ten years to pay off.[32] The Cash house consisted of five rooms. At 1,120 square-feet, the house was a tight fit for a family of seven (and two more children would be added in a few years). It was supposed to be equipped with a toilet, running water, and electricity, but the family had none of these things until years after settling in Dyess.[33] The property was valued initially at $2,684.90, which Ray Cash could pay off at 6 percent interest per year.[34] The price included not only the house but a prorated share of the infrastructure (roads and bridges), livestock, charges to date for items purchased at the cooperative store, the outbuildings, and the hospital.

Despite the bare-bones interior of their house, the Cashes had a new home. Ray Cash, however, was not a man for rejoicing. He was pleased to be in Dyess, but he wanted to get to work, and before he got his hands dirty, he walked the twenty acres of land on his property. At one point, he fell into a hole and sank up to his chest in cold water.[35] The Cash homestead consisted of twenty acres, but Ray would have to put in many hours of backbreaking work before the land was suitable for farming. Ray and his oldest son Roy, then only a teenager, had to wrestle farmland from a wilderness. His other sons, Jack and Johnny, were too young for the hardest work—cutting trees, removing stumps, and draining the land—and the Cash men would have to labor without the aid of heavy machinery.

In Dyess, the Cash family had to fight not just the depression but also the very land they lived on. Early in its history, Dyess was compared to the fertile Nile River Valley.[36] But in 1934, when the colony was built, the land was not suited to farming. Once cleared and drained, the land presented other problems. Dyess would become known for its "gumbo" or "buckshot" soil, a thick mud that was rich but unstable. Over time, buildings and other structures fought to stay upright. Today a visitor to Dyess can see slanted telephone poles and wavy roads, dramatic evidence of nature altering the landscape—and doing it more quickly than in other parts of Arkansas.

Americans have settled places far more inhospitable than Dyess, however, and without the tools of the modern era. The founding of Dyess was a classic American story in which settlers brought civilization to a frontier. Puritans moved to Massachusetts in the 1600s to build a "city on a hill." Later, Americans migrated to the West Coast to fulfill a "Manifest Destiny" in which the United States would stretch from "sea to shining sea." In Dyess, there were no hills, let alone seas, but the project had similar idealism attached to it. In the 1934 report by the Arkansas ERA, the reporter described Dyess as a "Utopia" and "Eden."[37]

Dyess may not have conformed to most people's idea of a Utopia, but for desperate Arkansas men, it offered room for advancement. It also served as a link between the men of the Great Depression and the Founding Founders. Jefferson himself was a planter, but he saw the United States' future as one of yeomen farmers. By the 1930s, farmers such as Ray Cash were hardly the wave of the future; within a few decades, small farming in Dyess was doomed. But for a little while, Ray enjoyed a stable life farming his own patch of land, where Johnny Cash grew to manhood. Dyess briefly seemed to fulfill the dreams of the Jeffersonian yeoman republic.

For White People Only

As was true of the Founding Fathers and frontier settlers, the citizens of Dyess did not act in the interests of African Americans. Dyess was an extreme example of a southern community excluding Black people and a marked contrast to the town of Wilson, where Lee Wilson's plantations thrived using vast amounts of cheap Black and white labor. Wilson was a paternalist of the old school. At his most generous, he saw himself as the head of a large Black and white family. He even built a school for his Black workers and in many respects treated them better than other white employers of his time.[38] But Wilson also demanded obedience and hard work, and he was no opponent of the racial status quo, which enforced Jim Crow law and lynch justice.

Arkansas has a sinister and twisted history of race relations. In 1860, a quarter of the state's population were enslaved African Americans. In Arkansas after the Civil War, white supremacists—as was true in other former Confederate states—defeated Reconstruction through murder, violence, fraud, and terror. With the "redemption" of the South came the oppression of the Black population through segregation, lynching, election fraud, and forced exclusion from communities. In the late nineteenth and early twentieth centuries, Arkansas became notorious for its "sundown towns," in which Black people were warned not to "let the sun go down on them" in certain communities, especially those in the northwestern part of the state, such as the virulently racist town of Harrison, which even in the twenty-first century has a prominent Ku Klux Klan presence.[39]

After Reconstruction, white Arkansans continued to purge African Americans from their communities and the seats of power.[40] Mississippi County was no exception when it came to racial violence. Nationwide, lynchings were most numerous in the 1890s (averaging almost one every other day in some years, just in the South), but the extralegal, brutal killing of African Americans by white community members intent on maintaining racial dominance continued well into the twentieth century.[41] One lynching in January 1921 in Mississippi County was especially horrifying. Henry Lowery, a Black man, shot and killed several white people after a heated labor dispute with his planter boss. Lowery managed to escape Arkansas before arrest, but he was eventually caught and returned. White justice in Mississippi County involved dousing Lowery with gasoline and burning him at the stake in front of hundreds of eyewitnesses. It took Lowery more than a half hour to die. The case inspired national and even international fury among civil rights activists.[42]

Despite the racial violence, terror, and torture they endured, African Americans in the Delta remained numerous—some even thrived.[43] Mississippi County had a large African American population, but Dyess did not, even though Black people in areas of Mississippi County comprised 84 percent of residents.[44] One of the colony settlers claimed he moved to Dyess because he could find no work, owing to the "increasing preference for cheap Black labor on the plantations."[45] Dyess residents were hoping to escape the wage deflation that gripped the South. Whites were also happy to be free of "the Negro."

The white administrators who built Dyess had no problem with using African American laborers, even if those same laborers were not permitted to live there. The first Dyess government report noted the construction of three mess halls: "two for white labor and one for colored."[46] A Black nurse was also employed during the earliest days of the colony.[47] But when it came to getting homesteads in Dyess, Black people need not apply. Whites literally were getting twenty acres and a mule, but once again, the South's systematic racism denied opportunities to African Americans. And this time, it happened in the worst economic period in American history.

Surviving the Depression

William Dyess died in a January 1936 plane crash, but by then, his town was a thriving farming community. By May, most of the houses were occupied. The *Colony Herald* started publishing issues twice a month to keep residents informed.[48] At the end of 1936, the program to clear the land for farming was 50 percent finished, and citizens had access to more of everything that made a cotton town work, from a café to a laundry, cotton gin, printing shop, and sorghum mill.[49]

People nationwide began taking notice. On June 9, 1936, Eleanor Roosevelt visited Dyess. Her trip had not been easy, entailing fifteen miles over "dusty roads after leaving the main highway." But she greeted thousands at the community center, had lunch at the café, and visited several residents' homes.[50] Roosevelt also gave a speech in front of the administration building. On that memorable Tuesday night, she told the gathering that people in Washington were watching the town's progress. Her words emphasized how hard-working people were struggling through no fault of their own. What she saw in Dyess—the largest homestead she had ever seen—was an opportunity for people to "work out their own salvation." Her words reinforced the Protestant work ethic, noting that people had to "prove . . . you are able to make the most of it for yourselves and your children." When a yapping dog threatened to drown out Roosevelt's words, she said, "I like dogs." And the dog "only wants to take the center of the stage." Roosevelt did what the Roosevelts did best: instill optimism and confidence. Mrs. Roosevelt said she had just come from a mining town in Iowa and believed the people there would do well in the end. Her speech was no paean to big government. Rather, it was a lesson for neighbors to help one another and work hard.[51]

And yet, the Roosevelts could not end the Great Depression, and they could do even less to alleviate the devastation caused by the natural disasters that marked the period. One such catastrophe was the Dust Bowl, which ravaged the Midwest. Another was the 1937 Mississippi and Ohio River flood. While not as well known as the great Mississippi flood of 1927, it was horrendous in terms of the property destroyed and the people displaced. For Johnny Cash, it was his first encounter with a flood of Biblical proportions.

The 1937 Flood

Mississippi County was no stranger to flooding. A 1934 ERA report complained of a work stoppage in January because of "high water in scattered sections of the colony," where drainage ditches were overwhelmed by heavy rains.[52] The flood of 1937 began with rain pounding down in January. The deluge lasted three weeks. Situated as the Cash family was in the Delta, not far from the Mississippi, the flooding probably would have been bad in any case, but Dyess was not helped by the clearing done over the previous two years. With the loss of so many trees and vegetation, the land could not hold as much water as it had before. As the flood waters rose, Dyess residents worried not just about the Mississippi, but also the Tyronza River, which cut through the colony. The Cashes were in danger of losing everything.

Ray Cash held on as long as he could. He had his first home and farm. He didn't want to leave. He had been in Dyess for not even two years when the flood struck, threatening to take everything from him. But even a man as stubborn as Ray was not prepared to put his family at risk. The Cashes evacuated their farm as the flooding worsened. Ray Cash sent his family to Kingsland but stayed behind to protect his property from looters.

Johnny and the rest of the family were put on a bus that took them to a train. In a story typically rich in detail, Cash said in 1990 that it was during the flood that he began to love trains. As he headed through West Memphis, the engineer let him ride in the cab. Cash said the train was like a "magic carpet taking us out of the flood country. I watched men on the front, on the cow catcher, poking a pole to see if there were logs on the tracks, with the water two feet over the tracks."[53] Cash would choose music over farming early in his life. But the flood, and the plight of farmers and other working people, stayed with him.

In 1959, Johnny Cash wrote about the ordeal in "Five Feet High and Rising." It became a classic. Written with great economy, the song, with its relentless boom-chicka-boom—as relentless as the rain must have seemed to residents of Dyess—clocks in at less than two minutes. Despite the song's brevity, Cash penned some of his most descriptive lyrics, singing of the "homemade boat" taking the family to the train, the water rising over the wheat and oats, and the chickens "sleeping in the willow trees." As he often did, Cash injected some humor, sarcastically noting that "looks like we'll be blessed with a little more rain." The song makes no specific reference to the 1937 flood or Arkansas, but Cash mentioned the song's historic roots when he played it live over the years. Oddly, Cash did not mention the flood in either of his two autobiographies. Perhaps he had talked about it so much over the years that he didn't feel the need to talk about it again.

The flood was severe, but the Cash family was lucky. They had relatives in Kingsland they could stay with until the waters receded. Such was not the case for the one million people the flood displaced. West of Dyess in Jonesboro, Arkansas, meningitis broke out. Further south, in Forrest City, camps were set up for those made homeless by the flood.[54] When Johnny and his family returned to Dyess—as Cash was fond of recollecting—the house was a mess. The floors were covered with mud and the livestock had the run of the place. But the house and barn were intact. After a little cleaning up, life for the family went back to normal.[55]

The flood was not a major setback for the colony. By the end of February, almost everyone in Dyess—487 families—had returned home. The flood had cost the colony $47,566.86 in damages. This was no small sum in 1937, but it was no catastrophe either. The government, however, was not going to pick up the tab. Rather, Dyess Colony Incorporated, which ran the town, paid for the losses mostly on its own.[56]

Despite the flood and the fact that the depression dragged on, Dyess residents, as Americans often are, were optimistic amid hard times. Floyd Sharp, the president of Dyess Colony Incorporated, said in July 1937 that

This image, taken as a train moved from Memphis to Forrest City, Arkansas, gives a good idea of what the Cashes experienced as they fled Dyess in the wake of the 1937 flood. The Mississippi River flood caused major disruption and damage to Delta communities, but it did not do lasting damage to Dyess. The Cashes returned home once the waters receded and made a bumper cotton crop later that year. On his 1959 album *Songs of Our Soil*, Cash wrote about the flood in "Five Feet High and Rising" but did not specifically mention Arkansas in the song. *Courtesy Library of Congress, LC-USF33-004179-M3 [P&P].*

in just three years, the area was "back at the 1929 level."[57] Dyess was built by the federal government, but it was run, much like the post office, by a company dependent on making money.

King Cotton

Dyess, however, was never profitable—and the problem was cotton. In 1962, Johnny Cash recorded a cover version of "Busted" (written that same year by Detroit native Harlan Howard) in which he mournfully sings, "Cotton is down to a quarter a pound." Depression-era farmers would have been delighted to have cotton at 25 cents a pound. In 1919, in the wake of a wartime boom, cotton prices reached 35 cents a pound. By 1931, the price had dropped to a mere fraction of that: 5.66 cents a pound. The reasons prices were so low were a deflated economy and overproduction. Despite government efforts to control cotton prices during the 1930s, farmers were prolific. In 1937, the United States produced more than 12 million bales, which fetched 8.13 cents per pound. The next year it grew more than 18 million bales at 8.6 cents per pound.[58] Cotton was still very much king in the South. Still, the bumper crop, as impressive as it was, meant at best sluggish prices for farmers, resulting in harder times for small producers such as the Cash family.

Even high water could not harm the Dyess cotton crop. The 1937 flood replenished the land, and during the next harvest, Ray and others did well—on the whole, Dyess farmers ginned 1,548 bales of cotton. Prices, however, had fallen from 1936 by more than four cents per pound.[59]

The Cashes were lucky; they were not at the bottom of the economic heap. They depended on cotton, but they were *not* sharecroppers (i.e., those who did not own land, or in some cases even houses, and were heavily indebted to landowners). Dyess farmers worked their own farms, which they could eventually purchase from DCI. Yet though the Cash family was not the worst off in Dyess, hard work was a way of life. The production of cotton in 1930 didn't differ much from how it was done in 1830. Southerners spent countless hours chopping cotton—cutting away weeds that grew between the plants. The picking in depression-era Arkansas was done by hand, whether Black or white. Machines would not become a staple of the southern farm until after the Second World War.[60]

"Jesus Was Our Savior, Cotton Was Our King," Cash wrote in his 1975 autobiography *Man in Black*. Cotton might have been king, but it kept Arkansas a poor and agricultural state. At an individual level, it was monotonous, backbreaking work, not at all suited to an ambitious and creative young man such as Johnny Cash. Cash said with dry understatement that "there really wasn't much to recommend the work. It exhausted you, it hurt your back a lot, and it cut your hands. That's what I hated the most. The bolls were sharp, and unless you were really concentrating when you reached out for them, they got you." He remembered that after a couple weeks his fingers were covered with "little red wounds, some of them pretty painful." His sisters, he noted, particularly hated what picking did to their hands, but they got used to it. Even so, Cash wrote, "you'd often hear them crying, particularly when they were very young. Practically every girl I knew in Dyess had those pockmarked fingers. Daddy's hands were as bad as anyone else's, but he acted as if he never even noticed."[61] By the time he was eight, Cash wrote, he was dragging a cotton sack with a tar-covered bottom, "six feet long if you were one of the younger children, nine feet long for big kids and grown-ups."[62] J. R. disliked working in the cotton fields, but at harvest time, which peaked in October, he became a good picker who could pluck from the bolls several hundred pounds of cotton in a day. Johnny never could pick as much as his dad did, but as things turned out, he had no desire to stay in Dyess long enough to surpass him.[63]

The cotton fields were a source of misery for many southerners, but they kept the Cash family and other Dyess colonists afloat economically. The most unfortunate of families in Mississippi County were the sharecroppers. Rosanne Cash has written about her father trading stories of his upbringing with his friend John Rollins. "Although by 1976 he was one of the richest men in the country," she said of Rollins, "he and my father would try to 'out-poor' each other at the dinner table with stories of their childhoods of abject poverty."[64] The Cash family did not live in abject poverty. Rather, it was the many sharecroppers in Arkansas and the South who were the poorest of the poor. Cash, however, was not the kind of person to feel superior. He never forgot the drudgery of cotton farming and the toll it took on people's lives—physically, emotionally, and economically. He remembered the dirt-poor migrant workers who asked the Cash family if there were crops they could pick. "They'd come with rags on their backs and maybe a skillet tied on their wagon," he told Christopher Wren. "Mostly they just walked in."[65] Sharecropper in Dyess reminded him that there were people far worse off than his family: people with no home, no education, no good jobs, and no prospects.

As 1938 arrived, the Cash family remained on their farm. By then, though, many residents had left, whether because of bad luck, homesickness, or frustration. In April 1938, the president of DCI wrote that between 100 and 150 families had moved out of the colony.[66] By the spring of 1938, nevertheless, the *Arkansas Gazette* boasted that the center of Dyess had a hospital, barbershop, service station, movie theater, poultry plant, shoe shop, garage, machine shop, feed mill, and post office.[67] Regardless, the DCI was bleeding money. Gov. Carl Bailey, one of the many Democrats critical of FDR and the New Deal, battled with the colony over tax issues and ultimately revoked its charter in the spring of 1939. As a result, the Farm Security Administration took control of the colony in 1940.[68]

Despite DCI's problems, the Cash family found itself much better off than many similar families in Mississippi County or the South generally. Farmers in Dyess could shop at the cooperative Dyess Colony Store, located two miles from the Cash house in the center of town. When Cash was a child, the store sold a pound of Luzianne coffee for 29 cents, a pound of chocolate for 15 cents, and bananas for 25 cents per dozen. The store also sold dry goods: shoes, shirts, shorts, hats, and ties. One advertisement from the store noted, "We Don't Mind Working for Your Smile!" Even though the cooperative was the most "socialist" aspect of Dyess, the advertisement for the town emphasized hard work. "Lots of histories of folks' lives tell a great deal about how they were lucky, and therefore, became successful," the ad said. "That may be so, but we're not intending to sit down and wait for our good fortune. Work, and lots of it, plus experience, ability, common sense, and reasoning judgment are thrown into the scale to insure success for us and satisfaction for you."[69] Hard work and luck—those were things that signified Ray Cash's survival as a farmer. They also had a lot to do with why Johnny was successful as a musician.

Cash and Pop Culture

Johnny Cash never let farming get into his blood. He was a child of pop culture. He devoured radio and the movies, both of which were still relatively new innovations when he was young. The radio became a staple of American life in the 1920s, followed by the advent of talkie films in 1927. Radio shows happened in Cash's head, but film presented him with larger-than-life heroes, especially the cowboys. Film was also a way in which Cash could hear music outside of his constant radio listening.

Cash saw his first movies in the golden age of the silver screen. Despite the Great Depression, Hollywood continued to create spectacles and epics that combined the ancient art of storytelling with visual magic and the latest technologies. Two Technicolor classics, *Gone with the Wind* and *The Wizard of Oz*, were released in 1939. As is true of so many young men, Cash internalized mass media and became obsessed with the entertainment world. He was never much for spectacle, however. Cash was a from a period in which performers never incorporated big stage productions or flashy costumes—not even Stetson hats or rhinestones. Rather, they aimed at being direct rather than bombastic—hence the eventual emergence of the Man in Black. But Cash certainly understood the relationship between audience and performer. Going to the movies as a boy helped him learn that whatever they were wearing, entertainers had to put on a good show.

Cash also learned empathy from film. Late in his life, he told *Walk the Line* director James Mangold that his favorite movie was the original *Frankenstein*, which came out in 1931. Cash liked it, he said, because the movie was about a monster made up of "bad parts," who "tries to do something decent."[70] *Frankenstein* might also have appealed to Cash's childhood sense of being an outsider, which later shaped his rebel image and made him resentful of the Nashville establishment. Considering that Cash at his worst was a destructive monster run amok, we can see why he connected to Boris Karloff's portrayal. But even a monster, *Frankenstein* shows, is capable of tenderness.

Cash traveled to the cinema many times as a boy. In 1947, a stand-alone movie theater was built in Dyess (the one there today is a replica). Cash never received an allowance, but the movies were cheap, and Cash once remembered selling peanuts with his brother for ticket money.[71] Another story was at once sad and endearing. Johnny went to the movies with a friend, who was too poor to afford the twenty-cent ticket. Cash agreed to pay, and the two boys rode a blind horse to get to the theater.[72] Some nights, Cash had to walk home after dark—no mean feat considering it was a 2.5-mile journey.[73] On one occasion, J. R. made his unfortunate younger brother Tommy walk home alone while Johnny drove off in a car with friends.[74]

It was not uncommon for small towns in the 1930s and 1940s to have a movie theater. Far more communities had one then versus today. Despite the Great Depression coinciding with film's so-called golden age, that term had more to do with the percentage of the population that frequented the theaters rather than the quality of the films. In the age before television, however, movies brought the wider world to average Americans looking for glamour, adventure, and romance. Directors during Cash's youth delighted in the technological progress that allowed them to make epic, emotionally charged movies blending visuals, dialogue, and music. The cinema was also a cheap diversion. Anyone with pocket money could enjoy the experience. Some of Cash's earliest memories were of going to the movies. Later, he starred in movies himself, usually those with an Old South or Wild West theme. Film made a lifelong impression on him.

New Deal Politics

While Johnny Cash sought diversions amid the tedium of school and the cotton fields, his parents worried about their financial state and the country's political situation. Ray and Carrie Cash were not political people, nor were they alone as such in lily-white Dyess. In January 1938, a reporter for the *Arkansas Gazette* asked a Dyess resident about his political beliefs. "Nope. We ain't interested in politics," he said.[75] Ray Cash couldn't have put it better himself. J. R. became political later in life, but never in any conventional sense. He also said he never voted.[76] It's likely that politics wasn't discussed much in the Cash household, or at least not in any constructive way. Ray might have supported FDR while also being sympathetic toward the race-baiting politicians that were all too common in the South.

Despite their state's place in the Solid South, many Arkansans began to organize politically in ways others previously would have deemed revolutionary. The New Deal, while well intentioned and experimental, was hardly a radical assault on American capitalism or the political process. Still, outspoken Americans, from reactionary Catholic radio figure Father Charles Coughlin to Louisiana governor Huey P. Long, wanted Roosevelt to take a different course.[77] In the summer of 1934, the Southern Tenant Farmers' Union (STFU) was created in Arkansas in the town of Tyronza, not far from Dyess. The STFU was one of the many labor groups that formed in response to the Great Depression. Unlike northern unions, which focused on factory workers, the STFU attacked abuses inherent in sharecropping and tenant farming that had existed long before Roosevelt took office. The STFU was also concerned that much of the money dedicated to New Deal programs—such as the Agricultural Adjustment Administration—ended up in the pockets of wealthy landlords such as R. E. Lee Wilson. In the United States in the 1930s, unions were nothing new, nor were southern farmers' organizations. What was striking about the STFU in Arkansas was that it was biracial: Black and white members alike sought to make life better for the poorest farmers. Not surprisingly, the STFU's opponents decried the organization as a communist plot to equalize the races.[78] The union endured threats and violence during its attempts to organize. It began to crumble in the 1940s, and by the time the United States entered World War II, it existed in name only.

Ray Cash was not interested in the STFU or any other of the more leftist ideas or organizations born of the depression. The union was active in Dyess, but Ray probably thought unions were dangerously socialist and that Dyess was socialist enough as it was. The Cashes are not found on the rolls of the STFU.[79] A veteran, Ray had no problems taking money from the federal government. But he was a man of the Solid South, raised in a time when virtually every small farmer was a Democrat. Unlike Democrats who backed unions, Ray's Democratic Party was dedicated to small government and white supremacy—a country of the white man, by the white man, for the white man. In his eyes, Black people could go only as far as a menial job would take them—and they were best seen and not heard, if they needed to be seen at all. Dyess was not only a racist town—it was unusual in its racism. No Black farmers or laborers worked or lived there. Such a setup was unrealistic in most of the South, where African Americans were essential laborers. White men in Dyess decided they were not essential, and the Ray Cashes of the world were fine with that—less competition for them.

Ray shared the racial attitudes of his day, but in a time of great economic stress and political unrest, he was not a political man. Progressive Arkansans, however, saw the STFU as a way of combating the worst excesses of the depression and the plantation system. The existence of the STFU shows that there were cracks in the South's conservative political structure. Ray, who was from the southern part of a conservative state, did not soften his racial views once he moved to Mississippi County. Some residents of Mississippi County joined the STFU, but Ray had no interest in upsetting the racial or political status quo. Likely, in his mind, he had risked enough as it was by settling there.

Ray Cash might not have been interested in the STFU, but there was something in the air politically in Dyess during the Great Depression that undoubtedly settled onto the shoulders of young Johnny Cash. Johnny's politics were nebulous and are still debated, but J. R. grew up to be much more progressive than his father ever was, or most white men of his time. For the rest of his life, Cash had liberal tendencies—even if he never voted or aligned himself with one party—and an empathy for the working class and the downtrodden, from soldiers and prisoners to Native Americans.

Religion

The Cash family might have been apolitical, but they were not areligious. Later in life, Cash remembered his mother's advice to him: "Put your trust in God."[80] Church was central to Dyess life. At first, religious services in town were nondenominational, with no freestanding Baptist or Methodist churches. Dyess might have been experimental in many ways, but the town's religious culture was typical of small southern communities. As one resident noted, he was willing to walk three and a half miles to go to a nondenominational service, but "when the time comes only a Baptist Church will satisfy me."[81]

Religion was as central to the Cash family's upbringing as it was to Dyess as a whole. In the summer, churchgoers would gather for picnics. Cash remembered riding to the Baptist church in the back of a pickup truck—apparently this was before the Cashes had a vehicle.[82] The Cashes were willing to go to Baptist and Methodist services. Johnny himself visited various churches throughout his life, so long as they were evangelical. True to this upbringing, Cash learned the Bible well. His favorite verse was from the New Testament, John 3:16: "For God so loved the world that he gave His only begotten son that whoever believes in Him will have eternal life."[83] Cash also apparently took to heart another Biblical passage: "praise him with stringed instruments" from Psalms 150:4.

Cash's earliest childhood memories involved listening to the preacher's sermons and partaking in church activities. Church was where farmers learned about what was happening in the community, talked about crops, gossiped, and heard the word of God. It was also where most of them first practiced singing and playing music. Johnny's mother Carrie played piano at church, and she taught Johnny the religious songs that made such an impression on him.

Religious holidays were modest affairs. J. R. did not have fond memories of Halloween. Perhaps his evangelical family disliked the holiday's Catholic and pagan roots. The present-day rituals of Halloween would have been impossible in Cash's time. Any costumes children would have worn were homemade. Trick-or-treating would have been difficult in a town where long walks were the norm and candy and other sweets precious commodities. Halloween was not the commercial juggernaut it became in the late twentieth century. Christmas, another holiday with much stronger roots in Catholicism than evangelical Christianity, was low key. Cash never remembered any men dressing as Santa.[84] He said the family put up a tree, but it was memorable as the one time of the year that the family had fruit in the house. Nevertheless, J. R. recalled that Christmas in Dyess was "always highly spiritual."[85] Whatever they might have had, the Cashes were appreciative and generous. Cash said on the day after Christmas, his family "sacked up left-overs, including fruit and nuts and took them to the share-croppers."[86]

School and Recreation

Religion was central to southern life, but Dyess residents were also serious about education. The first school in Dyess opened in November 1934, a few months after work on the colony began. Colonists built the school and chose the town's teachers.[87] By May 1935, there were four employees at the school. Building the school was a sign of progress in the colony and symbolic of the advances being made nationwide to combat the depression. Dyess residents made sure their children received a decent education, and J. R. was a decent student. By his own admission he was a mischievous boy with a penchant for minor acts of destruction. But Cash did not act mean-spirited or seem troubled. A report card for the 1948–1949 school year shows his highest marks were in conduct.[88] Surprisingly, Cash, who later became a celebrated songwriter and author, was a below-average student in English. Later, as a senior, he got mediocre grades in history, a subject Cash had much interest in later.

J. R. played sports, too, such as softball, but he was not a dedicated athlete. Cash said he didn't play many sports because he had to work the cotton fields after school.[89] The real reason was that Cash's interests were more artistic. He said he got good roles in the plays throughout middle and high school, his favorite being "So Help Me Hannah," a 1940 play by James Floyd Stone.[90] He sang songs in the fields and at school, and he wrote poems and stories. Cash's musical ability was almost entirely untrained. He apparently had one voice lesson. According to Cash, after he sang her some Hank Williams, his instructor told him his voice was unique and that he should never let anyone change it.[91]

In summer, J. R. had no school. When not working in the fields or at church, it was a time for fishing, swimming, and playing in the woods. A true country boy, Cash went barefoot in the summer and "stepped on everything from broken glass to cow patties."[92] J. R. took quickly to swimming, which no doubt explains why, when he was asked to help his younger brother Tommy learn to swim, Johnny simply threw him in the water.[93]

As is true of many southerners who become tired of the relentless summer heat, Cash looked forward to the fall. September is still summer in the South, but temperatures cool by October. Cash also enjoyed the fall because, as he remembered it, "there was no work in the fields until late October."[94] Winter wasn't as exciting for J. R. and the young people of Dyess, which could get bitterly cold. Cash claimed that during the Second World War, the Mississippi froze and cars drove over it.[95] While that might have been a typical Cash exaggeration, his point was that northeastern Arkansas wasn't always warm. And yet, even when there was snow, there were no hills for the children to sled on.

Ray Cash

Johnny Cash tried to be a normal student in a small southern town, but he had to deal with a troubled home life. The problem was Ray Cash. While he might have attended church regularly, for many years Ray was a violent, abusive drunk. Even at his most well behaved, he was the kind of man who almost never smiled for photographs. Michael Streissguth has described him as a "stump of a man whose face forever seemed on the brink of rage or tears."[96] Later in life, Johnny Cash would be gone for long periods, sometimes months, but Ray was around all the time—in fact, too often.

Physically, Ray was unimpressive. He was a small man, shorter than his wife. Small as he might have been, he was the authority figure in the household. Johnny was raised in a time when child abuse was rampant, but not talked about. "My dad used to drink all the time," Johnny wrote in a 1952 letter, "and it didn't make things so happy at home a few times. Maybe that's the reason I'm so set against it."[97] Alcohol would never be

Johnny's drug of choice, but he was no stranger to drinking. And while he was not a notorious drinker, his struggle with chemical dependence lasted his whole life.

Ray cast a dark shadow over the Cash family, and Johnny carried resentment and bitterness toward his father for his entire life. Rosanne wrote that her grandfather Ray "was burdened and overworked and not always kind or even civil."[98] Johnny never forgot the time that Ray shot his pet dog for sneaking into the coop and killing some chickens. But he and his father never spoke about it either. The family later got another dog; its name was Ray.[99]

Cash's second autobiography displayed a clear anger toward his father. Ray never seemed much impressed with Johnny's accomplishment, instilling in his son a lifelong insecurity, anxiety, and brooding nature. Cash tempered his anger and fear though his art and sense of humor. Dyess for him represented the lightness and innocence of youth as well as the heaviness of the adult world—hard work, stern religion, and his father's cruelty. Balancing light and dark is often the formula for making great music, and it formed the basis for Cash's best work. Johnny eventually found some emotional and spiritual release through his songwriting.

We will likely never know what Ray's upbringing was like and what demons he carried with him throughout his life. In Dyess, he survived and provided for his family, but he did not thrive. He was the only member of his immediate family to have moved hundreds of miles from home. Ray likely had resentments toward his upbringing, his financial struggles, his own family (namely, his brother Dave), and life in general. Only in his last years did Johnny feel comfortable talking about his father. By the time Cash published his second memoir, he had nothing good to say about Ray, and retold the story of his father killing his dog. Ray might have been active in the church, but Johnny underscored how Ray was a self-described "evil man."[100]

Country Heroes

J. R. escaped from his family troubles through music. From an early age, he loved music, an education that depended on the radio. The Cashes didn't have electricity in their house until after World War II, but before then, they had a battery-powered radio. Cash remembered "an oncoming storm meant that soon I could run from the toil in the fields to the magic in the house—turn on the radio, listen to the music made far away, let it take me where it pleased."[101] Cash ably summed up the feelings of many young music fans who have heard odd and fascinating sounds coming from the radio—whether new or old—and have been inspired.

Cash's musical influences were varied and extensive. Among them was the Black rock and roll pioneer Sister Rosetta Tharpe.[102] Born in 1915, she was a native of Cotton Plant, Arkansas. Sister Rosetta's family worked in the cotton fields before moving to Chicago in the 1920s, where she was a regular at the Cotton Club. Her first recorded song, 1938's "Rock Me" (written by Thomas Dorsey), was a revelation in how it showed her ability to sing and play guitar soulfully and with originality. Adept at playing lead and rhythm guitar, she mixed blues and gospel in a way that foreshadowed rock and roll. Cash certainly appreciated Sister Rosetta's call in "Rock Me," as Tharpe's biographer Gayle Wald has written, "for delivery from worldly cares through music."[103] Among her fans were not only Cash but also Elvis and Carl Perkins.

Sister Rosetta was strong willed and sexually liberated. She was also a talented pianist and forceful guitarist, playing electric and acoustic guitar in an era when virtually no women did so professionally. One of her songs, "Can't No Grave Hold My Body Down," Cash recorded late in his career. In his first autobiography, Cash remembered seeing Sister Rosetta on stage in Chicago in 1964, where her performance brought a wasted Cash to tears. Later, Cash's daughter Rosanne said Tharpe might have been her father's favorite singer. While it is debatable whether or not Cash had one favorite singer—given Cash's love for Jimmie Rodgers, Hank Williams, Hank Snow, and Ernest Tubb, just to name a few—it is clear that he was a fan of Sister Rosetta's music. He talked about her for a good portion of his speech during his induction into the Rock & Roll Hall of Fame.[104]

Cash's love for Sister Rosetta's music shows how blues and country music intersected in the early twentieth century. Gospel often was the bridge between the two. Blacks and whites were segregated in the South, but the sounds of the church were often where these groups could find common space, even if it was more metaphorical than literal. As Olivia Mather has shown in her overview of race and country music, there was nothing inevitable about blues becoming "Black music" or country becoming the domain of white Americans. People have referred, somewhat ironically, to country as the "white man's blues," a phrase that is both exclusionary (country is white music) as well as inclusive, suggesting how much country owes to the blues. As Mather notes, the "split" between country and blues in the 1920s was much the result of marketing strategy emerging in Jim Crow landscape after World War I. Country "has always been a multiracial enterprise in a racialized society," Mather has written. "Its sounds capture the range of interracial encounters and embody influences that have been inextricable from the start."[105] Even avid country fans might have difficulty naming popular African American country stars beyond Charlie Pride or Darrius Rucker (who himself began his career in the pop group Hootie & the Blowfish), but Black musicians' imprint on country music has been deep.

As the authors of *Hidden in the Mix* have shown, hip-hop and country often share the same sources, a connection made possible through earlier similarities between country and the blues. Cash's fellow Arkansan and bluesman Big Bill Broonzy described his music's source in a way that Johnny Cash would have recognized.[106] He once talked about the pain that came from a man who works "twelve months of the year as a farmer and don't come out of debt, and the boss has to give you food on credit 'till the crop is sold, you can't do nothing but get the blues."[107] Broonzy was talking about people even lower on the economic and social rung than the Cashes of Mississippi County. But Cash could understand the struggle Broonzy was talking about. During his career, Cash wrote not just blues-inspired songs, but songs with "blues" in the title.

Cash's connections to the blues of the early twentieth century and the hip-hop of the late twentieth and early twenty-first centuries are just one means by which to measure the enormous impact he has had on music.[108] It also indicates how he could filter so many influences into his early music. Cash did not learn a musical instrument until he was in the Air Force, but in the eighteen years leading up to it, he was a musical sponge. Cash's mother played piano, but apparently J. R. took no interest in the instrument—the guitar would be Cash's lifeblood. Still, when Cash's mother bought J. R. a mail-order guitar in Dyess, the boy took no interest in that either.[109] Cash's early artistic development instead focused on his voice and writing and thinking about country music.

One of his heroes was Jimmie Rodgers, an early success as a musician and movie star, back when talkies were in their infancy. Rodgers's influence on Cash and other artists was immense. In one tune Rodgers sang, "I'm going to shoot poor Thelma just to see her jump and fall." The line inspired Cash's notorious line about Reno in "Folsom Prison Blues."[110] Rodgers, born in 1897 and known as the "Singing Brakeman" (a moniker he disliked), was one of the earliest tragic pop music stars. He was born in Meridian, Mississippi, which borders Alabama. Rodgers achieved great success in the late 1920s and early 1930s before succumbing to tuberculosis at thirty-five. Cash was only a year old when Rodgers died, but because of modern recording technology and the radio, Rodgers could sing to Cash from beyond the grave.

Cash's voice might have been unique, but early on there was one singer who he most closely resembled: Ernest Tubb. Born in 1914 to a sharecropper father just southwest of Dallas in Crisp, Texas—which later became a ghost town—Tubb, like Cash, was inspired by Jimmie Rodgers. Tubb gained fame in the 1940s, scoring a major hit in 1941 with "Walking the Floor over You," an early honky-tonk classic. Tubb's catalog is not so well known today as it was in Cash's time, but he had enormous influence on World War II–era America.

Another major influence on Cash in the 1940s was Clarence Eugene "Hank" Snow. Unlike most of Cash's heroes, Snow wasn't from the South, or even the United States. He was born in Canada in 1914, but that didn't stop him from gaining credibility from the country establishment. He moved to Nashville in 1945 and became known as the "Yodeling Ranger." In 1950, he wrote "I'm Moving On," which a casual country fan might think is a Hank Williams tune. The song hit number 1 on the Country Chart, the first of Snow's seven top hits, and stayed in that position for an impressive twenty-one weeks. One of Snow's best-known songs—though written and recorded by earlier artists—was "Wreck of the Old 97," a tune Cash played in concert for years.

World War II

It is no wonder that as an adult, Cash the musician wanted to lift people's spirits. He came of age in one of the lowest times in human history. The Great Depression was traumatizing and was only ended by the most savage and destructive war ever fought. For two years after Germany's invasion of Poland, the United States tried to remain neutral as Europe and Asia were engulfed in flames. That changed in December 1941 with the Japanese attack on Pearl Harbor. After years of bitter fighting in Asia, Europe, and Africa, the US lost more than 400,000 lives. A triumphant United States emerged as the world's economic superpower.

Johnny remembered being at his brother Roy's house in Trumann, in neighboring Poinsett County, when he heard of the Pearl Harbor attack.[111] Despite the United States' massive mobilization, the war did not immediately affect the Cash family. Only one of Ray's sons, Roy, served in the military—the navy—during World War II, and he apparently never saw combat.[112] The Cash family was not unusual in this; the vast majority of men who served during WWII never heard a shot fired in anger.

Wartime spending lifted the United States out of the depression, but that did not mean everyone benefited. To win the war, the federal government shifted priorities away from many of its New Deal programs to focus on war manufacturing and planning. In 1943, victory was far from assured as the United States made massive efforts to feed, clothe, and equip troops around the globe. That year, the federal government severed all ties to the Dyess project through an act of Congress.[113]

Ray and his children were spared the horrors of World War II, but tragedy visited the Cash family anyway. In May 1944, Johnny's older and favorite brother Jack died in a Dyess mill accident. The day of the accident, Johnny wanted to go fishing with his brother. Jack refused, saying his wanted to earn some extra money cutting lumber. Jack, who was only fifteen, did the work himself, until something went horribly wrong. While cutting wood, his clothing got tangled in the saw, which pulled him in. The whirling blade cut him nearly in half. As was his namesake—boxer Jack Dempsey—he was strong and a fighter. He lingered for days before dying.[114]

J. R. idolized Jack, who dreamed of becoming a preacher. The two boys had shared a bed, and Jack's death haunted Johnny for the rest of his life. In 1975, he made an album of gospel music, *Johnny Cash Sings Precious Memories*, to honor Jack's memory. The album, however, did little to fill the hole in Cash's soul that Jack's death had left. He never completely recovered emotionally. *Precious Memories* was not one of Cash's more memorable recordings, but it was one of the many ways he chose to honor his brother's memory.

As tragic as Jack's death was, the year 1944 saw members of the family further embrace the teachings of Jesus. That year, at the age of twelve,

Johnny was baptized in the Tyronza River.[115] Jack's death apparently had a deep effect on Ray Cash as well, who was baptized that May.[116] Family records do not provide an exact date for it, but it seems likely that Ray saw Jack's death as a reason to become more religious. Ray also decided to put the bottle down. In 1952, Johnny said Jack's death was the only time he saw his father cry. "Up to that time my dad was hard hearted and cruel," he said, "but since then he's changed."[117] According to Johnny's first wife Vivian, as Jack was dying, he told his father that God was "taking me so you'll quit drinking."[118] Vivian certainly was not there, but the story of how Jack's death shook Ray to change his horrid ways made an impact on her. The night before Jack died, Johnny remembered, his father prayed through the night, while Johnny sat listening to his father's anguish.[119]

As the Cash family planted cotton and prayed for the soul of their departed Jack, the world war raged on. The most dramatic story to come out of the Cash family during the war was that of Cash's brother-in-law, Jordan Joseph "Joe" Garrett. Garrett—who looked a bit like Carl Perkins in one navy picture—was a native of Clark County, Arkansas, and the husband of Cash's sister Louise. Joe and Louise had grown up together in Dyess and fell in love when they were young. Joe, however, wanted to "see the world" and joined the navy in 1940 before he could get married. In March 1942, the Japanese sunk his ship, the *USS Houston*. Joe was captured and languished in a Japanese POW camp for years. Louise, believing him dead, married. When Joe miraculously returned, an overjoyed Louise decided to leave her new husband for Joe. The two married, had two sons and a daughter, and stayed together until Louise's death in 2003. Joe lived until 2007, dying in Hendersonville, Tennessee, the same town where Johnny, June, and his parents were buried. Not long before his death, Joe had been awarded the Purple Heart. The man who presented it to him was Roy Cash Jr., who himself had served in the navy.[120]

Young Outlaw

J. R. hit his teens during World War II. Without a doubt, he was a restless young man and by no means a perfect child. It was in Dyess that he picked up smoking, a habit he greatly regretted later. As was true later in his life, he could be destructive but also had a reputation for honesty. Despite an abusive father and the death of his brother Jack, J. R. was mostly well behaved. In one telling bit of advice, Cash wrote that for anyone who was angry, it was best to say nothing and take a walk until the anger subsided.[121] Johnny said later in life that he and his siblings got along very well. According to him, they never fought.[122] Cash, however, either forgot the many fights he had had or wanted to put the best light on family relations. In the early fifties, writing from Germany, Cash said he fought with his younger sister, Reba, "every day" and added, "I don't think there were many kind words between us until she got married."[123] Cash always had a gift for blending the virtues of the good-natured southern boy with an equally strong rebellious and self-destructive streak. He misbehaved enough to make life more interesting in Dyess, while never going so far as to disappoint his teachers or parents. His experiences as a young man in a small southern town were typical.

When not in school or at play, Cash helped his family in the fields. For fun, he enjoyed fishing—a lifelong obsession—and hunting rabbits and squirrels. As did many American boys, he also liked to play make-believe as a "cowboy hero."[124] The cowboy myth had great appeal for Cash, who identified with solitary men doing their best under hard circumstances. Cash's understanding of the cowboy was based more on popular culture and myth than reality. Yet J. R. was no different than most Americans in that regard.

The Wild West myth has built its foundation on loners—outlaws, sheriffs, damaged soldiers, and doomed Native Americans. Sometimes Cash's love of music and cowboys came together in one entertainer. His favorite movie star was Gene Autry, the "Singing Cowboy." Cash said the first movie he saw, at age five, was a Gene Autry movie.[125] And he likely saw Autry often—from 1934 to 1953, Autry made ninety-three movies. He also worked in radio and television. Were Cash born in a less western state, his fascination with the cowboys-and-Indians mythology might have been merely quaint. But even well into the twentieth century, the Wild West was alive and well in Arkansas. With Arkansas having one foot in the South and one in the frontier, one could say that Cash grew up west of the Mason-Dixon Line. And Cash was not the only Arkansan in love with the West: in 1968, when Cash's career was at its zenith, Charles Portis, a native of El Dorado, published *True Grit*, part of which is set in Arkansas.

The dark side of the American frontier followed Cash his whole life, and Arkansas had more than its fair share of horrid tales of frontier violence.

In his posthumously published *Recollections*, Cash wrote of an eighty-year-old man named Jim George visiting the family. According to Cash, the man "wore a yellow bandana around his neck. He said it was to cover up rope burns where they tried to hang him."[126] Cash said the family never knew whether the man's story was true or not. The mysterious Jim George, nevertheless, appealed to Cash's young imagination. Had the man been a cattle rustler? A common thief? If he had escaped the hangman's noose, how had he done it? In Arkansas, Cash absorbed stories of the Wild West and rough justice that inspired a long and prolific music career.

The Wild West appealed not just to Cash's darker side but also his desire to test boundaries, to travel, to be an outlaw. Cash much preferred to write songs about outlaws than sheriffs, even if a criminal ended up swinging from the gallows, as in "25 Minutes to Go" (penned by Shel Silverstein in the mid-1960s). Cash embraced varied sources, but many were close to home. Some of the greatest outlaws in American history, from Jesse James to Al Capone to Bonnie and Clyde, spent considerable time in Arkansas.

Ballad of a Teenage Cash

Cash had a love for history, but he was also very much a modern teenager who sought the latest diversions. The original plans for Dyess included a ballpark (Cash was never a dedicated athlete), swimming pool, and tennis courts. There was one hangout in town, where high schoolers could get a cheap bite to eat. And by the end of World War II, Dyess had a roller rink.[127]

It is not surprising that as a cash-strapped child of the depression, J. R. had a fleeting attitude toward money. He was never a good businessman. A story Cash related to his daughter is telling of his attitude toward money. He remembered throwing away a dollar bill as a child, thinking it was a scrap piece of paper.[128] A dollar, of course, was a good amount of money for a young boy in the Great Depression. Cash later made millions of dollars from his records, but he understood that it all came and went as easily as that dollar he tossed away as a boy. Cash was notoriously careless with money, wasting thousands on drugs, trashed hotels, and wrecked automobiles. He lived well, but he never fetishized money. He had a blue collar attitude: make money by performing and creating, not investing and collecting royalties. The Great Depression complicated his attitude toward finances. He learned that if you don't work, you don't eat. That instilled in Cash a good work ethic, but it also made him indifferent and perhaps even resentful toward money.

Cash was more reverent toward food. Raised on country fare, he said the first food he knew how to make was gravy, and among his favorites were bacon and fried chicken.[129] The family celebrated Thanksgiving, but Cash said they never had the luxury of eating turkey, as was true for most Dyess residents.[130] As an adult, Cash became known as one of country music's greatest eaters. He never sank to the decadent depths of Elvis, but Cash was known as a man who could consume large quantities of food and drink quickly. He impressed onlookers with how he could wolf down a steak or knock back a beer in seconds. By the 1960s, his cravings for drugs were also well known. Cash was a man of large appetites.

Cash grew up in a town of farmers, where hard work was a way of life. He did many chores, including hauling hay, which he hated. He also cut firewood, built fires, fed mules, pigs, and chickens, dug potatoes, and picked other vegetables (officials in Dyess required residents to grow their own produce).[131] He was a member of Future Farmers of America, but he had no interest in becoming a farmer. His first job was as a water boy, helping workers in the field. Cash remembered it was a "hard job, non-stop." He also worked as a janitor at a church for $3 a week.[132] But Cash wanted to play music, later saying he always wanted to be a singer, "never anything else."[133]

Ray Cash never had much use for music himself. J. R.'s mother Carrie was different. She played piano and knew a little guitar. J. R.'s guitar lessons in Dyess were few. He had a friend named Jesse Barnhill (a dead ringer for legendary guitarist Link Wray) who, despite being disabled by polio, played guitar. Cash would visit Jesse's house to learn a few chords. J. R. had a burning desire to learn as much music as he could. He claimed his friends nicknamed him "Guitar," not because he played one, but because he was such a music fan.[134]

Cash wasn't in a band in high school, but before World War II, young men didn't play in garages or basements—neither of which Cash had—the way they would in the 1950s and 1960s. Cash nevertheless enjoyed singing. When he was fourteen, he won a talent contest singing "That Lucky Old Sun," a tune covered by everyone from Louis Armstrong to Dean Martin and Willie Nelson and one Cash would revisit on his 2000 album *Solitary*

Man.[135] Cash must have appreciated the prize money, but he also learned the lesson that having talent—especially in music—could prove lucrative for someone willing to perform. It certainly was easier and more rewarding than long days of field work.

In Dyess, Cash developed an appreciation for music of all genres. Some of the orchestra-heavy songs he remembered were "Linda," released in 1946 by Buddy Clark; "Goodnight, Sweetheart," a 1931 song by a British trio—not to be confused with the later doo-wop hit, "Goodnite, Sweetheart, Goodnite"—though Cash probably knew that one well, too, as it was released in the mid-fifties. The Ray Noble Orchestra's version of "Goodnight, Sweetheart" is lush, but it has a brief, bluesy guitar intro. Writing to his daughter Tara later, Cash also remembered Dinah Shore and Tony Martin's "A Penny a Kiss" and Nat King Cole's "Too Young" (1951) and "Nature Boy" (1948). It might seem out of character for Cash to mention how he remembered string-laden pop songs. But later in his career, he was no stranger to filling out his own sound. During the two years of his ABC television show, he played some of his best songs of that period—"Flesh and Blood," "What Is Truth" and "Sunday Mornin' Comin' Down"—backed by an orchestra. Cash was always looking for a new sound, and he was well attuned to the pop market. If strings helped him sell records, he used them.[136]

A little-known favorite of J. R.'s was the Chuck Wagon Gang, a gospel group founded in 1935. The original members consisted of Carters from Lubbock, Texas—not related to the Carters that Cash later married into—but the Chuck Wagon Gang was a good example of the family- and religion-oriented nature of country music, something Cash embraced for his entire career. Anna Carter married Jimmie Davis, the segregationist governor of Louisiana best-known for the classic 1939 country tune "You Are My Sunshine."[137] Cash sang the song throughout his career and recorded his own version with Rick Rubin. Another song he loved growing up was "You'll Never Walk Alone," a 1945 tune from Rodgers and Hammerstein's *Carousel.* Many artists have covered the song, including Sinatra and Elvis and New Orleans gospel singer Mahalia Jackson. Later, true to Rubin's American Recordings aesthetic, the accompaniment was bare. Rather than a guitar, Rubin had Cash accompanied only by a church organ.

Johnny Cash traveled the world, but J. R. had few opportunities to leave Dyess. One exception was the weeks he spent in the Ozarks for Boy Scout camp. Cash remembered the "beautiful country" he visited.[138] He might not have been at camp for that long, but like so many young people who go to camp, the place had an enormous impact on him. Later in life, Cash discussed a novel he was working on based on his trip to camp as a boy. He was using *Hoxie Rock* as a working title. In 1990, he said he had written about two hundred pages. Apparently, Hoxie Rock was the place where Cash and his friends would "take a leak" when they stopped along the road to Hardy, where the camp was. Cash said he had brought back a slab of the limestone to Dyess to put at the front door of his house.[139]

Going to camp was a treat for Cash. Most of his Dyess days consisted of school, the farm, and trips to town. Cash's depression-era life was not easy. Every day, he lived under a roof with an abusive father amid the hardest of economic times. The Cash children did not lack for necessities, though Cash complained later in life about never having any money and not having many clothes.[140]

Cash's experiences as a teenager were normal. He said he didn't have a "very broad social life."[141] He had limited experiences with women. He envied one boy at his school, an athlete, who "had a car and lots of girls."[142] His first date apparently happened when he was sixteen. As Cash remembered it, his father let him use the family car—a 1935 Ford—to take a girl to the movies. Cash said he got her home by 9:30. He summed up his high school years: "No money for the girls. No car to drive. No dates."[143] As self-deprecating as Cash was, it is unlikely his Dyess classmates fared much better.

As is true for many country boys, Cash was curious about the opposite sex. As he put it in his second autobiography, "What *really* got me moving, of course, was sex. By about fifteen I'd discovered girls. They did a pretty good job with my loneliness. When the hormones started moving, so did I."[144] Robert Hilburn has been blunter about Cash's first foray into sex. According to Hilburn, Cash's losing his virginity was not a pleasant experience: he and two other boys had sex with the same girl, who might have been mentally disabled.[145] So began Cash's checkered sexual history.

Cash did not have much sexual experience before leaving Dyess, but he had plenty of experience with smoking. Cash said he smoked "a piece of grapevine" when he was twelve.[146] But he graduated to cigarette smoking as a teenager and remembered stealing his father's tobacco. Cash's experiences with sex and smoking, while hardly encouraged by the intensely religious Christian community in which he lived, were typical of many

In 1950, Cash graduated from Dyess High School. That same year, after a series of short-lived and unfulfilling jobs, Cash joined the Air Force. When he returned to the United States in 1954, he moved to Memphis and married his sweetheart Vivian Liberto. He would return to Arkansas—including Dyess—many times over the years. *Courtesy Dyess High School yearbook.*

teenagers. J. R. likely considered them a means of relief from the boredom and anxiety caused by staid country life. And his rebellious tendencies were not so bad as to jeopardize his chances of making it out of town.

Leaving Dyess

Once he graduated, Cash wasted little time in leaving Dyess. The first job he got was picking strawberries in Bald Knob, Arkansas, roughly a hundred miles west of his hometown. The job, which Cash said paid $3 for three days of work, was dismal. He hitchhiked home.[147] Dejected, he decided to move to Pontiac, Michigan, to work in the automobile industry. That job lasted longer than plucking strawberries, but not by much. After Cash returned home again, he worked at a margarine factory at Evadale in Mississippi County. He understandably found sweeping the floors and doing other odd jobs unexciting and unfulfilling.[148] But Johnny Cash's future would not be in a factory or on a farm.

A high school graduate now, Cash had little direction in life. Music had a strong pull on him, but he had no formal musical training and little skill beyond his voice. Though Cash's baritone proved a powerful instrument, in 1950 he had no reason to think that he would have a career in music. Instead, Cash chose the military, which would provide employment, structure, travel, and steady pay—not to mention time to decide what he was going to do with himself.

As his father did before him, Cash enlisted in the service, though he chose a branch that had not existed in his father's time: the Air Force, which had been established only three years before. He would be gone for four years. Ray Cash had never seen combat, nor would Johnny. But even more than was the case with his father, Cash came back a changed man.

Despite all his hardships, Cash looked back upon his childhood in Dyess with fondness. It was far from idyllic. The family worked hard in the fields in a state and country racked by depression and then world war. Cash lost his brother in a horrifying accident. And yet the Cashes fared better than many Arkansas families. Ray's farm survived these trials and he made good on his debts. Carrie never had to work full time as many mothers do today. Cash grew up in the era before the obtrusiveness of television, which Johnny didn't see until he was in the Air Force.[149] Cash instead had the radio and listened whenever he could. He summed up his experiences in Dyess: "I was actually very happy."[150]

But Cash would not have been happy had he stayed in Dyess, and he did not leave free of personal demons. Despite his father's abusiveness, J. R. developed an empathy for the unfortunate and the underdogs of American life. Johnny himself would prove guilty of monstrous behavior as an adult, but he never fell prey to self-righteousness. A frequent sinner, he did not judge others, because he struggled constantly to check his own vices and weaknesses.

By the 1950s, Dyess was a relic of an earlier era, when Americans still believed in small farmers. For a time, the Jeffersonian experiment at Dyess worked. The Cash family had taken advantage of a federal program, even though they had little interest in the labor movement or socialism. Dyess residents were people of the Solid South, who voted Democratic and supported the racial status quo. They wanted to pay off their debts and be left alone. But over time, it became obvious that men working twenty acres had little chance of competing with the likes of Lee Wilson's enormous plantations or other men engaged in large-scale farming, what became known as agribusiness. As David Hayden has written, by 1970 a farmer needed "at least 320 acres and a lot of expensive farm equipment to make cotton farming a profitable enterprise in Arkansas."[151] By the time J. R. left for Germany, Dyess had been worn out. Today, Dyess has a fraction of the population it had in the 1930s.

Dyess was a quiet place to grow up, but it had few opportunities for an ambitious and talented young man such as Cash. Small-town life bred in him a lifelong restlessness. As an adult, he lived in Memphis, California, and later the suburbs of Nashville. But the road would become his one true home. Cash would be a man everywhere and nowhere. One of his greatest recordings is "I've Been Everywhere." It was a cover, but Cash, like many of his contemporaries in country music, lived up to such a title.

Settlers in northeastern Arkansas took on the character of frontier people, building homes and structures quickly, living year to year and unsure of the economic future. The Cash family never had running water and initially had no electricity in Dyess. But despite setbacks and tragedy—the 1937 flood and Jack's death—the Cash family farm was successful, and the Cashes eventually owned their property outright. While primitive in hindsight, Dyess was a step up for the Cash family. Ray Cash enjoyed the advantages of a successful if middling farmer.

The Johnny Cash story is in many ways a classic American tale: a smart, ambitious young man from a small town goes to the big city, where he finds success and fame. But the Cash family thrived in Dyess because of two things: hard work and help from the United States government. The Dyess experiment was not, despite what Cash said, "socialism," but it was more socialist than Arkansans were used to or would have wanted under normal circumstances.

As was true of the New Deal South generally, Dyess was not a radical place. No one there had any interest in challenging the Jim Crow system. Black people were excluded, and rather than be administered by the government, Dyess was managed by private companies. Today Dyess might be forgotten were it not for Johnny Cash, but at the time it was a lifeline for many Arkansans. "Dyess Colony was our salvation," Cash told Christopher Wren in 1969.[152] The colony gave J. R. a house to sleep and play in, work to do, and a good secondary education. His parents—hardworking and religious people, apolitical and serious—reared their children to revere God and the church and earn bread by the sweat of their brow.

Cash's experiences in Dyess shaped much of his later social and political outlook. He grew up in a southern state that had severe problems with race, prisons, and the poor. As an adult, Cash never publicly challenged Jim Crow orthodoxy, but he championed the cause of those who had fared poorly at the hands of the system, whether farmers, criminals, or Native Americans. Dyess instilled in Cash an empathy for the common man that he never lost, despite all his wealth and world-wide fame.

At a basic artistic level, Dyess made Johnny Cash the deeply musical person he was. "It's amazing that such a nothing looking place could mean so much to you," Cash said in 1969.[153] Dyess instilled in him an abiding love and appreciation for songs and singers of all kinds. He passed long hours of boredom by humming songs on the way to school, walking to town, or as he chopped and picked cotton. Cash loved country music and would become famous as a country star. But various forms of music flavored his tastes, from gospel to pop, show tunes, and blues. At the age of eighteen, Cash wasn't sure what he wanted to do with his life just yet. He had ambitions of becoming a singer, but he did not choose music right away. He had a unique and untrained voice and a desire to make music. It would take several years, however, before he found his voice as a songwriter and performer.

3

Germany and Memphis

To make his music, Johnny Cash drew on his roots. Arkansas played a pivotal role in his growth as a musician and in the larger rock and roll scene that emerged in the mid-1950s. Writer Melvin Schwartz has described the personal and social makeup of the rockabilly heroes of the 1950s, who would be immortalized at Sam Phillips's studio in Memphis. They were "born between 1930 and 1935 into a low-to-middle-class home," he wrote. "Because he was not educated beyond high school, he worked in a trade, at a blue collar job, or on a farm. He served in the armed forces; West Germany and Korea were the most common assignments. The performer had a country music background mostly gained by listening to the radio, but he was also interested in music by Black performers."[1] Such a description ably sums up Johnny Cash. Music journalist Lester Bangs, as usual, was more blunt: "Everybody at Sun was white trash."[2]

Whatever they were, Cash, Elvis, Jerry Lee Lewis, Sonny Burgess, Roy Orbison, and Carl Perkins helped transform hillbilly music into rock and roll. Cash had always loved music, but he did not start singing or playing guitar regularly until he joined the Air Force. Later, Cash joked he was in the Air Force "for twelve years from '50 to '54."[3] To pass the time and alleviate the tedium in Germany, Cash wrote often to his future wife, Vivian Liberto, whom he had met while stationed in San Antonio before being shipped to Germany. He had spent little time with Vivian before deciding to marry her (as was true later with June Carter)—but his honest letters not only tell us about the man's personality but also provide insight into his evolution as a musician.

The Air Force

Johnny Cash left his hometown in 1950, the first year of a decade that saw the United States engaged in yet another bloody war in Asia. In 1950, the United States entered the Korean conflict, the country's first major effort to contain communism by force. Cash also joined the military that year, though he served in West Germany, not Korea. Cash wanted to do his "duty" by enlisting, as his father had done in World War I and his relatives did in World War II. "I think everybody should serve their time for their country," he would say in 1969. "I did. It's not up to every man to decide when it's time to go defend our country. We elect men to decide that for us."[4] As events turned out, Cash was a good patriot, but he was no diehard military man or jingoist. His patriotism did not depend on blindly following the country's leaders but on asking questions about where and when the nation was going wrong and how it must reckon with its history.

Cash began getting serious about music before his boat (yes, Air Force men arrived that way) landed in Germany in the fall of 1951. The ride to Europe was tedious. Cash sometimes had to wait several hours in the chow line. At least he had time to think, and music was always on his mind. Cash joined a singing group and bought a harmonica. On the boat, he met the American crooner Vic Damone, who was doing a stretch in the army. Cash wasn't impressed. "He won't do anything but sing overseas," he said of Damone, "but he tries to act like he's protecting his country."[5] In describing Damone, though, Cash essentially summed up his own career in the Air Force. Germany was a long way from the slaughter pens of Korea, and Cash's time there was most rewarding in how it spurred him to sing and pursue a music career.

Cash was excited about becoming a musician, but he also struggled with loneliness and depression. "Why does God make people this way?" Cash asked Vivian. "To be lonely and blue and can't find any peace within themselves? Why didn't he make a man so he could be contented alone when he had to be alone? I can't understand it."[6] Cash sought answers to such questions for the rest of his life. He was restless by nature, and a seeker—artistically and spiritually. Sometimes he could cope with loneliness through diversions such as hunting and fishing. Music and Jesus also helped. Life for him was a quest. But in Germany, he often found himself coping with tedium through drink and sex. For Cash, the Air Force was a godforsaken place. He would find no answers to his spiritual questions in Germany.

His time overseas made him think about his roots, and Cash talked about himself with customary self-deprecation. "I'm a country boy and I've still got a little of the cotton patch dirt between my toes," Cash told the Liberto family in an April 1953 letter. "All my people are Missionary Baptists [though his mother originally was Methodist] and the largest part of them live in the state of Arkansas. I'm proud of them of course. All of them are decent people, even though one of my uncles is known to be the biggest liar in the solid south, he's a decent liar."[7] The country boy with the cotton patch dirt between his toes was far away from his loved ones in the States. In the three years he was in Germany, Cash never saw Vivian or his family once.

Cash was honest about the stressful nature of his work, which involved staying in one spot for hours listening to Morse code in order to intercept messages leaving the Soviet Union—not an easy task for a naturally restless young man. Cash and his comrades were far from the battlefield, but the Cold War was at its height. Code breaking was "very hard on the nerves."[8] The pace of the work broke some men down. Cash empathized with one comrade who had become suicidal. "If they'd leave him alone" and "treat him human," he wrote to Vivian, "he'd be alright, but those dumb doctors do him more harm than good."[9] Cash's admonition to "treat him human" foreshadowed his public views on prisoners later. He always recognized the basic humanity of the hardest-hit people.

Despite the high tension between the United States and the Soviet Union, Cash had little interest in politics. At one point in June 1952, the men were made to watch a film on the Marshall Plan. Cash said he had about as much interest in the subject as he did in "Roy Acuff's dog."[10] Cash rarely could keep his mind off of country music. And while one could read too much into Cash not wanting to watch an instructional film, his years in the Air Force reveal how apolitical he was. In Germany, he was fulfilling a patriotic duty, but he had little interest in larger world events.

At a more personal level, Cash told Vivian not only about his and other men's drunken and obnoxious behavior but also dalliances with other women. Air Force men were young and overworked, and they relieved tension through booze, women, and fighting. Cash tried to be true to his sweetheart. He eventually proposed to Vivian—by mail. Cash took pride in the fact that he had not married early in life, the way some people in Dyess did. "They marry 'em young in them thar hills, except we don't live in the hills," he told Vivian.[11] He repeatedly spoke of his love for Vivian, but she had plenty of evidence that Cash had difficulty with self-control. He hoped that music could soothe the beast within him.

Cash didn't begin writing songs in earnest during his four years in the Air Force, but the words of his first smash hit, "I Walk the Line," could have been about his days in Germany as much as any other time. Cash was just another one of the brawlers and hard drinkers in the barracks, though the most important and constructive way he managed stress was through music. Cash bought his first acoustic guitar in Germany for twenty marks (then about $5), an instrument "so cheap that it didn't even have a brand name," Johnny wrote later.[12] In Landsberg roughly forty miles west of Munich, he met Orville Rigdon of Louisiana, who taught him how to play. Another friend and member of his band, the Landsberg Barbarians (a play on Landsberg, Bavaria), was Reid Cummins, a native of Pine Bluff, Arkansas, who had brought a guitar with him to Germany that he let Cash and others play.[13] Cash flirted with playing guitar in Dyess, but it was not until he arrived in Germany that he became a serious, albeit limited, student of the instrument.

As he tended to, Cash later embellished the story of his first guitar purchase, saying he had some beer before lugging his guitar back to base—a long and difficult trek amid a supposedly deadly snowstorm. "I walked back four miles," Cash told Christopher Wren, "me and my beer and my guitar in the snow. I had drunk enough beer to keep me from freezing. It was a blizzard and I kept losing my way. They said I looked like a snowman when I walked through the gate. My hair was covered with snow. Why I didn't freeze to death, I don't know."[14] We joke about adults sometimes telling their kids or grandkids stories about walking through three feet of snow—uphill both ways—to get to school or somewhere else. Cash's story of buying his first guitar was one such tall tale.

Whatever the facts of that fateful day, Cash soon started playing music with some of his Air Force buddies. He proved a hit with his bunkmates. In January 1952, Cash wrote to Vivian about his hillbilly band, "a pretty good one too," performing in the barracks. Cash said he sang every tune he knew, "some of them at least a dozen times."[15] That December, he wrote Vivian about his comrades, who after a hard night of drinking dragged him out of bed and forced him to play until they sobered up. Cash said he "wore off five sets of fingers on that guitar." He had no ego about his playing, saying his "Rebel buddies" liked his brand of hillbilly music when they were drunk, but added that they would "have to be drunk to listen to me."[16] Cash never lost his humility or sense of humor.

Nor did he ever shed his dark side. Despite the enjoyment he got from playing music seriously for the first time, Cash's letters to Vivian reveal a man often at war with himself. He spared Vivian none of the details of his troubling behavior. In one letter, Cash wrote about getting drunk at a bar, where he was pestered by a prostitute. When she began calling Cash names, he knocked her to the floor.[17] Cash also got into bloody fights with fellow Air Force men. While Cash was usually a genial man when sober, the story was different when he was drunk or on pills. The pills came later, but in Germany, Cash had his fair share of bad drinking nights.

Cash was a person who could not moderate his intake of drugs or alcohol—in short, a man cursed with an addictive personality. When drunk, he could be nasty, and he revealed an ugly racist side of his personality while in the service. In one slurring letter to Vivian, Cash—celebrating Vivian's birthday no less—wrote of how "some Nigger got smart and I asked him to go outside and he was too yellow. He thought he could whip everybody in the club but he wouldn't even fight me. He's [a] yellow coon."[18] At his worst, Cash was—as his father was—a violent, racist redneck. Given that he didn't know Vivian very well, he either assumed she was sympathetic to his racial views or that she was unlikely to protest. Vivian's letters have not been made available to the public, but one hopes she disapproved of such behavior. Given his drunken state while writing, Cash would have been wise not to have sent the letter, at least for posterity's sake.

But he did send it. One could perhaps excuse Cash's racism as the musings of a young, bored, drunken cracker, and clearly alcohol brought out the worst in the brooding Cash. The day after writing to Vivian about the "yellow coon," he was remorseful for having gotten drunk. Still upset about the incident involving the "smart Negro at the club," Cash tempered his language from the night before. But he was still angry at the Black man walking down the aisle "jigging" when he "pushed by me," whereupon Cash shoved the man back. After challenging the man to step outside for a fight, Cash's opponent backed down. "They're not so mean and tough when it comes to actually doing something," he concluded to Vivian.[19] Less than two weeks later, Cash had another unpleasant confrontation with a Black man who insulted a drunken Cash and then walked away. Cash "called him every name anyone has ever given a Negro." As the man left, Cash yelled "Coon," "Nigger," "Jig-a-boo," and "a few others." Cash told Vivian he went on for "a full 30 minutes that I could whip any Negro that walked on the face of the earth." He was again remorseful, vomiting the next day and writing that when he woke up, he was "so disgusted with myself that I want to die."[20]

Was Cash racist? Should Cash fans dismiss these incidents in Germany as an aberration? In researching this book, I have come across no such similar incidents in Cash's later life. Even so, Cash was a son of the racially segregated Solid South, where too often whites happily voted for openly racist Democratic candidates and kept Black people down in every way possible. Dyess was lily white, and Cash lived under the roof of the racist and abusive Ray Cash. The years he spent in Memphis, Nashville, and California were in white neighborhoods. Cash never fell prey to the kind of lifelong racism his father practiced. But he wanted to live as most southern whites did: in white middle- and upper-class areas.

Whatever the depths of his racism while in the Air Force, Cash remembered a tense atmosphere between Black and white men at the time. Cash arrived in Germany in the fall of 1951, three years after President Truman had integrated the military by way of Executive Order 9981. Truman was elected in 1948, a year that saw the rise of the racist Dixiecrat Party led by South Carolina segregationist Strom Thurmond. The ascent of the Dixiecrats foreshadowed massive resistance to civil rights in the 1950s and paved the way for racist demagogues such as George Wallace.

Cash later wrote of the supposedly messy results that came from mixing Black and white servicemen. In his 1990s memoir, he described a race riot in Bremerhaven upon his arrival in Germany. Cash recalled leaving the boat only to see his fellow servicemen "tearing at each other with everything they had." He continued: "I had no problem sharing a barracks with blacks, and I couldn't imagine hating them so much that I was willing to wage a private war on them." As his letters show, though, Cash indeed had problems being around Black servicemen in Germany, and he did not share barracks with them either. Yet the integration of the armed forces in Europe was mostly peaceful because few white and Black men were immediately forced to live and work together. Despite Truman's order, units remained segregated for years, and soldiers tended to self-segregate when on leave.[21]

It is sad to learn that Cash could have been so racist in Germany, but we should also believe him when he said in the 1990s, "I've certainly learned more about race hatred along the way."[22] Scholars have correctly treated Cash's Air Force racism as an anomaly in a life dedicated to championing underdogs and holding fast to progressive principles. "Like millions of other whites of his generation in the South," Robert Hilburn has written of Cash, "he felt that he eventually distanced himself from the earlier bigotry of the region, and for him that process began in Germany."[23] Later in his career, Cash booked Ray Charles on his TV show, had his picture taken with Muhammad Ali, and engaged in a mock gun battle with Sammy Davis Jr. outside a hotel. Cash's views evolved as he got older. He might have had some embarrassing racist lapses in the Air Force, but he apparently never repeated them. Cash was complicated and could be infuriating. But there is no evidence to suggest he had lifelong prejudices against African Americans. As Michael S. Foley has concluded, by the time Cash had his own television show in the late sixties, "his feeling for Black America, for the hardships African-Americans had endured, ran deep."[24]

As Cash neared the end of his time in Germany, race relations in America were poised for dramatic change after the landmark *Brown v. Board of Education* decision. Cash returned to the United States in May of 1954, the same month the Supreme Court ruled on *Brown*. As the economy, technology, and racial attitudes shifted, the South's Jim Crow society faced its greatest threat yet. The *Brown* ruling was not one case but five, involving various lawyers from different states. The decision was historic, but Jim Crow was not dismantled overnight, based as it was on the ambiguous decree in a follow-up Court ruling that desegregation happen with "all deliberate speed." In many parts of the South, it did not happen at all. State and local governments ignored the decision. Changes in the country's racial status quo did not come quickly. Nevertheless, a spirit of upset, change, and rebellion pervaded the 1950s and lasted well beyond the decade.

By the mid-1950s, as always in America, matters of race were sensitive at best and deadly at worst. Cash released his first song, "Hey Porter," on June 21, 1955,[25] nearly two months before the lynching of fourteen-year-old

Chicago boy Emmett Till in north Mississippi, and less than six months before the Montgomery Bus Boycott. Cash's classic period, running from 1955 to 1968, dovetailed with the emergence of the civil rights movement, but Cash never publicly embraced it.

Cash exhibited ugly, racist behavior in the Air Force; it was also where he developed problems with substance abuse. While in Germany, Cash took a liking to whatever alcohol he could get his hands on. In principle, he disliked drinking, as he saw the damage his father did to the family when drunk. Cash claimed that on the night of his brother Jack's death, he promised that were he ever to get married, he would not allow drinking in the household.[26] It was a promise he would not keep. Cash was never known for his drinking, but he drank more than his fair share in his life. In Germany, it was not easy to avoid excess, given the hard work and stress of military life, not to mention the fact that he and his men were far from home, loved ones, and social norms. Cash avoided some vices, though. In July 1953, he told Vivian he was taking a liking to wine but not playing cards.[27]

When it came to alcohol, Cash had a double standard with Vivian: Cash couldn't help himself, but he disapproved of her drinking at all. "You're not pure when you're drinking Vivian," Cash lectured his future wife. "You're filthy and unpure and unclean when you've got a drop of that in your naturally pure body."[28] As he condescended to his future wife about her drinking, Cash expressed guilt over his own sexual lapses.[29] He was no virgin, and he admitted as much to Vivian, from whom he asked forgiveness. "Vivian honey, can you forgive me for it, and not have any resentment or disgust for me for it?" He understandably sought sexual relief while deployed. In December 1954, he admitted he attended a strip show, then tried to persuade Vivian that he didn't know there would be one that night.[30] Even if it were true that Cash stumbled into the sex show accidentally, he didn't walk out disgusted. Being the good American he was, he had hang-ups about sex. The military has exposed countless enlisted men to all the vices they could want in faraway places. Until he got married, Cash had no healthy way of expressing his sexual urges.

As is true of so many people distant from family and friends, Cash thought longingly of home. In the Landsberg barracks, his mind was very much on Arkansas. He wrote to Vivian in November 1953 about plans for their first night back. Johnny had in mind a "special" trip to Blytheville or to the drive-in movie theater in West Memphis. Cash knew he wanted to be alone with Vivian and "sit on a river bank, or lake or something where it's quiet and romantic." He promised they would have a "wonderful night angel. I'll figger it out."[31] A few days later, Cash wrote that his father wanted to move to Osceola. He hoped the news wasn't true. "There's nothing to Dyess," he admitted, but he hoped the family would stay there. He believed his family "wouldn't be satisfied anywhere else after 20 years at Dyess."[32]

The Cashes remained in Dyess, but when J. R. was in Germany, the family moved out of the house in which he had grown up to a place near the center of town. As Marvin Schwartz has written, in the 1950s, "the last remnants of the Arkansas frontier faded away."[33] And the Cash family had given up the farm. With most of the children grown up and moved away, Ray could no longer make it work. In November 1953, Ray, Carrie, and the rest of the family still in Dyess moved to what Johnny was told was the "nicest, newest house in town," though Johnny added wryly, "it still wouldn't have to be too nice to be the best."[34] The selling of Cash's boyhood home made him feel nostalgic: "Every inch of that place makes me think of something different," he wrote Vivian, "something wonderful and precious that happened. I could walk over that place and think of things I'd never remember any other way. I can remember Roy and Louise and Jack and Reba so well when they were all kids. It's even sweet to look back over the hard work I did there with them."[35] Johnny's upbringing was far from perfect, but Dyess nevertheless made Cash feel rooted and sentimental.

Toward the end of his Air Force service, Cash made a recording of himself singing. By his own admission, it was unexceptional. He told Vivian that "after you play the record the first time you'll probably throw it away."[36] Even so, it was an earnest attempt by Cash to create music. He begged Vivian not to judge his singing too harshly, and he added that "I was tense, the guitar was no good and out of tune, and it was cold in the room and I was shaking."[37] Cash might have been self-conscious about his first recording effort, and it was likely nothing close to what he would do at Sun only a year later, but his letter revealed that he was earnest about making records. Cash had taken an important step forward.

When Cash left the Air Force, he had no desire to stay in the military. Compared to his later success, it may seem his years in Germany were wasted. But Cash felt he was doing his patriotic duty, and when he left the service, he was still a young man of twenty-two, who would need only a year back in the States before making hit records. Rather than being an anomaly in the trajectory of his life, his service set much of the template for his later life and career. Cash's letters from Germany are among the most revealing documents he left behind. They show a man struggling with sobriety and adulthood. He fought, got drunk, and encountered unpleasant people both in the service and Germany's streets, bars, and strip clubs. Cash showed he could be angry and violent as well as funny and romantic. Through it all was a man who absorbed all sorts of music and was intent to make his own. Cash's days in Germany had no shortage of dark moments. But Cash felt he had remained true to Vivian, even though he had related enough bad behavior to have scared off a more conservative woman.

Cash also showed that he could remain true to a solid work ethic, one that served him well later in life, when he was too sick to leave his bed, his room becoming a de facto recording studio. In an October 1953 letter to Vivian, Cash wrote, "Out of the 50 boys I work with, I've got the hardest, most important job there is. Because it's so important, I work harder than anybody there, and *every single day* that rolls around, somebody has something sarcastic. One guy especially is always calling me 'Airman of the Month.' Or somebody is always asking me when I'll make Captain." Cash didn't let such taunts distract him from his work. "I like my job," he reassured her, and "I don't like *any* job unless there's a lot of work." Cash added, "I've worked hard ever since I got here."[38] Cash's later drug use and missed concert dates might give the impression he was not a hard worker. In fact, his addiction to pills stemmed in part from his desire to keep working and traveling. Much of his work ethic was rooted in the blue collar life of the cotton fields. It also had much to do with Cash's natural restlessness. "I'm always looking for something but can't find it," he told Vivian in March of 1952.[39] He hoped to find "something" in his music.

As is true of great artists, Cash was on a journey—mostly personal, often spiritual—and as a musician, he was always looking for an inspired song, a new sound, a muse. When the muse did not come, Cash worked through it. Later in life, he felt the need to record two or three albums a year, even when the work was of mixed quality or uninspired. Once famous, Cash bore the enormous pressures of a man trying to balance life and career, while remaining energized, creative, and productive artistically. Such pressures could break him. He had seen that happen to men in Germany, and it would happen to him.

Whatever his future might have held by the mid-fifties, Cash knew it would not involve working the land. When talking about Dyess, Johnny noted, "I'd starve to death trying to make a living farming."[40] Cash could not have imagined how successful he would be as a recording star, but just as writers need to read the best books, Cash was listening to as much music as possible. He heard the Grand Ole Opry on the radio and was compiling a record collection consisting of many of the biggest stars in country music: Hank Williams, Faron Young, Eddy Arnold, Hank Thompson, and Hank Snow. Other influences included Webb Pierce, Kay Starr, Homer and Jethro (with whom June Carter recorded), the Maddox Brothers and Rose, and the Carlisles.[41]

While he never came close to combat, Cash emerged from the military a changed man. And he had the marks to prove it. He didn't get a Purple Heart for it, but he returned with his famous scar on his right cheek, the result of a doctor's bungled attempt to remove a cyst.[42] Vivian obviously didn't mind. In the spring of 1954, Cash returned to Arkansas. He married his beloved Vivian in San Antonio on August 7. Vivian's uncle, Father Vincent Liberto, a Catholic priest, conducted the service. Cash was a deeply religious man—though not always a great Christian—but he had no problem with an interfaith marriage. Vivian's family obviously took their Catholicism seriously, but the family also had colorful characters. Vivian's brother was "Wildman" Ray Liberto, a San Antonio pianist with a handlebar mustache, best known for his 1958 song "Wicked, Wicked Woman." The song sounded like a cross between Fats Domino and Randy Newman. Cash wasn't the only wild man around.

Johnny's wedding night was an awkward one for Vivian, who was still a virgin and self-professed "prude."[43] Whether or not Vivian was a prude, she thought Cash's parents were "very conservative and proper. They frowned upon outward displays of affection." She worried about hugging or kissing Johnny in front of them.[44] Johnny, however, was no prude, even though he was prone to self-righteousness and double standards when it came to Vivian's behavior. "Before we fell in love I had other girls," Cash had told her in November 1953.[45] Despite his dalliances, Cash told Vivian that he regretted his past behavior and feared she would be repelled or resentful.

Perhaps because of her Catholic nature, Vivian was forgiving—as events developed, probably too much so.

Memphis

Cash decided to move with Vivian to Memphis, the closest big city to where he grew up. At the time, Memphis was still the "capital of the Delta," with palpable vestiges of Old South gentility. It was in its Renaissance period, and Cash and Elvis were about to blow things open musically at Sun. The Peabody Hotel was where people went to be seen and where tourists could smile at the daily march of the ducks through the lobby. As Cash tried his hand at making music, Shelby Foote was writing his magnum opus: a three-volume Civil War narrative. In the mid-fifties, Memphis was a literary and musical hotspot. As Arkansas rocker Ronnie Hawkins later described it, Memphis had "special meaning. Saying you were from Memphis meant you had some connection with W.C. Handy and Beale Street and the blues. White kids were playing the blues, but that was rare anywhere except in Memphis." In Memphis, Hawkins concluded, "they played the kind of music I liked."[46] Sam Phillips wasn't the only one remaking music; in 1957, Jim Stewart, a country musician, founded Satellite Records. Four years later, he changed the name to Stax.

As Cash made his awkward introduction to "Mr. Phillips" at Sun, the South was becoming modernized. Air conditioners now cooled off movie theaters, homes, and hotels. People were dazzled by television. Cars were not only convenient, they were a necessity for millions of people traveling, seeking good-paying jobs, and enjoying a comfortable middle-class life in leafy suburban neighborhoods. The lucky ones had a swimming pool. The suburbs spawned a unique musical world, too: the garage band.

Johnny and Vivian moved in 1954 into a "horrible hot" upstairs apartment on Westmoreland Street in Memphis,[47] Tennessee's biggest city at the time. Cash had no future in Arkansas. Home to a vibrant music scene in the late 1950s, Arkansas was perhaps good for launching a music career but not sustaining one. Cash could not have had a long-term career there as a professional musician. Arkansas lagged behind nearly every other state in terms of economics, education, and crime. In 1959, two years after Gov. Orval Faubus shut down the schools in the wake of desegregation, Arkansas ranked forty-eighth in the nation in public school funding, with the worst teacher salaries in America.[48] Arkansas was, and is, the kind of state that people leave for better opportunities. Johnny Cash was no exception.

Today, no aspiring musician would choose Memphis over Nashville as a place to start a career. Such was not true in 1954. Memphis was a thriving city, with 400,000 people—larger than most American cities at the time—and was enjoying a postwar boom. It had quadrupled in size since 1900, and it would continue to grow until the 1980s. By the 1950s, Memphis was only beginning to confront its racist past, whether slavery, the Civil War, or the 1866 race riot in the city, where white police officers roamed the streets, killing Black people in cold blood, raping Black women, and burning Black churches, schools, and homes. Of the forty-eight people killed in the rampage, only two of them were white (one of them was killed by fellow whites).[49]

As is true of so many American cities, the geography of Memphis is synonymous with racial demographics and segregation. The city's western flank, where the downtown is located, abuts the Mississippi River. West Memphis is not in Tennessee, but across the river in Arkansas. As the city evolved, Memphis's Black population tended to live near the river, both north and south of downtown, with the white neighborhoods further east. Shelby Foote, when living in Memphis, crudely described his neighborhood as "niggertown," but he liked living there until his home by the river was bulldozed in the name of "urban renewal[50]—essentially a euphemism for the destruction of historic Black and poor white communities.

The civil rights struggle in Memphis is not as well known as that in other southern cities, but it was a hard struggle all the same. Black voters there were evicted by their white landlords from their homes and forced to live outdoors in what became known as "Tent City." Civil rights groups fought the evictions in court, but the federal government would not make a serious effort to stop Jim Crow–era voting practices until the 1965 Voting Rights Act. The law increased Black voting rates but couldn't end housing discrimination or systematic racism and injustice.[51]

In 1950s Memphis, one found a palpable collision of the Old and New South. Confederate general Nathan Bedford Forrest's statue still stood on Union Avenue, and Jefferson Davis's monument wasn't far from that. But the future was in the hands of new companies such as Holiday Inn (founded in 1952) and FedEx (founded in 1971 in Little Rock and moved to Memphis in 1973). Postwar Memphis was an exciting, fast-paced place, nowhere more so than Sun studios.

A few months after marrying Vivian, Cash sought out Sam Phillips at Sun Records, where Elvis got his start. Cash wanted to be a musician, and he was persistent. In Memphis, he had tried making a living as an appliance salesman; despite his natural charm, he was not good at it. "I hated every minute," Cash said in 1969 of his appliance days.[52] Vivian credited Johnny's success at Sun to his salesmanship. He was "relentless," she said. All those doors he pounded on selling vacuum cleaners prepared him for approaching Sam Phillips. As Cash later told interviewer Terry Gross, "the country boy in me tried to break loose and take me back to the country, but the music was stronger."[53]

Sam Phillips, the man responsible for the music revolution in Memphis, was born in 1923, nine years before Cash. By the time Cash arrived at his studio at 706 Union Avenue, Phillips had more than ten years of professional experience as a radio man and sound recorder. Unlike Cash and other rockabilly artists, Phillips had not served in the military. Born and raised in the Muscle Shoals region of north Alabama, Phillips had moved to Memphis after World War II. At the time, Memphis was one of the largest cities in the former Confederacy. Only Dallas, Houston, San Antonio, and New Orleans were bigger. For Sam, Memphis was where the action was.[54]

Memphis is on the western border of Tennessee, but in terms of United States geography, it is central. It is also central when one frames it in the geography of American blues music, which flowed from the Deep South and lower Mississippi Valley up the river to Chicago (after turning right at Davenport). Memphis is roughly 530 miles from Chicago and 400 miles from New Orleans. It's a southern city on Central Time. The Mississippi River has been central to Memphis's history, too: in the Old South, cotton traveled down from Memphis to New Orleans for shipping all over the globe. In the 1950s, Sam Phillips managed to turn this river town into a centerpiece again by making it a mecca for American blues and rockabilly musicians.

For someone from rural 1920s Alabama, Phillips was a man of remarkably progressive racial attitudes. He had grown up around Black cotton workers and had been enthralled by the songs they sang and the blending of white and Black music in northern Alabama. He had a musical background himself, though relegated to playing in his high school marching band. His brilliance lay in his approach to recorded sound. But his gift for spotting new talent and recording it in innovative ways would have been squandered had he not taken a democratic approach to the music process.[55]

Once he opened his recording studios in Memphis, Phillips welcomed virtually any artist that had the courage and talent to approach him. Not all of them were success stories. At first Phillips excelled at attracting talented African Americans such as B. B. King and Howlin' Wolf. For a while, he succeeded as a maker of "race records." Phillips was no activist, but he also had no interest in maintaining the racial status quo when it came to music: he wanted to *promote* and improve, not exploit, his Black roster. Jim Crow was a way of life when he founded his recording studio, but for Phillips, musical talent—not skin color—mattered most in a man.[56]

Sam Phillips showed that in Memphis, racial attitudes were changing. The postwar economy also was giving men unprecedented opportunities. Men such as Cash thrived in the flush 1950s, the golden age of the American white male. Memphis was not only big, it had great music, and white middle-class men such as Cash seemingly had their pick of career options in that decade. But in Memphis, Cash found that his Arkansas roots, and the fact that he was "country" in more ways than one, proved an asset rather than a liability. Ben Wynne notes in his book *In Tune* how some people consider Memphis the "capital of North Mississippi."[57] One could also call it the "capital of eastern Arkansas," given the influence Arkansas had on the rock and roll music that emerged from the city in the mid- and late 1950s. What was more, Cash's background was as humble as Sam Phillips's or B. B. King's.

Memphis is only about three hours by car from Nashville, but it feels and looks very different. The seat of the Tennessee legislature and the undisputed capital of country music, Nashville is centrally located in the state and has quintupled in size since 1960. In contrast, Memphis feels static, a Mississippi River town that historically has lured people from the margins of Arkansas, Mississippi, and west Tennessee, while lacking the flash and energy of New South Nashville. Unlike its neighbor to the east, Memphis feels haunted by the ghosts of slavery, war, and the unspeakable crimes of the Jim Crow era.

But in the 1950s, Memphis was much like the Nashville of today—growing and exciting. River towns have a reputation for wildness, and Memphis is no exception. In the history of rock and roll, Memphis plays a central role. There, the white stars of early rock and roll—Cash, Elvis, Roy Orbison, Jerry Lee Lewis, Carl Perkins, Charlie Feathers, and Sonny Burgess—got their start, making the records that changed popular music and modern life as we know it. The young men at Sun have inspired millions of musicians and non-musicians alike.

Memphis was not new to Cash or his family. As a boy, J. R. had visited Memphis's Cotton Carnival.[58] When he arrived in 1954, Cash had help settling into the big city from his brother Roy, who lived there and had modest success in the local music scene. Roy, who was ten years Johnny's senior, was in a band called the Dixie Rhythm Ramblers. They had played on a radio station in Blytheville—not far from Dyess—in the late 1940s.[59]

Sam Phillips had started Sun Records in February 1952, hoping to succeed in a music industry dominated by giants such as RCA and Columbia. Luckily for Phillips, he attracted incredibly talented and trusting young performers. Cash later recounted having difficulty getting hold of Phillips for an audience. But for years, Phillips had kept his doors open to all kinds of people. In January 1950, before establishing Sun, he had opened the Memphis Recording Service in a garage devoted to glass repair. In the true DIY spirit, Phillips had his own self-made studio in downtown Memphis. Elvis approached Phillips because he wanted to hear what he sounded like on wax. Eventually the greasy kid from Tupelo stumbled into making a rock and roll record—his cover of Arthur Crudup's "That's All Right"—once he had caught Phillips's attention. But "The King" could have ended up like so many other musicians who were attracted to Phillips's studio for the novelty of it, rather than ambition.[60]

As was true of Elvis, Cash quickly settled into the music business. His initial recording session with Phillips had him playing with Marshall Grant and Luther Perkins—who would make up the Tennessee Two—as well as a steel guitar player who panicked and couldn't make it through the session. Cash and his two remaining bandmates were not virtuosos, but Sam Phillips was not interested in that. That was for jazz and the big bands. His musicians were coming from a more primitive, though no less intense, musical place. Phillips's roster was made of up bluesmen, gospel lovers, former field hands, even prisoners—not trained musicians. What Phillips most wanted was a special sound. He didn't strive for perfection. Instead, he wanted a *feeling*, the emotion of men thrilled about their music and creating something new and compelling. Phillips was willing to stay up all night with musicians in order to get a memorable and spontaneous sound. "Mr. Phillips," as he was called, wanted to capture energy and emotion, not make polished records.

Phillips captured the youthful spirit that had emerged after World War II. The baby boomers were the biggest generation in American history, and they were the ones who would buy Cash's and Elvis's records. The men at Sun were setting themselves apart from the musical establishment. No one confused the Memphis sound with traditional country or whatever was happening in Nashville. Memphis was raw, more based in the blues, more African American in its sound and swagger. There was no place for an Ike Turner or a Howlin' Wolf or a B. B. King in Nashville. But they found a home in Memphis, albeit briefly, before moving on. Not long after, white musicians in Memphis followed their lead in remaking the American music scene.

Sun Records harnessed the energy of a generation recovering from the biggest and most destructive war in human history. Americans were enjoying their newfound wealth, but they were also nervous—about the Bomb, about communism, about race, and the stress and suffocating conformity of the modern world. Before the Beatles played their shows to hysterical teens, Elvis and Cash saw how mad young people were for a new music being unleashed in the 1950s—what became known as rock and roll.

The break from traditional country at Sun was as much about style as it was the music. Nobody at Sun wore cowboy hats. Cash and Elvis never did on stage, and nothing screams youth like a big head of hair. With their oily pompadours and sideburns, the rockabilly crowd looked young and dangerous. The Sun boys might have had one foot in the country tradition, but they looked more like killers from *West Side Story* than the hillbillies at the Opry. What it came down to, though, was performance. Cash, Elvis, Carl, and Jerry Lee had an energy that no one in country music could match. As men too young for World War II, and not much interested in fighting in Korea, they were making war on the music world. Fans responded with intense—at times even frightening—enthusiasm and devotion.

Cash and the Tennessee Two certainly had limitations as musicians. But no one could deny the unique sound they created with an upright bass, acoustic guitar, electric lead, and Cash's booming, otherworldly voice. What helped them was Phillips's unique "slapback" technique, which created a slight delay during the recording process, using two expensive

Ampex 350 tape machines played at the same time. The echo effect gave Sun its unique sound.[61] The slapback sound was especially suited to Johnny Cash's country baritone. Cash might never have had Elvis's singing range or his prowess as a performer. But Elvis didn't write his own songs, nor did he have Cash's intellectual depth and curiosity—not to mention Johnny's dark side, which would have made Elvis fans choke on their bubblegum. Other artists at Sun, such as Roy Orbison and Carl Perkins, wrote their own material, but Cash was the most successful at writing his own songs in Memphis. His writing matured without losing any commercial appeal. Most important of all, he created a signature sound. In a couple of years, Cash would produce stellar original material: arguably, he never surpassed the artistic heights he attained at Sun.

Cash's Sun singles were among his best, from "Folsom Prison Blues" and "Get Rhythm" to "I Walk the Line" and "Big River." As well as the Sun singles sold, Cash had to spend countless hours on the road to find an audience. He paid his dues as a touring musician, but they weren't hefty. He had a fast ride to fame. The American Dream is elusive, not only as a definable idea but as something obtainable for those seeking it—even in the best of times. Unlike many people, Cash knew what he wanted to do: make music. And that was all he wanted to do. Luckily for him, Cash was pursuing a music career in the mid-1950s. In the years following a global conflict that had decimated Europe and brought Japan to its knees, the American economy was thriving. Small towns throughout the country had one or more large factories. It was a time when men could walk into an employer's office, ask for a good-paying job, and get one. Blue collar families could survive on a husband's salary alone. Women were expected to raise children, support their husbands, and seek a domestic, bourgeois lifestyle. Johnny and Vivian Cash were no different.

Cash's success relied on talent, tenacity, and timing. Of what became known as the Million Dollar Quartet—Cash, Elvis, Jerry Lee Lewis, and Carl Perkins—Cash was the only one from Arkansas. Elvis was from Tupelo, southeast of Memphis (and actually closer to Alabama than Tennessee). Carl Perkins was from Tiptonville, a western Tennessee town north of Memphis. While they might have lived in separate states, Dyess and Tiptonville were only about seventy miles apart as the crow flies. Jerry Lee Lewis was from Louisiana. Before Sonny Burgess and Charlie Rich, Cash was the lone man from Arkansas at Sun.[62]

Sam Phillips was responsible for Cash getting a start at Sun, but in the studio, Cash worked more frequently with "Cowboy" Jack Clement. A man who country writer Peter Cooper has described as "Falstaffian," Clement acted as producer, writer, and musician for many of Cash's songs. The eccentric "Cowboy" Jack, who ironically "wore comfortable shoes and was frightened around ponies," was responsible for moving Cash in a more pop-oriented direction.[63] He composed "Ballad of a Teenage Queen" in 1957 for Cash, which, in contrast to earlier songs, featured piano and backing vocals. The tune was a hit. Also successful was "Guess Things Happen That Way," another Clement song. It was Clement, not Luther Perkins, who played lead guitar on the official version of Cash's masterpiece, "Big River." Clement and Cash collaborated for decades on a variety of projects.

Jack Henderson Clement was born in Memphis in 1931, but he knew Arkansas well. His maternal grandparents were Jefferson Davis and Ella Henderson Clement of Newport, Arkansas, which in the 1950s had a vibrant music scene. Clement visited Newport in the days before air conditioning. As a boy, he remembered sitting in bed on a warm night, when he heard girls singing "You Are My Sunshine" through the window. They "sang it so pretty," he remembered, "and I envisioned them as being beautiful. It's great to be in a sealed place and not have to sweat, but you can miss something good when you don't have those windows open."[64] Given Cash's success with Clement early on, Cash viewed him as something of a muse and good luck charm. Long after he left Sun, Cash returned to Clement for new material when he was in a rut.

Clement had ties to Arkansas, and he understood how distinctive the state's music was. The Arkansas sound, he said, was not "as lazy as Mississippi, all blues and slow pokey stuff." Instead, Arkansas, he said, was "younger," taking a bit from Texas's country and swing. "Thank God for Arkansas," Clement said. "Those Arkansas boys could rock."[65] It wasn't just Cash and Sonny Burgess who were making their influence felt on Memphis and the early rock and roll scene. Some, such as Levon Helm and Ronnie Hawkins, traveled to Canada to play music and make money. Others, such as Sonny Deckelman and his second cousin Bud Deckelman, made solid rockabilly records before fading into obscurity.

Cash and Clement's work on "Big River" represented one of the last and greatest songs from Cash's Sun period. Succinct, poetic, and up-tempo with a catchy guitar riff, "Big River" was another example of Cash's obsession with a sense of place. The song offers the listener a tour of the Mississippi in which Cash rattles off a list of river towns, including Baton Rouge, St. Paul, Davenport, Memphis, and New Orleans. The immensity of the river, however, isn't enough to hold the tears of the narrator: "The tears that I cry for that woman, are gonna flood you big river / Then I'm gonna sit here until I die." When writing love and heartbreak songs, it was hard for Cash to avoid getting dark.

Cash was a major force in creating an artistic bridge between 1950s and 1960s rock and roll, whereby the group identity in rock music eventually surpassed individual performers. Before the 1960s, musical acts were more dependent on single artists and their backing bands rather than a group identity. Casual listeners didn't care who was backing Elvis, and the biggest acts at Sun were all individuals: Roy Orbison, Jerry Lee Lewis, and Carl Perkins, not to mention Cash and Elvis. Even well into the 1960s, the biggest names in rock and roll were solo artists, from Black musicians such as Little Richard and Chuck Berry to white performers such as Del Shannon and Eddie Cochran. America likes to think of itself as a land of individuals. It is no surprise, then, that the golden age of American rock and roll, spanning from 1955 to 1963, was a landscape of individuals, while the British Invasion, begun in 1964, depended on combos such as the Beatles, the Rolling Stones, the Who, and the Kinks. America gave ambitious men like Cash the tools to achieve stardom more or less on their own. By contrast, in mid-sixties England, few internationally known acts were identified with one man.

What Cash and the other songwriters at Sun shared with their British counterparts was a desire to write original material. Despite the individualist nature of the early American rock and roll scene, Cash's fame depended more on his band's sound than other acts at Sun. Only three men played on Cash's early Sun Records: Johnny sang and played acoustic guitar, Marshall Grant was on bass, and Luther Perkins picked on his on Stratocaster. They were a "power trio of oddball savants," Marty Stuart said of Cash and the Tennessee Two, "who at times hardly tuned their instruments, and could barely change chords together."[66] Whatever the band's limitations, what they did musically worked—and what was more, sold well. Their sound was as stripped down as a backwoods Baptist church. And like a sweaty preacher firing up his congregation on an August Sunday morning, the

Tennessee Two could get people moving. Cash's "Get Rhythm" was a straight-up rocker that he wrote for Elvis before he cut it himself.

In retrospect, Cash's records were no more stripped down than Elvis's Sun sides. Carl Perkins might have had a drummer (WS Holland, who later joined Cash's band), but the rhythm section on his cuts was still fairly sparse. What was key on Sun's rock and roll records was the lead guitar, whether Scotty Moore's inspired playing on "That's All Right," or Luther's work with Cash. One cannot underestimate the importance of Luther Perkins in developing Cash's early sound. Cash was only ever a middling acoustic guitar player. His bassist, Marshall Grant, became an accomplished musician and songwriter and an intense performer. But it was Perkins's muffled electric rhythm and his crisp, understated solos that defined Cash's sound. Luther's deceptively simple-sounding licks gave energy and color to early hits such as "Folsom Prison Blues," "Hey Porter," and "I Walk the Line." Cash, Perkins, and Grant provided an enormous drive, despite the fact that for years they had no drummer. Indeed, country bands at the time were discouraged from having drummers.

Though they met in Memphis, neither of the Tennessee Two were from Tennessee. Luther Perkins was born on January 8, 1928 in Como, Mississippi, a town in Panola County in the northern part of the state and one county away from the Mississippi River. Luther was named after his father, Luther Monroe Perkins, born in 1901. Both Luther's father and his mother, Delphie, were natives of Mississippi. Como, as was true of Dyess, has always been a small, rural town dependent on agriculture. Cash biographer Stephen Miller notes that Luther's father was a Baptist preacher, but on the 1930 and 1940 census, Luther Sr. is listed as a farm laborer.[67] That is not to say that his father wasn't also a preacher, but he apparently did not make a living doing it.

Cash was not mechanically inclined, but his bandmates were. Marshall Grant, Luther Perkins—and later WS Holland—all worked as mechanics before joining Cash's band. Their knowledge of automobiles came in handy later when the band drove thousands of miles around the country and endured inevitable breakdowns and delays. At the age of eighteen, the lanky (six feet tall, 155 pounds) and ruddy-complexioned Luther moved to Memphis to weld for the Illinois Central Railroad and become a mechanic, where he eventually worked alongside Marshall Grant and Roy Cash.[68]

As was true of the Cashes, the Perkins family produced more than one successful musician. Luther's younger brother, the teenager Thomas Wayne Perkins, had a hit with the saccharine ballad "Tragedy," which hit number 5 on the *Billboard* Top 100 in 1959. Perkins never had another hit record, but his band, the DeLons, were recorded by Elvis's guitarist Scotty Moore. Luther was no singer. Nor was he a natural on guitar. In 2008, *Vintage Guitar* magazine called Luther's playing style "primitive genius."[69] Luther found he was good at playing Johnny Cash songs, and that was about it. Nevertheless, he was vital. "If it hadn't been for him," said guitarist Bob Wootton, who replaced Luther in 1968 after his death, "I don't know if there'd ever have been a Johnny Cash." Whether or not that was true, Luther was loyal. He only ever played without Johnny on a few instrumentals, "Bandana" and "Wabash Blues," and in concert when he would sometimes get a minute-or-so guitar solo. Luther was content to be the stoic man on stage, focused on his guitar and never upstaging the other players.

The other member of the Tennessee Two, Marshall Grant, was born May 5, 1928, in western North Carolina near the Tennessee border. Marshall's parents were William and Mary Elizabeth Simmons Grant. The couple had twelve children together, eleven of whom survived into adulthood. Marshall was the ninth. When he was eighteen, he married Mississippi-native Etta May Dickerson. In Memphis, Etta became good friends with Vivian Cash. Grant not only played upright bass maniacally on stage, he was the record keeper and road manager for the band—though mostly by default. Cash had no mind for business, and Luther apparently was content to let Marshall handle the grim details of touring. Grant's wife was as organized as Marshall was. When it came to Etta, Vivian Cash remembered "how perfect she looked at all times" and was a "meticulous housekeeper." She ironed all of Marshall's clothes, right down to his socks and shorts. She even pressed his towels.[70]

The history of Johnny Cash and the Tennessee Two started with all of them picking on acoustic guitars. "J. R. brought in his old guitar," remembered Grant, "which was the worst thing to try to play I'd ever seen."[71] Cash was still strumming the cheap guitar he bought in Germany. He had gotten his money's worth, though, and he was determined to make music with what he had. Grant, thankfully, handed him his Martin, a brand of guitar that Cash stuck with for the rest of his career. According to

Marshall, Cash used his guitar for all the Sun recordings,[72] and apparently had no interest in the electric guitar.

Cash and his bandmates soon realized they couldn't function as three acoustic guitar players. Cash's strength as a singer was never questioned, but he was the one who ended up with the acoustic. Grant picked up the bass, while Perkins got hold of an electric guitar. None of the men had any musical training to speak of. Even so, Cash and the Tennessee Two made the most of their limitations. What is amazing is that men in their mid-twenties— with day jobs and wives, and no musical training or understanding of show business—pursued music as seriously as they did. Becoming proficient on guitar is no easy feat, especially without lessons. As a guitarist, Cash kept to strumming and picking. Grant set himself to learning the upright bass, on which he attached pieces of tape so he could follow the notes on the fret board. The difference between upright and electric bass, Peter Cooper has written, is "like driving a tank and flying a plane."[73] Marshall eventually became adept at both.

As the group's sole electric guitarist, Perkins had the most difficult task of all three musicians in providing riffs and lead lines that gave shape to Cash's songs. Perkins painstakingly worked out his lead parts, note for note. His playing was primitive compared to the guitar wizards of the late 1960s and the 1970s. Even by 1950s standards, though, Cash and the Tennessee Two could not have kept up with contemporaries such as the Pennsylvania-based Bill Haley and the Comets. The solo on "Rock around the Clock" remains one of the best guitar breaks of all time. The Tennessee Two couldn't play like the Comets. Still, as a guitarist, Luther had one essential virtue: he was distinctive. And people—not least among them Perkins's later replacement, Bob Wootton—admired and emulated him. Luther might have been limited, but the stripped-down Sun style became the gold standard for rockabilly. Many of the most successful and revered bands, from the Rolling Stones to the Beatles, eschewed extended instrumental breaks. They took lessons from what Cash, Perkins, and others at Sun did: say it well in a song and do it in under three minutes. What Cash and the Tennessee Two created was "boom-chicka-boom" or the "Cash sound."

It is remarkable how quickly they managed to find this sound and get it recorded in a professional way. Cash initially wanted to record gospel music, but by the time he made it into the studio, his band's sound was more similar to the emerging force that was rock and roll. Cash and the Tennessee Two had that most slippery of qualities: authenticity. Cash's biographers and admirers have often used this term to describe him.[74] But what exactly does authenticity mean, and how does it apply to Cash? When discussing authenticity in music, critics have often praised musicians and bands that have it while deriding those that do not. One might lambast Milli Vanilli for not singing their own songs, for example, or the Monkees for too often not playing their own instruments (though they were accomplished musicians and singers in their own right). In such discussions of authenticity, punk, with its DIY aesthetic, is considered authentic, while more accomplished musicianship—as in progressive rock—is considered elitist or "ersatz shit," as Robert Christgau once described English proggers King Crimson.[75] "Ersatz, compared to what?" one might ask—Robert Johnson?

Even Christgau has described authenticity as a "philosophical black hole," though that didn't prevent him from using the adjective to describe musicians such as Tom Waits or, more infamously, accusing Jimi Hendrix (of all people) of being a "psychedelic Uncle Tom."[76] Christgau's embarrassing misread of Hendrix aside, there is a tendency among critics and fans to see "Black" music (i.e., the blues) as more authentic than "white" music (i.e., anything that isn't the blues or close to it).

Regardless of one's critical pedigree, it would be the rare person that would describe Johnny Cash as lacking authenticity. The authors of *Faking It: The Quest for Authenticity in Popular Music* have noted how Cash provides a "good example of how complex it can be to judge authenticity." Their analysis of Cash's late-career recording of "Mercy Seat"—about a condemned man—applies well to "Folsom Prison Blues," one of his earliest efforts at Sun. "Is it authentic? Of course not," they conclude of "Mercy Seat," but "our knowledge of Cash and his performance of the song give it an emotional charge that rides through the inauthenticity, creating an effective drama, even if it is not an authentic document."[77] Cash and his band's authenticity was based on the fact that they came from poor, working-class backgrounds and none of them were trained musicians. Rock and roll, especially in England and the American cities, with its songs about cars and motorcycles and its fans' fondness for leather jackets, drew on an urban aesthetic. But Cash and his band were country boys, who had spent much time in the cotton patches and evangelical churches of their youth before venturing to the big city. Still, as different as Cash and the Tennessee Two might have been from the rockers who followed them, they were essentially one of the first garage bands, suburban groups that became a staple of 1960s and 1970s middle-class youth culture. Thus, they have achieved a level of critical authenticity.

The repetitiveness of the "boom-chicka-boom" was the key component of the Cash sound. At its worst, repetition can be annoying, numbing. At its best, it gives a band drive, a catchiness, an almost hypnotic power. "Minimalism has a certain charm," Keith Richards has written. "You say, that's a bit monotonous, but by the time it's finished, you're wishing it hadn't."[78] Cash's sound seems as if anyone could have invented it, but no one else did, and it gets stuck in your head. Cash's straightforward, stripped-down rockabilly approach was appealing to the all-important and growing youth market. Unlike in the days of traditional country, jazz, or big band music, American youths seem to have found in Cash's records a music all their own. And what Cash did at Sun was of lasting value. Each generation since Cash's Memphis days has embraced him.

Cash and the Tennessee Two, like Elvis and the others at Sun, were bridging the gap between traditional country and the revolutionary emerging force that was rock and roll. Neither genre lacked virtuoso players. What proved essential to both was sincerity. Hank Williams could say a lot with three chords, just as Bob Dylan could. Thus, country and rock fans have often been unconcerned with technical brilliance, so long as a song feels honest. They have wanted great songwriting, melody, and a true and interesting sound with integrity. Country and blues often cross paths, but country did not mesh so well with the more challenging musical worlds of jazz or classical. Jazz records succeed—in fact, thrive—without words, just as classical has for centuries. But in country and rock, the voice was essential. Country singers didn't want their bands to overwhelm the voice or lyrics in a recording. Later, rock music would grow much louder and sophisticated. Lead singers would have to scream to be heard over the noise of pounding Ludwig drums and wailing Gibson guitars. In the 1950s, though, records were still emerging from the era of vaudeville and barn dances. Cash and the Tennessee Two were not going to overpower and audience with sheer volume. But they had the boom-chicka-boom.

It was no coincidence that the Cash sound emerged from a Memphis studio. Had Cash and the Tennessee Two recorded just a few hundred miles away in Nashville, their sound might have been (as later events proved) more country or religious, more attuned to the expectations of the Nashville establishment. Thankfully for Cash, Elvis, and the rest of the Sun stable, Sam Phillips was looking for a different kind of sound, one more similar to the race records he had produced before Elvis rather than anything being done in Nashville. Memphis and Nashville are both big Tennessee cities—and were never really rivals—but they were distinct from each other. Memphis, a Mississippi River town, evolved quite differently from inland Nashville, and it had the music to prove it.

Arkansas was not a place to make lots of money as a musician, though initially it might not have made a difference. "The money didn't matter," Sonny Burgess once said of an aspiring musician. "You just wanted someone to listen to you."[79] And people quickly began listening to Cash. Vivian later recalled that "word spread that Johnny was an everyman's man. And it did say a lot about Johnny's character. He never felt above anybody else. He didn't have an ego. People everywhere just couldn't help but like him."[80] One could question whether or not Cash had much ego—after all, some inner force was driving him to record, perform, and write—but Vivian was correct in noting that Cash's music had honesty and authenticity. Unlike Elvis, Cash might have been too dark for the teenyboppers, but for a time, he made music marketed toward them, without giving away any of the sincerity that allowed him to ingratiate himself later with soldiers, prisoners, and Native American activists.

In keeping with the standards of the time, Cash and the Tennessee Two dressed well, usually in suits and ties. Cash sometimes wore bright red or other colors—the Man in Black was not the Man in Black until the late 1960s. Nor was he especially somber. Cash was fine with playing the clown if it made audiences laugh. Despite the band's concessions to 1950s norms—suits and ties, and all of the band's members being married—Cash gave his audiences a show. Luther Perkins stood like a wax figure. Marshall Grant snapped his chewing gum and danced to the beat, slapping his upright bass (once he moved to an electric, the dancing stopped). Despite Marshall's gyrations, Cash was the center of attention—introducing songs, making patter with the audience, and cracking jokes. Cash, ironically, was much more a wild man on stage before the worst of his drug period. The highlight of his performance often was his Elvis impersonation, where he threw his long hair forward and shook his hips. He would run a comb through his hair and throw it at Marshall as if it were a dead bat. Cash did his Elvis impersonation well into the 1960s.

Cash's Elvis impersonation was pure shtick, but he took seriously one aspect of his stage persona: how he held his guitar. Given Luther's responsibilities as the melody maker on lead, and the fact that the band had no drummer, Cash played his guitar like a percussion instrument and wielded it like a weapon. On the Sun recordings, Cash slipped a dollar bill between the strings, giving his playing a snare drum effect as he strummed. On stage, when the band launched into "Big River," Cash pointed his guitar at the audience like a machine gun.

In Memphis, Cash solidified his place as the forerunner of Outlaw country. With the Grand Ole Opry as the centerpiece of its musical culture, Nashville had always embraced tradition more than Memphis. In contrast, the Memphis scene was a Wild West for young talent, with Sheriff Sam Phillips trying to maintain law and order. The performances Cash and Elvis were perfecting were much closer to later rock and roll than anything ever seen at the Grand Ole Opry. The shows Carl Perkins and Sonny Burgess put on, too, were more in the spirit of the juke joints of poor white and Black communities of the Deep South than the staid traditions of the Ryman Auditorium. Cash's generation had come of age amid the Great Depression and World War II. Thankfully for them, they were young enough to have avoided combat. Restless, they were putting their energies into music. And the music business was booming.

Of the friendships Cash forged at Sun, one of his deepest was with Carl Perkins. Both had led similar lives up to that point. Perkins was born on April 9, 1932, roughly six weeks after Cash, in Tiptonville, Tennessee. Carl Perkins Highway (Highway 78), which runs through the town today, is about a mile from the Mississippi River. As was true of most southerners, Perkins was raised in the shadow of the Civil War and racial violence. Perkins grew up not far from Island Number Ten, site of an important 1862 battle, where seven thousand Confederates surrendered to Union general John Pope. In 1901, much of Tiptonville was burned in the wake of the lynching of Ike Fitzgerald, a Black man accused of raping a white woman. It was thought the blaze was started by one or more members of the Black community, but its cause remains unknown.[81]

Unlike Cash, Perkins was born to a sharecropper family—the lowest of the low on the southern white social ladder. Being a sharecropper meant the Perkins family did not own their farm. Neither Perkins nor Cash lived in a home with running water or electricity, but the Cash family's Dyess house was a middling farmer's home, not a shack. Perkins, however, grew up in a house where on cold nights "frigid winds would rush through the newsprint papering the walls, under the shack's foundation, and between the cracks in the floor."[82] Both men knew their way around a cotton patch.

As musicians, the evolution of Cash and Perkins was not at all similar. Cash did not seriously play guitar until he was in the Air Force. Perkins, though, managed to get his hands on one at a young age. He played it religiously, picking up lessons here and there from an uncle, making progress from constant practice—just as countless teenagers with dreams of rock stardom later would. Perkins's inspiration came from many of the same radio sources that inspired Cash. Neither man had the luxury of hearing records at home growing up. Cash's love of singing alleviated the drudgery of sweating in the cotton fields. Perkins likewise hated field work. His best hours were spent back in the family shack, mastering the guitar.

Perkins was a few weeks younger than Cash, but his professional career began much earlier—in his teens. Why? For one, Perkins did not spend four years in the military, as Cash did. Perkins was also a high school dropout, whose family was more permissive than Cash's was. As was true of Ray Cash, Buck Perkins, Carl's dad, could be an abusive drunk. Ray gave up alcohol around the time Johnny entered junior high school. Unlike Ray, Buck had no self-control when it came to drinking—he was a carouser.

As was true of Johnny, Carl's encouragement in music came from his mother, Louise. His family was wilder than the Cash clan. Sharecropping was not a path to a prosperous, stable existence. Luckily, music gave Carl an outlet for his youthful energy. By the age of fourteen, he was playing in juke joints—ramshackle places not classy enough to be considered bars, known for hard drinking, dancing, and fighting.[83] They were the kind of places Ray and Carrie Cash would not have let Johnny go, had there been any in Dyess. The honky-tonks, immortalized in countless country songs, may have had a rough, romantic charm to them, but they certainly were no place for a teenager. Very quickly, Carl was drinking just as hard as the customers he was entertaining. He also enlisted the help of his two brothers—Jay on rhythm guitar, Clayton on upright bass. The Perkins brothers soon earned a reputation as a raucous live act. And given the brothers' intensity, they sometimes had fistfights on stage. Perkins, nevertheless, stayed focused on his music. Years before Cash, he was writing songs and developing a rockabilly sound.

Long before the Beatles turned American youth into screaming mobs, Carl Perkins confronted the first wave of rock and roll hysterics. The Beatles, who knew something about unhinged teens, covered Perkins more than they did any other artist.[84] "Blue Suede Shoes"—which Perkins claimed he wrote on a brown paper sack—was one of rock music's earliest anthems.[85] The first song Perkins recorded was "Movie Magg," released in March 1955 on Sun. The song was about a young man taking his date to the movies—not in a car, but on the back of a horse. It was the kind of song Cash could have written, though he might have made "Becky" a mule rather than a horse. Perkins had written the song as a teenager, and it was a fitting tune for 1950s rock and roll. Nothing said American pop more than a tale of two teenagers going to the movies. For a first record, "Movie Magg" did well, though it was released on Flip Records rather than Sun (Phillips owned both labels). The seminal "Blue Suede Shoes" was recorded in late 1955 and released in January 1956. Elvis had an even bigger hit with it, but Perkins had written it, one of hundreds of songs he would pen throughout his career.

Cash had the idea for what became "Blue Suede Shoes" in 1955 while the band was hanging out with Perkins backstage one night in Bono, one of the many small towns that characterized northeastern Arkansas (and still do). Cash told Perkins that he had a friend in the Air Force who was always complaining of people at dance halls stepping on his blue suede shoes. The idea of "don't step on my blue suede shoes" had a nice ring to Cash. Perkins agreed and wrote a song about it—the most popular he ever wrote.[86]

To say kids in the 1950s were excited about rock and roll is an understatement. Perkins dealt with fans who were out of control and rushed the stage at various shows in the South. At one point, Carl actually considered quitting touring because the fans were so violent.[87] Cash never dealt with fans as wild as that, but he leaned more heavily toward country. In the mid-1950s at Sun, though, no hard lines existed between rock and roll and country acts.

Cash and Perkins had different memories concerning when they first started playing together. Cash remembered his first show with Perkins being in Parkin, in northeastern Arkansas, at a theater. "There was no toilet in the place," Cash said, "and Carl and I, before the show, went around the back of the theater, on the ground, like country boys do, and we talked about it then. We were still country boys, playing the big theater in Parkin—I don't know but it would seat two hundred people, but it was a big deal for us."[88] Perkins remembered playing his first gig with Cash in Marianna, Arkansas, in the Mississippi Delta—about forty-five minutes southwest of Memphis—in the spring of 1955. "We played in a football field, on a flatbed truck," Perkins remembered. "He came with the Tennessee Two, and I came with my brothers, Jay and Clayton." Perkins said his first big break came at a gig in Texarkana, which entailed a long drive across the diagonal length of Arkansas. Many other exhausting drives were to follow. "I spent most of the time in John's car," Perkins said, "and we wrote songs together."[89] Over the course of these many dates and rides together, Cash and Perkins became good friends.

In the early stages of Cash and the Tennessee Two's music career, the three men's noodling around in Cash's house in Memphis presented no threat to domestic life. Vivian supported her husband's singing and his ambitions to become a professional musician. Unlike her character as portrayed in the film *Walk the Line*, Vivian was not dismissive of the band's abilities. She said she enjoyed hearing them practice, while she played cards in the living room with friends.[90] She also accompanied Johnny on early gigs in 1955 to places in northeastern Arkansas such as Lepanto and Osceola.

To further complicate his life, within a few months of being married, Vivian became pregnant. She gave birth to her and Johnny's first child, Rosanne, on May 24, 1955. It was a few weeks before the release of Johnny's debut single, "Hey Porter." According to Vivian, Rosanne was a combination of the nicknames Johnny had given to her breasts: Rose and Anne.[91] The story, however, may be apocryphal; Johnny had a grandmother named Roseanna. But if true, it ably summed up Johnny's attitude toward fatherhood, as well as the flippant attitude certain fathers in the 1950s had toward parenting.

Many men of the 1950s had rigid ideas and unhealthy habits concerning fatherhood. Those that fit the generational stereotype of the sexist, aloof, boorish father and husband—and there was no shortage of those—were resented by a generation of wives and children who bore the scars of their callous behavior. Furthermore, physically and verbally abusive behavior toward wives and children in the 1950s was common and not necessarily scandalous. Pop culture, as on the brilliant TV show *Mad Men*, portrays Cold War–era fathers as psychologically and emotionally unavailable authority figures, men who were both workaholics and alcoholics, breadwinners given great license to smoke like fiends and spend as much time away from home or their families as they wanted.

When it comes to the history of fatherhood, however, the 1950s are complicated. Neanderthal attitudes were changing. Even before World War II, there emerged what Ralph LaRossa has called a "new fatherhood," which spurred men to be more involved in children's lives.[92] Unfortunately, for too much of his career, Cash put music far ahead of family. He was a seriously flawed father. He was never physically abusive and was a better father than Ray had been. But Ray's was a low standard. What is clear is that the longer Cash was a father, the worse things got for him and his family.

For a while, Cash's ineptitude was charming. Vivian referred to Johnny's messy diaper-changing style, unbeknownst to him, as "Johnnying it"—meaning, "when you're rough-like with anything or doing something haphazardly."[93] In time, Cash's shortcomings as a father became less amusing, more cruel and heartbreaking. Even so, things did not get bad until the family moved to California. Pictures survive of Johnny at the Memphis zoo with Rosanne. They show a child and daughter not yet worn down by the stresses of fame, neglect, and addiction. As for Vivian, she would have been happy to stay in Memphis. She never imagined how far Johnny's music would take them, and she didn't want the pitfalls that came with her husband's international celebrity.[94]

Elvis had a head start on the other rockabilly artists at Sun. His version of "That's All Right" hit record store shelves in July 1954, the same month Cash was honorably discharged from the Air Force in New Jersey. But events for Cash moved quickly. By August, Cash had married. On September 9, he auditioned for Sam Phillips. The following March, Cash cut "Hey Porter"—his first single with Sun, which was released in June.[95]

It is fitting that Cash's first recorded song was about trains. Cash described "Hey Porter" as a "daydreamin' kind of thing," and it was one of many train songs he cut throughout his career.[96] The song was about a man riding a train to return to the cotton fields. For Cash, that meant Dyess—where some of his family members still lived—even though the song only referred to Tennessee. For his first release, Cash put a decidedly southern spin on the universal desire to return home. It could have been sentimental stuff, but the song had a locomotive propulsion courtesy of the Tennessee Two that made it a tune more about postwar impatience than nostalgia.

The reason for Cash's referencing Tennessee rather than Arkansas might have been practical: Cash was living in Memphis by then, and his music career had started there. Besides, it's easier to make a lyric rhyme with "Tennessee" than "Dyess" or "Arkansas." In any case, after he and the Tennessee Two cut "Hey Porter," Cash experienced something close to ecstasy: in his hands, he had a song of his own. Cash said it was "the most fantastic feeling I ever had in my life." Despite his elation, Cash said that when he gave the record to a disc jockey to play, the man broke it. Cash had to wait another day to get a new copy.[97] As is true of any addict, Cash chased the ecstasy of making his first record for the rest of his life.

Before Cash released "Hey Porter," he worked small gigs in early 1955, mostly in the Memphis area, northern Mississippi, and Arkansas. Marshall Grant remembered an early date at a rustic setting in Parkin, in northeastern Arkansas, not far from Memphis. "The building had a dirt floor," Grant remembered, "and seating consisted of two-by-eight boards nailed to stumps. I don't think more than thirty-five people showed up for the show, but at least we played that night and made a few bucks."[98] It was all part of a new band paying its dues. And really, playing before a crowd of several dozen people is a respectable start for an aspiring band (or even an established one).

Cash's big break came with the release of "Cry! Cry! Cry!" on the first day of summer 1955. Cash apparently wrote the song in a matter of minutes.[99] However quickly written, the song was a hit, reaching number 14 on the country chart. On July 30, Cash recorded "So Doggone Lonesome," though it was not released until December as the B-side of "Folsom Prison Blues." "So Doggone Lonesome," written in the style of Ernest Tubb—one of Cash's heroes—performed well, climbing to number 4. Cash was quickly becoming a singer of note. For a time, he and the Tennessee Two liked to play dates near Memphis. But soon—and much to Vivian's dismay—Cash's fame took him far beyond.[100]

"Folsom Prison Blues" was released on December 15, 1955. At the time, no one had yet discovered that "Folsom" stole heavily from "Crescent

City Blues," a 1953 song written by Gordon Jenkins (based on an earlier instrumental piano blues of the same name). Cash got the idea for his iconic Folsom song while he was in the Air Force. In October 1951, he wrote to Vivian about seeing *Inside the Walls of Folsom Prison*, a crime picture that would have been forgotten were it not for Cash's connection to it.[101] It seems Cash did not write a song about Folsom until much later—at the time he saw *Inside the Walls*, he was not playing guitar or writing songs. "Folsom" became a hit for Cash at Sun, but it caused him headaches later and a $75,000 settlement after Jenkins sued Cash for theft.

Anyone who compares the lyrics of Cash's "Folsom Prison Blues" with "Crescent City Blues" would convict Cash of stealing. Yet Cash's version made some unforgettable lyrical changes, and the two songs also differed quite a bit musically. The 1953 song was sung by Beverly Mahr (the wife of Gordon Jenkins) and was told from a woman's perspective. Cash turned a charming song about romantic frustration into a lonely, mournful tale of a prisoner doing hard time. As the name implies, "Crescent City Blues" is an ode to the slow, sensual ennui of New Orleans. Cash's "Folsom" makes key rewrites. He released it as an up-tempo rocker, complete with vital and slashing Luther Perkins guitar breaks. Cash kept most of the line about rich folks in the dining car, but he wisely changed "pheasant breast" and "eastern caviar" to "drinking coffee and smoking big cigars." His most brilliant change was giving the prisoner the most nihilistic and psychotic reason for killing someone. The notorious line, "I shot a man in Reno just to watch him die," was Cash's take on the Jimmie Rodgers line, "I'm gonna shoot poor Thelma just to see her jump and fall," and put a much darker shade to the material than Jenkins could have imagined. It quickly became a staple of his live shows, and Cash had a hit with the song twice—once at Sun and later with his live version for Columbia in 1968.

Cash might have remade (and markedly improved) "Crescent City Blues," but there is no doubt he passed off another artist's song as his own. It is understandable that Cash would have borrowed heavily from another artist at the time. As a young songwriter, he was drawing on every creative resource he could in order to deliver good material, and his ideas about Folsom—as derivative as they were—provided inspiration for a classic song. Rock music then had no template for performers, and Cash probably had no idea "Folsom" would become so popular. Without excusing it, theft has always been a part of the entertainment industry, especially in a time when copyright laws were not so rigidly enforced as they are today. Cash was no worse than some of his peers when it came to "borrowing" from other artists.

Had "Folsom" been based on much older material, Cash might have had no later legal problems. But "Crescent City Blues" was recorded only two years before Cash cut "Folsom." Cash could have saved himself trouble by giving Jenkins songwriting credit on "Folsom," but by the time Jenkins realized what Cash had done, it was impossible not to associate Cash with the tune. Theft aside, Cash remade the song in his own unique style, much as he would later with "Ring of Fire" and countless others written by different artists. As is true of many accomplished musicians, Cash was a great interpreter as well as a gifted songwriter.

At an August 1955 show in Little Rock, Cash played on a bill that had Webb Pierce as a headliner. Pierce was native of West Monroe, Louisiana, only about a two-hour drive from Cash's birthplace, and was yet another country star who had emerged from the cotton fields. In 1955, he had a huge hit with his version of "I'm in the Jailhouse Now," recorded by Jimmie Rodgers and others, that spent an incredible twenty-one weeks at number 1 on the country chart. Elvis also appeared at the August Little Rock show along with Red Sovine, Wanda Jackson, Bud Deckelman (who, as with Cash, was a native Arkansan and Air Force veteran who settled in Memphis), Charlie Feathers, Scotty & Bill, and Sammy Barnhart. Cash's name did not appear in the *Arkansas Gazette* advertisement for the show. But no one could argue with the ad's claim that the audience would see "America's Greatest Country Stars!"[102] It was quite a lineup.

Cash and his Sun mates were having little trouble finding an audience. A few weeks after his Little Rock show, Cash, along with other acts, appeared with Elvis in Forrest City, Arkansas, at a Country Music Jamboree at Smith Stadium. Cash was no touring veteran at that point, whereas Presley was called the "King of Western Bop." Both Elvis and Cash were rising to superstardom, but Forrest City had more mundane concerns. The Labor Day concert raised money for a wire fence around the St. Francis County Fairgrounds.[103] Luckily for the fundraiser, attendance set "an all-time record."[104]

Cash was doing what any successful musician has done: support more established acts until his name rose on the billing. The *Texarkana Daily News* of November 17 had Cash placed at the bottom of a show that included

Elvis, Hank Thompson, and Charline Arthur. Arthur was a Texas blues and rockabilly singer whose hits included a version of "Wildwood Flower," made famous by Maybelle Carter (though written in 1860). Thompson, a native of Waco, Texas, later inspired the novel and film *Crazy Heart.* Cash was at the bottom of the bill, but it was a talented one. If Cash were the kind of man to take comfort in such things, the *Daily News* had Elvis listed as "Elis" Presley.[105]

Cash was gaining acceptance as one of the best rockabilly performers. Ralph Gleason, a critic who helped found *Rolling Stone*, headlined a story about Cash: "It Looks as if Elvis Has a Rival—from Arkansas." Gleason noted that unlike Elvis, Cash had "no bumps and grinds in his routine." Cash's guitar playing was "fair-to-middling" (using an expression common among cotton farmers), but he noted that Cash had penned his first four records himself. Cash's Sun label was "relatively unknown," Gleason wrote, but Memphis had become ground zero for innovative music. Cash's fan clubs were multiplying, and Gleason noted Cash's desire to "live calmly" and not buy Cadillacs "by the gross." Cash instead contented himself with a serious fishing habit.[106]

Cash was not going to "live calmly" for much longer. As he worked hard to become a professional songwriter, northeastern Arkansas was seeing an explosion of live music, featuring some of the best musicians of the 1950s and 1960s. Ironically, it was in the deepest notches of the Bible Belt that one could catch the earliest smoky whiffs of the "devil music" that was rock and roll.

Perhaps the best music in Arkansas was found in Newport, a town with historically high aspirations. Citizens built an opera house in 1890, and William Jennings Bryan spoke there in 1911—three years after his third and last run for president. Newport experienced a boom during World War II, courtesy of a large military base that doubled the town's population and produced lucrative farming operations.[107] In 1951, Jackson County—where Newport was—ranked among the wealthiest counties *in the country* in cotton, soybean, and rice production.[108] Young people, though, weren't moving to Newport to farm: they were there for music. "Newport was one of the best club scenes I ever played," remembered Fayetteville, Arkansas, native Ronnie Hawkins. "It was always full. It was always rockin'."[109] Revelers in Newport could visit the Bloody Bucket, where a bear on a chain guzzled beer until it fell over drunk. Others could indulge in the plentiful prostitutes on Front Street.[110] At the north end of Newport was the Honky Tonk: a place so rough, WS Holland said, "they would sell bricks at the door."[111] Also rocking was the town of Swifton, seventeen miles north of Newport along Route 67, now known as the "Rock and Roll Highway."

In December 1955, Elvis played the Swifton High School gymnasium, where Cash and the Tennessee Two were the opening act. Later that day, Elvis appeared at the King of Clubs in Swifton, owned by Bob King. The venue, located about a half-hour drive north from Newport, was a wild, un-air-conditioned place known for its loud music and sweaty dancers. Large fans blasted revelers as the music blared. The fans might have helped, but they also forced musicians to tune their instruments constantly.[112] Carl Perkins was a regular in Newport. The same month Elvis and Cash played in Swifton, Perkins recorded "Blue Suede Shoes," which Sam Phillips released in January 1956. It was the height of the Sun period, and Arkansas was taking advantage of all the musical acts coming out of Memphis.

The rockabilly greats may have been having fun playing in Arkansas, being chummy with one another, and offering encouragement and song ideas, but it wasn't always easy. One night at the King of Clubs, Elvis asked Bob King to give Cash $10 to sing a song. King said no, but he'd give Cash $20 to sing three songs. Cash was not amused. According to Sonny Burgess, he had to give Cash a pep talk about staying in the music business. Cash apparently was not pleased with having to open for Elvis for a mere $20. Burgess said Cash might jeopardize his career if he didn't play his set.[113]

It is doubtful Cash was ready to abandon his music career at that point. Music was all Cash wanted to do. But what Burgess probably did was give Cash some confidence on a night he was not feeling at his best. Cash was still a budding musician, and opening for Elvis was a great boost to his career. By the time Cash was touring, however, Elvis was becoming too big for playing small gigs in Arkansas; his December appearance was the last time he played the state.

Cash and Sonny Burgess were from the same region—northeastern Arkansas—but their styles were quite different. Burgess's music and stage act were more in the spirit of big band and Texas swing. Sonny and his band, the Pacers, numbered six people—two guitarists, bass, piano, drums, and a horn. Burgess became best known for his singles "We

Wanna Boogie" and "Red Headed Woman" (about Burgess's wife). Just as it is hard to imagine Cash with an electric guitar in his hands, so was it difficult to imagine Burgess with an acoustic. Cash's music has proven more popular, but Burgess was more modern, embracing rock and roll in a way Cash never did. Burgess's tunes were much more electric and up-tempo, and Cash's performances never reached the frantic heights of the Burgess and the Pacers' circus-like live show. Burgess might extend a song for a half an hour or more. Band members liked to form a human pyramid, and one night, Burgess injured himself after jumping more than ten feet off the stage.[114]

Albert Austin "Sonny" Burgess had an upbringing similar to those of Cash and Carl Perkins. He was almost three years older than Cash, hailing from Newport, seventy miles due west of Dyess. At the time of his birth in 1929, it was home to fewer than five thousand people. Burgess rode a horse to church as a kid, and like Cash and Perkins, he knew the cotton fields firsthand. Burgess could have spoken for either man when he said, "One day picking cotton really makes you want to play music." Sonny listened to music on a battery-powered radio, and he learned guitar early on. He was an exceptional baseball player who received a scholarship to play at Louisiana State University. Burgess was drafted in 1951 and served in Germany, where he first started playing for audiences. Sonny said he always wanted to play like Scotty Moore and sing like Elvis.[115]

Burgess and others from the Sun stable popularized Porky's Rooftop Club in Newport, the more redneck alternative to its more respectable Newport rival, the Silver Moon. At the time, the Silver Moon was the largest club in Arkansas.[116] Regardless of which venue musicians played, they were in good company. Over the years, Porky's hosted Elvis, Hank Thompson, Wanda Jackson, Roy Orbison, and Conway Twitty.[117] Porky's had a rough reputation, but it was suited to players like Carl Perkins and his brothers. The place had gambling in the back room, where Clayton Perkins was talented at losing money.[118]

Their musical styles might have differed, but Burgess and Cash were fellow travelers in the early rockabilly music scene. Burgess and the Pacers traveled with Cash to California to play with him in 1958. But for the most part, Burgess didn't enjoy leaving Arkansas. After achieving some early success, he grew discouraged in the early 1960s and was soon working a day job.[119]

To the benefit of the music world, Sam Phillips was managing to find one superior talent after another at Sun. In early 1956, a few months after Perkins released "Blue Suede Shoes," Cash penned "I Walk the Line." Not surprisingly, Cash's music was still drawing heavily on Arkansas influences. The memorable humming intro to "I Walk the Line," Cash wrote later, was based on a doctor from Dyess. "He hummed all the time," Cash remembered. "I always thought if Dr. Hollingsworth could have put his humming to music, he might have had a hit."[120] Along with the great Cash vocals, Luther's slow southern-drawl guitar intro, which has the heavy feel of a man expressing his love for a woman, further made the track unique. Cash not only had a smash with "I Walk the Line," it became a classic. *Rolling Stone* has called it the greatest country song of all time.[121] Upon its release, Cash was not even two years into his recording career.

In May 1956, Cash played Little Rock. Carl Perkins, billed as "Mr. Blue Suede Shoes," was the headliner. Second on the bill was Cash, whom the *Arkansas Gazette* called "tall and handsome" and a man with a "great ability in writing songs." The *Gazette* praised him "as one of the most distinctive new country stars to come along in many years." Touring kept him on the road a lot, the paper continued, but there was "always time between dates to stop and fish for a few hours in a handy lake, and to have an occasional fish-fry in a wayside park."[122] Also among the country boys was Warren Smith. A native of Mississippi, Smith had been in the Air Force and moved to West Memphis after he left the service. Another one of Sam's Sun babies, Smith's hit at the time was "Rock and Roll Ruby," a song Cash had written.[123] At the Little Rock show, Smith had third billing. Beneath him was Roy Orbison. Tickets were one dollar.

Cash was off to an astounding start at Sun, and eventually the money came in. Vivian remembered the first royalty check Johnny received was for $2,000. It was "a fortune when you're borrowing just to survive," she wrote.[124] By the summer of 1957, Cash had released only a handful of singles, but he had crafted stellar material and was compiling a good backlog of songs at Sun.

Cash and the Tennessee Two, meanwhile, kept grinding out shows. In Warren, Arkansas, in May 1957, in the south-central part of the state, the response was ecstatic. With Cash and Perkins were Jerry Lee Lewis and the Tennessee Mountain Boys as well as Onie Wheeler and His Band. "The total effect," the local paper concluded, "should be about the same as if they were giving away dollar bills at the rodeo arena." In June, Cash played at Warren's tomato festival. His two-hour nighttime show took place at the rodeo arena. A square dance followed. The venue might have been less than glamorous, but it was the kind of show Cash played in his early days—in fact, he never lost touch with his rural audiences. The "Johnny Cash Show," as the paper called it, also featured Carl Perkins. His show in Warren revealed Cash could stretch out his performances and attract other talent to perform with him.[125]

In the 1950s, singles were much more important and commercial than albums. Nevertheless, in October 1957 Cash released the first of his two full studio albums for Sun Records, *Johnny Cash with His Hot and Blue Guitar*—a play on a popular Memphis radio program "Red, Hot & Blue," hosted by amphetamine-popping disc jockey Dewey Phillips. The album contained Cash's biggest hits such as "Folsom Prison Blues," "Cry! Cry! Cry!" and "I Walk the Line," as well as unreleased material. Cash was the first Sun star to release a full album. It was an impressive debut and included the classic Cash ingredients: a train song, love songs, prison songs, and talk of the country life.

The train song was the opener: "The Rock Island Line," one of many locomotive songs Cash released in his career. Cash's version came a few years after Lonnie Donegan's, recorded in 1954 and a hit in England. Not surprisingly, Cash's version was faster and sounded more southern. It also had more verses than Donegan's. The song had roots in Arkansas music history. It was written in the late 1920s by Clarence Wilson, an African American member of the Rock Island Colored Booster Quartet. Wilson penned the song while working in a freight yard in Little Rock. "Rock Island Line" was popularized by Lead Belly, the bluesman who had served hard time at Louisiana's Angola prison farm and who had his version recorded by folklorist John Lomax (father of ethnomusicologist Alan Lomax). John Lomax's 1934 recording of "Rock Island Line" features prisoners singing at Tucker prison farm in Jefferson County, Arkansas. A version later that year was made at Cummins, the biggest prison in Arkansas and the setting for a memorable show Cash performed in 1969 (discussed in chapter 5).[126] Cash was familiar with the Lomax recordings. "Rock Island Line" was part of the rich library of music he kept in his mind, one obsessed with trains, prisoners, redemption, lovers, working men, and the downtrodden.

The 1934 John Lomax recording of the original "Rock Island Line" contains references to Jesus. Cash, despite his own deep religious beliefs, instead made it a song about trains. The arrangement was miles away from songwriter Clarence Wilson's 1929 version—done a cappella. Cash and the Tennessee Two's "Rock Island Line" might be the definitive recording. It's something of a hillbilly mini-opera, benefiting from a Cash vocal performance that is, in parts, locomotive fast. The band manages to pack much more music into the 2:10 running time than one would think possible. The song has plenty of drive, with tempo changes and an ending that mimics the sound of a speeding train engine. It was an exciting first song on Cash's first album and quite a feat for a three-man band with no drummer.

Robert Christgau has written that Cash was "the countriest at Sun"—that is, more country sounding than Elvis or Jerry Lee Lewis.[127] True to his roots, on his first album, Cash included the autobiographical and nostalgic "Country Boy." He played it himself on acoustic guitar, using a simple (E-A-D) chord progression. With its romanticized talk of a shoeless boy working under the hot sun, roaming the countryside, hunting, and frying fish and rabbit, it was a thick slice of Dyess life. At a deeper level, in saying "you're lucky free . . . I wish I was you and you was me," the song suggested that Cash longed to be that country boy again. Despite the darkness that always seemed to be following Cash, he thought of brighter days—some in the past, others in the future. It was always the present that seemed darkest. In "Country Boy," Cash's nostalgia suggested that adulthood was taking its toll.

Johnny Cash lived a quarter of his life in Arkansas. His time in Memphis amounted to only a few years. But in that time, Cash recorded exceptional music and many of his most enduring hits. He moved to Memphis at a special time in the city's history and the history of American popular music. No period in this country's musical past was more important than the mid- to late 1950s, when Sam Phillips recorded a roster of rockabilly artists that included Elvis, Cash, Roy Orbison, Jerry Lee Lewis, Sonny Burgess, and Charlie Rich. It was more talent than Sam Phillips could handle. By January 1956, Elvis was recording at RCA; by August 1958, Cash had left Sun for Columbia.

Cash and Phillips did not separate on good terms. Cash essentially left without being honest with Phillips about why, and he later regretted it.[128] All the other talent at Sun left within a few years. But in the several years

Cash and his peers were at Sun, Memphis solidified its reputation as the birthplace of rock and roll. Elvis might have departed Sun in 1955, but he never left Memphis, and Graceland became a mecca for his fans. When Sam Phillips discovered in the 1990s that the Rock and Roll Hall of Fame was destined for Cleveland, he was furious.[129]

Memphis made Elvis, and it made Johnny Cash, too. Memphis was not Dyess, but for Cash, it was as close as he could be to his home and still make a name for himself. Until he left Dyess for the military, Cash had spent virtually every hour of his life in Arkansas. Once he returned to the United States from the Air Force, he left the horizontal life of the country for the vertical life of the city. Within a couple years as a musician, he was playing concerts in Canada—a few years after that, Germany and England. In Memphis, through his own immense talent, luck, and the confluence of events, Cash had the most brilliant run of his life.

In the history of country music, the Memphis scene falls between the rise of Nashville and the development of the later "Bakersfield sound" in California. Memphis was different from those places to be sure, for it incorporated more of the blues, more sounds of the Delta. It is no wonder rock and roll started in Memphis rather than Nashville. Memphis was a true river town. And as someone who grew up along the Mississippi, Cash fit perfectly in Memphis. Memphis had absorbed much of what was happening along the length of the Mississippi, which included the sounds of poor whites and African Americans making music. Sam Phillips, in essence, recorded artists who were reimagining the blues for the nuclear age.

Johnny Cash was made by Arkansas. With the vast musical knowledge he had acquired in Dyess, he began developing his guitar playing and performance chops while a serviceman in Germany. One he was back in the United States, Cash helped make rock and roll and the city it hatched in—Memphis—famous. And despite his success in western Tennessee, as the 1960s approached, Johnny Cash was just getting started.

4

California and Nashville

The story of Johnny Cash and the 1960s is a highly dramatic and nearly tragic one, where Cash rode mountain highs and descended into subterranean lows. For him the decade was like an extended nervous breakdown, where an extraordinarily talented man fell prey to personal demons, drug abuse, and the sins of the flesh. In his wake, he left smashed hotels rooms, broken-hearted family members, and literal scorched earth. But out of it all came great art. Cash had the promise to be perhaps the greatest country star of all time—if he lived.

For a while, Cash seemed capable of living up to the high standards of middle-class, 1950s America. As he continued to record, write, and tour later that decade, his family kept growing. Rosanne was born in May 1955, followed by Kathy in April 1956. Johnny and Vivian's third daughter, Cindy, was born in July 1959 in Memphis. In five years of marriage, Johnny and Vivian had three children. As Johnny's music became an all-consuming career, Vivian struggled to run the household. A new child and new home in California—Johnny and Vivian moved there in the summer of 1958—only added to the Cash family's pressures. The move came on the heels of Cash signing with Columbia Records that August 1. Cash had increasing money and fame, but he was also spending less time around his wife and daughters.

California

Cash and the Tennessee Two were a hardworking band in the age before regular air travel. Given the group's touring schedule, the move to California made no logistical sense. Memphis, centrally located in the United States, had its advantages, especially since the tours were not handled as they are today, where bands minimize travel time. Cash and the Tennessee Two literally were all over the map. But Cash wasn't alone in his desire to live on the West Coast. Luther Perkins also moved to California with his wife Birdie, though she ended up hating the place and returned to Memphis without her cheating husband (whom she eventually divorced). Marshall Grant never bothered moving to California.

Things began to change dramatically for the Cash family once they settled in California. Cash wanted to be near Hollywood, and he hoped to start a career in movies once there. Had Cash been serious about a movie career, he might have been wise to live in Hollywood or somewhere else in Los Angeles. Instead, Cash moved the family outside the city—effectively in the country, which was cheaper and where he might have felt more comfortable. What he ended up doing was putting the family in a remote location that only added to Vivian's sense of isolation. Worse, Cash's personality changed more from Jekyll to Hyde the longer he stayed there.

California, nevertheless, offered opportunities for an aspiring entertainer. Coming as it did on the heels of his move to the big time at Columbia, Cash wanted to be at the center of the entertainment universe and not—it is important to note—Nashville, where Columbia's studios were. One popular country music venue was *Town Hall Party*, a three-hour, late night Saturday radio and television show featured on Pasadena and Los Angeles stations. Recorded in L.A., *Town Hall Party* could have been filmed in Nashville or Shreveport. The hoedown, fiddle-friendly introduction of the show was pure country, and the producers of the show wanted guests to perform songs that were short and danceable. Cash obliged.

In 2003, the Sundazed label released an album of Cash's November 1958 appearance on *Town Hall Party*. As music writer Rich Kienzle has said, the show featured a "young feral Cash, full of piss, vinegar and sly orneriness."[1] By 1958, Cash might have been performing for only a couple years, but his band was in fine form on the show, with Cash ribbing Luther about how pretty and small his wife was (though the couple was having marital problems around that time). His stage persona was already well defined. As would be the case throughout his career, he brought an energy and honesty to his performance that transcended his band's limitations as players. Even so, the Johnny Cash sound was there, and his set on *Town Hall Party* was impressive.

Cash opened with one of his best rockers, "Get Rhythm," before settling into calmer numbers such as "You're the Nearest Thing to Heaven" and the

1955 Fern Jones religious song, "I Was There When It Happened." As was true of Cash, Fern Jones had lived for years in Arkansas, when she made a name for herself writing religious songs. Jones sounded a bit like Patsy Cline, and she was a fan of one of Cash's favorites, Sister Rosetta Tharpe. Jones only put out one album in her career, but she made an impression, especially on Cash.

Cash also sang "Frankie's Man Johnny," an updated version of the murder ballad "Frankie and Johnny." The song had its roots in the nineteenth century. Cash kept the song's theme of a lover's fidelity, but his was a sanitized version, more suited to the teen market of the time. In Cash's telling, Johnny is a "long legged guitar picker," with a "wicked, wandering eye." Cash also made it funny, writing that Johnny had eyes for a woman who was—unbeknownst to him—Frankie's sister. When he finds out who she is, she slaps him, and he is scared back into Frankie's arms.

Cash closed the program with "Suppertime." The song sounded like it could have been written by Cash, but the sentimental tune was composed by New Mexico–born Midwest evangelist Ira Stanphill and made popular by Jimmie Davis. Cash kept "Suppertime" in his live repertoire for years, effectively making it *his* song. With its message of the goodness of going home, Cash liked to close his set with a tune that was not only nostalgic but spiritual, talking about the "great suppertime" in the afterlife, where families break bread with Jesus.

On *Town Hall Party*, Cash was playing in support of his first album on Columbia, not-so-modestly titled *The Fabulous Johnny Cash,* released in November 1958. On it, Cash kept to his roots: songs about the soil, love, and the West. The album included "Pickin' Time" and "Suppertime," both meaningful as statements about his youth in Dyess and long-time live Cash staples. Other songs included "Frankie's Man Johnny" and "Don't Take Your Guns to Town."[2] The album also featured "I Still Miss Someone," a song Cash wrote with his nephew, Roy Cash Jr., and that became the B-side to "Don't Take Your Guns to Town."

"I Still Miss Someone" proved one of Cash's most enduring songs, appearing as it did on *At Folsom Prison* in 1968. Roy did most of the writing, though Cash helped with the lyrics. Roy said he began composing the song during a dull accounting class he was taking at Memphis State University.[3] It was one of the many times Cash called upon his kin to help him musically, though it was unusual for him to collaborate so closely with extended family. Later, country musician and former Dyess resident

Buddy Jewell said that "I Still Miss Someone" was the first song he learned how to play.[4]

The Fabulous Johnny Cash proved a smooth transition from Sun to Columbia. Cash kept his signature sound, but he progressed as a songwriter. Cash always knew how to tell a good story—"The Rock Island Line" was a stellar example of that. On *The Fabulous Johnny Cash*, however, he began telling stories that were steeped more in American history and the history of Johnny Cash. On "Pickin' Time," Cash needed only a minute and fifty-nine seconds to tell the story of a struggling cotton farmer and his family, whose economic stress is relieved when the crop is harvested. Cash approaches the song from the farmer's perspective. He doesn't mention Arkansas, but the song clearly was autobiographical and traditional. The song's tune is reminiscent of the popular lullaby "Hush, Little Baby," which originated in the South in the early twentieth century. With its reference to coal oil costing a dime, "Pickin' Time" was set in the pre-electrification era, one that Cash knew well. The song could have been called "Dyess" or "My Father Ray." Instead, Cash took a more universal approach, speaking for hardworking farmers everywhere, especially in the South of his childhood.

"Pickin' Time" examined aspects of American life—small farms and long days in the fields—that were disappearing. While Cash knew cotton farming firsthand, tales of cotton picking probably would have seemed like a story from the nineteenth century for many listeners accustomed the modern world's air conditioning and TV sets. Another track, "Don't Take Your Guns to Town," approaches history from a different perspective, delving into the mythos of the American West. Cash said it was the first "Western" song the band had written.

The song, while taking place in the Wild West, was not worthy of Saturday morning serials. As was customary of Cash's life's work, the song eschewed romance and stereotype for a darker and truer sense of human tragedy. Cash tells the story of a young man named Billy Joe who, as the title notes, insists on wearing his pistols into town, despite the warnings of his mother not to do so. At a saloon, he has his first drink of whiskey and thinks he "had become a man." A "dusty cow poke," however, is not impressed. He laughs at Billy Joe, and a standoff ends quickly with Billy's death. Despite the dark subject matter, the song was a hit, reaching number 1 on the *Billboard* country chart. It inspired Cash to record more music set in the Wild West. He never stopped doing it.

The song is classic Cash in many ways. It begins with Luther hitting the same four notes on his guitar before Cash starts singing. The setting is unspecified, but it could have been anywhere from the dusty streets of western Arkansas to a muddy mining town in California or the Dakotas. The setting, nevertheless, is American through and through. It also has a moral: son, obey your mother. In a way, "Don't Take Your Guns to Town" was Cash rewriting *Lone Bull's Mistake*, his favorite book from childhood, to boom-chicka-boom. In Cash's brand of storytelling, it is a young cowboy who, like Lone Bull, fails to heed a warning and suffers because of it. Whatever the moral, the song represented an early example of a Cash murder ballad. In the course of his career, Cash's songs would rack up a high body count, but he was just drawing on his roots. Arkansas was a place with a history of Western-style violence and rough frontier justice.

California might not have seemed like a natural choice for a country singer such as Cash to settle in, but both California and Cash's native South are a land of cowboy hats, guns, ranches, unrelenting heat, and intense religious belief. California saw the emergence of its own country scene in the 1960s with the Bakersfield sound, epitomized by California native and one-time San Quentin inmate Merle Haggard and Bakersfield transplant Buck Owens. It was in California that Arkansas-born Bob Wootton—who replaced Luther Perkins in 1968—first heard Cash's "I Walk the Line."[5]

The most noticeable musical break Cash made by leaving Sun for Columbia was his choice of religious subject matter. In May 1959, Cash released his first Christian album, *Hymns by Johnny Cash*. It was gospel, the type of music Sam Phillips had not wanted Cash to record for commercial concerns. Religious music didn't sell, Phillips believed, and—at least when it came to Cash—he was correct in that assessment. But Cash wanted to record gospel songs and albums anyway. While not nearly as popular as Johnny's other works, *Hymns* has enough of the boom-chicka-boom sound to satisfy fans not partial to gospel music. The album represented Cash taking advantage of his new artistic freedom. In 1962, Cash released another religious album, *Hymns from the Heart*. It was a forgettable collection of songs, though it did have a great cover, with a well-dressed, dark-suited Cash standing in front of a wooden church like a preacher from a Flannery O'Connor story. It was the last gospel album Cash recorded before *The Holy Land* (1969). It is no coincidence that in his worst drug period, Cash cut no spiritual albums.

Cash took strength from religion, family, and history, all of which he sang about on *Songs of Our Soil*—a title that fairly well sums up the idea of roots music. For the album, released a few months after *Hymns by Johnny Cash*, Cash wrote "Five Feet High and Rising," a companion to "Pickin' Time." Both songs had universal meaning for cotton farmers and those living in the Delta, but they also had meaning for Cash, who had spent so much time in the fields. "Pickin' Time" was about a family trying to hold on financially until the crop was in. "Five Feet High and Rising" was a drama about flood waters threatening to wipe out everything a farmer had. For the song, Cash drew on his experiences in the 1937 Dyess flood. The song worked well, and he played it for years afterward at live shows, where he would introduce it with a personal story about growing up in Arkansas.

Despite its rootsy and autobiographical feel, *Songs of Our Soil* was more eclectic than earlier efforts and seemed a departure from Cash's trademark Sun sound. The album nevertheless showed Cash's readiness to tackle different themes, from class issues ("The Man on the Hill"), family and nostalgia ("My Grandfather's Clock," "Don't Step on Mother's Roses," and "I Want to Go Home"), Native Americans ("Old Apache Squaw"), and religion ("The Great Speckled Bird"). "Great Speckled Bird" was the title of a southern hymn, but it was also the name of a song penned by Roy Acuff in 1936. Many country and folk artists have covered the song or made references to it since then. When it came to Cash, the song had a fitting double meaning. "Great Speckled Bird" was a reference to Jeremiah 12:9, with speckled bird being a "bird of prey," sometimes translated as "vulture." "Great Speckled Bird" was also slang for the amphetamines popular in Nashville at the time.[6]

As the title suggests, *Songs of Our Soil* showed Cash staying close to his roots: family, faith, and a sense of place. Given the money and freedom he had as an artist working at Columbia, Cash felt comfortable veering from secular to religious material. By 1959, he was developing a pattern in which he interspersed religious albums with better-selling secular work. In the late 1950s, though, Cash's songs were drawing more and more on American history for inspiration. His Sun material came from the heart, but his Columbia recordings often sprung from Cash's reading and education—as folksy as it might have been. As was true of the folkies, Cash had an intellectual depth, curiosity, and fondness for dark material that few of his peers had. Elvis certainly didn't.

"As a youngster," *Time* wrote in 1959, "Johnny had something to cry about." He was famous now, but despite his new-found success, Cash had "remained a country boy."[7] And he had time to return home. Cash's obligations in California did not keep him from traveling to Little Rock in mid-May of 1959 for the Fifth Annual Arkansas State Horse Show, one of several concerts Cash performed in Little Rock that weekend for mentally disabled children. They were the first shows he had played in Arkansas since becoming famous. Reporter Bob Troutt heralded Cash's return with the article "Country Music by a Country Boy," discussing Cash's roots in Kingsland and Dyess and his father's struggles during the Great Depression. Cash said he was "looking forward to a real homecoming."[8] He played four dates at the Barton Coliseum, which included two shows on Friday and Saturday. The front page of the *Arkansas Democrat* featured a smiling Cash with a smiling Miss Little Rock, who was strumming Cash's guitar and nearly sitting in his lap.[9] It was the kind of photograph that might have made Mrs. Cash jealous—had she ever seen it. But Vivian was back in California.

Cash stayed several days in Little Rock for the four-day horse show, which ran from Wednesday to Saturday. At the opening night event, Cash played before a crowd estimated at 750 people—a much larger audience than at past concerts. Attendees showed "enthusiasm for the high-quality show horse entries" as well as Cash, who played his hits, including "I Walk the Line" and "Folsom Prison Blues," standout tunes in an ever-growing set list.[10] On Friday night, Cash played his recent "Pickin' Time" and at least one gospel song, "Swing Low, Sweet Chariot." A reporter not acquainted with the stoic Luther Perkins thought he "seemed a little downcast." The reporter added, however, that Perkins's demeanor might have had to do with the fact that Luther and Marshall Grant walked to the venue, while Cash had a convertible deliver him. Cash agreed to sign autographs after the show, but only on programs—and for fifty cents.[11] At the Saturday night show, roughly 2,500 people turned out to see Cash, whose jokes from the previous nights "got the same enthusiastic reception."[12]

Back in California, Cash had film aspirations. His acting career never took off, but by the late 1950s, Cash's music was becoming more theatrical. Once he left Memphis, his music and persona had more of a Western flair. He was in full Western garb on the cover of his *Ride This Train* album (also released as *Come Along and Ride This Train*), holding a gun on a cliff overlooking a desert scene of a locomotive passing below him. The cover, though, was misleading. It was not an album about the Wild West.

The subtitle of *Ride This Train*, released in September 1960, was "A Stirring Travelogue of America in Song and Story." The subtitle might have been ambitious, considering the album consisted of only eight songs (half attributed to Cash) in a run time of thirty-two minutes. And despite the cover image, Cash focused on southern stories. Cash nevertheless managed to cover quite a bit of ground, from songs about an Oregon lumberjack, coal mining in Kentucky, a woman in Louisiana, and a convict who wants to break free of a chain gang working on a levee and run to Memphis ("Going to Memphis," a Hollie Dew and Alan Lomax song that Cash rearranged).

Arkansas was still very much on his mind. On the first track, Cash rattles off a list of place names, much as he would later on his cover of "I've Been Everywhere." The last Anglo name in his list is Bald Knob, Arkansas. Cash then launches into Native American tribe names, including the Quapaw and Caddo, who were not among the more famous tribes but were prominent in central Arkansas. The album, ironically—especially for Cash—contains no actual train songs, but Cash connects each track by doing a spoken-word, first-person segment over locomotive sound effects. *Ride This Train* was Cash's first true concept album, and it was a successful one. It also served as a dry run for his ABC show's "Ride This Train" segment—Cash's favorite segment on the program.

In his introduction to the song "Boss Jack," written by actor and songwriter Tex Ritter, Cash went deep into plantation culture. He begins his tale in Dyess. Cash tells a cotton story, but it's not about the time in which he grew up. Instead, he goes back to 1855, when the narrator, "Boss Jack," says he "had the best bunch of slaves you ever saw. And I treated them right. A lot of them even stayed with me after the war." Boss Jack had a rule that the slaves had to return by night. But one day, he finds "Uncle Moses" out in the fields after the sundown curfew. It's a punishable offense. Boss Jack, however, hears Moses singing "Swing Low, Sweet Chariot" and does not discipline him. In fact, he gives Moses a job in the house, where Boss Jack enjoys listening to Moses's singing every night.

Cash's story was right out of Old South moonlight-and-magnolias mythology, where plantations were home to happy, singing, loyal "darkies" and caring, paternalistic masters. It was the kind of story no respectable musician would record today. *Ride This Train* came out in 1960, but Cash's depiction of the antebellum period was like something out of *Gone with the Wind.* In the 1950s, historians such as Kenneth Stampp and Stanley Elkins began demolishing Old South plantation myths. Still, it was not the kind of history most people were reading, and apparently not Cash either.[13] It is no wonder that "Boss Jack" is not one of Cash's better-known songs. Though fine musically, the song's spoken-word introduction provides, by today's standards, an unfortunate and embarrassing backstory for Boss Jack.

More important, though, than Cash's conservative views of antebellum life on "Boss Jack" was why he was becoming so obsessed with history—in fact, more so than any artist of his stature at the time. America's past clearly gave Cash material for the albums he was now producing at a regular clip. He obviously couldn't write songs about the hotels he was trashing or the drugs he was taking. He might have delved into the darkness of his romantic life. Instead, he looked to the past for inspiration. History songs might have put an emotional distance between him and his audience, but by trying to cover so much territory geographically in his songs, Cash connected to his fans all over the country. He couldn't write about every place he had been to or read about. His stories nevertheless revealed an interest in and even empathy for those living in the less glamorous or forgotten parts of the country and a growing desire to tell their stories. Cash's history songs were the product of a man with a deep intellectual curiosity about where he came from and how the country had evolved. Cash loved traveling and living on the road, and there was no easier way to travel than through history: time travel made possible by opening a book. For Cash, history was interesting, but it was also a way of escaping the everyday.

When it came to the West, movies and TV shows tended to put things in terms of black and white, heroes and villains. Cash was never one to do that. On *Ride This Train*'s "Slow Rider," he acted the part of the notorious killer John Wesley Hardin (1853–1895), the Texas outlaw who supposedly once shot a man for snoring. Hardin, whom Wild Bill Hickok called "Little Arkansas," was killed in a saloon by a shot to the back of the head. Hardin was a good example of living by the gun and dying by the gun, but he had folk hero credibility. Within a few years, Cash was more willing to depict the white man as the enemy. Still, he would never abandon his love of singing about the Wild West—or Hardin for that matter, who returned on Cash's *Ballads of the True West* album.[14]

Cash's increasing shift toward becoming a storyteller focused on American history, especially the West, was fitting for a man of his time and place. Cash was from a South that prided itself on its storyteller tradition. Northerners might like to talk, but southerners like to tell stories. Storytelling in the South has a long history. Slaves loved to tell tales about Brer Rabbit. And after the Civil War, Mark Twain—who claimed to have fought briefly in the Confederate army—emerged as one of America's finest storytellers. That gift for storytelling only seemed to gain strength in the twentieth century, when southerners were on the cutting edge of narrative storytelling, whether in the controversial work of Kentucky filmmaker D. W. Griffith or the novels of William Faulkner. Cash, too, was a natural storyteller. From the first, his songs told stories. As his career progressed, the music began taking a backseat to the story Cash was trying to tell. To augment his sound, he was adding piano, fiddle (called violin up north), and dobro (an American invention) to give his songs a richer, more Americana flavor.

What is Americana exactly? One might find Johnny Cash records at a hip vinyl store—as this author does in Richmond, Virginia—in the "Americana" section. Americana is not synonymous with country music, but it is also hard to categorize. One author has relied on the Americana Music Association's definition, which has Americana as infused with country, folk, roots rock, R & B, blues, and bluegrass. It relies heavily on acoustic instruments, but also can feature a full electric band. It taps American and especially southern music traditions, but is not necessarily played by Americans—as the success of Mumford & Sons has shown.[15] In the twenty-first century, Americana bands like to dress like The Band and pose in wheat fields or on front porches, even though you have to go to YouTube to hear the groups' mandolin AC/DC cover. What is Americana? Maybe it is like Justice Potter Stewart's notorious 1964 cop-out when defining pornography: you know Americana when you hear it.

Getting dusty and talking about the West doesn't hurt one's American credibility. By the time *Ride This Train* appeared, Cash was taking advantage of the seemingly insatiable American appetite for Westerners—the 1960s were their golden age. Cash had grown up watching movie Westerns—a genre as old as cinema itself. The first true motion picture ever made, 1903's twelve-minute-long *Great Train Robbery*, was a Western. By the time Cash was getting his tickets torn, Westerns were not just popular serials but a genre that produced some of the best films ever made. The

1960s began with *The Magnificent Seven* and ended with *True Grit*. By the end of the 1960s, the genre got ultra-violent with spaghetti westerns and *The Wild Bunch*. The famous line, "When the legend becomes fact, print the legend," was not just a famous line from *The Man Who Shot Liberty Valance*, it also applied to men like Johnny Cash.

Westerns were even more popular on television. In 1954 and 1955, Walt Disney set off a coonskin hat craze with its popular *Davy Crockett* program. In the 1960s, viewers could watch *Maverick* (1957–1962), *Wagon Train* (1957–1965), *Rawhide* (1959–1965), *Bonanza*, (1959–1973), *Gunsmoke* (1955–1975) and *The Rifleman* (1958–1963), just to name a few. In April 1961, Cash released "The Ballad of Johnny Yuma/The Rebel—Johnny Yuma," the theme song to the TV series *The Rebel*. Cash hadn't written the song for the show (though he had written an earlier song, "Johnny Yuma Theme" in 1959, which wasn't used for the program). According to the show, Yuma had fought in Robert E. Lee's army until the general's surrender at Appomattox Court House in 1865, then traveled to Texas. Cash played the song at shows for years afterward. He also appeared on the program as a guest star. Cash wasn't a great actor, but when he was effective, it was in Western roles.

In 1961, Cash was featured in a full-length movie, but it wasn't a Western. It was the B-grade film noir *Five Minutes to Live*. The movie, in which Cash plays a machine-gun-toting, guitar-playing criminal named Johnny Cabot, was not a critical success. But the film made a profit and produced an odd and interesting theme song, also called "Five Minutes to Live." The song doesn't make any sense when taken out of the context of the movie, though for Cash fans, it is a morbid curiosity, sounding like a cross between "I Walk the Line" and his mid-sixties song "25 Minutes to Go." The movie was rereleased in 1966 under the new name *Door-to-Door Maniac*. By that point, it was a fairly good summation of Cash's drug problem.

In California, Cash began partying with his Stewart Carnall, who co-managed Cash with Bob Neal. A tall, thin Illinoisan, Vivian Cash said Stu—as he was known—was "a nice enough guy" but one who liked the "California lifestyle" of staying up late, drinking, and playing the horses.[16] Family, faith, and a sense of place kept Johnny Cash rooted. Drugs, drinking, and being away from home for long periods did not. By mid-1960, Cash's drug problem was worsening.[17] Initially while in California, Cash maintained connections—symbolic though they might have been—to his former life. Vivian said Johnny "still remained a simple Arkansas farm boy at heart." She remembered him planting some cotton in the yard from seed he had brought from Dyess. Johnny had never liked work in the cotton fields, but as Vivian noted, "he didn't want to let go of those roots for anything."[18] Over time, it became clear that Cash never really felt at home in California, and it was the scene of many of his darkest, scariest, and loneliest moments. The farther Cash got from Arkansas, the worse things got for him.

Through it all, however, Cash stayed a productive and inspired musician, seamlessly crossing from rockabilly into country and showing how he could excel as a songwriter and interpreter. The transition is especially smooth when one listens to Cash's early Columbia material from the late 1950s and early 1960s. One would be hard pressed to find a more country album than *Now, There Was a Song!*, released in March of 1960. The album was unusual in that it featured no Cash originals. Even so, *Now, There Was a Song!* sounded as if it all could have been written by him.

The album was subtitled *Memories from the Past*. Cash certainly loved history and older country music. On the cover, he looked like someone out of the nineteenth century. He featured material from his heroes Hank Williams and Ernest Tubb, but the album had tunes from recent stars too, such as Marty Robbins, George Jones, and a young Kenny Rogers. Cash also covered his druggiest song yet, T. J. Arnall's "Cocaine Blues," the title of which Cash changed to "Transfusion Blues." It would be a few years before Cash could sing about cocaine without negative consequences for his career. In fact, in a few years, singing about cocaine would *help* his career.

What made *Now, There Was a Song!* sound more distinctly country than most of Cash's work was the addition of steel guitar (courtesy of Nashville session player Don Helms) and Gordon Terry's fiddle. Adding to the country flavor was the cover. At the Liberto family's San Antonio ranch, Cash leaned on a fence in a torn-at-the-elbow work shirt and shit-kicker hat, which made him look like he'd just come back from roping a steer. The cover could have been shot in Dyess or in California dry country. It certainly didn't look like Memphis. Cash wisely chose a country cover for a country album.

After his 1959 Little Rock shows, Cash—called "one of the nation's top music stars" by the *Cleveland County Herald*—traveled to his birthplace. There he saw some of his relatives, including his beloved aunt, Mabel

McKinney, and his uncle Russell Cash.[19] Around that time, Cash posed with his good friend Johnny Horton on the steps of the Kingsland post office. That year, Horton had scored a hit with "The Battle of New Orleans." Born in Los Angeles, Horton was raised in eastern Texas and became a regular on the *Louisiana Hayride* broadcast out of Shreveport. Horton is best known for his history-based storyteller songs such as the aforementioned New Orleans track, "North to Alaska," and "Sink the Bismarck." But as was true of Cash, Horton started out as an artist who could rock with the best of them on such risqué songs as "I'm Coming Home."

Cash and Horton spent lots of time together. Avid fishermen, Cash and Horton—the latter known as the "Singing Fisherman"—started the Cane River Bait Company in Natchitoches in northern Louisiana. The company produced several lures, including the Ole Fire Ball Fishing Lure.[20] Their relationship reflected the incestuous nature of the country community. Horton's wife at the time of his death was the beautiful Billie Jean Horton, the widow of Hank Williams, with whom Cash was romantically involved.[21] The friendship between Cash and Johnny Horton ended tragically in November 1960 when Horton was killed in a car accident in Milano, Texas. Cash grieved for his friend and paid tribute to him musically. Over the course of the 1960s, Cash embraced a storyteller persona worthy of his late friend.

Cash likewise could have ended up as one of the casualties of the early 1960s, which took not only Horton but also killed Eddie Cochran and seriously injured fellow rocker Gene Vincent (who already suffered from a bad leg injury for which he wore a brace). Cash was not much of a driver himself, later surviving crashes while he was high on pills. Driving long distances in the 1950s was treacherous given the lack of interstate highways. That didn't stop Cash and his band from covering hundreds of miles a day, only to repeat that feat again the next day. When not difficult, long-distance travel was tedious.

In some cases, there were no bridges spanning large rivers. Drummer WS "Fluke" Holland remembered crossing the Mississippi at Dyersburg, north of Memphis, while traveling with bandmates Carl and Jay Perkins. With no bridge, the three had to take a ferry, where the ferryman on the other side was signaled with a lantern. They had to wait as the ferry crossed, giving Carl Perkins and his brother time to start beating each other up.[22]

In March 1956, Perkins and his band suffered a serious crash while traveling to New York to appear on *The Perry Como Show*. All of them survived the crash, though it killed the driver whose pickup they hit. Fluke Holland was thrown from the car but was miraculously unhurt. Carl Perkins, however, was in the hospital for some time.[23]

Cash and the Tennessee Two might have had good luck avoiding accidents on the road, but Cash's lifestyle was exhausting. Amid touring and the craziness of rockabilly life, he tried to maintain ties to Arkansas, though it was proving more difficult than ever.

In June 1959, Johnny Cash's uncle Dave—Ray's brother, who had so much political and economic pull in Cleveland County—died. As a prominent sheriff, judge, and landowner, Dave Cash was a powerful but unlikable man, whose cruel behavior earned the ire of relatives. His obituary—adjacent to a story about the rising number of polio cases in Arkansas—was bloodless, listing his accomplishments in county law enforcement, as a businessman, and a Mason.[24]

Dave's death symbolized the changes occurring within Cash's family as well as the South as a whole. Dave Cash was born in the nineteenth century and was a man of that time—when lynching and Jim Crow assured suffocating racial control. Johnny, however, was a man born in the mid-twentieth century, a time of hardship and change in the South and all the contradictions that came with it. Johnny was a throwback in many ways, and he struggled with personal demons and problems, but he revealed how much the South was changing. Racism was still profound there. The Supreme Court, however, had ruled "separate but equal" unconstitutional, and the civil rights movement was changing the landscape. In contrast to his father and his uncle Dave, Johnny represented something different—liberating. Johnny was a rock and roller—a fast-living, pill-popping outlaw, whose life depended on loud music, air-conditioned motel rooms, and television. Cash was a wild child of the modern South. But he was also one who sang about Jesus. Cash was being pulled in many directions, further worsening an already intense battle within him: a Manichean war between good and evil. His native South was just as torn.

And as was true of the South, success did not come without risk, pain, and tragedy. The loss of Johnny Horton was a serious blow to Cash's delicate psyche.[25] But other people were becoming a fixture in Cash's life and career. On August 5, 1960, Fluke Holland played with Cash at the Three

Rivers Club in Syracuse and soon became a permanent member of the band. The Tennessee Two became a Three and could now boast of an actual member from that state.

WS Holland was born in 1935 in Saltillo, located on the southern border of Tennessee on the left bank of the Tennessee River. Saltillo was originally named Davy's Landing, but in 1849, Scott Terry, a veteran of the Mexican–American War, renamed the place after the Mexican city of Saltillo. Holland's humble beginnings made Dyess look like Memphis. He later remembered "how a simple country boy from Saltillo, Tennessee could end up where I was. I have to admit, I still don't have the total answer."[26] His initials "WS" never stood for anything and thus needed no periods after each letter. In 1954, having finished high school, Holland was working on cars and air conditioners before he started playing music. He got his nickname when he was working on cars. He liked to joke that certain tools were a "flukas." Rather than say, "Hand me that crescent wrench," he would say, "Hand me that flukas." Other mechanics got to calling him "Flukas," which soon became "Fluke." The moniker stuck.[27]

Fluke eventually hooked up with Carl Perkins, who was then playing with his two brothers in the Jackson area. Holland liked to sit in with Perkins's band, but he had no drum set and no idea how to play drums. When Perkins had the opportunity to record for Sam Phillips in Memphis, he asked Holland to bring some drums along to the session. Holland hastily borrowed a set from a man he knew and spent the next couple of days playing. This made Holland yet another member of Cash's band who was musically self-taught. Fluke was even unsure of how to set up his drum kit. The right-handed Holland positioned his drums as if he were left-handed (in contrast to Ringo Starr, who was left-handed but played as if he were right-handed). Despite the left-handed setup, Holland played the high hat with his right hand, but with the high hat to his right, not his left (thus refusing to cross his wrists the way most drummers do). Holland might have had innocent confusion early on as to how to approach his instrument, but the unorthodox style worked for him. He never abandoned it.

Holland played with Perkins for years. Many of their dates were in Arkansas, including Helena, a Delta town with its own rich music history. Holland remembered three girls there in 1955 who "tried to get me to stay in Helena and party. I decided to play in a band the rest of my life."[28] In fact, though, nothing about Fluke's career in the music business was assured. By 1960, when Cash contacted him, Fluke was ready to retire. He had enjoyed his time as a drummer, but he was running out of money. WS had spent much of his earnings on fancy clothes and boats, the latter of which became a lifelong passion. By 1960, Carl Perkins had left Sun for Columbia, two years after Cash had done the same. Fluke was about ready to go back to the air conditioning business, but Cash's offer to follow him on tour in late 1960 changed Holland's life. The year was a significant one in another respect: Fluke married his one and only wife Joyce, with whom he had two children.

Holland and Perkins came out of a more defined rock and roll scene than Cash did. From the first, drums were an essential part of rock and roll. Such was not the case in country music, where many legends played solely to acoustic guitar accompaniment. Even in the 1960s, drummers at the Grand Ole Opry did not appear on stage with a full kit. Thus, one can find photographs of Holland playing with Cash at the Ryman in a standing position, beating just one drum. Traditionally, country music has never been a place for flashy or inventive drum work. The Ryman also had a small stage early on, which discouraged bands from having the drummer play a full kit. Not until the late 1960s were full kits a regular feature at the Opry. The traditions of the Nashville establishment have died hard.

Holland and Marshall Grant were the sober members of Cash's band. They did not smoke either. By the time Holland joined, Cash was well into his pill addiction, and Carl Perkins was an alcoholic, though both Cash and Perkins decided to sober up by the late 1960s. Despite the madness, Holland enjoyed life with Cash, even when Johnny was out of his mind. Holland encouraged and took part in the many practical jokes and acts of vandalism that characterized life on the road.

June Carter

The addition of Fluke Holland gave Cash's music an even more driving beat. But the most fateful change in the Johnny Cash Show was the arrival of June Carter in late 1961. June's interest in joining Cash on tour was both romantic and commercial. While their relationship was anything but easy, it changed their careers for the better, eventually making them an immortal country couple. Others were not so durable. George and Tammy divorced. Neither Porter and Dolly nor Loretta and Conway were ever married. But Johnny and June stayed together until "death do you part."

Valerie June Carter was born in Maces Spring, in Scott County, Virginia, on June 23, 1929. Scott County shares a border with Tennessee, and June's hometown is a short drive from both Kentucky and North Carolina. It is fitting that her home is closer to Nashville than it is to Richmond, Virginia—both cities where June lived later in life. Richmond is the capital of Virginia but would never be a destination for aspiring musicians; it is a city of politicians, lawyers, and historians. Nashville has these people in abundance, too, but its fame as the capital of country music outstrips its importance as the capital of Tennessee.

June was the middle child in her family, just as Johnny was. As was true of the Cashes, June's interest in music came from the maternal line. Her mother, Maybelle Carter, was a musician, but her father, Ezra "Eck" Carter, worked as a mail clerk for the railroad company, earning enough money for his family to travel and support their musical life. In 1927, Maybelle began recording with her brother-in-law, A. P. Carter, and his wife (and Maybelle's first cousin), Sara Carter. They cut their first songs in Bristol, a city split between Tennessee and Virginia.

By 1930, the Carter Family had sold hundreds of thousands of records on the Victor label. Their travels took them across the country and not always to parts well known. In 1938, the Carters moved to Del Rio, Texas, which was within walking distance of Mexico. There they played on a Mexican radio station with a signal powerful enough to reach across the United States. The family soon moved to San Antonio, where the Carter sisters began playing music with their mother, A. P., and Sara. As a young performer, June played autoharp and liked telling jokes. She did not have her mother's gift for guitar playing, nor did she have a voice as beautiful as her sister Anita. Instead, she combined her good looks, energy, charm, and musical ability with her willingness to play the clown to emerge as the standout performer in the family.

In the fall of 1942, the Carters moved to Charlotte, North Carolina. A few months later, in March 1943, the original Carter Family broke up, leaving Maybelle to carry on with her daughters. A. P. and Sara had been divorced for several years by then, though their relationship had crumbled in the early 1930s. A. P. ended up moving back to western Virginia, while Sara wound up in a trailer with her second husband—and a first cousin of A. P.—Coy Bayes, in Lodi, California.

After the breakup, Maybelle and her daughters moved again, this time to Richmond. June graduated in 1946 from John Marshall High School, where she played basketball, but the Carters would not call Richmond home for long either. The family moved to Knoxville, Tennessee, then Springfield, Missouri. June first performed at the Grand Ole Opry on May 29, 1950. It was at the Opry, six years later, that she first met Johnny Cash.

Because of her mother's success in the Carter Family and her father's steady income, June enjoyed a comfortable middle-class upbringing. In contrast to the cramped Cash house in Dyess, June was raised in a nine-room house that "hugged the side of Clinch Mountain."[29] But as was true of Johnny, she was religious, growing up worshipping with Methodists, Baptists, and other church members. At fourteen, she became a true member of the church. She recalled that she "shot up like an arrow, crying, singing, and the fire was all around me."[30]

For June, as for Cash, travel became her prison and her liberation. She covered thousands of miles crammed into a vehicle with her sisters and mother, but she loved the openness and freedom of the road. She called the early days of her career the "last of the vaudeville days, and the yearning to keep on singing or traveling just a little farther never left."[31] While the road led to fame, she also found that fame led to feelings of emptiness and an unending quest for something better.

Naturally restless, she began recording with musicians outside of the Carter Family in 1949. That year, she cut "Country Girl" and a *Hee Haw*–worthy spoof of "Baby, It's Cold Outside" with the comedy duo Homer and Jethro. The latter did well commercially, hitting number 9 on the country chart and rising to 22 on the pop chart.

In July 1952, June married country musician Carl Smith. The couple had their daughter, Rebecca Carlene, in 1955. While married to Smith, June recorded her own songs such as "Juke Box Blues" and "No Swallerin' Place (co-written with Frank Loesser, author of "Baby It's Cold Outside"). Two years later, she married again, to Rip Nix, a Nashville native, former football player, inventor, boat racer, and sheriff's deputy. With Nix, June had one child, another daughter, Rozanna Lea. The couple divorced in 1963, the year—not coincidentally—Johnny Cash's "Ring of Fire," based on June's song, "Love's Ring of Fire," debuted.

By the time she was playing regularly with Cash, June's second marriage was crumbling. The fortunes of the Carter Family were little better. They were the most important family act in the history of early country music, but by the 1950s, despite having sold millions of records, they were receiving no royalties.[32]

When she met Johnny, June was an accomplished musician, songwriter, and actress. Her stage routine often depended on lowbrow comedy and cornpone humor, but with the encouragement of director Elia Kazan, she had studied acting in New York City under Lee Strasberg.[33] By the 1960s, June was a seasoned road warrior and accomplished entertainer—someone who had known country royalty intimately her whole life. As a performer, she was something of a cross between Minnie Pearl and Judy Garland. June could carry a tune, but didn't have a terrific voice or great musical chops. Yet she was the most outgoing of the Carter Family, and she could hold her own around other country stars both on stage and off. She had known Hank Williams at his worst. She survived the gun-toting, thoroughly intoxicated Williams when he was mad with jealousy over his second wife leaving him. She was not with Williams when he died, but she attended his funeral in January 1953 with her then-husband Carl Smith.[34]

By the end of 1961, Johnny had four daughters. His musical family was also growing: June and Fluke had joined his show. With June came the Carter Family—her mother Maybelle and her sisters Anita and Helen. Other musicians toured with Cash, who remained the headliner, including such luminaries as George Jones and fellow Virginian Patsy Cline (who, unfortunately, introduced June to pills).[35]

As Cash's musical family grew stronger, his relationship with his real family was unraveling. In September 1961, Cash moved from Encino (near Burbank and Los Angeles) to Casitas Springs, roughly fifty-eight miles west. The family took up residence in a new, large ranch. It was supposed to be the Cash dream home. The five-thousand-square-foot house symbolized Cash's desire to live in a place a Dyess boy could only have dreamed of, but the move isolated him—and more importantly, his family—from the outside world. Encino had been a small city, but Casitas Springs was tiny. The entire population could not have filled one of the theaters Cash regularly played. In June 1961, Saul Holiff, Cash's manager, had heard about the impending move to the new home in Casitas Springs. "The description of your new home sounds like a Paradise and the fulfillment of a dream," Saul wrote him. "It's exactly what I would like, only I'm still dreaming."[36]

The supposed dream home proved more a house of horrors. Tara Joan Cash was born in August 1961, but the new addition to the family did not make Cash a better father. Quite the opposite. Johnny's amphetamine addiction made him irritable, erratic, violent (though apparently never physically abusive), and self-destructive. Vivian recalled that in Casitas "everything, I mean everything, started to fall apart."[37] Johnny was on the road more than he was home. As Cash's family, fame, and fortune grew, he had little time for the duty that mattered most: being a husband and father. Cash's loyalties had shifted to music and life on the road. The pressures of stardom—combined with a personal background that, in contrast to June Carter's, had nothing whatsoever to do with his present lifestyle—loosened his grip on what usually had grounded him: family, faith, and a sense of place. The Johnny Cash of 1961–1967 is the story of a man coming apart.

To handle his career and increasingly chaotic personal life, Cash had replaced Stu Carnall in 1960 with Saul Holiff, a Canadian music promoter and manager. At first glance, the two might have seemed an unlikely pair. Holiff was Canadian and a Jewish atheist—about as far removed from the cotton fields as one could be. But the men were also alarmingly similar. Both Saul and Johnny had been in the Air Force, were determined hustlers, and had dreams of making it not just in the music business, but Hollywood, too. Holiff had suffered growing up with an abusive father. He was prone to substance abuse and depression (and ended up taking his own life in 2005). In July 1963, Saul complained of Cash's "emotional and irrational" behavior at a time when he himself was "preoccupied with death."[38] Saul also was fond of wearing black and was not the only one who was buying lots of pills. In a 1961 letter, Holiff told Cash, "enclosed is a brief account of a new tranquilizer." Saul said he had bought "$1,000 worth, and have on order a million pills for future delivery."[39] As was true of Cash, Saul would disappear for long stretches without explanation. He was a workaholic who could be aloof and verbally abusive at home. Holiff, however, was a shrewd, no-nonsense manager, who had no problem putting Cash in his place when things went wrong.

He managed Johnny at his lowest and highest points in his career. Appropriately enough, Saul's company was named Volatile Attractions. In 1961, Cash wrote on stationery that listed him as a "Singer, Song-Writer, Guitar Picker and Cotton Picker." Fittingly, he did not add "Businessman." In July 1961, singer Johnny Western—a Minnesota native who had spent time on an Indian reservation as a kid—told him that Cash was "wandering in a fog," "*not* a good businessman," and a "big star on the brink of disaster."[40]

Cash preferred losing himself on the road or in wide-open spaces, hunting, fishing, or camping. At home, he felt confined and stressed out. The

California desert gave Cash plenty of time outdoors, but it was not a good fit for him professionally or personally. Without Johnny around, Vivian and her daughters found life in a big house on a dusty hill in California lonely, even terrifying. Johnny Cash later told his daughter Tara that he found her staring a rattlesnake one day when she was two. "You thought he was pretty," Cash wrote.[41] Rosanne's recollections were not so fond. Snakes slithered across the property and scorpions sometimes entered the house. Rosanne's father usually was not there to protect her from such terrors, as he should have.

When Johnny *was* at home, he could put the family at risk. Rosanne remembered a time when her father's sparking tractor caused a brush fire that set the mountain ablaze. Looking back, she wished her father had burned the whole mountain to "save us all a lot of unnecessary psychic torment on that lonely, arid, snake-infested hillside."[42] In the farming culture in which Cash grew up, fathers were around all the time. When it came to his own wife and kids, however, Johnny was often away for interminable stretches. Yet when he was home, he seemed lost in his own world. In many households, it was the era of "leave daddy alone" when he was behind closed doors. Cash's manager Saul Holiff was the same way.[43]

At home, Johnny's behavior often ranged from the obnoxious to the bizarre. The neighbors, for one, did not like him. One Christmas, they complained about Cash blaring loud music from speakers. The *Star-Free Press* in Ventura printed an article titled, "Johnny Cash Has a Blue Christmas."[44] Cash would act aloof, playing records in a room with the door shut. Vivian said when he was around, he was "always on edge." She remembered Johnny sitting nervously at the kitchen table, drinking endless cups of coffee, tapping his feet to the Morse code setting on the radio.[45] Rosanne remembered her father once putting two dead puppies in a box on the roof of the house. She never figured out why. She thought it might have had something to do with Cash's Native American obsession. Perhaps in her father's drug-deranged mind, the poor dogs were given a spiritual burial that way. In any case, it frightened his oldest daughter every time she passed that corner of the house.[46]

Cash wandered the desert for days, thinking, brooding—avoiding people and his responsibilities, wrestling with his demons, seeking relief in the welcome expanse of the open sky, spending nights alone under the stars and moon like a lost, broken cowboy. "Saul, my only cure is solitude," Cash told his manager. "Too many things work against my peace of mind.

Only the desert, with its purity and silence can help me now."[47] As had so many seekers—spiritual or otherwise—before him, Cash thought he could find himself in the desert.

Cash might have sought peace of mind, but life in the wilderness provided a path to self-destructiveness, too. He drove vehicles through the desert like a maniac.[48] It was miraculous he did not kill himself during one of his reckless excursions. Cash was literally and figuratively lost—not so much as an artist, though he had struggles, but as a man cracking under the responsibilities of being a husband, father, and leader of a successful band for which he was the sole singer, composer, and creative force. Many people depended on Cash, and often he simply shut down and became unavailable. In the process, he was destroying his marriage and unraveling his family ties.

Songwriters are much like athletes: they usually do their best work in their twenties. By 1963, Johnny had entered his thirties. He hadn't had a hit song since 1959, and his contract with Columbia was to expire in December. Worse, he was addicted to drugs and not selling records like he used to. Cash had become unhealthy and unreliable. At Carnegie Hall in 1962, his amphetamine-parched voice gave out. It was an embarrassing disaster.[49]

His musical gift had not left him, though, and even when he was not writing great songs, he remained a masterful interpreter. June had been with the Cash show for scarcely a year when she gave Johnny one of his biggest hits. In March 1963, Cash recorded "Ring of Fire." He took June's slow, folksy "Love's Ring of Fire," shortened the title, and kicked up the tempo. June's sister Anita had first recorded the song. Her version is lovely and light. Johnny Cash's version burns like a cattle brand. As June originally wrote it, the tune was a love song. When Cash refashioned it, he put emphasis less on the love and more on the fire. Crucial in Cash's remake is the inspired blast of mariachi horns at the beginning—courtesy of Jack Clement—that provided the song its signature riff. What's more, the horns give it heat. Few places, after all, are hotter than Mexico.

The way Cash sings "Ring of Fire" adds a darkness and menace that Anita and June neither intended nor could have provided. "Down, down, down," Cash sings, like a man being pulled into the pits of hell. His affair with June was tearing apart his marriage. His pill addiction was killing his body and mind. The perpetually stoned Cash was in a dark place when he recorded "Ring of Fire," but the man with a scarred cheek and sunken eyes gave the song the brooding twist it needed to make it a huge hit. The song was released in April 1963.

Musically, Cash did to "Love's Ring of Fire" what he had done to "Crescent City Blues." In the latter case, he took a slow, sexy number and made it into a stark tale of a prisoner's anguish. Without changing the lyrics of the original version, "Ring of Fire" had a heat and depth that came from Cash's evangelical upbringing, sweaty days and nights on pills, and tortured private life. The song suggests not reassuring love or even sexual release, but the literal fires of hell. All those days Cash spent in the churches of Dyess had not been misspent. Any boy who labored in the fields under a blazing Arkansas sun could have imagined an eternal, fiery torment. And why not add some mariachi horns to intensify the heat? Cash was going down a lonely and self-destructive road, but he had lost none of his canniness as an artist.

The flipside of hell is salvation, and Cash was a man obsessed with the idea of redemption. His religious worldview depended on it. On "Ring of Fire," Cash managed to put more heart into the song than on any of his gospel records—it has an urgency that most any other song lacks. After years of adultery, self-abuse, verbal abuse, stupid fights, drug abuse, crashed cars, sleepless nights, and family neglect, Cash was clearly a tortured man—worried about his life, his career, his relationships, and what might await him in the afterlife. You can hear the fear in his voice.

Cash so transformed "Love's Ring of Fire" that people assumed he must have written it himself. Anyone could have made that mistake, although Cash's wife Vivian—who understandably hated June—wrongly believed he had composed it and given it to June as some kind of gift.[50] More important, the success of "Ring of Fire" put Johnny back at the top of the charts and became one of his signature tunes. He had recorded "Ring of Fire" in the style of previous hits, the mariachi horns effectively spicing up his familiar boom-chicka-boom.

"Ring of Fire" was a smash single and became one of Johnny's classic songs, but at the time Cash was concerned with concept albums. His newfound inspiration came courtesy of America's thriving folk scene. Cash always gravitated toward "authentic" music. As Jonathan Silverman has written, "folk music is *the* authentic American music, not only because it comes from the people but also because it eschews commercial motivations."[51]

In early 1963, Cash released *Blood, Sweat and Tears*, best known for "The Legend of John Henry's Hammer." As he had shown on *Ride This Train*, Cash was making concept albums years before *Sgt. Pepper's Lonely Hearts Club Band* or *Days of Future Passed*. Cash's take on the John Henry legend was his longest song ever, clocking in at 9:03. "John Henry" incorporated spoken word, tempo changes, sound effects, and multiple speaking parts—in essence, it was musical theater. Cash's trademark boom-chicka-boom served as the foundation for a story of the Virginia-born, African American steel-driving man who works himself to death. The most memorable sound effect is the clinking of a hammer, which Cash reproduced on stage by clanging two metal bars together. Cash played the role of the muscle-bound John Henry (despite the fact that the historical Henry was African American) and was joined on record by various members of the Cash troupe as voice actors.

The historical foundations of the John Henry story tell us much about race relations in the nineteenth century and the shocking exploitation of African Americans and their labor. Scott Reynolds Nelson has argued that the historical John Henry may have been a prisoner sent to work as a steel driver in West Virginia—one of the thousands of victims of the horrific convict-leasing system in the post–Civil War South, a system that proved a veritable death sentence for those charged for minor crimes forced at hard labor. Nelson has asserted that Henry succumbed to silicosis contracted from the mining dust and may have been buried on the grounds of the former White House of the Confederacy in Richmond. Cash might have built an entire concept album around the John Henry legend itself, but he did not. And he certainly did not use the story to address racial issues. His story is more a tale of man versus machine: John Henry versus the steam-powered drill. In telling the story, however, Cash was aligning himself with the folkies, who were making music based on working-class and historic themes.[52]

Whatever his personal faults by the mid-1960s, Cash remained a driven and inspired artist. His sound always defied genres. He never liked to think of himself as a country act, but by the time *Blood, Sweat and Tears* hit the shelves, Cash had become obsessed with the folk movement, which was using songs of the American past to tell stories about the stormy political climate of the 1960s.

As he delved into the folk scene and Americana, Columbia was releasing more commercially minded material. In August 1963 his first Columbia compilation, *Ring of Fire: The Best of Johnny Cash*, appeared. The album contained no music from his Sun period, which Sam Phillips was reissuing with regularity, but did include his recent titular hit as well as more obscure material, such as "Forty Shades of Green," which has proven an enduring classic among Irish fans. The album went to number one on the country charts.

In November, Cash released a new album of holiday material, *The Christmas Spirit*. Being the artist that he was, Cash was not content to issue Christmas standards. Some of the songs were traditional. Others he wrote himself. On "Christmas as I Knew It," Cash recalled a Christmas from his years in Dyess, when his brother Jack was still alive and he family seemed happy, even though "the cotton crop hasn't been too good this year" and "there's just no spending money." Cash also remembered whittling a whistle for Jack. Despite the occasional fights between the brothers, "when I gave Jack that whistle he knew I thought the world of him." To a degree, the song is nostalgic, but the wistfulness is tempered by the reality of a farming family where "Christmas was lean." The song takes an even more somber tone when Cash talks about a sharecropper family to whom his family brought food. The story was based on truth and could fairly well sum up the Christmas spirit: giving to others and remembering there were people worse off than you.

Cash's somber mood carried him into the new year. The year 1964 was a particularly memorable one in a tumultuous decade. One of the biggest changes for American musicians came on February 9, when the Beatles played on Ed Sullivan's show. Already a huge band in England, the Beatles' performance on live TV to over 100 million viewers unleashed the British Invasion. Among developing musicians, the day became a "BC/AD" for American pop music. After the Beatles, music would take on new and magical forms.

Along with the British Invasion, the country was experiencing political tumult. The civil rights movement continued to inspire and divide Americans. At the same time, the United States was becoming more deeply involved in Vietnam. The same month the Beatles played on *The Ed Sullivan Show*, the Gulf of Tonkin Resolution gave President Lyndon Johnson a blank check to deal with the spread of communism in southeast Asia. This meant more troops, more bombings, more casualties, and billions of dollars in war spending. Johnson was also committed to expanding domestic programs and defending civil rights workers. In 1964, with

LBJ's backing, Congress passed the landmark Civil Rights Act and the law that created Medicare and Medicaid.

Johnson's presidency signaled the triumph of postwar liberalism. His Great Society programs sought to create a more inclusive America by ending segregation, expanding entitlement programs, and eradicating poverty. His policies, however, created a political backlash that culminated in the 1964 presidential campaign of Arizona senator Barry Goldwater. Goldwater lost in a landslide that November, but his new brand of conservatism—where, as he put it, "extremism in the defense of liberty is no vice"—launched a new brand of Republican politics that drew its greatest support from the Sun Belt and eventually overtook formerly solid Democratic states such as Cash's Arkansas. The riots in American cities that occurred in Johnson's second term—whether Watts in 1965 or Detroit in 1967—further emboldened the conservative movement and forces of extremism, whose adherents saw the end of Jim Crow and the expanding welfare state as an existential threat to the American way of life.

Dylan and La Farge

In 1964, Cash also became more political, but he would embrace an unusual cause: rectifying the wrongs done, and still being done, to Native Americans. Cash began by befriending singers who were more political than he was. Hanging out in small clubs in New York, he became intimate with the emerging folk movement. Among the singers Cash embraced was Bob Dylan, with whom he later collaborated on Dylan's *Nashville Skyline*. Dylan was also the first guest on Cash's television show.

Cash and Dylan were about to travel down different paths that year: Dylan wanted to go electric, while Cash chose to get folky. The two men had much in common, though. Both became known for fusing country, rock, and folk music. They were wordsmiths, prolific songwriters obsessed with early American music and the songs of lone-wolf balladeers such as Woody Guthrie and Hank Williams. They were quintessentially American musicians from Middle America. By the time he met Dylan, Cash must have appreciated the young (he was nine years Cash's junior) Mr. Zimmerman's stripped-down aesthetic and purist view of the art form. Dylan didn't think of himself as a folk singer, because he was writing original songs—albeit in a folk style. Cash also liked Dylan's defiant attitude in going electric, and he supported him in a November 1964 letter to *Broadside: The National Topical Song Magazine* in which he said "SHUT UP! . . . AND LET HIM SING!"[53] As was true of Dylan, Cash liked to raise a middle finger toward the establishment and its efforts to categorize him. In Dylan, Cash had found a kindred spirit.

Dylan's early act relied on his voice, his guitar, a harmonica, and a stack of songs. The coffeehouse version of Dylan appealed to Cash, who by then was supporting a large touring show and playing before big crowds. The folk scene wasn't just vital music for Cash, it was an escape. New York was about as far away as he could get from his family and business obligations in California. In a dark, smoky New York café or club, Cash could watch a new type of music take hold of American culture. He was watching performers doing music that was even more sparse than Cash's own spartan early music had been. And it was just as powerful.

Cash eventually recorded some Dylan songs, but instead of covering Dylan right away, he embarked on one of the most unusual and ambitious projects of his career. What ultimately became Cash's fixation on Native American culture might have seemed odd, given that no other major musician of the time had much interest in the subject. But by 1964, Cash was seeking to move in new directions artistically. Even when he was not writing hit songs himself, he knew a great song when he heard it. With Dylan inspiring him, Cash's admiration for folk music harmonized with his deep interest in Native American history and culture, a fascination that had followed Cash since his Dyess days watching movies and reading books such as *Lone Bull's Mistake*. Cash had always been a student of the Wild West, both the cowboy mythos and its counterpart, the saga of the American Indian. His obsession with Native American life and music was part of his effort to move in a new direction while remaining grounded in traditional American music. His devotion to the cause of Native Americans culminated in a concept album, *Bitter Tears: Ballads of the American Indian*, released in October 1964.

Cash knew there were millions of Black Americans who had gotten a raw deal from his fellow southerners and the rest of the country. Yet Cash never embraced the Black civil rights cause in any profound way, and he never immortalized Black people in song the way he did Native Americans. Why not? Cash probably could not have done for Black people what he did for Native Americans, even had he wanted to do so. It was one thing to embrace the cause of Native Americans. Cash could do so without upsetting his white southern base. But for him to ally himself with African Americans in their fight for racial equality—however morally justified and in keeping with his Christian beliefs and political leanings—was something else. Many folk artists embraced the Black civil rights movement, but Cash was never a true folk artist. And for a man who wrote so often about the South, the plight of Black southerners was something he was not going to march or fight for. Had he been a vocal supporter of the civil rights movement, his beloved South would have turned on him.

Country music has long appealed to reactionary white elements in American society. Cash certainly was a country musician. But for some, he wasn't conservative enough. Some country musicians have at times been openly racist, far more than any individual in rock and roll or other genres. Ohio-born David Allan Coe, for example, released songs in the early 1980s that have been attacked for their racism. One track on his *Underground Album* is called "Nigger Fucker," which ridicules white women who have sex with Black men. Cash never sank to such depths. But at the height of the struggle, he was not going to address head-on the cause of African Americans, either. Cash was raised in a fully segregated community in which a white person could be openly racist with little consequence. Cash was an intelligent man, who knew about the South's dark racial past. He could have tackled the issue of race directly, as some folk singers of his era did. American musicians, however, generally have avoided the issue of race as too controversial and commercial suicide. By the late 1960s, southern bands such as the Allman Brothers were including a Black member. But there was also Lynyrd Skynyrd, a group that proudly flew the Confederate battle flag well into the twenty-first century. Being the good American he was, Cash liked underdogs. But he had his limits. The cause of Black Americans was not one he was willing to champion with much force. Despite featuring some terrific African American musicians on his TV variety show such as Ray Charles, Charley Pride, Stevie Wonder, and Louis Armstrong, Johnny Cash's life was mostly a lily-white affair.

Cash, of course, embraced causes that had Black people at the center of the struggle. His advocacy for prisoners, while never race specific, shed light on the plight of many Black men doing hard time. America's institutionalized racism has assured that African Americans have suffered disproportionately at the hands of the justice system. Cash was ahead of his time on *Bitter Tears*, but when it came to Black Americans, Cash took no great risks.

Cash's writing a concept album about Black life in the Delta—or some such subject—is one of country music's great might-have-beens. Cash could have broken historic ground had he sung at length about Black life in America, and he probably could have done so with great artistry and sensitivity. Such material, however, might have been too tricky for an artist of his stature in the mid-sixties. Cash had no great insights into Black life, and African Americans were just fine writing their own music and speaking for themselves. Cash might have felt that Black people could make their own art without his help. An album on which Cash tackled Black issues overtly probably would have perplexed his fans and have had little commercial appeal. As it turned out, *Bitter Tears* had its own controversy, when Cash berated disc jockeys whom he believed would not play "The Ballad of Ira Hayes."

Cash clearly found the tragic story of Native Americans compelling. Whites had evicted tribes from their homelands, waged war on them for centuries, and nearly driven them to extinction. The true story had not been told in white America. Despite Cash's erroneous claims to Native ancestry, there was not much crossover in the mid-1960s between white life and Native American culture—nothing like the mixing that occurred among white and Black Americans. Despite the dictates of life under Jim Crow, when it came to Black and white in the South, there was considerable blending concerning language, family life, music, work, and food. But Native American culture was far more foreign to whites. To Cash, the world of Native Americans must have seemed exotic and alluring. On *Bitter Tears*, Cash gave them serious attention in a time when pop culture almost universally depicted them as embarrassing stereotypes.

Cash had an interest in his possible American Indian roots well before he was famous. His family seemed to think it had a Native American connection. "I really don't know what nationality I am except a little Indian," Cash wrote to Vivian while he was still in the Air Force. "My dad can't trace his ancestors any further back than his grandfather," he told her. "It seems some of the Indians were kind of peaceful in those days. My dad shows Indian blood a lot more than I do."[54] For a long time, Cash claimed he had significant Cherokee roots. "We're both part Cherokee Indian," he said of himself and June Carter in 1970. "My wife and I are about one-eighth to one-quarter Indian, but we men in the family have all of the Indian features."[55] By that he meant high cheekbones, dark hair, and hairless complexions. Over time, it was revealed that Johnny Cash had no Native American ancestry, or at least none that he or the family could document. June perhaps put it best in her second memoir. "I've seldom met an American that doesn't claim to be part Indian," she wrote in 1987. "They all will claim that honor. I've also noticed they sure like to pick their Indian."[56] Anyone who bought *Bitter Tears,* however, might have mistaken Cash for an American Indian. On the cover, Cash, with his dark skin, headband, and exhausted expression, could have been mistaken for a defeated tribesman who had just seen Federal cavalry burn his village down.

Cash was an increasingly strange man at that point, and he collaborated with a songwriter who was just as odd. Most of the songs on *Bitter Tears* were written by Peter La Farge, a mysterious, brilliant, and troubled musician. He was born Oliver Albee La Farge in New York City in 1931 into an upper-class family. His father was Oliver Hazard La Farge, a novelist, anthropologist, and great-great-grandson of Admiral Perry, the hero of the Great Lakes battles of the War of 1812. Peter's father had studied at Harvard, graduating with a master's degree in 1929 and winning the Pulitzer Prize that same year for his novel, *Laughing Boy*, concerning a young Navajo man's efforts to assimilate into white culture. In 1934, the novel was turned into a movie of the same name.[57]

Peter La Farge boasted of his Native American heritage, and one Cash biographer has described La Farge as a "Hopi Indian."[58] La Farge, however, was no more Native American than Cash was. And despite La Farge's focus on Native issues, he was a child of the white Southwest, an excellent horseman and roper who dressed like a cowboy even after he moved to New York City. For *Bitter Tears*, he penned five songs for Cash (who wrote the other three, one co-written with Johnny Horton) that addressed famous events in United States history involving Native Americans. They included "Custer," about the fateful battle of the Little Bighorn, and "As Long as the Grass Shall Grow," about a broken treaty from George Washington's time. La Farge also covered more recent events, such as the tragic Marine, Pima Indian, and alcoholic Ira Hayes. Hayes fought at the horrendous battle of Iwo Jima, where he helped raise the flag at Mt. Suribachi. He died mysteriously one cold night in January 1955 in Sacaton, Arizona, south of Phoenix, on Native American land. On an album that often sounded decidedly un-Cash-like, "The Ballad of Ira Hayes" employed the reliable boom-chicka-boom sound to tell Hayes's sad story.

Bitter Tears was a commercial and artistic success. The album hit number 2 on the country chart. The now classic "Ballad of Ira Hayes" rose to number 3 on the country singles chart and made it to number 47 on the pop chart. Cash, nevertheless, was infuriated by what he saw as Nashville DJs refusing to play the song. In a full-page letter in *Billboard*, published in August 1964, Cash was even angrier than he was toward the Dylan haters he had called out earlier in the year. "Where are your *guts?*" he demanded. "Teenage girls and Beatle record buyers don't want to hear this sad story," Cash continued, and he was no doubt correct. But that had nothing to do with the particular truth Cash was singing about and wanted people to hear. He knew "Ira Hayes" wasn't a typical country record, or maybe not country at all. He instead called it "strong medicine," and with his customary flair for the dramatic, he compared the record to recent unrest in Rochester and Harlem, New York, and Birmingham, Alabama, as well as the war in Vietnam, then turning into a major conflict. Cash reminded readers of the success "Ira Hayes" enjoyed at the recent Newport Folk Festival, where Cash played in front of an audience that was not "hillbillies" but "an intelligent cross-section of American youth." Toward the end of his letter, Cash disingenuously said he found himself "not caring if the record is programmed or not," he just wanted to know why. And as a last claim to authenticity, Cash said, as an "almost a half-breed Cherokee-Mohawk (and who knows what else?)," he said he had to "fight back." The letter was classic Cash: honest, misguided, melodramatic, desperate, angry—and above all, passionate about his music.[59]

As a concept album, *Bitter Tears* was a success. With its stripped-down arrangements, it has aged well. Most of the tracks trade Cash's signature sound for acoustic guitar and drumming that doesn't follow the usual 4/4 rock pattern. In short, it sounds unlike any other Cash album. It also showed that Cash's move to California might have been a disaster personally, but artistically, his distance from Nashville helped his music, allowing him to explore new ideas and remain an independent thinker. Being out west and spending many days in the desert further deepened Cash's appreciation for the mythos of the Wild West and the frontier. In his addled state, Cash probably thought his "strong medicine" made him some kind of Native shaman.

When it came to incorporating Native American culture into pop music, Johnny Cash was a pathbreaker. *Bitter Tears* again established his credentials as a roots musician. Few of his contemporaries had been adept at playing rockabilly, folk, and country in such unique and stimulating ways. Cash began a Native American fad that lasted for the rest of the 1960s. Other artists sometimes took a Native American posture that was stereotypical and embarrassing, as in the case of Loretta Lynn's cover for her 1969 album *Your Squaw Is on the War Path.* Clad in a skimpy Native outfit complete with Land O'Lakes–style hair, Loretta peers into the distance, holding a tomahawk. (The music, thankfully, has aged better than the cover.) Less offensive was the Native American fashion seen everywhere at the 1969 Woodstock festival, where some audience members were clad in Native American garb and Jimi Hendrix and Roger Daltrey strutted on stage in Indian-inspired fringe jackets.

By the mid-1960s, Cash's artistic choices were far better than his personal ones. In 1965, his missteps, erratic behavior, and self-destructiveness reached new lows when he managed to burn down thousands of pristine acres of California forest land, a bungle that took hundreds of firemen days to put out. Cash was slapped with an $82,000 fine, and in court he was unrepentant, even rude to the judge. Cash, nevertheless, had supporters. Native Americans helped Cash during his court battles. The Tribal Indian Land Rights Association of California said that unless the suit against Cash was dropped, they would "reclaim the entire Los Padres National Forest." They also erroneously declared Cash a Cherokee and his sister (who owned the camper) Choctaw.[60] The wildfire was an embarrassing, irresponsible, and expensive mistake for Cash to make, but it added to his outlaw image. It seemed as if he were acting out the lines of John D. Loudermilk's "Bad News," which Cash had released on his *I Walk the Line* album in the spring of 1964. "Bad News" sounds like the devil having a hell of a good time on record. On the song—one perfectly suited to him—Cash can hardly make it through a verse before he growls or laughs in contempt. It tells the story of a man who was hanged for his crimes but "broke the rope" of the hangman's noose and had to be let go.

Cash was, by all accounts, bad news by this point—escaping death was not just the stuff of his songs. But when Cash did show up for a concert, he could still prove an electric performer. In summer of 1965, Cash swung into Arkansas for two shows. The first was in Little Rock at Barton Coliseum, the other at the convention center in Hot Springs ($2.75 for adults, 30 cents for kids under twelve). Cash always loved playing in his home state, but once he had moved out of Memphis, his trips home were infrequent. The Little Rock show was only his second in Arkansas since he had released his "I Walk the Line" single.

By 1965, he had become a legendary figure in his home state. The *Osceola Times* reported on Cash's long-overdue return to Arkansas. Under a headline that called Cash "Tops in the World of Music"—the *Times* quoted Dewey Fielder, an insurance salesman, as having grown up next door to the Cash family in Dyess. According to Fielder, he remembered Johnny as "always having a guitar in his hand" and that Cash was "about the most popular boy in high school."[61] It is debatable just how popular Johnny was as a teenager. What is certain is that Fielder did not see Cash always with a guitar in hand, for the simple reason that he didn't own a guitar until he was in the Air Force. Thus is the power of myth and the fuzziness of human memory. But this historian, for one, is prepared to forgive Dewey Fielder.

The *Arkansas Gazette* was positive in its coverage of the Little Rock show. The paper's accompanying photo showed a haggard but intense Cash playing his guitar as if he were about to smash it to pieces. The show revealed the fine line Cash walked between a good show and a disastrous one. Reporter Robert Shaw noted Cash "bounced onto the stage without his guitar." Cash went to get it and then broke a string on the first song, but kept playing despite it. "The audience of several thousand persons loved it," Shaw wrote. It was clear that Johnny's performance in Arkansas—one of several dates played in the South that summer—made him feel at home. He felt a connection to people there as he did nowhere else. With typical hyperbole, Cash said that half the audience was "cousins, uncles and aunts." Cash had arrived only about an hour before the show from Columbus, Georgia. Despite the typically rushed nature of his life at that point, he found time to meet Harvey Clanton, one of his classmates in Dyess. "They said he could sing real well back then," Clanton said, "and I guess they were right."[62]

Cash was still on good terms with fellow Arkansans. Such was not the case with the man who had discovered him, Sam Phillips. In July, Cash sent a letter to Saul Holiff saying he had been to Memphis, where he had a bitter fight with Phillips. Cash said he was so angry he could have punched

Phillips, but he held back. "His mind is completely soaked in alcohol," Cash said, "and I'll never speak to him again."[63] While Cash might have been dismayed by Phillips's drinking, he was out of control himself.

Cash planned on returning to Arkansas on October 10 for a family reunion. He also wanted Holiff to arrange a visit with Jimmie Driftwood for the day after. Born in 1907, Driftwood was a fellow Arkansas musician, known for writing "The Battle of New Orleans" and "Tennessee Stud." Cash, though, didn't make it to Arkansas that month. The reason was that he got busted in Texas. On October 4, authorities caught Cash trying to smuggle hundreds of pills from Mexico with him into El Paso. It was his first arrest, and not his last, and the story made international headlines. Once again, Cash's personal stumbles and problems were keeping him from home, whether California or Arkansas.

Despite his personal problems, Cash remained productive. In 1965, he put out two albums. He released *Orange Blossom Special* in February; that September, fans could buy his double LP, *Johnny Cash Sings the Ballads of the True West* (later edited down to one record issued as *Mean as Hell!*). The state of Cash's health was evident in photographs taken of him at the time. He looked weary and sweaty on the *Bitter Tears* cover. His Western costume on *Ballads of the True West* hid his ever-thinning frame, as did the shot of him smoking on a train on the cover of *Orange Blossom Special*. Two other albums—*Everybody Loves a Nut* (May 1966) and *Happiness Is You* (October 1966) featured artist's renditions of Cash, though even *Happiness* contained an unflattering picture. By the time he released *Carryin' On with Johnny Cash & June Carter* in 1967, Cash looked positively skeletal.

Cash was literally disappearing, which gave some of his better songs a haunting quality. His version of "The Long Black Veil" on *Orange Blossom Special* was one of his best moments on record. It's a tale of a man who chooses the death penalty for a crime he didn't commit rather than admit he had been making love to his best friend's wife at the time of the murder. It was the kind of dark material that suited Cash. On the whole, however, *Orange Blossom Special* was another eclectic mix of songs. "Long Black Veil" was a dark moment, but Cash employed up-tempo boom-chicka-boom on his inspired cover of the title track, complete with West Virginia native Charlie McCoy's sparkling harmonica work and a saxophone solo.

Orange Blossom Special showed how much and how little Cash's music had changed since moving to Columbia. Some of the songs, such as "Long

Black Veil" or the title track, could have been featured on any number of Cash albums. But by 1965, Cash was under the influence of Bob Dylan, who he covered three times on *Orange Blossom Special* with "It Ain't Me Babe," "Don't Think Twice, It's All Right," and "Mama, You've Been on My Mind." Cash also dipped into his traditionalist music bag on the old Carter Family number "Wildwood Flower" and the classic "Danny Boy," written by Englishman Frederic Weatherly in 1913 to the tune of the Irish song "Londonderry Air."

On "Danny Boy," Cash included a long spoken-word segment that went back to his father's youth in Kingsland. The period was modern, but Cash painted a picture of an Arkansas barely removed from the Wild West, saying "the way of life didn't change very fast back home" He said his father Ray "rode a horse about ten miles every Sunday to see Miss Carrie Rivers, in those days when everyone in the country either rode a horse or wagon or walked." According to Cash, his father met an Irish immigrant working on the Cotton Belt Line who dreamed of going back to Dublin one day and told him the story of "Danny Boy."

Ballads of the True West proved a virtual who's who of the Johnny Cash world. The album included songs by Cash, June Carter, Ramblin' Jack Elliott, Merle Kilgore, Tex Ritter, Shel Silverstein, Jimmie Driftwood, and Peter La Farge, who died a few weeks after the album was released. *Ballads* yielded one of Cash's best songs, Silverstein's "25 Minutes to Go," about a condemned man sweating out the last moments of his life before swinging from the hangman's noose. It was dark. It was funny. It had Cash doing his patented spoken-word style singing to boom-chicka-boom accompaniment.

Cash's sense of humor—as dark as it often was—kept him grounded. That humor was never more apparent than on his 1966 album, *Everybody Loves a Nut*. C. Eric Banister has said it is "the first album many fans of the dark and brooding version of the Man in Black eliminate from conversations about his career."[64] For fans, the songs might have seemed as odd and irreverent as *Mad* magazine artist Jack Davis's wacky cover art. Even so, Cash played the album's "Dirty Old Egg Sucking Dog" (written by Jack Clement) at live shows, and the irreverent "The One on the Right Is on the Left" was a hit, reaching number 2 on the country chart. And for diehard fans, Cash offered a murder ballad he penned himself, "Austin Prison."

Cash's "Black" Wife

Everybody Loves a Nut was a lighthearted departure for Cash. Less funny were the encounters he had with white supremacists in early 1966. In the wake of Cash's late 1965 arrest in El Paso, vocal racists in the South saw a picture of Cash with his dark-complexioned wife Vivian and assumed she was Black. The controversy came at a time when racial tensions were high in America and artists were feeling the brunt of the civil rights backlash. The accusations against Cash, originating in the Deep South publication *The Thunderbolt*, called Cash "scum" and accused him of spending money on "dope and Negro women." Racists plagued Cash for a while. In October 1966, the White Citizens' Council of Mobile spoke of Cash's "Negress" wife and four "mongrelized" daughters. Saul Holiff was prepared to sue for libel, but nothing ever came of the threat.[65]

Ironically, Cash had publicly avoided any serious discussion of the race issue when it came to African Americans, and his music on that score contained nothing the white South would have found bothersome. In fact, Cash had embarrassing racist incidents on his ledger when he was in the Air Force. A song like "Boss Jack" from *Ride This Train* would have pleased any redneck who might have had "Dixie" hanging in his garage or flying in his front yard. But for a time, none of that mattered. It was a dangerous time for outspoken pop stars. Cash's problems with white supremacists—and accompanying death threats—came the same year as John Lennon's statement that the Beatles were "more popular than Jesus." Lennon's comments were originally given (and mostly forgotten) in a March 1966 interview for an English magazine. In July, however, a teen magazine in America reprinted the interview. Lennon's thoughts on religion sparked outrage and were especially offensive in the South, where unamused whites burned Beatles records and Klansmen made threats against the band. In a decade where civil rights was often center stage in American politics, reactionaries in America were not taking kindly to pop stars who had views on race and religion that differed from their own.

Cash quickly corrected the error concerning Vivian, but white supremacists wouldn't believe him. "Johnny and I received death threats," Vivian remembered, "and an already shameful situation was made infinitely worse. The stress was almost unbearable." Their strained marriage didn't help matters, and Vivian thought her husband handled the controversy poorly. "To this day I hate when accusations and threats from people like that are dignified with any response at all."[66] It was the mid-sixties, and the South, not to mention the rest of the country, was seething with racial tension, if not exploding into open violence. The controversy over Vivian's "Blackness" made her miserable and created headaches not only for Cash and his band—depending so much on tours through the South—but his manager Saul Holiff, who had to handle damage control. It was no easy task for anyone, let alone a Jewish foreigner—not a popular combination among hate groups.

To review Vivian's heritage, her parents were Thomas Peter (1905–1971) and Irene Robinson Liberto (1913–1979). Both were natives of Texas. Both were listed as white in the census. Thomas's parents were Frank (1874–1940)—a native of Sicily—and Angelina Rinaudo Liberto (1880–1924), also from Italy, though they settled in Texas at the turn of the twentieth century. Irene's parents were George Edgar (1884–1955) and Dora Minnie Robinson (1890–1988), both likewise listed in the census as white. George's parents—Benjamin Franklin and Mattie E. Haynes Robinson—were listed as white people from Alabama and Mississippi, respectively. As is true of so many Americans, Vivian's family was of varied stock. Her Sicilian heritage certainly contributed to her "ethnic" looks.

And yet, Vivian did have African American ancestry. On a 2021 episode of the PBS show *Finding Your Roots*, Henry Louis Gates Jr., presented Rosanne Cash with DNA evidence showing that she had some African American ancestry (though she was more than 90 percent of European heritage). How? Irene Robinson, who married into the Liberto family, had a grandfather named Lafayette Robinson. He was the son of a slave woman named Sarah A. Shields. Her father was William B. Shields, a planter in Alabama. Sarah's mother is unknown. But in the 1830s, Sarah, herself of mixed race, married Anderson Robinson, a white man—even though such unions were then illegal. Sarah was legally freed in 1848 by her father, and her children were able to "pass" as white in the South.

Despite the recent genealogical revelations, the debate surrounding Vivian's African American ancestry has, in a sense, advanced no further than it did in 1966. One can see whatever one wants to see in Vivian's ethnic background. She certainly was not as Black as the white supremacists of the 1960s thought her to be. And they had no hard evidence to support their claims of her being a "Negress." At the same time, her great-great-grandmother had been born a slave, albeit one of mixed race. Vivian certainly qualified as Black if one measured such a thing by the racist standards of the "one drop" rule in the South—a standard that terrorized many people into denying their African American heritage in order to pass as white. As for the Cashes, it is unclear how much she or Johnny knew about her ancestry at any time. It is unlikely that Johnny would have married a woman in 1955 who he thought had a significant African American background, especially given his own racial prejudices at the time. Were Johnny's and Vivian's denials simply damage control? If so, they managed to keep the family's African American heritage a secret even from one of their own daughters.

That white supremacists thought Cash was a race traitor for having wedded the "Black" Vivian Liberto put a further cloud over their marriage. By the time Cash released his 1967 album, *Carryin' On with Johnny Cash & June Carter*, his affair with June essentially was in the open. The question was whether Cash would live long enough to have a future with her. By the autumn of 1967, Cash was in freefall. His drug use was out of control, and it seemed that if he did not get help soon, he might die. He was a man who had received more than his fair share of second chances. His desire to seek help from his family and medical treatment from Dr. Nat Winston of Nashville to overcome his addiction was a logical and necessary step in his life and career. In November 1967, Cash was arrested again—this time in northwestern Georgia, not far from Chattanooga, where he had been stumbling around the small town of Lafayette. The sheriff locked him up for the night and let him go, but not before giving Cash a much needed and heartfelt reprimand.[67]

At the nadir of his drug addiction in the fall of 1967, Cash wrote a poem about Arkansas called "Crowley's Ridge," concerning the 150-mile hilly formation between the Mississippi River and the Ozarks in northeastern Arkansas. The story was about a man riding his horse from Lepanto—next door to Dyess—to Hardy (a good distance north and bordering Missouri). The poem, with its pastoral imagery, seems set in the nineteenth century. But Cash mentions "the river had washed out the WPA bridge," thus revealing that the poem was set in Cash's lifetime. In his poem, a woman swims across the river to be with the narrator, who hesitates to take her away from her family in Hardy. She agrees to ride on with him, and the poem concludes that the couple rode the horse "Till the land got flat / For like the cotton / Love grows good / In ground like that."[68] In a tale of two lovers, Johnny found a few moments of calm amid his deeply troubled life.

Nashville and the Nickajack Cave Story

By 1967, Cash had decided to settle in the Nashville area, though "settle" is not the right word. His battle to overcome drugs had only begun. His first marriage was over. The quality of his music was erratic. Johnny Cash's road to Music City was a long and rocky one. His humble beginnings playing country songs in Air Force barracks had led in a few years to stardom on the Sun label. More hits followed at Columbia, but the pressures of stardom ruined his marriage and nearly killed him. Cash usually had his greatest success when he stayed true to his boom-chicka-boom sound, but his ambitions as an artist had led him to experiment with folk sounds, Native American themes, and concept albums. Yet, by 1967, Cash had fallen as far as a man could.

The last record Cash put out before his recovery and the seminal *At Folsom Prison* was the January 1968 album *From Sea to Shining Sea*. It was another of Cash's concept albums, containing songs about God, prison, farming, Native Americans, coal mines, gas stations, and the fishing boats of America. What strung the songs together was Cash's spoken-word narration included at the beginning and end of the album. All the songs were written by Cash. Some were autobiographical, such as "The Frozen Four-Hundred-Pound Fair-to-Middlin' Cotton Picker," where Cash again sang about the farm work he detested so much as a boy. *From Sea to Shining Sea* is listenable and holds up fairly well, but the strain in his work was showing. He had once again stayed close to his musical roots, but the album mostly feels like standard-issue Cash. "The Walls of a Prison," a song Cash said he wrote after a show at Folsom, borrowed the melody from "Streets of Laredo" on *Ballads of the True West*. His reference to the "Red Man" on "The Flint Arrowhead" is a step down from *Bitter Tears*. But another song, "The Whirl and the Suck," could have been from that album.

In the liner notes, Cash claimed "it was a half mile inside Nicajack Cave that I wrote *The Whirl and the Suck*." The song concerned the Nickajack (or Nicajack as Cash called them) Indians, a "barbarous tribe" (Cash's words) of the Cherokee in southwestern Tennessee. Cash's recounting of the Nickajack tribe combined solid history with certain exaggeration and perhaps outright fabrication. Songwriters tend not to write songs a half mile inside caves, though it is likely a bad idea to take Cash's words literally. And one supposes Cash might have been the kind of person to write a song inside a cave. In any case, according to Cash's liner notes, the Nickajack took positions at a bend in the Tennessee River near Chattanooga, where "there were whirlpools and suckholes, and the water was swift and deep." There, the Nickajack rolled boulders down upon unsuspecting white families. Those not killed by the falling rocks or drowned in the river encountered Nickajack warriors who would "slaughter the survivors in the most horrible way they could conceive."

Cash was obsessed with Nickajack Cave. The place's history undoubtedly influenced his later suicide story of crawling into the cave to die around the time he recorded *From Sea to Shining Sea*. Cash described the mouth as being 150 feet wide and 75 feet high. The labyrinth of passages and tunnels ran for forty miles. In what was a forgivable exaggeration, Cash wrote that "ten million" bats flew out of the cave at dusk.[69]

Cash clearly wanted to paint a colorful picture of the area. Without a doubt, the Nickajack tribe and the cave that bore its name had a compelling history. Despite claims about Nickajack ferocity, however, in 1794, United States forces crushed the Nickajack in one battle in southeastern Tennessee. The Americans suffered only three casualties, all wounded, while killing dozens of Nickajack villagers. As one historian has written, while the details are unclear, it "may have been more a massacre than a battle."[70]

Nickajack Cave might have been an interesting source of inspiration for an entire concept album of Cash tunes, given the rich history of the area and Cash's fascination with it. Nickajack is near Chattanooga, a mid-size city today and an important Civil War site. Confederate forces laid siege to Union forces there in the fall of 1863. A gateway to the Deep South, Chattanooga was a vital source of salt for Rebel munitions. In November 1863, Ulysses S. Grant punched a hole in the Confederate siege before attacking the Rebels. They retreated into Georgia following his victories at Lookout Mountain and Missionary Ridge. It was a story Cash knew well.

And yet the standout track on *From Sea to Shining Sea* had nothing to do with bats, caves, Rebel troops, or warring Native Americans. It is "Cisco Clifton's Filling Station," where Cash offers a relaxed, folksy, spoken-word assessment of a small-town gas pumper. Cisco Clifton has seen business drop over the years, largely due to the construction of the highway. But despite hard times, Clifton, with his "rough hands soiled" and finances "always in the red," continues to provide warm and helpful service to the people who pull in. The song laments how the plight of the working man and the human touch—a "howdy and a checker game" as Cash puts it—has been lost amid the force of "progress." It was not a song about Nashville. Cash might have been writing about Dyess, but really the song could've been about many small American towns.

From an artistic point of view, the album showed that Cash's music hadn't progressed much from *Songs of Our Soil*. *From Sea to Shining Sea* was recorded in April 1967 and released in January 1968, but it could have hit record shelves much earlier in the decade. *Sea,* nevertheless, was true to Cash's love of place. "I have been in all 50 states," Cash wrote in the album's liner notes, "usually though on a schedule which prohibited explorations of my own. But occasionally a song seemed to be begging to be written about some of the things I did see, or do."

By 1967, Cash had found a new home in Hendersonville, just outside of Nashville. And writing about the Nickajack was an outgrowth of how much time he was spending in Tennessee. Cash might have been getting more settled, but his music needed a jolt and a new direction. First, however, he needed to clean up his act. As was fitting for Cash's life and career, he wrapped his personal transformation in a shroud of myth in which the singer literally emerged from the darkness of his personal despair to a closer embrace of Christianity. By late 1967, Cash had reached the worst point in his life. As he told Patrick Carr, in October 1967 he traveled to Nickajack Cave in order to kill himself. Cash supposedly had the idea to enter the cave and never return. He claimed he brought a light in with him but eventually it went out. Cash moved around the cave in total darkness, but somehow, as the story went, he found his way out. He did so by following the cold air that he knew must be belching from the entrance to the cave.[71]

This was the story Cash told Carr in his 1997 autobiography. As far as this author can tell, the Nickajack Cave story was first recounted in a thirty-nine-cent Christian comic book, *Hello, I'm Johnny Cash*, published in 1976. The book was an honest attempt to show the male celebrity temptations of loose women and drugs. *Hello, I'm Johnny Cash* also portrays Johnny's supposed brush with suicide inside Nickajack Cave. In the comic, after seeing visions of June and his mother Carrie, a muscular, shirtless, well-coiffed Cash storms out of the cave, looking a bit like the Incredible Hulk. To say the least, it was not an accurate depiction of Cash's physical condition at the time. But the book, in showing that Cash, even at his lowest moments, was a heroic figure, added to the Cash myth.[72]

Oddly, the story did not appear in the best early biography on Cash, *Winners Got Scars Too*, published only about four years after the Nickajack Cave incident supposedly happened. Nor did Cash relate the cave story in his 1975 autobiography *Man in Black*, though it would have been perfect for that book's narrative of sin and redemption. Cash told the story to an interviewer in 1983, and the Nickajack cave incident got its most popular retelling in Cash's 1997 autobiography.[73] Serious biographers of Cash are skeptical of the cave story.[74]

Assuming it is untrue, why would Cash have wanted to tell it? A natural storyteller, Cash knew the tale had dramatic impact. People, after all, are born from darkness into the light, and Cash's cave story—where Johnny is in a tunnel that barely allows him room to crawl—becomes a symbolic second birth. It was also a myth ripe with religious metaphor. The cave has long been used in religious and philosophical literature, from the Book of Genesis (whether it is Lot staying in a cave or Abraham burying Sarah in one) to Plato's "Allegory of the Cave," the Gospels, and the story of St. Paul and the Cave of Ephesus. The Nickajack story has Cash going into a literal underworld—as Jesus had—before his resurrection. According to some interpretations of the New Testament, Jesus was born in a cave, not a manger. And Cash's cave story also echoed the tomb Jesus was placed in after his crucifixion. For Cash to emerge from a cave so far from home—leaving a literal and spiritual darkness and emerging again into the world, one in which he was determined to be sober—made for a compelling tale. For him, it was a story of literally hitting rock bottom and finding the light. Addicts, after all, are encouraged to seek a "higher power." Cash already had one, but it was one that he had not embraced for a long time. In the cave, as his story goes, he connected in a deep way with God.

Cash repeated the cave story over the years, but there are good reasons to doubt its authenticity. It is unlikely that Cash would have traveled all the way to Nickajack to take his own life. Death by spelunking also seems an unusual method for someone with suicidal depression, especially given Cash's access to easier methods: booze, pills, automobiles, and guns.

Marshall Grant, for one, believed the cave story did not happen.[75] The cave, furthermore, was not even accessible to explorers in late 1967. The previous year, its entrance was flooded by the construction of Nickajack Dam. "By 1967," one expert has written, "the dam was complete and water backed up into the mouth of Nickajack Cave leaving only the top 30 feet visible." Nevertheless, the entrance of the cave apparently is an "impressive" sight from Highway 156.[76]

It is doubtful Cash went into a cave in October 1967 to kill himself, but there is no doubt that he was at an extremely low point that autumn. In the depths of his drug addiction, Cash's relationship with his parents was often strained. Before getting sober, he could be downright violent toward family. The bad news concerning Cash's drug abuse and arrests "really hurt Mama," said Cash's sister Joanne.[77] A few months before he cleaned up, Johnny sucker-punched his brother Tommy in an airport. Cash had been acting erratically on a plane into Tennessee. An understandably frustrated Tommy, with his parents present, yelled at his brother once they were at the terminal. Tommy asked, "Is your show about over for today?" whereupon Johnny called him a punk and hit him.[78]

What is clear is that to redeem himself, Cash needed to improve physically—and quickly. By January 1968, he was looking better and had gained weight. His drug intake persisted, but was manageable. The same month *From Sea to Shining Sea* was released, Cash recorded his historic *At Folsom Prison.* The year 1968 was a comeback year for Cash as well as a homecoming. His dark days in California were behind him. He had a new home in Nashville with June Carter, and he was grateful for a second chance at life.

As was the case when Cash was riding high, he returned triumphant to Arkansas, where he would draw even more strength from the people and the place. In February 1968, Cash, the man with the "twangy, lonesome baritone," returned to Dyess, where he gave his first concert in Arkansas in three years.[79]

Cash was home.

5

Arkansas

For his Dyess homecoming concert, Cash played at the high school. The man who organized the February 4, 1968, concert was Gene Williams, who grew up in the area and went to Dyess High School, though he and Cash were not classmates. Williams was six years' Cash's junior. After leaving his hometown, Williams worked in radio and television in various places, and his booking agency later represented Tommy Cash. Williams became known as the most successful music promoter to come from northeastern Arkansas. Later in life, he settled in Branson, Missouri. At Cash's Dyess show, Williams acted as emcee, but he made sure to keep the focus on Cash.[1]

The Homecoming Concert

Cash's arrival in Dyess was big news for his hometown. Columbia had not yet released *At Folsom Prison*, but Cash was always a good draw as a live act. According to the *Osceola Times*, Cash was remembered as a "very nice boy with talent for entertaining."[2] Mayor Fred Dallas declared that Sunday "Johnny Cash Day" in Dyess. School superintendent (and childhood friend of Cash's) Lynn Cox assured that he would give Johnny a "warm and cordial welcome home,"[3] adding that he and Cash had gone rabbit hunting years before. Cash apparently had told Cox that he had wanted to play a show in his hometown, but he couldn't find the time. Now that Cash was more sober than he had been in years, he was better at keeping to schedule and following through on promises.[4]

Cox recalled that Cash "was a good student, but I don't particularly remember him being different." In an affectionate blend of fact and fiction, Cox remembered what Johnny was like as a kid. He remembered Carrie Cash playing piano for children on Saturdays. He added that Carrie "played and sang spirituals and country and western songs" and taught Johnny how to play guitar. Carrie might have sung religious songs, but it was Johnny, not his mom, that would have been singing country. Cox remembered, "Johnny always carried his guitar around, humming or making up a verse or two."[5] Johnny had not been a serious guitar player until he was in the Air Force. Cox, nevertheless, was right in saying how important music was to the young J. R. Cash.

The Johnny Cash Show, which included the Statler Brothers, Carl Perkins, and Mother Maybelle and the Carter Family, accompanied Cash to Dyess. Also appearing was the local opening act, the Country Junction Band. To get in, adults paid $2, children $1. The mayor made sure that two thousand seats were available for the show, a number much larger than the population of Dyess at the time, which had dwindled to about four hundred. As the *Arkansas Gazette* noted, the place had "three filling stations, two cafes, a movie house and the Blue Eagle Malt Shop." The once "stately" administration building at the center of town was run down and had been chopped up into apartments. The Church of Christ had bought the community center. "Everything in town is closed on Sunday," the *Gazette* noted. When a gas station patron was told he couldn't use the toilet because the station was closed, the proprietor offered to let the visitor use his bathroom at home.[6]

Fans came from as far as Little Rock. Others, as the *Arkansas Gazette* reported, poured in from West Memphis, Blytheville, Jonesboro, Tomato, Bassett, Delpro, and Cottonwood Corner.[7] Cash apparently had little trouble filling two thousand seats. He also played a smaller second show for five hundred people.

As usual, Carl Perkins opened the festivities. "Like Cash," the *Arkansas Gazette* said, "Perkins is a big, tough-looking country boy."[8] For Perkins, as for Cash, 1968 was a turning point for him. That year, Perkins, who was suffering from hallucinations caused by alcoholism—he had visions of spiders and dinosaurs—decided to sober up.[9] Perkins had been with Cash at the seminal Folsom concert, though his songs were not included on the original record. With Cash, he was getting a deserved second chance.

When Perkins finished playing "Blue Suede Shoes," the Sunday crowd was so entranced, Mike Trimble of the *Gazette* wrote, that they "forgot for a moment that Cash was the man they came to see."[10] The Statler Brothers were next. They combined music and comedy with their "outlandish faces, broad puns, and jokes about toilets." Then came the Carter Family, and for the *Gazette*, Mother Maybelle was "clearly the . . . the class member of the Sunday afternoon." Her rendition of "Keep on the Sunny Side of Life" delighted Trimble, who thought it the highlight of the show up to that point.

Trimble, however, made it clear who the star of the show was. Cash drew "the greatest response with his jerky motions, his downright scary voice and those steely dark eyes that bored big bullet holes in the back of school custodian E. O. Woodie's brand new gym."[11] Phil Mullen of the *Osceola Times*, however, emphasized the vulnerability that Cash showed as a performer that afternoon. He wrote that Cash "sometimes was as awkward as an overgrown teenager, and as exuberant as a neophyte . . . and there was a sweet sentimentality and bubbling happiness in this very special show of his." Cash told the crowd, "This is what I'd rather be doing than anything else in the world. This is my home town." Cash said he wanted to do a meet and greet after the show, but added that he was "slow on some names" and asked the crowd to "remember that I have travelled a million miles and seen a million new faces." Among the crowd were many children, and when a baby girl approached the stage to dance, Cash picked her up and danced with her.[12]

Cash was trying to help a community that had fallen on hard times. Ironically, Dyess's glory days were during the Great Depression. Trimble wrote, too optimistically, that things in Dyess were "looking up" with its "impressive new school" that replaced the one that had burned in 1963. The highway running through the town, 297, was to be paved. Trimble wrote that not much in the way of entertainment came to Dyess anymore. Cash, with his appeal "almost universal," was an exception. Trimble couldn't avoid taking a shot at teen culture: "Every acne-plagued rural teenager in America would like to imagine himself a man like Cash—handsome, Mean as Hell (the name, incidentally, of one of his albums) but still a good old boy." Cash performed songs that were grounded in his experiences in Arkansas, including "Five Feet High and Rising" and "Pickin' Time." By the end of the show, the audience was "clapping itself silly."[13] Cash talked with and mixed with fans after the show. Some who had seen the first concert stayed for the second. It was a good idea to get their fill of his music, because it was the last time Cash played a concert in his hometown.

The Dyess show revealed that Cash was ready to return home, and it was another major event in what was the most eventful year of his life. In January 1968, he had played his seminal concert (actually two shows, both recorded) at Folsom State Prison in northern California. The resulting album, *At Folsom Prison*, was a multi-platinum smash and rebooted Cash's career. Amid his new popularity, Cash also began to get his personal life together. In March, he married June Carter in Franklin, Kentucky, a short drive from Nashville. Why Kentucky? It required no waiting period for couples seeking to wed.

It would take two years before Cash completely sobered up (albeit not permanently), but by the end of 1968, Cash was a changed man. Ironically, he was pulling himself together in a year where the United States seemed intent on tearing itself apart. But if the Vietnam conflict and American politics were chaotic, it was also a time of incredible musical variety and creativity. *At Folsom Prison* was a back-to-basics album in a period when nothing seemed basic anymore. In the face of war, unrest, and assassination, musicians such as Cash were returning to a more rock and roll and rootsy sound. In 1968, the Beatles and the Rolling Stones released albums that were free of psychedelic-era ornamentation. The Stones's *Beggars Banquet* was mostly an acoustic record with a homemade feel. On their double album *The Beatles*, better known as the White Album, the Fab Four employed a more rock and roll approach on "Back in the U.S.S.R.," "Birthday," "Yer Blues," and "Savoy Truffle." The blank cover of *The Beatles* was a nod to the avant-garde. It also spoke to the band's more stripped-down aesthetic, as if the Beatles literally wanted to start from a blank slate.

Pop music, more than ever, was seeing crossover between country and rock and roll. When Eric Clapton played his farewell show for Cream in late 1968, he was dressed like a Nashville session man. The Beatles and Stones were offering fans generous helpings of country-inspired songwriting. In 1968, the Beatles dug into the songs of the American West on "Rocky Raccoon"—set in the Black Hills of South Dakota—and Ringo's fiddle-friendly "Don't Pass Me By." The year 1968 also saw the emergence of American roots rock bands such as the swampy, Delta-obsessed Creedence Clearwater Revival, who released their first album in May. *Music from Big Pink*, the Band's first album, released in July 1968, sounded southern even though only one member—Arkansan Levon Helm—hailed from Dixie.

Whatever the Band's geographical makeup, *Music from Big Pink* became a classic of roots rock. A month later, the Byrds reinvented themselves as a country rock band with *Sweetheart of the Rodeo.* It's no coincidence that roots music was emerging around the same time as the hippies—they wanted honest music, answers to big questions, and were looking to the South and the American West for inspiration.

Cash had a head start on bands who were embracing their own roots as well as early rock and roll. Cash's sound had always been stripped down—he hadn't added much to his core band since 1955 aside from Fluke Holland, the only permanent addition. Carl Perkins and even June Carter were more of a sideshow than the main event. On record, Cash sometimes added backing vocals, a little piano or slide guitar, but he had rarely diverged much from a minimalist sound.

The fact that *At Folsom Prison* became a blockbuster was not inevitable. It could have gone the way of his other underperforming records. The album mostly showed Cash as he always was on stage. But the perceived directness of *At Folsom Prison*—despite the fact that Cash's straightforward nature had made him a mainstay in country music—appealed to a wide audience looking for honesty and sanity in an era of government lies and obfuscations.

True to the American roots music revival, the year 1968 was a homecoming for Cash. In that year, he spent more time in his native Arkansas than he had for a long while. By then, Cash and his family had long since left his native state. But he returned to Arkansas for personal and political reasons. Whenever Cash went back to Arkansas, he again found his roots. And in his roots, he found strength.

The Concerts for Rockefeller

A more sober Cash was a more reliable performer and one more willing to play in his home state. He never completely shook his drug problem, but by February 1968 he had gained weight and looked healthier. On June 6, Cash played the Municipal Auditorium in Fort Smith on the Arkansas–Oklahoma border. Cash's time in Arkansas, however, soon took on a greater political importance. In the late summer and fall of 1968, Cash traveled throughout Arkansas with Gov. Winthrop Rockefeller as he sought reelection.

Rockefeller was Arkansas's first Republican governor since Reconstruction. As an adult, Cash identified with Republicans who were closer in their ideology to FDR than Calvin Coolidge or Ronald Reagan. Whatever his politics, Cash's notions of prison reform were welcome to many in Arkansas, especially Winthrop Rockefeller (nicknamed WR), who saw the penitentiary as a barbaric relic. Rockefeller, the grandson of oil magnate John D. Rockefeller and the brother of New York governor Nelson Rockefeller, was elected in November 1966 on the strength of his reform platform. WR had lost in 1964 to the popular segregationist Orval Faubus. Two years later, with the help of Arkansas's large (though minority) Black population, Rockefeller beat the openly racist Democrat Jim Johnson to win the state's highest office.[14]

Once in charge, Rockefeller appointed African Americans to important positions, including the Prison Board and the Office of Economic Opportunity. He cracked down on gambling in the old gangster playground of Hot Springs and campaigned for tax increases to pay for new programs. When Martin Luther King Jr., was assassinated in April 1968, Rockefeller was the only governor in the former Confederacy to hold a memorial service, where he held hands with Black leaders on the steps of the capitol and sang "We Shall Overcome."[15]

With the understanding that Rockefeller would clean up the prisons, Cash supported the governor in his reelection campaign.[16] In his January 1967 inaugural address, Rockefeller had called the Arkansas prison system the worst in the country. He emphasized the need for "major reforms" that would help in "clearing up deplorable conditions within our prisons, our probation and parole systems."[17] His two terms as governor would see the largest efforts by the state to modernize and democratize its prison system.[18] Prison reforms, however, did not happen without great controversy, which put enormous strain on the governor and Arkansas's national reputation.

In 1966, under Rockefeller's predecessor, Orval Faubus, the Arkansas State Police began a report on the horrifying conditions at Tucker farm, the smaller of the two prisons (the other was the much larger Cummins farm). The report revealed systemic abuses, including torture, rape, prostitution, beatings, drunkenness, and graft—the latter perpetrated not just by prisoners but also officials working there and in the local community.[19] Faubus suppressed the report. Not until Rockefeller took office were its

In 1968, Cash supported Gov. Winthrop Rockefeller at a handful of rallies throughout Arkansas. Cash was attracted to Rockefeller's stance on prison reform. With Cash's help, Rockefeller—the first Republican governor of Arkansas since Reconstruction—was reelected that November. It was the most Cash ever performed for any political candidate. *Courtesy Republican Party State Headquarters Collection, UA-Little Rock Center for Arkansas History and Culture.*

contents made known to the public. Even though Rockefeller had heard rumors of abuses at the prison since he had moved to Arkansas in 1953, the report shocked him. His wife, Jeannette, remembered it made him physically ill, and he would not discuss it with her.[20]

The prison report spoke of rampant corruption and spine-chilling torture at the prisons. The most notorious instrument of abuse was the "Tucker Telephone" an old-fashioned crank telephone used to send electric shocks through inmates. The torturer would attach one end of the wire to the phone and the other to the prisoner's toe or genitals. A prisoner would then be "rung up." That was bad enough, unless the man had the misfortune to receive a "long distance" call from the deranged warden, Jim Bruton, which meant prolonged torture.[21]

To help clean up the prisons, Rockefeller brought in Tom Murton, a penologist from California who had previously worked in the Alaska prison system. Murton was put in charge of Tucker farm. Murton was shocked by what he found there. He remarked on the lack of any meaningful rehabilitation in the penitentiary—not just an absence of psychological counseling but also no educational or vocational programs.[22] Murton found he had to change the inmates' and the larger public's perception of what a prison should be. He defined reform as "a program that would enable [inmates] to survive with some dignity as human beings while they served their sentences."[23] As he had found in Alaska, his aggressive tactics quickly brought him into conflict with administrators, whom he believed were moving too slowly both from a reformist point of view and on things as simple as receiving bulk food shipments for the prisoners.[24]

In keeping with Jim Crow orthodoxy, prisoners at Cummins and Tucker were racially segregated in their living quarters. Furthermore, when it came to punishment, whites disciplined whites and Blacks disciplined Blacks (at least in theory). By the late 1960s, Tucker was all white, with the exception of death row inmates (Tucker then housed the state's facilities for administering capital punishment). Despite the differences in their demographics, Tucker and Cummins were more alike than not. Both institutions were based on the Old South plantation model, in which men worked against their will to grow cotton, rice, and other crops on large farms, overseen by men on horseback with guns. The prisons had superintendents at the top of the administrative structure, with wardens below them. But it was the trusties—so called because administrators supposedly could trust them—who ran daily operations and enforced discipline.[25] With the inmates in charge, corruption was rampant. Convicts were forced to bribe those above them for better food, jobs, and even things as simple as receiving their mail.[26]

Murton might have been far more professional and ethical a person than his predecessors, but he proved no less controversial as a prison manager. After successfully cleaning up Tucker prison farm, he was given the job as the head of Cummins, a much larger facility. His tenure at Cummins, however, proved brief. In late January 1968, with members of the national media on hand, Murton, helped by Cummins prisoner and informant Reuben Johnson, unearthed three skeletons buried within sight of the guard towers. Murton was convinced both that these men had been murdered and also that there were as many as two hundred more bodies—men that had been declared escapees by prison officials but whom he believed had been killed.[27]

Murton's grisly discovery put Arkansas's prisons in an ugly national and even international spotlight.[28] It also undermined Rockefeller's efforts to control the public relations battle over reform efforts. Believing himself a scapegoat, Murton refused to back down from his claim that the skeletons were of men who had been killed, and he wanted to dig for more. Murton's critics claimed that he had acted without authorization and that the deaths had not been violent. They believed Murton had found nothing more than a pauper's grave.[29]

In 1968, as he tried to find the right man to run the prisons, Rockefeller worked hard for reelection in a state where the governor served only a two-year term. He enlisted the help of Arkansas entertainers, one of whom was Johnny Cash. By then Cash was Columbia Records' top-selling country musician. Cash had not lived in Arkansas since 1950, but he never forgot his home state. As a performer, he had a wealth of prison songs with which he could entertain inmates.

Cash may never have served time in prison, but he sympathized with the plight of convicts, and he was a true believer in reform and rehabilitation. "The culture of a thousand years is shattered with the clanging of the cell door behind you," he wrote in 1968. "Life outside, behind you immediately becomes unreal. You begin to not care that is exists. All you have with you in the cell is your bare animal instincts. . . . Behind the bars, locked out from 'society,' you're being re-habilitated, corrected, re-briefed, re-educated on life itself, without your having the opportunity of really reliving it . . . How could this torment possibly do anybody any good. . . . But then, why else are you locked in?"[30] Part of Cash's belief that prisoners could change stemmed from his conviction that all men could change. It was fundamental to his Christian beliefs. In Cash's mind, if a man such as he could escape the prison of drug addiction, inmates at American prisons could also overcome their demons and the wrongs that had driven them to crime. Cash's views were certainly not unusual in the reform-minded 1960s. But he was raised in a state with a notoriously brutal prison system, which made him rethink the wisdom of retributive justice.

Rockefeller's prison reforms coincided with immense cultural and political shifts occurring within the United States. The civil rights and student movement were rocking the political establishment, with women, African Americans, and Native Americans demanding equal treatment and respect from the traditional white male power structure. When Rockefeller took office, Arkansas was emerging from the shadow of Democratic one-party dominance and the evils of Jim Crow. The Little Rock crisis—where Governor Faubus blocked access to Central High School to avoid integration, before President Eisenhower sent in federal troops to allow Black students in—was roughly a decade past, but the state had not fully integrated. Two of Rockefeller's greatest accomplishments in prison reform—the abolition of the lash and the integration of barracks—had actually been outlawed before he became governor. The Faubus administration, however, had not made serious efforts to implement such measures.

Attracted by Rockefeller's efforts at prison reform, Cash and his band played six concerts in support of the governor. The band accompanied Rockefeller at large rallies at Winthrop, Fayetteville, Harrison, Monticello, Pine Bluff, and Hot Springs. It was one of the most political moments in Johnny Cash's career.

With June Carter at his side, Cash seemed happier and more popular than ever. But in the summer of 1968, tragedy struck when Cash lost Luther Perkins in a horrifying accident. On August 3, Luther fell asleep while smoking in his Hendersonville, Tennessee, home.[31] The fire consumed his house, and Luther, badly burned, managed to get out of the house alive, but barely. He was rushed to Vanderbilt Medical Center, but he died two days later from his burns. He left behind his second wife, Margie, and four daughters. The funeral was held two days after his death. Cash and the rest of the band acted as pallbearers.

Cash was soon back on the road, but Luther's death had deprived him of the most important component of his signature boom-chicka-boom sound. Cash's earlier music featured many great guitar breaks courtesy of Luther, but the deeper Cash dipped into his Americana music bag, the less prominent Luther had been on record. As *At Folsom Prison* showed, however, Luther was still integral to Cash's stage shows, providing the drive and raw energy need on tracks such as "Folsom Prison Blues" and "Cocaine Blues." Despite the loss of Luther, Cash was not one to stop performing. He carried on with the rest of his band. Carl Perkins filled in on lead guitar and sang his hits.

On August 24, the Johnny Cash Show made its first stop for Rockefeller in tiny Winthrop. Though not named after the governor, the town was founded in southwest Arkansas in 1912, the same year Rockefeller was born. The event was the first in Rockefeller's reelection campaign, which, compared to present-day campaigns, was mercifully brief. The rally for the governor—a World War II veteran and philanthropist trying to modernize one of America's most backward states—was the first of twelve regional rallies he held. A local paper said the Winthrop event was the first "political rally on wheels," referring to the Rockefeller Victory Special Campaign Train. The train represented an obvious connection to American political campaigns, when candidates spoke from the caboose to attentive crowds. Rockefeller's was a modern train, not a steam-powered one, but his campaign had an obvious connection to the past. In addition to Cash, at Winthrop, Rockefeller provided free watermelons, carnival rides, and balloons for the kids.[32]

On stage with the governor was Rockefeller's second wife, Jeannette, and Arkansas congressman John Paul Hammerschmidt. Chet Lauck (pronounced "Lock") introduced Cash. Lauck was an Arkansan best known for his work as the character Lum on the *Lum and Abner* radio show and related movies. *Lum and Abner*—a show now known to few people, even inside Arkansas—did nothing to better the state's reputation as a hillbilly heaven. But Rockefeller and Cash were trying to change that. Before Cash appeared on stage, the crowd listened to the Dixieland All-Stars, a traditional jazz band out of Little Rock.

Cash's Winthrop show was exceptional only in the absence of Luther. He played what the people wanted to hear: his classics, including "Big River," "I Still Miss Someone," and "I Got Stripes." He also played "Five Feet High and Rising," about the 1937 flood. Cash briefly introduced the song by noting how he was five when he had to take refuge in Pine Bluff when the water got too high.

Born in New York, the tall, heavy-set, chain smoking and too-fond-of-martinis Rockefeller was wisely surrounding himself with as many Arkansans as he could. WR had moved to Arkansas in 1953, a year before Cash left it. Now they were on stage together. At Winthrop, a Rockefeller supporter wrote, Cash provided "foot-stomping music for the crowd."[33] Despite Cash's support for Rockefeller, the singer liked to champion individuals and causes, not political parties. Just as Cash blended folk, rock, blues, country, and gospel into his music, his politics were unique to himself. Cash once said that he had grown up "under socialism." More accurately, Cash had grown up in a land that prized rugged individualists.

In the summer of 1968, Cash and WR might have seemed an odd pairing. But they were alike in many ways. Both were veterans and wealthy men who understood hard work (WR had once been a roughneck in Texas) and had a sympathy for common folks. They also had a deep concern for Arkansas and wanted to see it succeed. When he was in the Air Force, Cash had once written Vivian, agreeing with her that the life of rich people was unenviable. Cash said he would work hard to make Vivian comfortable, "but I don't ever want to be rich," noting he was "always so proud that I was a plain country boy." When he saw a "big shot driving a new car, smoking a cigar," he said that he would "breathe a prayer of thanks that I was poor." Cash said his "life's ambition was to walk up to John D. Rockefeller [Jr., who died in 1960] and tell him rich people don't go to heaven."[34] WR was as close as Cash came to meeting John D. Rockefeller, and one presumes he did not tell WR that rich men did not go to heaven. Besides, at that point, Cash had long been a wealthy man himself. Obviously, he no longer believed that rich men—now that he was one—couldn't be saved. Even so, Cash's status among the rich probably added to his spiritual and personal discomfort.

His second concert for Rockefeller was at Hog Heaven in Fayetteville on September 17. It proved a historic day for Cash and his band. Chet Lauck again was there. As emcee, he introduced Cash by saying, "We here in Arkansas take great pride in claiming Johnny Cash as a native son." Lauck added, in a bit of bumpkin hyperbole, that Cash was raised "so far back in the stix they had to grease their wagon twice to get to town."[35] In fact, Cash could easily walk to the center of Dyess. In any case, with two members of his band grounded because of bad weather, Cash was forced to go on stage with just June and Fluke Holland. Even though Cash was never better as a performer, the Fayetteville show demonstrated that he had two essential qualities: confidence and vulnerability. The prospect of going onstage with only his drummer could have led him to cancel the show, but he performed anyway. He did the best he could to entertain the crowd.

Bob Wootton

Luckily for him, a young guitarist named Bob Wootton was among the 6,500 people in attendance.[36] The story of Bob Wootton joining Cash's band at Fayetteville is one any fan or aspiring musician should know. It was, in short, a fantasy come true. As was true at Folsom in the case of Glen Sherley—an inmate whose song "Greystone Chapel" was played at the show—Cash had turned a fan into a star. Robert Charles Wootton was an Arkansas native, born March 4, 1942, in Red Branch, part of Paris, a small Ozark town of about 3,500 people. Bob was the son of Rubin C. Wootton and Noma Lucilla Moore Wootton. Wootton's family, like Cash's, was large; Bob was one of six children. Both men were from humble, rural Arkansas backgrounds.

Being from the hill country rather than the Delta, Bob's musical influences were different. Even more so than Cash, he grew up where music was central to family life. The people in Wootton's mountain community called it hillbilly music, though Bob said "what they was playin' was actually what they call bluegrass nowadays." Wootton's first love was gospel. "I just played in church," he remembered in 2008. "We had a guy who played guitar, my dad played mandolin. My uncle played guitar, and I just played rhythm guitar. I didn't try to play lead or anything. I'd always get up and sing a song when they'd ask me to. My dad had a very high voice, like Bill Monroe."[37] An early favorite was the Louvin Brothers and their album *Satan Is Real*. Bob's first guitar hero was Billy Byrd of Ernest Tubb's Texas Troubadours. Another influence was Merle Travis, whose finger-picking style impressed Bob. Wootton initially wanted to be a singer, partly because he could sing well and also because he thought guitarists didn't get much credit. Indeed, when Wootton was young, there was no such thing as a "guitar hero."

Wootton's father worked as a coal miner rather than a cotton picker. Like the Cashes, however, the family was willing to travel for better opportunities. For a working man, Rubin Wootton wisely decided the West Coast made more sense than small-town Arkansas. In 1950, the family moved to Taft, California, not far from Bakersfield—the epicenter of West Coast country, giving rise to artists such as Merle Haggard and Buck Owens. By 1953 Bakersfield was broadcasting a daily television show dedicated to country music. The host of KCPO's *Trading Post* was disc jockey Cousin Herb Henson, who invited Wootton to appear on the show. Convinced that country was the "devil's music," Bob's mother stopped him. Wotton said his mother only wanted him to perform gospel songs. He might have been thwarted in his first attempt at fame, but he remembered *Trading Post* fondly as the first show on which he saw Buck Owens. It was also the first time he heard Johnny Cash's music.[38]

When Bob first heard "I Walk the Line" in 1956, he liked it so much that he bought it, even though he didn't own a record player. The song's unique composition mystified Wootton. "It didn't dawn on me what it was," Wootton remembered. "I just thought it was strange. He kept changin' keys and whatever. I thought, 'How weird!' But when I heard John do it with the guitar sound behind, and his low voice, I just couldn't believe it."[39] The song kick-started Wootton's obsession with Cash, and Bob dedicated himself to learning how to play like Luther Perkins.

In 1958, the Wootton family moved again, this time to Tulsa, where Bob graduated from high school two years later. Believing that employers would not want to hire someone likely to be drafted, Wootton enlisted in the army, where he spent fifteen months in Korea. There he made a friend named Chavez, who he said "played pretty good, and taught me some of the stuff that Luther did, even though his guitar wasn't electric."[40] Wootton formed a country band in Korea called Johnny and the Ramrods. A sergeant was the leader of the group, and Wootton's abilities as a singer got him light army duty.[41] Bob was awarded a job in the mail room, where he had time to sing and make recordings to send home.

After returning from Korea, Wootton left the army. Once home, he spent his remaining military pay on a Regal electric guitar, a Fender amplifier, and a Gibson Hummingbird acoustic guitar. Wootton returned to Tulsa, where he got married and kept gigging in local clubs with his band, the Comancheros. To pay the rent, he drove trucks and bartended. In 1966, Wootton went to see Cash play at Cain's Ballroom in Tulsa. It was one of many shows that Cash did not show up for around that time, but Wootton managed to get his picture taken with Luther Perkins. Johnny Western was forced to fill in for the missing Johnny. Bob heard no Johnny Cash music that night. "I was just so disappointed," Wootton remembered. He wasn't alone. Cash was letting nearly everyone down in 1966.[42]

In a couple of years, though, Cash had turned his life around. After Luther's death, Wootton mourned the loss of his hero. He also saw an opportunity to join Cash's band. Bob called Cash at one point but could not get a hold of him. Not long before the fateful Fayetteville show, a Greyhound Bus driver heard Wootton singing at Caesar's Lounge, a Tulsa bar. The driver told Bob about the Cash show happening in Fayetteville, Arkansas.[43] Wootton was determined to see Cash again.

When he travelled to Fayetteville, he was twenty-six, just a few years older than Cash had been when he got his break at Sun. Bob was accompanied by his girlfriend, though he was still married at the time. Bob's lady friend managed to get the attention of June Carter. With thousands of people waiting for the rest of the band to arrive, June told Johnny that Wootton could play pretty well. Cash decided to take a chance on Bob and a bass player also in the crowd. "This time, um, I'm as anxious as you are to hear how it's gonna sound," Cash told the crowd as he introduced Bob and his guest bassist (whose name is unclear on the audio of the event). "I understand these two fellas are great musicians. They come from around this part of the country." Wootton nailed the audition. He gave a much-needed jolt to such classics as the rocker "Big River." "Play it, Bob!" Cash shouted in the middle of the song.[44] After opening with "Big River," Cash went into "Five Feet High and Rising," "Wreck of the Old 97," "I Walk the Line," "Folsom Prison Blues" and "Cocaine Blues."

Cash liked the confident young Wootton, who reminded him of himself in his Memphis days. Cash wrote about the Fayetteville concert in his 1975 autobiography, *Man in Black*. He asked Bob if he could play like Luther Perkins. "Nobody can do that," he remembered Wootton saying. "But I'll try if you want me to."

"Get out there and plug your guitar in," Cash told him. Wootton claimed to know some songs better than his hero did.

"Key of C!" Cash yelled to Wootton before beginning one song.

"You recorded it in D!" Bob shouted back.

"But I want to sing it in C," Cash insisted.

"OK," said Bob. "But you recorded it in D."[45]

Cash's recollections were accurate. Audio of the concert reveals Cash and Wootton talking about which key they should be in, especially on a rather messy version of "Orange Blossom Special," which required Cash to change harmonicas midway through. "We'll figure it out later," Cash quipped at the end. Wootton ended the set with a guitar solo that sounds like a pure rush of adrenaline. For Wootton, the experience must have been surreal. But the thrill of playing with his hero had only begun.[46]

Marshall Grant and Carl Perkins eventually made it to Fayetteville using Governor Rockefeller's plane. By the time they arrived, the gig was over. That night, Grant recalled, Cash told him the whole story of Bob showing up to the concert and filling in. Grant discovered from Cash that Wootton "had everything down—every song, the keys, the kickoffs, the breaks, the endings—he had all of it down pat. It was absolutely amazing. Nobody, short of Luther, could have done the job that Bob did that night." Wootton, Grant concluded, "was a godsend."[47] Cash's recruiting of Wootton underscored Johnny's open-mindedness, accessibility, and eye for new talent. Fortunately for both Cash and Wootton, the gamble on the young guitar picker from Tulsa paid off.

Marshall Grant remembered that the band's next date after the Fayetteville show was a week later in Memphis. In fact, the next gig was on September 19 in Harrison, Arkansas, for another Rockefeller rally. With Perkins and Grant on stage this time, the Tennessee Three was complete. Wootton was much more nervous than he had been at Fayetteville. Adding to his nerves was the fact that his red Naugahyde Kustom amplifier kept rolling around on the uneven flatbed. Bob thought, "Well, I can kiss this goodbye. I can't even control my amplifier (from) rollin' off the stage!"[48] But the performance went well.

The show took place at the city baseball diamond, where the WR people were busy dispatching—by the *Northwest Arkansas Times*'s count—7,500 hot dogs. With Cash's help, WR reached "twice as many people as he drew on a campaign stop here in his successful 1966 bid for the governorship."[49] In the course of the governor's fifteen-minute speech, the crowd applauded twelve times. Rockefeller was popular, but so was Cash, who boosted turnout. "Apparently the most popular person at the Rockefeller rally," said the *Harrison Daily Times*, was Cash, a man "besieged by autograph seekers at every turn."[50] Cash obliged, signing copies of *At Folsom Prison* and posing with smiling young females. Clad in the turtleneck and blazer combo fashionable at the time, he shook hands with a blind man as well as a disabled person too ill to be taken out of the back of his vehicle.

After the Harrison show, the band hit Charlotte, North Carolina, and then Norfolk, Virginia, before playing Memphis.[51] Grant remembered Wootton sitting out the band's date at the Mid-South Coliseum in Memphis and not joining the tour until Cash played Knoxville. Of the Memphis gig, Grant wrote, "This wasn't a little campaign-rally show where we probably played to no more than a thousand people; this was the Mid-South Coliseum, which was completely packed with more than 11,000 screaming fans." The Rockefeller rallies, however, were not "little," having crowds numbering at times five thousand or more people. Grant recalled that Bob was in the audience in Memphis (not playing full time yet) and was intimidated by the spectacle. He was "about ready to get up and go home," Grant remembered. Wootton, however, was determined to go onstage and play the Johnny Cash songs he knew so well. At Knoxville, he was again in good form.[52]

Bob Wootton got a once-in-a-lifetime opportunity at Fayetteville, and he performed well under pressure. All those hours listening to Luther Perkins and playing gigs in Tulsa had paid off. At Fayetteville, Bob had done Cash a favor, and Johnny was determined to repay him. He rewarded Bob with a blue Jazz Master and Twin Reverb amplifier he used at the San Quentin show and on the later ABC variety program. Even more important, he made Wootton a full-time member of the band. Cash said of Wootton, "One thing I came to appreciate about Bob was his knowledge of and love for the hymns and gospel songs I'd recorded," Cash wrote in *Man in Black*. Bob knew those as well as Cash's secular material. Cash also liked Bob's "easy-going manner and ability to adjust and get along with people, plus his love for and devotion to his job."[53] Johnny wasn't the only one who had a deep admiration for Bob. June Carter's sister Anita did too, and eventually they wedded in 1974. Cash needed a guitarist who would "treat everyone in the group as if they are [a] blood brother or sister."[54] By marrying Anita, Bob became a part of the family in every way.

WR's Reelection Fight

As Cash reorganized his band, the governor's race heated up. Until late into the 1968 campaign, Rockefeller trailed his conservative Democratic opponent, Marion Crank. The prisons continued to grab unwelcome headlines. Crank,

Arkansas's speaker of the house and a native of southwestern Little River County, criticized Rockefeller for wanting to turn the prisons into some kind of country club. The prison farms were far from that. Rockefeller and Bob Sarver, head of the newly formed Department of Corrections, were committed reformers, but they were struggling to maintain control over the prisons and the public opinion battle.

The more Cash played for the governor, the more he helped him. On October 1, Cash and his band performed for WR yet again at Monticello, a Delta town in the southeastern part of the state. The people who came enjoyed a free barbecue at Hyatt Field in McCoy Park. Rockefeller said, "I kid Johnny Cash a little bit and I tell him I don't know whether people came to hear his singing or whether they came for the free food or whether a few of them came to hear me. I said it makes no difference. They came and they stayed and they listened." Turning more serious, Rockefeller spoke of officials "using slave labor at the prison farms."[55] Such serious talk likely did not detract from the festival atmosphere. The Monticello *Advance* agreed with Rockefeller's sentiments concerning the rally: "They came to eat free barbecue, be entertained, see the governor and, probably last of all, hear political speeches."[56]

The prison issue, however, was not going away. On October 14, a shooting occurred at Cummins prison farm, where guards fired birdshot at inmates sitting outside and protesting ongoing abuses. No inmates were killed, but the violence again showed how far Arkansas had to go when it came to establishing a humane and stable penitentiary. Rockefeller defended the actions of the guards at Cummins. He regretted that violence was necessary to keep order at the prison, but he noted that other recent prison uprisings in Oregon and South Carolina had ended tragically. "I will not put up with any foolishness at the prison," Rockefeller vowed.[57]

Voters wanted him to continue his work. Cash undoubtedly helped Rockefeller, but WR was also saved by a nepotism scandal that undermined Crank's campaign. Crank had been putting members of his family, including his eight-year-old daughter, on the payroll. In November, Rockefeller was elected to another two-year term. He defeated Marion Crank by thirty thousand votes, a victory made possible not just by Cash's performances and Crank's scandals, but the African American vote.[58]

In late 1968, some Arkansans might have had bad things to say about Rockefeller, but no one seemed to have anything bad to say about Cash.

The year was one of controversy and struggle in Arkansas, but it was a great year for Cash. Tragedy had struck with the death of Luther Perkins, but *At Folsom Prison* was a smashing success, and the addition of Bob Wootton at Fayetteville gave the Johnny Cash Show a young member who could provide an essential element to the band's sound. On New Year's Eve 1968, Cash wrote a letter to himself in which he reflected on the year's events. For Johnny, it had been a time of tragedy and triumph. "I feel that this year, 1968 has been, in many ways, the best year of my 36 years of life," he wrote. "It has been a sober, serious year. Also probably the busiest year of my life, as well as the most fulfilling." He remembered the sad death of Luther Perkins. But he also noted the many high points, including the concerts for Governor Rockefeller and the "accidental" discovery of Bob Wootton in Fayetteville.[59]

Cash at Cummins

Cash and Rockefeller met again at Cummins prison farm in April 1969. It was the one and only time Cash played for prisoners in Arkansas. On that day, Johnny took the stage under a deep blue sky. It was a warm April day at Cummins in Lincoln County, Arkansas, roughly an hour northeast of Kingsland. The temperature that day hit the mid-seventies. Clad in a long jacket, striped pants, and boots, his face sweating under the bright afternoon sun, Cash and his band played classic songs from a well-established set that included "Ring of Fire," "Folsom Prison Blues," "I Walk the Line," and "Jackson." Standing before the crowd of eight hundred to nine hundred men and women, Cash also played a song he had written for the occasion, "When I Get Out of Cummins." The song, played in a shuffle tempo—somewhat like the song "San Quentin" recorded a few months earlier for inmates in California—told of a prisoner storming out of Cummins, not stopping until he reached the steps of the Capitol in Little Rock, and demanding change from the legislature:

When I get out of Cummins,
I'm goin' up to Little Rock.
I'm gonna walk right up those Capitol steps,
And I ain't gonna even knock.
And if the legislature's in session,

> There's some things I'm gonna say.
> And I'm gonna say, gentleman . . .
> You say you're tryin' to rehabilitate us,
> Then show us you are.[60]

With Gov. Winthrop Rockefeller and Commissioner Sarver in attendance, Cash shouted, "There's a lot of things that need changin', Mr. Legislator Man."[61] No one would have argued with Cash, who was by then the biggest country star in America, selling more albums in 1969 than the Beatles.[62] Cash's Cummins concert never became as famous as his performance at Folsom or San Quentin, but in terms of visibility and influence, it was one of the high points in both Cash's public efforts to promote the cause of rehabilitation at America's prisons and of Governor Rockefeller's reform drive. It was the last time they shared the stage, but it was a memorable and influential final appearance together.

Cummins prison farm had a long and dark history. In 1902, against the wishes of the governor—who thought the site too far from the capital—Arkansas bought ten thousand acres of flat, treeless former plantation land to construct Cummins prison farm. Today, Cummins spans 16,600 acres, roughly the size of Dyess. Its construction was part of a turn-of-the-century southern decision to build prison farms as a way to deal with crime.[63] Located on prime farmland along the Arkansas River in Lincoln County, roughly seventy miles southeast of Little Rock, the area was ideal for a prison. Growing crops promised great returns for the state's coffers. Prisoners were isolated, with no large towns or cities nearby, especially in an age before wide automobile use. The featureless landscape proved difficult for escapees to maneuver in, and those that tried to climb the levee and swim across the Arkansas River might drown in the attempt.[64]

Cummins was the headquarters of the state penitentiary, and it has remained the largest prison in Arkansas, both in physical size and population. Its existence represented a clear continuity between the Old South plantation and the New South penitentiary. Still, at the time it was built, Cummins was an improvement on the lingering convict leasing system. In December 1912, Arkansas's governor, George Donaghey, pardoned hundreds of white and Black prisoners, an act that effectively destroyed the normal operations of convict leasing. In February 1913, his successor, Joseph T. Robinson, signed legislation that abolished the practice.[65]

In April 1969, Cash (here, with June) and Rockefeller met again to perform at Cummins prison farm in Lincoln County. It was the only time Cash performed for inmates in his home state. It was also the last time the two men appeared on stage together. While Rockefeller had made progress reforming the prisons, in 1970 a federal judge ruled the entire prison system in Arkansas unconstitutional—the only such ruling in US history. *Courtesy Winthrop Rockefeller Collection, UA-Little Rock Center for Arkansas History and Culture.*

Cummins was meant to house African American inmates, though from the prison's early days, white convicts also lived there; by the 1930s, all of Arkansas's adult convicts resided at Cummins. By the 1950s, Cummins housed the state's female prisoners in a separate facility, the Women's Reformatory. It was a converted chicken house.[66]

Though far less well known than his Folsom or San Quentin shows, the Cummins concert revealed Cash at a crossroads in his career. By the spring of 1969, Johnny Cash's popularity had only increased since his visit to Arkansas the previous year for the Rockefeller rallies. He recorded *At San Quentin* in February 1969 and released the album in June. That same month, with two huge live albums to his credit, he was about to make the leap into network television. Although Cash played a more supportive (if well-publicized) role when performing for the Rockefeller campaign, at Cummins he was the undisputed star and center of attention.

The prisons were excited about Cash's visit. "Next month every country music fan in Cummins should flip," the *Pea Pickers Picayune*, the uncensored, inmate-penned prison paper, wrote in March 1969. "The Folsum [*sic*] Blues Warbler, Johnny Cash, will perform here." The editor of the *Picayune* urged prisoners to avoid escape attempts or other behavior that might land them in the "hole" and would "cause you to miss the man who gives out the music."[67] On the long-awaited day of the concert, Cash took Rockefeller's jet from Pine Bluff to Cummins.[68] But Rockefeller and the other Arkansas officials attending the show were not seated up front—Cash reserved those seats for the convicts.[69]

Cash's ability to connect with prisoners relied on many things. He empathized with them. They enjoyed his music. And with his homemade haircut (June was his barber) and sideburns, Cash looked like a prisoner. His scar gave the appearance of someone who had come out on the wrong end of one too many bar fights (though that was not the case). He chafed at conformity. "Every hair cut is a bad experience," he wrote later in life.[70] Cash had as little interest in regular haircuts as he did in neckties. Had the prisoners known such things, it would've been another reason to like him. Johnny Cash was not the kind of guy to get expensive haircuts.

At one point during a break at the Cummins concert, Governor Rockefeller spoke to the inmates about Sen. Thomas J. Dodd of Connecticut. Dodd had been partly responsible for keeping Arkansas prisons in the national spotlight. In March 1969, Tom Murton had testified before the United States Senate Juvenile Delinquency Subcommittee, where he again recounted the horrors of the Arkansas penitentiary, which had no minimum age for men doing hard time (hence his testimony concerning juveniles). One of the Committee members was Dodd, who had been censured by the Senate in 1967 for misappropriating campaign funds. Dodd was sympathetic toward Murton. But a few days after Murton's testimony, Commissioner Sarver and criminologist Austin MacCormick—employed by Rockefeller as a consultant—attempted to refute Murton's testimony, especially his assertion that conditions at Tucker had worsened since Murton left. Senator Dodd, however, proved hostile toward Sarver, who became noticeably frustrated during the two-hour ordeal.[71] On stage at Cummins, Rockefeller took swipes at Dodd, saying, in effect, the senator should have been in the audience—as a prisoner.[72]

As politicians battled over prison reform, Cash took a more straightforward approach to the penitentiary problem. He could help inmates through his presence and music, though he was prepared to do more than that. He believed prisoners were his best audience, and the men and women at Cummins were clearly pleased with his performance. During the concert, Wade Eaves, editor of the *Pea Pickers Picayune*, presented Cash with an honorary life sentence.[73] The concert broke, at least briefly, the usual drudgery of prison life. The day of Cash's visit to Cummins, the *Picayune* said, inmates had "virtually *flipped*!"[74] The paper dubbed Cash the "King of Cummins." The Man in Black "came, he sang, he mingled with the inmates," the paper reported, "and fired morale to a tempered, glittering high seldom if ever seen." Cash, the *Picayune* opined, "became a bona-fide hero to the Cummins Crew." The editor said meeting Cash "is a real experience. Your pre-conceived expectations get knocked silly. He somehow greets you with the same glowering, even smoldering, restlessness of a big Kodiak bear standing in a steel trap." The paper also noted Cash's gift of $5,000 to raise funds for the building of a chapel at Cummins.[75]

Commissioner Sarver was also impressed with Cash's performance, noting that Cash had said "some things I've been afraid to say." Cash reassured Sarver, noting that, as a country singer, Cash had "nothin' to lose."[76] Cash's feelings about prisoners were similar to Thomas Murton's. For reform to happen, outsiders needed to recognize inmates' basic humanity. "I think these men are very, very human," Cash said before he left Cummins. "And some people ought to be more careful about how they treat human beings."[77] To show how people should treat them as humans, Cash had lunch with inmates and also visited the men on death row.

Cash gave a total of $10,000 for the construction of chapels at Cummins and Tucker,[78] but at the time of the Cummins concert, the Tucker chapel was well under way. It was finished in the fall of 1969. Called the "Island of Hope," it was the first prison chapel built in Arkansas.[79] Newspapers reported that Cash had been put in charge of the Cummins chapel fund after his concert at the prison, but apparently this position turned out only to be honorary.[80] In any case, Cash would not have had time to deal with the fund; he would soon be busy working on a weekly television show for ABC. It would take prison officials years to finish work on the Cummins chapel. Management of its fund eventually was handled by Winthrop Paul Rockefeller, the governor's son, who later served as Republican lieutenant governor under Mike Huckabee.[81] The Cummins chapel finally opened in January 1977.[82]

After the Cummins concert, Cash went on to even greater fame. *At San Quentin*, another smash hit, was released in June 1969. That month, his ABC program, *The Johnny Cash Show*, debuted, garnering high ratings but lasting only two seasons. And unfortunately for Rockefeller, Johnny Cash alone could not bring about meaningful change in the Arkansas prisons. In February 1970, federal judge J. Smith Henley, an Arkansan, ruled in the second of two decisions in the landmark *Holt v. Sarver* case (named for attorney Lawrence J. "Jack" Holt and prison commissioner Robert Sarver) that the Arkansas prison system was unconstitutional: the prisons violated the Eighth Amendment's prohibition against "cruel and unusual punishment" and the Fourteenth Amendment's right to equal protection. Henley called the prisons a "dark and evil world completely alien to the free world, a world that is administered by criminals under unwritten rules and customs completely foreign to free world culture."[83] Among the prison system's deficiencies was the lack of rehabilitation programs. The *Sarver* decision, noted the *Harvard Law Review*, was "the first in which an entire prison system faces possible abolition on constitutional grounds."[84] The state's lawyers appealed the decision, but it never went beyond the Eighth Circuit Court.

By 1971, Arkansas was not alone in dealing with a nightmarish prison problem. That September, prisoners at Attica in upstate New York took guards hostage following anger over the death of George Jackson, a California inmate and Black activist who had killed six guards while trying to escape from San Quentin. It was Gov. Nelson Rockefeller, brother of Winthrop, who ordered state police to take control of Attica. The police stormed the prison and restored order, but at a cost of thirty-nine lives, the vast majority of them prisoners'.[85]

As the Arkansas penitentiary worked to comply with constitutional standards, Johnny Cash continued to talk about the need for prison rehabilitation programs. In July 1972, he testified before the Senate Subcommittee on National Penitentiaries, which was considering parole legislation. With him was fellow songwriter and ex-convict Glen Sherley. Cash had been instrumental in getting Sherley released early from prison. Before the Senate committee, Cash spoke of the need for prisons to focus more on rehabilitation as a means of bettering inmates' lives. He did not speak at length about Arkansas, though he mentioned having heard about the plight of a fifteen-year-old prisoner, incarcerated for car theft, whom fellow inmates raped repeatedly. The unfortunate teenager died the next day. Cash again shared his belief that prisoners must be treated as human beings. "If they are not," he said, "they are not going to act like human beings." Cash stressed the need for spiritual development among inmates by people who "really care for these men" and "not just somebody who comes here because he is paid $200 a week to do it." Cash also urged the Senate to lessen the punishments for first offenders, especially those convicted of crimes involving marijuana. Cash's own struggles with drug addiction were well known by that point, and had he not been rich and famous—had he just been another poor kid from Arkansas—he likely would have fared poorly in the justice system. Cash worried about a man convicted of minor drug crimes becoming a lifelong criminal. Such men emerged "an educated, well-trained criminal in the ways and in the skills of crime. And I think that is a crime in itself to do that to a man."[86]

Cash not only testified before the Senate that July; he also met with President Nixon to discuss prison reform.[87] Cash's attempts to rehabilitate the troubled Glen Sherley, however, were unsuccessful. Despite speaking well of Sherley at his 1973 concert in Sweden's Österåker prison, Sherley remained a disturbed and violent man. According to Marshall Grant, one day on the tour bus, Sherley threatened him with death for no apparent reason. Cash decided it best to get rid of Sherley soon after. Sherley moved to California, became homeless, and died by suicide in 1978. Sherley's death, Michael Streissguth has written, represented the "death of [Cash's] passion for prison reform."[88] In 1980, Cash played his last concert for prisoners—at Angola in southern Louisiana.

By the time of Cash's last prison concert, the country's turn to the Right had resulted in an intensified drug war, which, combined with states embracing capital punishment and other retributive models, led to an explosion in the US prison population. Still, Cash had made an imprint on the history of prison reform. The chapels Cash helped build at Tucker and Cummins lived on. In 1985, Bill Clinton wrote that the chapels "have proven to be time and money well spent."[89] And yet in the 1980s problems continued to plague the Arkansas prison system. It was not until 1982 that federal courts deemed the Arkansas penitentiary compliant with constitutional standards. In the 1990s, ugly headlines about the system appeared, including an international blood plasma scandal in which the prison had been selling tainted blood to other institutions.[90] Nevertheless, in 1996, Cummins prison obtained certification from the American Corrections Association.[91] By then, Arkansas had come far in aligning its prison policies and conditions with national standards. The reforms that Winthrop Rockefeller's administration inaugurated, and which Johnny Cash championed, began the process of making incarceration more modern and humane, but the process of reform was a slow and painful one. By the 1990s, the prisons were much like penitentiaries in any other state. But cleaner, safer, and better-run prisons did not mean that Arkansans had erased injustices within the system itself.

The Arkansas penitentiary's darkest days ended with the reforms of Winthrop Rockefeller. Conditions for inmates unquestionably improved from the late 1960s onward, but the state's prison population has only increased since Rockefeller's governorship. The state now spends hundreds of millions of dollars annually to keep criminals locked up. The reforms of the Rockefeller period represented a quantum leap in the state's understanding of how to run a modern penitentiary, but Arkansas now has an unwieldy prison-industrial complex. When Johnny Cash played at Cummins, there were fewer than 1,500 people in the Arkansas prison system. In 2010, there were more than 16,000—so many that some prisoners were housed in local jails due to overcrowding.[92] As one man, Cash could only do so much to reform an institution as complex and troubled as the Arkansas prison system, but in 1968 and 1969 he did some good in Arkansas. Without a doubt, Rockefeller had an important ally in Johnny Cash.

Cash was at the height of his fame at the end of the 1960s. It was a period of personal rebirth. He was doing what he had always done—making music—but now he could thank a more sober lifestyle, a new wife, a rejuvenated band, and the blockbuster live albums they recorded. It is no surprise that he chose to spend so many days of his comeback in his home state, where he hoped to affect positive political change. Whenever Cash was doing well, he spent lots of time in Arkansas. And by returning to his roots, he could recommit himself as an artist, bandleader, TV star, activist, father, husband, and Christian. With so much success at the end of the decade, Cash felt he had to reassess his relationship with his lord and savior. It was one of many changes he made in the 1970s.

6

Hendersonville, Kingsland, and the New Johnny Cash

Americans are a nostalgic people who like to break up modern history into convenient chunks of time, usually separated into sequential ten-year periods. Ever since the 1920s, it seems that Americans have been eager to fit history into neat decades. Nostalgia aside, there is good reason to do so. The Eighteenth Amendment and Prohibition started the Roaring Twenties. The stock market crash of 1929 brought on the grim and dusty 1930s. The German invasion of Poland in September 1939 ended people's preoccupation with the depression and turned their energies toward winning World War II. The next major war America fought was the Korean War, which, conveniently for historians, began in 1950. The election of Kennedy, which contributed to the rise of America's youth culture, happened in 1960. The 1960s ended, so conventional wisdom goes, at the tragic Altamont concert in December 1969. And so on. While it also may seem too convenient, for Johnny Cash, 1970 was an important transition year.

By late 1969, events had turned people against hippie culture. In August 1969, the cult followers of Charles Manson committed a series of grisly murders in Los Angeles. A few months later, Hells Angels killed a Black audience member during the Rolling Stones' chaotic set at Altamont in northern California. The Woodstock festival had made history as three days of peace, love, and music. But by the end of the year, it seemed the country had changed. Richard Nixon was president, and the Vietnam War still raged. The hippies hadn't been able to change either of those things.

As the 1960s became the 1970s, Johnny Cash was at the peak of his popularity. At the Country Music Association Awards in October 1969, Cash was declared "Country Music Entertainer of the Year" while also racking up honors for best male vocalist; best single, "A Boy Named Sue"; best album, *At San Quentin*; and best vocal group with June Carter. As Cash's popularity soared, the weight of his celebrity pulled more people into his inner circle. His mansion in Hendersonville, outside of Nashville, became a palace for country music royalty and visiting dignitaries. Through it all, though, Cash tried to remain ever the country boy.

Hendersonville and the House of Cash

Cash was again embracing family and friends as the sixties ended. After his first major attempt at sobriety in late 1967, Cash's family returned to center stage. Ray was at Cash's seminal Folsom concert in January 1968. In late April 1970, Carrie appeared with Johnny on his ABC television program, where she played piano. On March 3, June gave birth to her only son, John Carter Cash, and according to Marshall Grant, 1970 was the year when Cash truly became clean and sober.[1] In addition to sobering up, Cash stopped smoking (though, as was true with Cash and his vices, the halt was temporary). Cash's control over his drug problem would not outlast the decade, but kicking drugs temporarily allowed Cash to dedicate himself more than ever to his family. Unlike the 1950s and '60s, when the relentlessly touring Cash was gone for long periods, Johnny decided to keep his family on the road with him. The result was that John Carter followed his father everywhere. Long gone were the days when Cash and the Tennessee Two piled into a car for long drives. Cash now had a tour bus.

While in the Air Force, Cash wrote to Vivian saying he wanted their firstborn to be a boy.[2] Instead, he got Rosanne, followed by Kathy, Cindy, and Tara. Johnny had always loved his four daughters, but he had never given them the kind of attention he gave John Carter. When Johnny was not away on tour, he acted aloof or strange when he was home. But when John Carter was born, Johnny rededicated himself to fatherhood.

In 1970, Cash, who had little interest in the business end of music, made his sister Reba the general manager for his publishing companies House of Cash (for BMI) and Sound of Cash (for ASCAP) and the office manager for Johnny Cash Enterprises. Reba, whom *Billboard* called "a striking brunette" and one of the "youngest-looking grandmothers in Tennessee," initially had been put in charge of her brother's fan mail.[3] Cash's previous attempts to keep the family involved in the music business had not gone so well. In 1964—roughly in the middle of the worst of Cash's drug period—Tommy Cash took charge of his brother's office on Music Row in Nashville, overseeing operations of JC Music and South Wind Music. Johnny, however, had little respect for his brother's efforts to keep order. Cash stormed into his offices at night, overturning cabinets, smashing coffee pots, and committing other acts of destruction. He wouldn't stop the vandalism, so Tommy quit. Tommy said later, "Until a person wants help they're not going to get it. They have to decide they want to change."[4]

The 1970s represented a new departure when it came to Cash's personal life, but such was not the case artistically. He continued to speak out for two of the most marginalized groups in America: prisoners and Native Americans. In December 1968, near the anniversary of the Wounded Knee Massacre of Indian women and children in 1890, Cash visited the site amid the bleak South Dakota landscape and performed a benefit show for the Native Americans there.

Cash still was deeply interested in Native American history. In the spring of 1970, he portrayed Chief John Ross in *Trail of Tears*, a drama on National Education Television Playhouse, concerning the removal of Native Americans from Georgia during Andrew Jackson's administration (a policy that continued under his successor, Martin Van Buren). Ross was born in 1790 and was a Cherokee chief from 1828 until his death in 1866. Despite the fact that Cash was a southerner who lived in Tennessee, it was Jack Palance (born Volodymyr Palahniuk), a Pennsylvanian actor known for the hissing villains he often portrayed, who played Jackson. The filmed play is not well remembered today, but it again showed how Cash sought to combine his political and artistic interests. Cash's turn as Ross likely further confused those who thought he was part Native American, which was not helped by the singer's continued insistence that he had Cherokee ancestry. Ironically, though, in keeping with the entertainment industry's refusal to give lead roles to ethnic minorities, Arthur Smith Junaluska—a full-blooded Cherokee—appeared in the show, but in a supporting role.[5]

Several scenes of the movie were shot in Massachusetts, where the December weather in the western part of the state gave authenticity to winter scenes (with some help from a local ski resort snow machine). A reporter for the *Berkshire Eagle* of Pittsfield met up with Cash and some Native American actors—imposing Mohawk brothers Malcolm and Lynwood Harris—at a local bar. Sipping drinks with them was Bob Wootton. The

Harris brothers praised Cash for being a "straight guy," whom they considered "one of the boys." Cash and Wootton couldn't help having some fun with the locals by passing off Wootton as Cash's brother. Wootton also might have had some fun with the *Eagle* reporter: Wootton said he was part Cherokee and had come from the cotton fields. Neither of these were true.[6]

Musically, Cash was white hot as the sixties became the seventies, and his success rested on what he had consistently done throughout his career. He continued to blend the sacred with the secular, releasing *The Holy Land* in January 1969, a recording sandwiched between *At Folsom Prison* and *At San Quentin. The Holy Land* was the last album to feature Luther Perkins, who died before its release. The record was the product of Cash's second trip to Israel. He had traveled there in 1966, but the 1968 trip was special because Cash was on honeymoon. It was June, however, not Johnny, who insisted they go there.

A mix of songs and spoken narration about Jesus, *The Holy Land* was not an exceptional album. It did have one stellar track—the Carl Perkins contribution, "Daddy Sang Bass," a song about family, the spiritual life, and "making a living out of black land dirt"—all things to which Cash could relate. Fittingly, Cash and June sang on it as well as the Statler Brothers, who had been a part of the Cash touring show for years. The song incorporated the popular hymn "Will the Circle Be Unbroken?" which had been written in 1907 but was made popular decades later by the Carter family.

Cash remained political in the 1970s, but in a way that appealed to the Left and the Right. His activism for Native Americans and prisoners endeared him to liberals, while his patriotism and Christian beliefs kept his more conservative fans happy. Cash was not a militaristic person, and he was not ideologically in favor of the Vietnam War, but he supported the troops and the president. Cash had faith that Nixon would do the right thing.

During the 1968 campaign, Nixon talked about ending the war, but as president, he expanded the country's commitment in southeastern Asia. In 1969, troop levels in Vietnam reached their peak, at more than 500,000 soldiers. The year was the second bloodiest of the conflict, with nearly 11,780 servicemen dying.[7] The war eventually spread into Cambodia, and under the leadership of Nixon and Henry Kissinger—Nixon's and Gerald Ford's national security advisor (from 1969–1975) and secretary of state (1973–1977)—the US unleashed its most intense bombing campaigns yet.

When it came to the Vietnam War, Cash became part of the phenomenon whereby people ideologically opposed to a war support the continuation of it late in its progress. They act on motives of patriotism and loyalty, but also a fear that not supporting it may lead to not only defeat but a societal collapse in the warring country. They also fear abandoning the war would betray the sacrifice of Americans who had died fighting it. Thus, even if a person such as Cash rejected the war initially, by 1969 there was no point in debating why the country started the conflict—only how it might end it.

Nixon, and many Americans along with him, believed the United States had a moral duty to end the war responsibly. As Nixon termed it, he wanted an "honorable end" to the conflict, and Cash agreed. He was also willing to visit the troops. In January 1969, Cash and his retinue went to Long Binh—a ward in the large city of Bien Hoa in southern Vietnam, not far from what was then Saigon—to play for the troops. During the trip, Cash was not at his best. He had come down with pneumonia, and all-night enemy shelling deprived him of sleep. After singing "Wreck of the Old 97," Cash joked with the troops about not feeling well, saying he went to the dispensary doctor, who told him he shouldn't sing because he had a temperature of 102. "Hell, my normal temperature is 110," Cash quipped to the raucous troops.

While he might not have been in top form, Cash had the opportunity to see the war firsthand and play before an appreciative crowd. Among the usual classics such as "Big River" and "Tennessee Flat Top Box," Cash played a history song, "Remember the Alamo," written by the Texas songwriter Jane Bowers. The song was recorded by the Kingston Trio in the late 1950s and by English folk rocker Donovan in 1965. Cash's studio version had appeared on his 1963 compilation *Ring of Fire*. At Long Binh, Cash didn't introduce or explain "Remember the Alamo"—though the symbolism of singing about the Alamo on Vietnamese soil was ominous. The Alamo, as is true of the Vietnam War, represents many things to Americans—bravery and futility, heroism and tragedy, disaster and defeat. Why did Cash sing about the Alamo? He understood the link between the past and the Vietnam War. The technology had changed between the 1830s and the 1960s, but again, young men were fighting for a cause that, while bloody and historical, was destined to go down as one of America's military defeats.[8]

Cash was struggling with supporting the war as well as his own addiction. At Tachikawa Air Base in Tokyo, the exhaustion of his illness, the stress of playing for troops, and the long flight made Cash's throat give out. His voice was also dried up by the pills he took before the show. His songs became mere whispers.[9]

Cash's Asia trip was another reminder that amphetamines were ruining his life. But his trip to see the troops in 1969 resulted in one of his classic songs, "Singin' in Viet Nam Talkin' Blues" (not to be confused with Phil Ochs's 1964 song "Talking Vietnam"), released in May 1971. In the song, over breakfast, Cash and June discuss visiting the troops in Vietnam. The detail of Cash having seconds of "country ham" during their talk underscores the difference between the lifestyles of those at home (especially the rich and famous such as Cash) and what the soldiers were going through overseas. For Cash, playing for soldiers was a lot like playing for prisoners: he wanted to entertain and treat as human the men stuck in dehumanizing, violent, and extreme situations. In "Singin' in Viet Nam Talkin' Blues," Cash was political, but the song also revealed his lifelong gift for empathy. As Johnny and June hear the bombs fall in the distance, June says how scared she is. "I'm scared, too," Cash responds.

Cash said he didn't like the war, and he wanted the troops home as soon as possible, but he supported Nixon's efforts in Vietnam. Cash saw himself not as a hawk, but as a "dove with claws." If people wouldn't stand behind Nixon, he said, "get the hell out of my way so I can stand behind him." When asked about his support for Nixon, Cash put things in Biblical terms, hoping that under Nixon's leadership, "all our boys will be back home and that there will be peace in all the mountains and all the valleys"[10] Cash's rationale for the war in 1969—respect and support the troops, trust the president, fight them "over there" rather than "over here"—might have been morally dubious and not in keeping with his Christian beliefs. His conviction, nevertheless, that Americans should "support the troops" resonated later with those who were committed to later invasions of Iraq and the "War on Terror."

Amid a hideously divided America, in April 1970 Cash traveled to the White House to play for Richard Nixon. The concert proved controversial, for Cash did not play several songs Nixon requested, including "Welfare Cadilac" (spelled with one "l") and "Okie from Muskogee." The controversy, however, was slight. Nixon obviously knew nothing about country music or the etiquette of requesting songs that were not Cash's own. Cash's political sympathies were in keeping with neither Merle Haggard's classic (if right-wing) "Okie from Muskogee" nor Guy Drake's crass take on the poor in "Welfare Cadilac." In any case, Cash didn't know either song, and he wasn't going to learn them when he had so many other great tunes in his repertoire. Nixon actually made light of the "Welfare Cadilac" faux pas, saying Cash "owns a Cadillac, but he won't sing about them." The president noted that Cash was from Arkansas and may have moved to Tennessee, but "belongs to the whole country," calling his songs "American music that speaks to all Americans." For Nixon and the country, it was a triumphant day. Not only was Cash giving a historic concert, Nixon began the evening expressing relief and gratitude for the safe return of the Apollo 13 astronauts to earth.[11]

By 1970, it was not uncommon to talk about Nixon and Cash in the same breath. In December 1969, Nixon had visited Fayetteville for a critical football game between Arkansas and the University of Texas at Austin. It was the biggest event in Fayetteville since Cash's visit the previous year. And as one salt-of-the-earth local put it, "you can't get much bigger than Johnny Cash."[12] Cash and Nixon were both enormously popular figures, but at first, it would seem they had little in common, despite their fame. One was an Arkansas singer known for his honesty, the other a career politician made infamous by his lies, moral corruption, and impeachable behavior as president. But the two men were from similar backgrounds. Both had come from nothing. They even shared musical talent, though Nixon's instrument was the piano rather than the guitar, and he played with more virtuosity than Johnny ever mustered on his Martin. Nixon was from Yorba Linda (meaning "beautiful Yorba" and named after the Spanish soldier José Antonio Yorba), a small city in Orange County, California, roughly thirty-seven miles southeast of Los Angeles. As was true of Dyess's most famous family, the Nixons were poor farmers—though in the Nixons' case it was a ranch. And they were religious, too, being Quakers as compared to the Baptist Cashes.

Born in 1913, Nixon was old enough to have been Cash's father, but he was only sixteen when the Great Depression hit. He could have avoided the military during World War II, but as was true of Cash, Nixon felt a duty to serve and eventually became a naval officer. Both men lost a brother while young. In Nixon's case, his brother Arthur died from tuberculosis and at a younger age than Jack Dempsey Cash. Nixon and Cash obviously had diverging views on politics, but they were both self-made men capable of historic comebacks, which they experienced in 1968.

The entirety of the White House concert is lost to fans and historians, but some of the audio survived. Cash made no attempt to hide his humble roots from the crowd. "We hope to show you a little bit of the soul of the South tonight," Cash noted at the beginning.[13] To do that, he played well-worn songs such as "Wreck of the Old 97" and "Five Feet High and Rising." Cash also got political with "What Is Truth"—one of his best political commentaries. More sober than he had been in years, Cash became a better performer on stage. "Is he always this good?" one Secret Service agent asked at the show.[14]

Cash also seemed better on record. In the early 1970s, he produced some of his best work, from "Man in Black" (released March 1971) to "What Is Truth" (February 1970). Both were political in their own way, addressing the youth culture, the Vietnam War, and how events tested one's deepest convictions. Cash could also rock as hard as ever, as on the sexually charged track "Blistered," a Billy Edd Wheeler tune that Cash cut in October 1969, helped by searing guitar work from Carl Perkins.

By the fall of 1970, it seemed Cash could do no wrong. He had a hit TV show, and he continued to find good material, helped in part by the contributions of a new member of the Cash musical family: Kris Kristofferson. Kristofferson wrote one of Cash's best and most melancholy hits, "Sunday Mornin' Comin' Down"—a perfect song for Cash, who could sing with conviction about depression, restlessness, and substance abuse. As Michael Streissguth has written, Kristofferson was part of "an authentic and modern outlaw tradition that settled into Nashville beginning in the early 1960s."[15] Kristofferson's music was finding a wider audience by 1970 courtesy of Johnny Cash, who by then wasn't writing the kind of songs that had made him famous. His "songwriting productivity had plummeted," said Streissguth.[16] But Cash knew a good songwriter when he heard one. Kristofferson became not only a great collaborator but also a close friend.

Kristofferson was a Texas-born army brat, pilot, and (as everyone feels compelled to point out) Rhodes Scholar. When Cash had discovered him, he had been working as a studio factotum at Columbia Records, sweeping floors and putting away tapes. Kristofferson had worshipped Cash. Early in their friendship, Kristofferson had sent song lyrics to Johnny and June with no success. An Army pilot, Kristofferson rented a helicopter and flew to Cash's Hendersonville property to deliver demo tapes. It was the kind of dramatic "rock and roll" gesture that Cash could appreciate.

It also helped that Kristofferson was a good-looking, brilliant songwriter. In her 2010 memoir, Rosanne called Kristofferson "my dear friend and the closest link I have to my dad now." Kris and his wife Lisa, she added, "were perhaps closer to Dad and June than anyone else outside the family."[17] Cash's version of "Sunday Mornin' Comin' Down" was a smash, hitting number 1 on the country chart. It was also nominated for a Grammy. As a single release, Cash released his cover of Kristofferson's tune between "What Is Truth" and "Flesh and Blood," a more conventional love song. Both were penned by Cash, and they were hits, too.

In a November 1970 *Playboy* interview, Cash was portrayed as a man at the top of the music industry, but one still attached to his roots. Cash by then was in his enormous, quarter-million-dollar house in Hendersonville, where he had tried to make Tennessee a home as much as possible. He had bought the place in 1967, and it was where he started sobering up after a hellish decade of abusing pills. The new house was an unusually designed mansion that he bought on impulse. He saw it, liked it, and made the owner an offer he couldn't refuse.[18] The living room could seat a hundred people. There, Cash hosted gatherings of musicians and friends such as Shel Silverstein, Kristofferson, and Bob Dylan. They were "guitar pulls," where Cash and other songwriters tried out new material on one another.

In Hendersonville, Cash was geographically close to Nashville recording studios and the country music establishment. As much as he could, he tried to remain a country boy who loved a chance to connect to American history. Hendersonville was rural enough, but in 1972, he and the family also purchased a farm, Bon Aqua, about forty miles west of Nashville. "He could go there and decompress, sit on the front porch and listen to the birds and the cows," said Johnny's niece Kelly Hancock. "It brought him back to who he was," she added, "a country boy from Arkansas."[19] The farm, with its two-story house, was originally built by William Loch (or Locke) Weems in 1837. Weems built cabins on the property, where visitors could take in the good water—hence the name, "Bon Aqua." With Weems's death the land passed to his son, Philip Van Horn Weems. Major Weems fought in the Civil War for the Eleventh Tennessee regiment and was mortally wounded at the Battle of Atlanta in July 1864. He was only twenty-six. Buried in Georgia, he was exhumed in the 1880 and brought back to Tennessee to be buried at Bon Aqua. It was the kind of story that made for Johnny Cash songs.[20]

According to *Playboy*, Cash was making $3 million a year. But in his living room, he had a shelf with a display of cotton on the stalk. Cash demonstrated for his interviewer, Saul Braun, "with no self-consciousness or hesitation," how to pick cotton. Braun found it odd that Cash enjoyed talking about his childhood, considering "the dismalness of American rural poverty in the Depression years," and "how rejected the rural South feels and has felt" and "the tragedy that dogged the Cash family." As a New York City writer, who likely didn't know much about Cash's childhood—especially considering *Winners Got Scars Too* had not yet appeared—it might have been easy for Braun to make assumptions about Cash's upbringing. Cash had grown up poor, but he wasn't the poorest of sorts. He and his family could have been far worse off during the Depression. Besides, Dyess was the only place Cash really knew. Just because he was a wealthy man didn't mean he didn't appreciate where he had come from. He had been poor longer than he had been rich.[21]

As Cash graced the pages of the nation's most famous men's magazine, back in Arkansas, the *Osceola Times* published a piece that humbled Cash. The paper wrote that in Dyess, "his old friends just weren't all that excited about J. R. Cash being the greatest country music entertainer in the country." School superintendent Lynn Cox said he had not watched the Country Music Awards, and he seemed annoyed that Cash wasn't returning his phone calls concerning "an important community project." When it came to the CMAs, the mayor of Dyess, E. O. Woody, also didn't tune in. Woody claimed to have taught Cash how to "pick a guitar." He had seen Cash in 1968 at his Dyess high school show, when Johnny had announced, "Open the door and ask that old man in. He taught me to play a G chord on the guitar."[22]

Woody was a longtime resident of Dyess. He might have been unexcited about Cash's recent accomplishments, but he defended white people's role in creating country music. "The colored people think they have invented soul music," Woody said, but believed "country music has been soul music for millions of us for many years." Woody apparently told Cash at one point, "J. R., as long as you remain yourself, as long as you remember your beginnings, then you will be a success. If you ever try to act sophisticated, or go long hair, then you're a gone gosling." In fact, Cash's hair—which the *Times* said looked like that of a "Mississippi gambler"—was longer than it had ever been, and he was more successful than other country musician in history.[23] So much for the advice of small-town mayors.

Folks in Dyess might have kept Cash at a respectful distance, but Cash stayed true to his roots. On a Sunday in October 1970, he returned to Rison for a family reunion. At the gathering was Cash's cherished aunt, Mabel Cash McKinney. Cash flew from Nashville to Pine Bluff, where he was met by his cousin Otis Cash from nearby Warren. Cash joined his family in song, including the hymn "The Uncloudy Day." Despite the sunny nature of the tune, Cash cut his visit short because of an approaching storm that threatened his travel plans. "I am proud of my heritage and my people and it is good to be here with you this short time," he said. With Cash that day were his father, his brother Roy, and his sisters Reba and Joanne. Dozens of other family members were there, too, including those from the McKinney, Overton, Wolley, and Miles families.[24]

By 1971, Cash's career was in its zenith, and amid his enormous success, he chose to look backward rather than forward. For a man obsessed with history and comfortable with reflecting on his past glories and mistakes, this made sense. Musically, however, it would create problems. Cash was a man who loved to cross genre boundaries, but in a decade that unleashed onto the world flashy rock operas, ARP synthesizers, and Spiders from Mars, the Man in Black could offer little in the way of musical innovation. Country was about lyrics and melody rooted in the American soundscape, not the dark side of the moon. The appearance of Christopher Wren's biography of him in 1971, as he was reckoning with his past, was therefore well timed.

Further evidence of Cash's willingness to look behind him came on February 28, when he appeared on the popular and thoughtful TV show *This Is Your Life*. The episode featured a parade of folks familiar to the Cash story, and Cash looked emotional—on the verge of tears at times. Shot at the Grand Ole Opry, the program included Cash's Dyess schoolteacher, Mrs. Ruby Cooley; Reid Cummins, a member of Cash's Air Force band, the Landsberg Barbarians; Marshall Grant; Stu Carnall; Ventura, California, pastor Floyd Grissom; Georgia sheriff Ralph Jones; and Dr. Nat Winston. Glen Sherley appeared via a filmed segment (he was still in prison), as did Cash's four daughters. At the end, the usual suspects from the Johnny Cash Show charged the stage, including June Carter, Mother Maybelle, and his parents. In a telling moment, Cash gave his mother a big hug, while he offered his father Ray only the slightest of handshakes. It was well that Cash was looking back on his life. He had, after all, reached the ripe old age of thirty-nine.

Sober, immensely popular, and a father again, Cash also rededicated himself in another important way: his religious faith. It happened on May 9, 1971. Cash did not have his spiritual rebirth at a Baptist or Methodist church, the churches of his youth. Instead, it happened at a Pentecostal church outside Nashville run by Pastor Jimmie Rodgers Snow, Hank Snow's son. It seemed fitting that Snow's son put Cash on his new spiritual quest. Hank Sr. had helped Cash on his musical journey as a young man in Dyess. Snow's famous father was Canadian, but he died in Madison, a neighborhood in northeastern Nashville. Rev. Jimmie Snow had tried his hand at music. Rather than pursue a music career—and after surviving his own struggles with drugs—he decided to become a preacher.[25]

The New Johnny Cash

As was true of so much of what Cash did, his decision to recommit himself to Christ occurred within a family context. In 1970, Cash's sister Joanne, the second youngest of the Cash siblings, made a profession of faith in the same church before the same preacher, Jimmie Snow. Joanne had had personal troubles similar to her brother Johnny. According to author Russell Chandler, she had "accidentally" and almost fatally overdosed on drugs twice in her life.[26] In October 1970, she flew home for a family reunion. During the horrendous flight through bad weather, she thought she would die. She decided to become more religious, describing a conversion experience in a way that her brother Johnny could have understood. "I literally felt the drugs, sins, depression, and so much feeling of the past lift off me," she told Chandler, a Christian writer. "It was as if it came from my toes and gradually came upward. It was like black uncovering white. It was like 10,000 light bulbs just beginning to flash on. I felt clean and assured. There was not a doubt in my mind that I was saved. It was like for all the Christmases of my life I had never gotten a single present and now I was getting them all at once. It was beautiful!"[27]

Joanne had come a long away from the irresponsible seventeen-year-old who had left for Germany to marry a soldier. While overseas, she developed a fondness for pills that made her feel "terrific."[28] In *Man in Black*, Johnny described such feelings as "A Demon Called Deception."[29] By 1969, Joanne was working at a rental car place in the Houston airport when Johnny asked her to come work for him in Tennessee. She did, and she soon began a new life.[30]

Cash's public expression of a spiritual rebirth might have occurred in 1971, but the roots of his closer embrace of the Gospels had been building for some time. Cash's concerts for Rockefeller and prisoners, his marriage to June and commitment to sobriety—even his Nickajack Cave story—were all part of his personal rebirth and efforts at redemption. His interest in Nickajack Cave was also an outgrowth of his obsession with a sense of place. Despite his thousands of hours on the road, Cash liked to immerse himself in the landscape and history of wherever he was living. His years in Memphis drew heavily on the Delta. Once in California, he wandered the desert near his ranch, wrote songs about cowboys and the West, and became an advocate for Native Americans, whose culture and people were more palpable west of the Mississippi River than east of it. Now, in Tennessee, Cash apparently was so fascinated by the place that he would—according to him anyway—think nothing of exploring deep into the bowels of Nickajack Cave.

Cash's fascination with the cave—whether or not he intended to kill himself inside—revealed how a place can be as suffocating as it is liberating. Cash first discovered this in Arkansas. Dyess was created as a land of opportunity, but one with serious limitations that made a nearby city such as Memphis attractive and exciting. As a young man in a poor, rural state, Cash knew there were few opportunities for a talented young man. But through the radio and singing songs, he found liberation through music. The Air Force freed him from the cotton fields. But Cash again encountered limitations in the rigid routines and mind-numbing repetition of his decoding work. Neither his brilliant years in Memphis nor his sojourn to California satisfied him. In running from place to place, Cash was running from himself, his family, his responsibilities, and his god.

By the 1970s, his wandering seemed to have come to an end. Cash still was a road warrior, but he looked like a man at peace with himself.

Recommitting himself to the Lord in Nashville was fitting for Cash. According to chronicler Paul Conn, Cash went from being "an apparently-irreligious man to one who is, by any yardstick, deeply and permanently committed to personal discipleship with Jesus Christ."[31] Anyone who had thought of Cash as "irreligious," however, hadn't paid much attention to his career or his gospel music.

In any case, Cash had a tighter grasp on his faith, and he was not alone. Granted, he had intense personal reasons for his newfound Christianity, but he was also one of millions of Americans who were swept up in what historians have called the Fourth Great Awakening. By the end of the decade, an artist as seemingly secular as Bob Dylan had had a spiritual awakening, whereby the Jewish Dylan became a Christian. Americans were searching for meaning in old and new myths. In 1977, *Star Wars* broke box office records. With its return to a classic battle between and good and evil and discussion of the mystical, all-encompassing Force, the Me Generation had found even science fiction could be spiritual and uplifting.

Americans are a religious people (though not always moral), and Christianity has played a central role in the nation's development. Many of the most well-known events in the country's religious history have resulted from change and uncertainty—whether the political tumult in New England several years before the Salem Witch Trials, the market revolution that spurred the Second Great Awakening of the 1820s, or the military defeats that led to revivals in the Confederate army during the Civil War. Crisis has often led Americans to a closer embrace of God and Jesus Christ. Cash himself was lucky to have survived the 1960s. His drug abuse fueled self-destructive behavior that could have killed him any number of times. Cash could've been just another tragic musician—another Hank Williams. But through determination and the support of friends and family, he emerged victorious at the end of the 1960s to become the biggest country star in the nation, with hit records, armfuls of awards, and a successful television show.

Cash's re-embrace of Christ was an important step for him personally, though many Cash fans have little interest in the singer's spiritual music. For them, it is the least memorable part of his career. The cynical Nick Tosches, whose 1977 book *Country* says nothing good about Cash, wrote, "There are several offensively pious men in country music. Johnny Cash and his God are a particularly tedious act. The strongest drink Cash serves at his parties is non-alcoholic fruit punch."[32] Tosches finds more amusing the psychotic hijinks of hillbilly brute Jerry Lee Lewis. Perhaps Tosches had picked up on Cash's tendency to overcompensate—a tendency that goes against Cash's usual "authenticity." But if Tosches suggests that Cash had suddenly become pious, he was wrong. Cash was raised in Arkansas communities that were deeply religious, and he had recorded many spiritual songs throughout his career. Tosches was not wrong, however, in suggesting that what the public most wanted from Cash was secular music along the lines of "Folsom Prison Blues" and "I Walk the Line." Perhaps Tosches also saw something disingenuous about Cash's newfound religiosity—perhaps it was something more based in guilt than "seeing the light." What is certain is that the change wasn't permanent. Cash would relapse in the late seventies, not long after Tosches wrote *Country*. The twenty-something Tosches, furthermore, was writing in 1977, when the Sex Pistols rented a boat on the Thames during Queen Elizabeth II's silver jubilee so they could sing about how Her Majesty was subhuman. To a young music writer desperate for street cred, Cash might have seemed as cutting edge as Fat Elvis.

No doubt Cash's secular music sold far better than his religious albums. Such was true of the Sun years, his live prison albums, and the period when he recorded with Rick Rubin. None of Cash's later American Recordings albums were religious in nature, though they contained spiritual songs. Cash's religious records are not as highly regarded as his Sun singles, *Bitter Tears*, or the prison albums, but they were no less important to Cash himself—more so, in fact. According to Rodney Clapp, Cash pledged early in his career to "tithe" one in every ten songs to religious subjects, though Clapp has estimated the number was close to one in four.[33] The Folsom and San Quentin live sets might have rocketed Cash to superstardom and wealth, but they were entertainments—cut in a day—not albums that would cleanse his spirit or make him contemplate his personal salvation.

Cash's "coming to Jesus" happened in the same year as the publication of his first serious biography, Christopher Wren's *Winners Got Scars Too*. Though it was not the first biography of Cash, Wren's was the best researched and written to date, and it contained the most firsthand testimony of any book yet written about the Man in Black. *Winners* was published to capitalize on Cash's enormous success at the time, but it was still a solid account of Cash's upbringing and music career that gave plenty of space to Cash's family too.

Christopher Wren had an interesting life and career before he met Cash. Born in California in 1936, he was the son of Sam Wren, a movie executive, and Virginia Sale, who acted in more than a hundred movies. He attended Dartmouth as an undergraduate and then went to Columbia for his master's degree. As was true of Cash and so many of his generation, Wren joined the military, rising to the rank of lieutenant. After leaving the military he pursued journalism, a path that took him to Greece, Vietnam, China, and the Soviet Union. His writing career eventually landed him a job at the *New York Times,* where he became a gifted reporter. In 1969, Wren penned an article, "The Restless Ballad of Johnny Cash," for *Look*, featuring pictures of Johnny and June at Cash's vacant house in Dyess.

Thus began a relationship Wren had with Cash for several years. Wren had access to Cash and they became close. June conceived John Carter Cash in 1969. Wren's wife was pregnant at the same time. While on the road together, Wren's wife and June would sometimes pull the car over so they could both throw up.[34]

Cash deserved his newfound success, but his rise to superstardom in the early seventies coincided with an explosion in country music that continued throughout the decade. Everything from the network variety show *Hee Haw* (which ran from 1969–1971 on CBS before beginning a long life in syndication) to the 1980 films *Urban Cowboy* and *Coal Miner's Daughter* brought country music to a popular audience. On the rise, too, were Outlaw artists Willie Nelson, Waylon Jennings, and Kris Kristofferson. By the end of the 1970s, some stars, such as Dolly Parton, showed they could cross over from music to TV and movies.

Cash was not alone among the living legends of country. Country music had matured in the fifties and sixties "from back porches scattered through the South to a $100-million-a-year industry," Little Rock writer Rod Lorenzen observed in September 1970. While Cash was the industry's biggest country star, he still avoided easy categorization. "All attempts to label Cash have failed," Lorenzen wrote. "He seems to defy everything, except his profound belief in God." In 1971, Cash's days of self-destructive behavior and wild road life seemed behind him.[35]

A few weeks after Lorenzen's article appeared, Cash played again in his home state, this time in Little Rock for the Arkansas State Fair. Cash was at Barton Coliseum for an afternoon show. As usual, June and the Carter Family, the Statler Brothers, and Carl Perkins were also there. Other acts at the fair included Roy Clark and the "Hee Haw Gang," Hank Williams Jr., and Doug McClure, a California-born actor best known for his cowboy role on the television show *The Virginian*. Bill Lewis of the *Arkansas Gazette* covered Cash's show, and it was no fluff piece. Lewis noted Cash "looks not unlike the convict whose plight he champions. He carries a tune like he may drop it any minute. And his diction hasn't passed the marbles-in-the-mouth stage." The house was not full on that October afternoon, but Cash gave them a good show running more than two hours. The audience, Lewis said, "embraced him for what he is—one of them." Cash had no problem connecting with the crowd. Lewis reminded his readers that Cash was an "Arkansas country boy," but the singer had not changed his act in many years. The songs might have changed some—the more recent "A Boy Named Sue" was now a staple of the live set—but his sound still depended on the Tennessee Three. Lewis described the band's sound much as if Cash were a rock or punk act, playing "to a driving, rubbery, thump-thumpy beat," making the band capable of "fearsome volumes."[36] After the show, Cash, accompanied by a guard of state troopers, signed autographs.

Cash was at the height of his fame, but his hometown was not doing well. Dyess had been slipping for decades. By the early 1970s, the town's population had fallen to a scant 412 people. Ron Russell of the *Gazette* said that besides Cash's house, little was left from the depression era. The town, nevertheless, had tourists who were curious to know where Cash had grown up. Jimmy Allen, principal of the Dyess grade school, told Russell that he had recently met tourists from Pennsylvania. Lynn Cox, the school superintendent and Cash's childhood friend, provided the usual stories of the two getting into trouble as well as an account of Ray Cash catching Cox stealing watermelons from the Cash melon patch. Russell also spoke with Vera Pickens. Her son-in-law was Roy Cash, who had married Vera's daughter, Claire. According to Vera, Cash's 1968 concert in Dyess had meant more to him than any he had done before. Russell's article featured a photograph of a Dyess resident pointing to the Cash house. The caption noted—incorrectly, but perhaps optimistically—that the house was being renovated by the current owner. The house looked better than it had in 1968, when Cash visited it for the pictures that ran with Wren's 1969 *Look* article.[37] But nothing like a true renovation of the house would occur for decades.

The *Gazette* claimed that Cash still slipped into Dyess once a year "unannounced" to talk with residents. One should probably not take such a claim literally. While Cash enjoyed visiting his home state, his immediate family had long since left Dyess. Anyone else with ambition had, too. Dyess, as was true of so many small towns of the 1970s, was a symbol of what became known in the Jimmy Carter years as the "national malaise."[38] The 1970s might have been the decade of porn chic, bouncing disco, and piles of cocaine, but for salt-of-the-earth residents in places such as Dyess, there was little fun to be had, let alone rampant hedonism. Since World War II, Arkansas had seen declines in both the family farm and plantation agriculture. Cotton farmers did not need small armies of pickers anymore. By 1972, the Arkansas cotton crop was 100 percent machine harvested.[39] Dyess was part of a national trend in which small, formerly thriving places—old cotton communities in the South and small factory towns in the North—were becoming economic dead zones and cultural wastelands. As the Cold War and Vietnam War ground on, Americans found themselves battling high gas prices (from the Middle East oil embargo) and stagflation (inflation without accompanying economic growth).

Towns such as Dyess might have been withering, but the Sun Belt was growing in size, wealth, and political influence. From 1964 to 2004, every elected US president was from the South or California. In the 1950s, Atlanta's population increased by half, while in the 1960s, Las Vegas nearly doubled in size. In March 1972, Cash played Vegas for the first time in nearly ten years. "Sin City" has become shorthand for American excess. It has also become a metaphor for the declining fortunes of once great musical acts, such as Elvis. Cash was no stranger to sin and excess, but his Vegas show underscored his aversion to artifice. Unlike other performers, he avoided making the show a bloated production. He chose not to have a comedian open for him and declined using an orchestra. Cash instead offered his usual show—just him, the Tennessee Three, June, Carl Perkins, and the Statler Brothers. Cash clearly was determined not to be the next Elvis.[40]

Johnny Cash understood the plight of the common man. He still spoke out on behalf of prisoners, and throughout the decade his music had a blue collar quality that fitted the times. As noted, this concern led him to travel to Washington in July 1972 to testify before the Senate Judiciary Committee concerning prison reform. More specifically, he was there to discuss how the system abused young men. During the same trip, he spoke with the President Nixon about the prisons.

Cash had performed at the White House at Nixon's invitation in April 1970. Even so, the ever-paranoid Nixon saw Cash as a threat. Cash made the Nixon administration nervous amid the 1970 US Senate campaign in Tennessee. During the race, country star Tex Ritter briefly ran against the more conservative establishment candidate, Bill Brock. Murray Chotiner—a close associate of Nixon—wanted to make sure the administration "neutralized" any support Cash might have had for Ritter, who had named Cash a statewide finance chairman (an honorary post and one funny to anyone who knew Cash's business history). The larger point was that Ritter allowed Cash to take part in a campaign where Cash's name could lend him credibility and garner support from average people.[41]

Cash had no idea that Nixon thought him a threat. And he likely had no idea of the depths of Nixon's duplicity and paranoia. In the time before the Watergate scandal, despite the usual doubters and critics, Americans were not yet cynical about the presidency. The country had no shortage of people who opposed the administration, but as the decade progressed, Americans became less partisan and radical.[42]

Despite the fact that Nixon had failed to end the Vietnam War, in 1972—a reelection year—Cash still supported the president. With Cash at his 1972 meeting with Nixon was Senator William Brock of Tennessee. Nixon, trying to find common ground, told Cash that he had toured San Quentin prison in 1948 during his senatorial campaign. The president had been impressed with how young the men were. Nixon believed such men "can be saved." Cash agreed, and he gave views on prisons that were consistent with those he had offered during the height of the Arkansas prison scandals. Cash said that a prisoner needs to know that "somebody cares for him." Cash's intentions were to see an overall reduction in crime. The fact is, most men who go to prison are released someday, and Cash, like the ill-fated warden Tom Murton, wanted to combat recidivism. "The prisoner has to be treated like a human being. If he isn't when he gets out, he won't act like one," Cash was quoted as saying during his meeting with Nixon. Cash brought two former prisoners to the White House that day: Glen Sherley, who had been free for nearly a year and a half, and Harlan Sanders, who had been out for only a week. Sanders had been imprisoned in California for murder and robbery. Sherley and Sanders talked about the brutality of prison life, where men depended on drugs, violence, and homosexuality in order to survive. Sanders noted that one time, "I had to break a guitar over one guy's head." Cash himself couldn't have brought together the two worlds of music and convict life any better.[43]

But in hindsight, Cash's commitment to prison reform was on the wane. He issued his last official prison album in October 1973, documenting his 1972 concert at Österåker prison in Sweden. By the mid-1970s, Cash was losing interest in playing for and advocating for prisoners. For the rest of the decade, his religious beliefs were his central focus.

The "New Johnny Cash" of the 1970s took on various forms, but his music hadn't fundamentally changed. Cash was one of the lions of country music, and he had always had solid credentials as a rock and roll artist. Rock critics and journalists appreciated how Cash had bridged the rock and country communities in the 1950s—the golden age of "pure" rock and roll. By the 1970s, artists such as Waylon Jennings, Willie Nelson, and Kris Kristofferson were carrying on what Cash had done.

In 1973, *Rolling Stone* recognized Cash's importance as a rock star by publishing its first interview with him. The man who talked with Cash was Robert Hilburn, who forty years later would publish a stellar biography of Cash. Back then he was music editor at the *Los Angeles Times*. His history with Cash went back further than the *Rolling Stone* article, though. When he was twenty-eight, Hilburn had been the only music writer at the seminal 1968 Folsom concert. That performance revived Cash's career, but at the time, he was the kind of singer the bigger press outlets avoided because of his lackluster sales and general unreliability.

Hilburn had made a name for himself in Los Angeles, but he was a southerner by birth. As was true of Cash, he was a country boy, born in Natchitoches (pronounced "nack-a-dish") in northern Louisiana. He spent much of his youth on his grandfather's cotton farm in nearby Campti. The family later moved to Dallas, but Hilburn's early days "in the fields" were a good primer for a lifelong obsession with Cash's life and music. To live in Campti likely rendered Dyess much more understandable. "That's cotton country," Cash told Hilburn when he heard Hilburn was from north Louisiana.[44]

Cash did not see his recovery from drugs as separate from his spiritual betterment. As he told Hilburn, "The growth of love in my life and the spiritual strengthening came at about the same time. Religion's got a lot to do with it." Cash had been raised in a religious household in the Bible Belt, but his family was willing to attend both Methodist and Baptist churches. Cash always thought of himself as a sinner, and the drugs had only deepened this feeling. In the early and mid-1970s, though, it seemed that freedom from pills and drink and a closer embrace of Christianity gave him some relief. "Religion, love, it's all one and the same as far as I'm concerned, because that's what religion means to me. It's love."[45] Cash knew he could not have carried on without the love of others. It was that love that got him through the worst of his drug addiction. With June and a son, his life seemed complete, or at least more full of love. Cash felt his newfound spiritual strength made him a better performer onstage, too.

Hilburn's interview began with Cash's upbringing in Dyess. Cash described working in the fields as "drudgery," noting that "I don't know how much good it ever did me." It was clear that by 1973, Cash's days chopping cotton were long behind him. His life in Dyess, nevertheless, instilled in him a strong work ethic. Cash might have had no love for the cotton fields, but his musical career was as exhausting in its own way. "I don't think a man can be happy unless he's working," Cash said. Never one free of insecurity, Cash said he lost sleep some nights worrying about how good his songs were and whether he was progressing as an artist. His people kept him honest, too. Hilburn asked what the reaction was when he returned to Arkansas. "I was still the country boy to those people," Cash said. Despite his success, fellow Arkansans would say, "Boy, I remember when you used to bring me buttermilk every other Thursday." Regardless of how many records he was selling, Cash maintained an active touring schedule—he had to keep the people to whom he used to bring buttermilk happy.[46]

Toward the end of the *Rolling Stone* interview, Cash again turned to religion. Hilburn asked about Cash's 1969 *Holy Land* album. Inspired by Cash's second Israel trip and recorded in 1968, *Holy Land* was one of Cash's better-known religious records, though not necessarily a fan or critical favorite. The album nevertheless was part of Cash's personal and career turnaround, whereby he could satisfy those who wanted Johnny the outlaw and Johnny the spiritual seeker. Now, in 1973, Cash discussed with Hilburn his most ambitious spiritual turn: *The Gospel Road*, a double album containing music and narration of the life of Jesus that served as the soundtrack to a full-length movie of the same name.

For those who like to see Cash as one of the progenitors of rock and roll or even punk, his religious output seems a by-product of an otherwise tortured and darkly poetic artist. But Cash's religious music came from the same place as his secular songs. Neither critics nor fans put Cash's religious albums on par with his prison albums, Sun singles, or concept albums. But listeners should take them seriously, for Cash put more effort into several religious projects than he did for any other artistic endeavor.

The Gospel Road was Cash's spiritual magnum opus. He financed the project—shot on location in the Holy Land— himself. He cast himself, friends, family, and unknown actors in the film. His sister Reba played Mary, the mother of Jesus. June, in the film's largest speaking part, played Mary Magdalene, a woman, Cash said in the film as he walked alongside water, who was the "subject of more speculation and controversy than any woman I've ever heard of." The film did not portray her as a prostitute or otherwise "fallen" woman.

Bob Elfstrom directed the picture and played a blonde-haired, blue-eyed Christ. His son, Robert Jr., played young Jesus. Cash had previously worked with Elfstrom on the 1969 documentary *Johnny Cash! The Man, His World, His Music*, where Elfstrom followed Cash to various locations, including Dyess. That film contained no narration, but for *The Gospel Road*, Cash himself narrated the life of Jesus. The movie, not surprisingly, was loaded with music.

For Cash, the film was true to his understanding of the Bible and his personal faith. Christians who saw it agreed. And while not a financial windfall for Cash, it was an artistic success in the sense that Cash conceived, executed, and promoted a work that articulated his religious vision. As Cash noted in a radio spot for the movie, it was "something worthwhile" and a "very personal film." *The Gospel Road* was an orthodox take on Christianity, but its earnestness was not likely to put off nonbelievers. In any event, Cash would never again undertake so ambitious a religious project.

The Gospel Road was released on March 31, 1973. A few months before the film came out, George Vecsey of the *New York Times* wrote an article about Cash and the movie. Vecsey noted how Cash's physical appearance had improved, saying he looked ten years younger than he had at the nadir of his drug abuse. Cash was forty-one now, but Vecsey said he "bounces like an athlete when he walks." The article put the best light on Cash's life and his relationship with June. Cash joked that he was able to make *The Gospel Road* with the help of "a lot of faith and a lot of June's money"—$500,000, according to Vecsey.

As was so often the case whenever Cash talked, the conversation drifted back to his life in Arkansas. Vecsey noted Cash made a public profession of faith when he was fourteen and living in Dyess. Despite the fact that he grew up in the Bible Belt, Cash felt his new film had resonance in New York as much as anywhere. *The Gospel Road* showed Jesus crucified in the desert, but the sequence segued to where Jesus was dying in the same way in New York, Las Vegas, and Hollywood. "Christ is real to me everywhere," Cash noted, and he added that he was not looking to make any money on the film. Instead, it was an expression of his faith.[47]

The Gospel Road never enjoyed a wide release. It didn't have a New York premiere until nine months into its run. In contrast to today's brief-run cinema, in the 1970s a film's future did not depend on its opening weekend; it could build an audience. Vecsey noted that the film was slowly making its way north and east after "moderate success in the Fundamentalist South." Hal Sherman, a promoter for the film's distributor, 20th Century Fox, said that the movie had more appeal for southerners, who tended to embrace the Bible and fundamentalism more closely than Americans elsewhere. Sherman was honest about the commercial challenges the movie faced: filmgoers wanted entertainment more than they wanted a lesson in the New Testament.[48]

To accompany his film, Cash released his double album *The Gospel Road* in April 1973. The album included songs not only from Johnny but also Kris Kristofferson ("Burden of Freedom"), Larry Gatlin ("Last Supper"), John Denver ("Follow Me"), Joe South, and Christopher Wren. Wren wrote the title song and "Jesus Was a Carpenter." Back in Arkansas in February 1974, the *Osceola Times* reported that the movie was playing for three days at the Murr Theatre (which closed three years later, another casualty in the increasing decline of small-town theaters).[49]

In *The Gospel Road*, Cash had made a film on a limited budget that could appeal to his more spiritual fans without pandering to them. Despite little fanfare, the film found an audience in Arkansas and beyond. But

Hal Sherman was correct: few movies at the time were taking on religious themes as overtly as *The Gospel Road*. Religious stories had been at the core of *Ben-Hur*, *The Robe*, and *The Ten Commandments*. Even so, these movies were relics of Old Hollywood, which relied on gaudy spectacle, historical inspiration, and melodrama. Religious or not, those kinds of movies were no longer being made.

Cash was no auteur or even a filmmaker, but *The Gospel Road* was worthy of the era's innovative directors, done in the spirit of John Cassavetes or the French New Wave. The 1970s is known for smaller budgets and grittier, realist films—more than at any other time in Hollywood history. It was a period when young actors and directors were seeing their vision through, regardless of their inspiration and source material. *The Gospel Road* was made six years before Monty Python's absurdist religious satire, *The Life of Brian*. The two films were opposites in terms of their tone, intention, theology, and willingness to offend. But they were both made in a decade of low-budget movies (Python's being funded by George Harrison's Handmade Films) that were not afraid to take on tricky subject matter, film on location, and use nontraditional actors. Cash's and Python's small, non-mainstream films were not the kind being made a decade later, let alone in the twenty-first century.

The Gospel Road soundtrack hoped to show Cash in a more spiritual light than ever. But two other albums he released in 1973 continued his habit of not letting his religious songs surpass his secular material. In January, Cash released *Any Old Wind That Blows*, featuring a windswept Cash on the cover. As with much of Cash's 1970s output, it was a mixed bag. One of the best songs was "Oney," written by native Kentuckian Jerry Chesnut about a factory worker who, on his last day on the job, takes revenge against his boss. Given Cash's working-class roots, the tune was a good fit for him, recorded with his trademark boom-chicka-boom sound.

Some of Cash's best sides in the 1970s were working-man's songs, and one wonders what he might have done had he recorded a concept album that tackled class issues in a decade known—at least in film—for its worldly realism, from *Blue Collar* and *Taxi Driver* to *Dirty Harry* and *The French Connection*. Cash, however, played "Oney" for laughs, and listeners responded to it well. The song made it to number 2 on the country charts.

Another standout on *Any Old Wind That Blows* was the Cash-penned "Country Trash." The song doesn't mention Arkansas, but it speaks to

Cash's experiences there growing up. Looking back, "Country Trash" serves as a companion piece to the earlier "Country Boy" and "Pickin' Time." As the song goes, "The wind's from the south and the fishing's good / Got a potbelly stove and a cord of wood / Mama turns the leftovers into hash / I'm doin' alright for country trash." Decades later, Cash re-recorded the song with Rick Rubin during the American Recordings sessions, when Cash got back in touch with the soul of his music and Americana.

In August, Cash released the third of his studio albums for 1973, *Johnny Cash and His Woman*, co-credited to June Carter. Again, it was a hit-and-miss collection of religious and secular material. Cash's sister Reba contributed her own composition, "We're for Love," which she cowrote with M. S. Tubb. The album, however, is most notable for Cash's take on "The City of New Orleans," written and recorded by Steve Goodman in 1971. Cash released his cover a year after Arlo Guthrie's better-known hit version; Johnny had been offered the song first but turned it down. Cash's cover is serviceable, but doesn't measure up to Guthrie's version. Perhaps Cash was too late with it. Or too early; Willie Nelson recorded "City of New Orleans" in the mid-eighties and it went to number 1 on the country charts.

Cash was riding high in the 1970s on the energy of being a new father and more devoted Christian. But he was also getting older in a music industry that prized younger acts—if not younger in years, at least in terms of their exposure on the country scene. In short, Cash was losing star power. Being a better dad and Christian might have given him some peace, but it did not make him hip, nor did it move records. His spiritual rebirth and turn inward, nevertheless, was appropriate for one living in the "Me Decade." As Paul Conn put it, Cash was a "moody and introspective" man, "a private person in the best sense of the phrase."[50] For Cash to focus more on himself was typical in a time when people were joining what University of Rochester professor Christopher Lasch called the "Culture of Narcissism." For many Americans, the decade brought a loss of inhibitions that manifested itself in drug use and sexual experimentation. It was also a decade of self-help books, twelve-step programs, psychiatry, health crazes such as jogging and vegetarianism, and the emergence of a politically powerful evangelical movement.

Cash had the money and fame to share his "new" self with the wider world. Unlike 1970s icon Woody Allen, Cash was not one for the therapist's couch. For him, religion was his therapy, but he knew he could not maintain self-improvement alone. Cash's friends, family, and band members were supportive. He also grew closer to Billy Graham, the most famous evangelical preacher of his time.

Graham was born in Charlotte, North Carolina, in 1918. He attended college at the Florida Bible Institute (now Trinity College) in central Florida before studying at Wheaton College, a Christian liberal arts school in suburban Chicago. In 1947, he began his annual Billy Graham Crusades. From 1950–1954 he also hosted a popular radio show, *Hour of Decision*. Graham's learning, media savvy, and ecumenism had wide appeal. Before Graham met Cash, he had worked as a spiritual advisor to presidents Eisenhower and Johnson. He was particularly close to Johnson, a fellow southerner. Graham later became the darling of conservative evangelicals and Republican politicians, but early in his career, he preached the Social Gospel—a religiously progressive take on class and racial issues. As a native of upcountry North Carolina, he was concerned about the shocking levels of poverty that persisted in postwar Appalachia. Even before the *Brown v. Board of Education* decision, Graham was literally tearing down barriers between the races. At one 1953 rally in Chattanooga, Tennessee, Reverend Graham dashed the ropes that separated Black and white rally members. He warned whites in the crowd that hell might await those too proud to take down such dividers. Graham was no civil rights radical, and in the late 1950s, he claimed to avoid "politics," but he was a proponent of Johnson's Great Society measures that sought to alleviate poverty and end legal racism.[51]

The fact that Graham's message went beyond individual churches appealed to Cash. In May 1970, he made his first appearance at one of Graham's Crusades in Knoxville at a stadium that attracted 62,000 worshippers. Graham, as was true of Cash, was willing to use the modern media to attract as many listeners as possible, but what Cash liked most was his message. In the following decades, Cash and June would accompany Graham at more than thirty Crusades.[52]

Cash's devotion to Graham's preaching became clear on his 1971 album, *Man in Black*, where Graham spoke on the first track, "The Preacher Said, 'Jesus Said.'" Of the album, Cash said, "I have never been prouder of an album than I have of this one." That was quite a statement coming from Cash. The album produced two singles, "Man in Black" and "Singin' in Viet Nam Talkin' Blues," both by far the most memorable from the album. "Man in Black" became Cash's signature song.

Black is many things. Black is cool, simple, and mysterious. It's what artists and preachers wear. It is also serious, powerful, and funereal. Cash said he wore black for the "poor and beaten down" and the prisoners, the non-Christians, and druggies who had suffered bad trips, the "sick and lonely old" as well as the "hundred fine young men" dying each week in Vietnam.[53] The song was brilliant in its summation of both Cash's religious beliefs and his vision as an artist. The song was a hit, to the point that Cash has become synonymous with being the Man in Black.

As was true of Billy Graham, Cash had an ecumenical attitude. Cash was raised firmly in the evangelical tradition, but his family contained Baptists and Methodists, and his first wife was Catholic. Cash strayed often from his faith, and by the time his personal life had hit rock bottom in the mid-sixties, he was not one to judge others for their bad behavior. At a theological level, he preferred Baptist and Methodist churches, but he never drew hard lines between denominations. Intolerant of intolerance, he would have rejected the fire-and-brimstone approach of more conservative churches. Cash was a sinner, but he believed in redemption. No stranger to anger or darkness, he nevertheless was a man who preached love rather than hate.

When it came to worshipping, Cash was willing to go to whatever church he liked. His openness to other faiths began in Dyess. His sister Joanne remembered, "We used to hitch a ride to church with our neighbors—sometimes to the Baptist church and sometimes to a little Pentecostal church a little piece away on road #14."[54] Later in life, Cash behaved much the same way, and he felt comfortable enough with the Pentecostal Church to make his public profession of faith with Reverend Snow.

By the mid-1970s, Cash had become the embodiment of American values, from his evangelical faith and patriotism, to his love of the outdoors and embrace of small-town life. The year 1976 was America's bicentennial, and it was a good one for Cash. He continued to build his reputation as a man redeemed. In 1975, he published his first autobiography, also named *Man in Black*, through Zondervan, a Michigan-based publisher of religious books. The book sold over a million copies, and it is essential reading for any serious Johnny Cash fan.[55] The memoir provides an honest account of Cash's life and struggles with drug addiction. Written in a simple and direct style worthy of Cash, it provides a detailed look into his upbringing in Arkansas, including the horrid death of his brother Jack. In the face of Cash's struggles with pills and his frequent brushes with death in the California desert or on his Tennessee farm, the book has an overarching religious theme: Cash's redemption.

It was Cash's first book, and to write it he had the help of Peter E. Gillquist, an author and archpriest in the Antiochian Orthodox Christian Archdiocese of North America who also worked at the University of Memphis and the Thomas Nelson publishing house in Nashville. Gillquist, Cash wrote, "spent many days with me talking about my life, helping me to remember, questioning, advising," and "correcting my 1950 high school grammar along the way." Cash dedicated *Man in Black* not to June or any member of his immediate family, but rather June's father, Ezra "Eck" Carter. A kind man with a Biblical name, Ezra, Cash said, "TAUGHT ME TO LOVE THE WORD."[56] Ezra had died in January 1975. Born in 1898 in Virginia, Ezra was no musician himself, but he had supported his wife Maybelle and the rest of the Carter family as they toured and sang. Ezra had married Maybelle in 1926, a year before the fateful Bristol sessions. Ray Cash, in contrast, was never much of a music fan. Unlike Ray, Ezra, by working as a mailman for the railroad, kept his family middle class. The Carters had their struggles, but they were never poor, and never as desperate as the Cash family had been.

Despite Ezra's Biblical name, and the fact that he and Maybelle were Christians, they were not judgmental. They had given Johnny a place to crash when he was strung out in Nashville. Cash often recovered at their home, and the couple allowed Johnny back even when he was unhinged. Ezra was a likable spendthrift, a good old boy, a man obsessed with gadgets, and an avid fisherman.[57] He was much more like Johnny than Ray was. In essence, Ezra was the father Johnny wished he'd had.

Even so, in *Man in Black*, Cash paid homage to his father Ray. In hindsight, one is struck by Johnny's overwhelmingly positive appraisal of his father as a provider and hard worker. Ray would bear much harsher scrutiny in Cash's second, 1997 autobiography. But in *Man in Black,* Cash accentuated the positive. Forgiveness, after all, is the Christian thing to do. And Ray and his son had a lot to be forgiven for.

The same year *Man in Black* appeared, Cash's life became the subject of the thirty-nine-cent comic book, *Hello, I'm Johnny Cash*. This otherwise obscure comic is worthy of discussion both for featuring the Nickajack Cave story and reflecting how deeply Christian Cash's projects had become. *Hello, I'm Johnny Cash* was one in a series of fifty-nine editions of Spire Christian Comics. House of Cash held the copyright to the book, but the publisher, Fleming R. Revell Company, specialized in Christian books. The comic was a collaboration between well-connected evangelicals.

Cash's name and image were on the cover, but the book was written by Billy Zeoli and illustrated by Al Hartley. Hartley had drawn for Archie comics as well as the risqué *Adventures of Pussycat* comic, featuring a buxom female spy in a perpetual state of undress. But around the same time *Pussycat* appeared, Hartley became a born-again Christian.

Zeoli was no lightweight. He graduated from Graham's alma mater, Wheaton College, in 1955 and became well known for heading Gospel Films (later Gospel Communications). Zeoli took his message to Billy Graham's Crusades (which Cash had attended), worked with professional sports teams and politicians, and was White House chaplain during the Ford administration, composing devotionals for the president. Gerald Ford was an Episcopalian, but Episcopalians have an evangelical history, and Zeoli had become friends with Ford when he was serving as a congressman from Michigan. The fact that Zeoli would have his name on a Johnny Cash book made sense in the mid-seventies: it was the coming together of men deeply invested in the arts, politics, and evangelical Christianity.

One man who wasn't buying Cash's spiritual deepening was Saul Holiff, who had quit as Cash's manager in the fall of 1973. Months later, Cash tried to smooth things over between them. Cash believed they had enjoyed a "fine relationship." He thanked Saul for the "good reading habits which I have developed" and had given him "a lot of growth mentally and spiritually."[58] Cash invited Saul to visit him at his Cinnamon Hill plantation house in Jamaica. A month later, writing from Jamaica, he told Saul about his "spiritual autobiography" *Man in Black*. Cash told Saul he still considered him a "friend and advisor" and a "wise man." But Cash couldn't stop there. Despite Saul being ethnically Jewish and religiously an atheist, Cash asked him if he thought Jesus was the Messiah and did Saul "believe in His Divinity?"[59]

Saul was in no mood to play nice. He had quit Cash's employ on bad terms, and he had no patience for Johnny's born-again, holier-than-thou attitude. What irked Saul were problems stemming from Cash's recent endorsement deal with American Oil. "Only a handful of people know what you are really like, and I am one of them!!" Saul wrote in a blistering December 1974 letter to Cash. Saul thought Cash's dealings with him were "unethical, decidedly not honorable, and, depending on various interpretations, un-Christian." For Saul, Cash's actions clearly did not line up to his public image. Saul brought up some of the more upsetting and complicated problems of the past, from Cash's frequent missed dates to his run-ins with white supremacists (though the latter were hardly Johnny and Vivian's fault). Despite what he saw as Cash's "Brobdingnagian ego" he said, "I don't envy you; I feel sorry for you. Nature, God, or whatever forces control our destinies will surely deal with you, and those who have influenced you, in an appropriate manner." He closed his letter to Cash with another cutting remark. "You're just like all the rest of them," he said. "I haven't changed my mind."[60]

Despite Saul Holiff's hex, *Man in Black* was a bestseller, and Cash's career was again ascendant. In the fall of 1975, Cash gave a candid interview with Larry Linderman of *Penthouse*. Given that the interview was done at the height of Cash's born-again period, it might seem odd that he would talk with someone working for a pornographic magazine (even one tame by today's internet standards). And yet Cash was never one to turn away a reporter, especially an earnest one. Cash knew he had all kinds of fans, whether their favorite reading material was *Penthouse* or the Bible. "I'm a country boy and I'm a country singer," Cash noted at the interview's outset.[61] Nevertheless, Linderman credited Cash with bringing country music to both a younger and more urban audience than ever.

Cash gave the interview from a hotel room in Las Vegas, where he was playing a string of lucrative dates. Cash didn't like Vegas much, but it was part of a musician's life to play shows everywhere, especially ones that paid well. Cash was customarily honest with Linderman. The interview touched upon the usual subjects, such as Cash's efforts at prison reform. Cash gave an update about some changes taking place in Tennessee, such as creating work release programs and building new facilities to help with overcrowding. He also advocated for looser marijuana laws. Cash seemed less interested in talking about prisoners than he did the power of his religious beliefs. "The spiritual strength I have is real," he said. But Cash made it clear that religion was not a new part of his music, noting that "they're the songs my mother sang to me."[62] What had changed was Cash's enthusiasm for the religious songs he knew so well and loved to sing on stage with June.

The "new" Johnny Cash also took the opportunity in his *Penthouse* interview to correct certain myths. Cash laid to rest the idea that he had Native American ancestry, saying "the higher I got, the more Indian blood I thought I had in me." Cash was even less patient with his glib take on the Vietnam War. Looking back, he thought "dove with claws" was a "stupid line." While he might have had regrets, Cash sought to bring together various views of the world. His ongoing concerts for prisoners, he said, were really an extension of the Christian idea of giving. He might have cringed when thinking of the "dove with claws" claim, but he remained a patriotic person. His patriotism, he told Linderman, came from his father; Ray had given him "a sense of history and a strong love for my country."[63]

Cash was a self-professed Christian and patriot, but when it came to his music, the hits came from a different place. In the spring of 1976, he released "One Piece at a Time," written by Wayne Kemp. Born in 1940, Kemp was an Arkansan native of Greenwood in the western part of the state. "One Piece at a Time" was Cash's first number 1 country hit in a long time, and his last. It was a novelty song about a man who travels to Michigan to work on an auto assembly line, much as Cash did briefly in 1950. The man decides to steal car parts over a span of years until he can build his own automobile. The punch line is that when he finally assembles the vehicle, it is a Frankenstein's monster of odd parts from various production years. In one of the instances of life imitating art, a man named Bruce Fitzpatrick—at the behest of record promoters—built a car made from various pieces of Cadillacs. In April 1976, Cash had his picture taken driving the car, with Fitzpatrick looking on, smiling. The car still lives in Tennessee.

"One Piece at a Time" is a catchy and clever song, and America certainly needed a laugh in the wake of the Watergate scandals and its defeat in Vietnam. Much of the song's success had to do with Cash being faithful to his roots. In a way, it is yet another song about a criminal, though it has none of the darkness of his early records. The tune opens with a classic rock and roll guitar riff and is set to the familiar boom-chicka-boom sound courtesy of the dependable Wootton-Holland-Grant combo, with some tinkling piano thrown in. Cash also provides vocal calisthenics at the end, rattling off the years of manufacture ("It's a 49, 50, 51, 52, 53, 54, 55, 56, 57, 58, 59 automobile") faster than any take since "The Rock Island Line."

The song also tapped into what was popular at the time: the CB (citizens band) radio craze. At the end of the song, Cash's narrator talks on a CB, saying he's in a "psychobilly" Cadillac, a phrase that served as the inspiration for psychobilly: a subgenre that mixed rockabilly and punk. Despite all his past musings about trains, in 1976 Cash had his first hit song about a car. It was a good time for drivers seeking some levity: Americans love and depend on their cars, and they were recovering from a painful mid-seventies oil embargo. Despite the recent shortages, no one knew about America's "Wide Open Road" better than Cash, and he released "One Piece at a Time" when road pictures were becoming increasingly popular, from Steven Spielberg's *Sugarland Express* to *Smokey and the Bandit*, the latter of which was a vehicle not just for Burt Reynolds but also raucous good ole boy and master guitar player and singer Jerry Reed.

Anniversaries are a good time to start over, and the year 1976 was one of celebration of the country as well as rebirth. Despite its power and money, the United States still had much of the underdog about it. It was, after all, a year that saw the soft-spoken peanut farmer and evangelical Jimmy Carter elected president and the release of the bittersweet, low-budget boxing movie *Rocky* (which would win Best Picture the next year). It was fitting then, that Johnny Cash—a man who knew about failure and struggles for redemption—served as an unofficial ambassador for the United States bicentennial. Cash was a patriot who knew how to connect with common folks. As was true of his country, he had not always avoided disaster despite money, power, and good fortune. He was one of America's biggest stars, but he was a man who relished comebacks—a man who was both an underdog and their champion.

The 1976 Cleveland County Concert

Cash had come from nothing. He was born in a shack in 1932 in rural Arkansas. He traveled the world and back, but it took him forty-four years to play his first concert in his birthplace. By then, Cash was synonymous with being the Man in Black, who used his dark dress as a protest against the wrongs being done to Americans of every stripe. When he arrived in Cleveland County in 1976, his outfit had changed a bit. For the bicentennial, he wore a black suit emblazoned with eagles. Cash never identified with any political party, but he had the credentials of a Cold War–era patriot. He was a veteran of the Air Force and an outspoken supporter of the troops in Vietnam. His 1974 song "Ragged Old Flag" lamented America's sorry state. Cash was no ideologue, but people, especially in Arkansas, appreciated his patriotism and relatability. He was popular with blue collar workers and country folk. Arkansans always saw Cash as one of them.

But in recent years, Cash had not done many shows in Arkansas. In 1973, he played at the Robinson Center in Little Rock and in Jonesboro—not far from Dyess—for a Fourth of July concert. In June 1975, he performed at Barton Coliseum. But in 1976, the concert he played on March 20 in Rison had special meaning for him—not solely because of the personal thrill but because of how the event honored his family.

The Johnny Cash Show had long been a family affair. June and the Carter Sisters and Mother Maybelle had played with Cash for over a decade, and in May 1974 in Las Vegas, Cash's guitarist and fellow Arkansan, Bob Wootton, married Anita Carter, June's sister, who was blessed with a singing voice as striking as her looks. Cash and Anita had been carrying on an affair around the time of June's pregnancy with John Carter. The affair had been rumored for years and discussed in the pages of *National Enquirer*, but it wasn't until Robert Hilburn's Cash biography was published that it became widely known.[64] The affair, however, has done little to hurt Cash's reputation among fans. Regardless of how much was known about the affair in the mid-seventies, news of it was kept in the family.

Despite the backstage drama, Cash tried to maintain the façade of the ideal Christian and ideal father. By 1976, Cash had his son John Carter with him everywhere. Cash's parents, who lived in the same Hendersonville neighborhood as Johnny and June, also were frequent concert attendees. The ever-unsmiling Ray Cash had been at Cash's Folsom prison show. And he would feature prominently in the Cleveland County festivities in 1976.

Cash's birthplace was ready for him. The *Cleveland County Herald* noted, "The Johnny Cash phenomenon is the biggest thing that has happened to country music since its recorded beginnings a half century ago."[65] Everyone close to him and close to his birthplace wanted to be there for the show. Paul McKinney, one of Cash's cousins from Irving, Texas, traveled to Cleveland County for the concert, as did relatives from

Florida, Oregon, and Rhode Island. Cash became the centerpiece of a celebration that spanned the entire weekend. The *Herald* not only covered Cash's visit, it also had copies of *Man in Black* in its office waiting for sale. According to the *Arkansas Gazette*, the county's young sheriff, Joe Paul King, was "biting his nails and working overtime" in anticipation of Cash's arrival. Residents were getting everything ready for what promised to be the "wildest celebration in the county's history." Cleveland County was expecting between ten and twenty thousand visitors and Cash fans. Harvey Hewitt from Pine Bluff was going to sell hot dogs, hamburgers, popcorn, and soda at the event. "I've been all over the state the past few weeks and the Johnny Cash show is all the people want to talk about," Hewitt said. Sheriff King was worried he wouldn't have enough men on hand, so he called in help from the nearby Jefferson County Rescue and Mounted Patrol, the National Guard, and the state police. King was also worried about public drinking; at the county's centennial celebration back in April 1973, alcohol use had been a problem. King expected worse at the bicentennial event on Saturday, even though Cleveland County technically was a dry county.[66]

Cash's concert was the result of five years of hard work by the Cleveland County Historical Society. Now that the historians and preservationists had gotten him to visit, the concert in Rison, wrote the *Arkansas Gazette*, "promises to be the wildest blowout in the little city's history."[67] The show would help raise funds for the historical society and serve as the highlight of the weekend's Bicentennial Pioneer Crafts Festival. The festival, however, had other ambitious activities going on, including a history pageant with a cast of 175 people marking two hundred years of history.

Lois Moore (referred to in the papers as Mrs. James L. Moore), had led efforts to get Cash to Rison. A graduate of Hendrix College in Conway, not far from Little Rock, she headed the bicentennial committee and was one of the founding members of the Cleveland County Historical Society. As is true of any good historian, she was persistent. What also helped her in her quest to get Cash to Cleveland County was a family connection: she lived near Cash's aunt. She talked to Ray Cash on the phone, too, and Ray persuaded his son to make the trip. Lois also contacted railroad executives to get the Cotton Belt Line to organize a special train for Cash. Not only was the special train a logistical challenge, the railroad also had to cover the high insurance costs. The train would carry June and Johnny as well as Governor Pryor and Rep. Ray Thornton, whose Fourth Congressional District included Cleveland County.

Johnny and his entourage arrived in Kingsland on the Friday before the Saturday morning concert, having taken his own bus for the four-hundred-mile trip from Nashville. In Kingsland, Cash met Joe Purcell—lieutenant governor and head of the Arkansas Bicentennial Commission—and Representative Thornton. Cash also met several of the executives of the Southern Pacific Railroad, who had flown in from San Francisco for the event. The Southern Pacific arranged to have three brightly colored Spirit of '76 locomotives take Johnny into Rison.

People had come from far away for the festivities. Visitors from twenty-two states had registered at the exhibit building and courthouse (which Johnny's father—according to family lore—had helped build). Not everyone, however, was star struck. One man in attendance told the *Arkansas Democrat* that Cash was "just another man, like me. Nothin' too special about him. He just got a few more breaks than me. I used to play with him when he was a little runt. And he was a mean little fellow, like me."[68] People in Arkansas had a tendency to put themselves in the Cash story. In Dyess, everyone seemed to have watched Cash stomp around with a guitar (even though he didn't own one then). And while they wanted to be part of the Cash story, Arkansans also wanted to keep Cash humble. To think that Cash had won fame and fortune because he got just a "few more breaks" was the kind of thinking that kept the American Dream alive, even if it was an oversimplification at best and dismissive at worst.

The day of the concert threatened rain. Cash arrived in Kingsland around 9 a.m. As he descended from his touring bus, he was met by a crowd estimated at four hundred people, not to mention television crews. As Cash said hello to friends, fans, and family, National Guard helicopters passed overhead. Before Cash boarded the train for the ten-mile trip to Rison, Kingsland Baptist Church preacher James Glover spoke on the platform. He praised Cash's deep faith, saying Cash and his family were "unafraid to identify with Jesus Christ." Rev. Glover said a prayer before Cash boarded the special train and asked God to hold back any rain. He also talked about the days when Kingsland was thriving economically. Unfortunately, those days were long behind it.[69]

In March 1976, Cash returned to his birthplace to play a show in Cleveland County. He visited Kingsland and performed at the high school for thousands of people in nearby Rison. Cash wore his bicentennial shirt for the occasion. The event inspired a song about his father, "Ridin' on the Cotton Belt." With him in this picture are June and Cash's son, John Carter. *Courtesy Stan Sadler.*

Before boarding the train that took him there, Cash and his family visited with relatives at the Crossroads, where Cash was born in 1932. Johnny and June were a little beat up. Cash recently had broken a bone in his foot during a motorcycle accident in Jamaica. June had hurt herself in a separate incident, though it had resulted only in bruises.[70] As they stood at the train, the mayor of Kingsland, L. R. Granderson, presented a key to the city to Ray Cash. Johnny had lived in Kingsland only three years, but Ray had called Kingsland home for nearly half of his life. Ray was not one for ceremony. The son of a farmer-preacher, he was a man who wandered Cleveland County during the Great Depression, scraping by doing factory work, killing livestock, and picking cotton. For most of Johnny's childhood, his father was an abusive drunk. But for the time being, Johnny seemed to have forgiven him, or at least tried to pretend their relationship was normal.

Ray was seventy-nine years old, and on this March day in 1976, Cleveland County honored him. After being presented with the key to Kingsland, he quipped, "Since I have the key to the city, where's the bank?" It was a line worthy of his son. "Nobody is more deserving than my daddy," Johnny said.[71] The women in Johnny's life were also honored. Roses were given to Carrie Cash and Mary Easterling, the midwife who had helped deliver Johnny into the world. Before the train departed from Kingsland, Cash made a few remarks from the back of the train. With him were June, Ray, and Southern Pacific president Benjamin F. Biaginni.

As was true of Cash's Rockefeller concerts of 1968, political candidates were getting in on the act. Among Cash's companions to Rison were Frank Henslee, a native of Pine Bluff running for secretary of state, and Gov. David Pryor. Pryor gave Cash a painting of a "black dog looking over a wall." He also declared it "Johnny Cash Day."[72]

On the train, Cash gave an interview with Geraldo Rivera, who was then working for the ABC television show *Good Night America*. Rivera later gained fame—or perhaps infamy—on his 1986 program *The Mystery of Al Capone's Vaults*, which revealed, despite much hype, that the vaults were only full of dust, bottles, and other 1920s junk. Rivera nevertheless went on to host his own talk show and later became a commentator on Fox News. Camera crews recorded the train ride, which took about twenty minutes and passed within a few hundred yards of where Cash was born. Cash told Rivera he was "more relaxed" than at any time in his life.[73] "It feels good to come home," he told him. "I just wish I could stay more than five minutes." Even so, Cash said it was "good to see the old faces." The train ride brought back memories for Johnny as well as his father. The Cotton Belt Line evoked nostalgia from Johnny, but it brought back darker memories for Ray: the death of his brother-in-law, killed by a Cotton Belt train. Ray also noted that he had had eight friends in Rison, but three of them were dead. He wanted to see the others while he was still in town.[74]

The train stopped at the foot of Main Street in Rison, where thousands of people met Cash, including members of the Johnny Cash International Fan Club "on the brink of hysteria."[75] The mayor of Rison, Ed Olmstead, gave Cash the key to the city; now two Cashes had a key to a city. Cash was also given a county centennial medallion by Rufus T. Buie, the president of the historical society. In another opportunity for his father to share the limelight, Ray gave a brief speech in which he mentioned men he had grown up with in the area. Before the parade started, a twenty-one-gun salute was fired. An estimated twelve thousand people lined the streets for the "longest, most colorful parade in the history of the county."[76] Cash and his family made their way through the streets of Rison in a horse-pulled buggy. Ray, the "vivacious and charming" June, and John Carter were with Johnny in the carriage.[77] The parade also featured Shriners on motorcycles, a marching band, and clowns. A carriage pulling parade marshal Johnny Cash through the streets of small-town Arkansas was a sight to see, but Cash was not the only rarity that day. Also unusual was the Arkansas Coonhunters Association, whose float featured a real tree containing live raccoons with men dressed as hunters and holding dogs.

After getting out of his carriage, Cash stopped for a few minutes in the home of Lois Moore, who had arranged for his visit to Cleveland County. Her five years of hard work had paid off. Then it was time for the concert. At the football field where he performed, Cash played for a crowd estimated between five and seven thousand people. Dressed in his black bicentennial suit stitched with red, white, and blue eagles, he started his show at a quarter after eleven. He opened with "Ring of Fire" and played for about an hour. The weather, overcast and drizzly, was unsettled—typical of March—but the sun also broke through at times and the rain mostly held off. Cash played a typical set that mixed hits and spirituals. Cash had the Tennessee Three with him as well as an additional guitarist, Jerry Hensley, with Larry McCoy on the piano. The Carter sisters also entertained the crowd.

Johnny Cash was "expressive—as no one else, perhaps," the *Cleveland County Herald* wrote, "of the natural strengths and elemental rhythms that Arkansans like to associate with themselves." The *Herald* had expected Cash to belt out more train songs, but still, Cash didn't disappoint. The paper admired the fact that he "hasn't forgotten the poor people, the prisoners, the busted wanderers, who come alive in those deep-voiced songs." The *Herald* remembered Cash refusing to sing "Welfare Cadilac" at the White House back in 1970 but wrongly believed that Cash also refused to attend the White House because of the controversy. Such was not the case, but the *Herald* was accurate in noting Cash was an entertainer among those not willing to "sell their souls."[78] As Cash might have said, he risked losing his soul many times to drugs. But he had never been keen on selling his soul to anyone.

Spectators often liked to comment on Cash's appearance or his voice. Those who covered the Rison show were no different. At six-foot-two and well over 200 pounds, Cash was an imposing man. The *Gazette*, though, thought Cash's "weathered face was much thinner than before." Regardless, Cash's everyman looks were part of his appeal. Even though he had given thousands of concerts in his career, he still broke a sweat. The *Gazette* noted Cash's "stern face, dripping with perspiration, seemed to beam." Cash called it "the most exciting day" of his life.[79] At his Cummins show in 1969, Cash performed a song he had written for the occasion, "When I Get Out of Cummins." That day in Rison, he performed a new song that had special meaning for him and his listeners: "Ridin' on the Cotton Belt," about his dad's adventures as a "working hobo" during the Great Depression.

Cash closed with "Ragged Old Flag," which he said he wrote when "all that bad stuff was going on up in Washington." Another inspiration for writing the song was his son. Cash said he wrote "Ragged Old Flag" after going to the movies with John Carter. Cash lamented how the flag had been "abused" and "burned, dishonored, denied, and refused," while the government was "scandalized throughout the land." The song typified Cash's wearied sense of optimism: despite the trials the country had gone through, the United States had seen worse and would endure. On stage at the Rison show—in the wake of the Watergate scandal and Nixon's resignation—Cash took comfort in the fact that America still was an intensely religious place, especially in southern Arkansas. He said with pride that "the great percentage of the people of this country are Christians, and that includes me."[80] Cash appreciated church officials meeting with him on the day of the concert, and he assured the crowd that "God will heal our land." Many in the crowd muttered an "amen" and applauded.[81]

Despite the religious overtones and the appreciation of the crowd, it was—more than anything else—a day for Cash's family. At the concert, Johnny gave a shout-out to his father, and he mentioned his aunt, Mabel McKinney, who lived near the football stadium. Johnny noted how he would like to have visited the grave of his great-grandfather, Moses Reuben Cash, the Georgia native who brought the Cashes to Arkansas and died in Cleveland County in 1880. But it's not clear whether he did so.

When it came to June, the *Arkansas Gazette* described her as something of an outsider at the festival, noting how her "bright blue eyes took in the madhouse."[82] She was from Virginia, but she also considered Arkansas her home. She couldn't help making a clever line about how "Johnny picked the cotton and I wormed the tobacco." Johnny had spent many long hours in the cotton fields, but June was no tobacco worker. Cash, nevertheless, was generous in his praise of his wife. "She saved me from drugs," he said, "and the Lord did the rest."[83]

Given Cash's legendary status, it was no surprise that the day mixed fact and fiction. Bill Lancaster of the *Arkansas Gazette* did June's line about worming tobacco one better, reporting that Cash had "returned to these parts occasionally in early childhood and hitchhiked along U.S. Highway 79 to Pine Bluff to play his guitar in a band."[84] It is uncertain where Lancaster got his information. Whatever its source, it was pure fantasy. Cash had never seriously played music in Cleveland County as a youth, let alone with a band. The *Cleveland County Herald* was more factual, noting that Cash did not buy his first guitar until he had joined the Air Force.[85]

After the show, Cash and his retinue returned to Lois Moore's house for lunch, then boarded his bus for Dyess. Cleveland County kept the festivities going with Cash in mind. On Saturday night, *The Gospel Road* was shown at the Kingsland First Southern Baptist Church. Worshippers at Rison's Methodist Church watched it that Sunday, and churches showed the film throughout the week.[86]

For years, the most lasting monument to Cash's 1976 visit was a marker in Kingsland, located near a church. The marker features a plaque as well as a large, painted stone guitar. The marker notes that Cash was "renowned in country, western, and religious music." It might also have added rock and roll to that list. Later, Cash would be the first man inducted into the Country Hall of Fame (and the youngest man given that honor), Rock and Roll Hall of Fame, and Gospel Hall of Fame.[87]

Cash wouldn't perform again in Cleveland County for eighteen years. He didn't forget his Rison visit, though. Later that year, he recorded an eight-minute acoustic version of "Ridin' on the Cotton Belt" in the studio.[88] Cash began the song with a spoken-word introduction in which he layered memories of the 1976 show with tales of his father in Rison. Cash said he was grateful for Rison honoring him with a homecoming. But he said it was really his parents' day. "Johnny Cash Day" had allowed his father to return to the place where he had lived as a "barefoot boy." Johnny talked about his father on the day of the Rison concert waving to people he knew from the buggy. For Cash, it was "one of the biggest kicks of my whole life and career."

Cash couldn't help but romanticize the story of his father during the Great Depression. As "Ridin' on the Cotton Belt" tells it, Ray had jumped on trains without paying. In Brinkley—roughly a hundred miles northeast of Rison—Ray managed to talk his way out of certain punishment at the hands of a detective who had caught him hopping the rails. Ray pleaded for forgiveness, saying he had just been paid for a job and he needed to get home to his family. The detective let him off with a warning, and Ray finished the trip by jumping off the train at Saline Siding, where "cut and bleeding like always," he brought his money "home to momma." With "Ridin' on the Cotton Belt," Johnny was still trying to please his daddy, despite the fact that Ray had few redeeming qualities. As usual, though, Cash could mix fact and fiction in ways that made for good songwriting and storytelling.

Cash also recorded a much shorter version of "Ridin' on the Cotton Belt," done with the Tennessee Three and vocalists accompanying him. It appeared on Cash's 1977 album *The Last Gunfighter Ballad*. That same year, Cash played the tune on *The Arthur Smith Show* with his full band. Arthur Smith was a native of South Carolina who had an early hit with "Guitar Boogie" in 1945. The tune sold so well that Smith became known as "Guitar Boogie" Smith. The song contains many of the musical elements of rock and roll—long before anyone had heard of Elvis or Chuck Berry. In 1955, Smith released another influential tune called "Feudin' Banjos," the basis for the enormously popular "Dueling Banjos" featured in the 1972 film *Deliverance*. Smith had worked as a producer for James Brown on "Papa's Got a Brand New Bag" (1965) and had written the religious "I Saw a Man" in 1954. Cash recorded it in 1959 on his first album of religious music, *Hymns by Johnny Cash*.

On the 1977 broadcast, during the banter before he launched into "Ridin' on the Cotton Belt," Smith asked Cash to "sing something that hasn't been a national tremendous international hit that you like."

"Well, I could pick most any of 'em," Cash quipped.

Smith asked about whether there was any competition in the Cash family—namely the rising fame of his daughter Rosanne and stepdaughter Carlene Carter. "They ain't gonna run me off yet," Cash assured Smith. "The old man's still got a few kicks left."[89]

Cash was facing competition not only from his daughter but his peers. By 1976, the Outlaws were remaking Nashville and country music. Michael

Streissguth has called Cash the "godfather" of Outlaw Country.[90] But the Outlaws—as exemplified by Waylon Jennings, Willie Nelson, and Kris Kristofferson—were decidedly Texan in spirit. In 1976, RCA put out *Wanted! The Outlaws*, containing music from Waylon, Willie, Arizona native (and Waylon's wife since 1969) Jessi Colter, and Nebraska-born Tompall Glaser. The album was the first country album certified platinum.

Michael Streissguth and Nadine Hubbs have lumped Cash in with the Outlaws, including not just Waylon and Willie, Colter and Glaser, but also David Allan Coe, Billy Joe Shaver, Merle Haggard, Kristofferson, Tanya Tucker, and others. As Hubbs has written, the Outlaws were "a species of hard country understood as a reaction against the Nashville sound and countrypolitan style."[91] Some of the better-known Outlaws were not exactly new to the scene. Willie Nelson had a long career as a songwriter before becoming the omni-toking, headband-wearing darling of Austin, Texas, and President Carter. He had, after all, written Patsy Cline's early-sixties hit "Crazy." Jennings, too, was no rookie, having recorded his first album in 1964. His records did well, but he didn't have a number 1 album until 1975's *Dreaming My Dreams*.

Cash had a good year in 1976. But in contrast to the Outlaws, he stumbled commercially after "One Piece at a Time." Cash's Rison show was a triumph, but his next concert in Arkansas was not nearly as memorable, though it reflected where he was in his career at that point. On January 15, 1978, Cash played Pine Bluff, a place best known for being the center of the Arkansas prison industrial complex. Cash played at 7:30 on a Sunday night at the Pine Bluff Convention Center. The weather was cold and snowy, though the *Pine Bluff Commercial* said Cash gave a "warming performance." It reported "a few thousand persons" had "braved a bitter wind" to see the show. Cash played with his usual lineup. June was described as a "glamorous country girl with a knock-'em-dead voice." She, along with Johnny, "warmed the crowd into a mellow mood." Cash gave a shout-out to his friends and relatives in nearby Cleveland County, sang "Ridin' on the Cotton Belt" from his recent album, *The Last Gunfighter Ballad*, and performed the usual hits and duets. His show also included a movie screen playing clips to accompany songs. "One Piece at a Time," noted the *Commercial*, featured a "Keystone Cops-style" movie. Cash also played scenes from *The Gospel Road*. The interplay between Cash and June evoked the "unmistakable warmth of family love."

Other than the blizzard, the show was not an especially memorable event in the history of Johnny Cash concerts. By 1978, Cash was driven more by professionalism than inspiration. Despite the success of "One Piece at a Time," for the rest of the 1970s and into the 1980s, he struggled to find not only hits, but good material that fit his voice and sound. Even more of a challenge was staying relevant and original in the post-Outlaw, post-punk period. As the *Pine Bluff Commercial* noted, Cash's January 1978 show was pleasing, but contained no surprises. The *Commercial* likely said more than it intended when it claimed the show provided an evening of "old songs" and "easy listenin'."[92]

On the day of Pine Bluff show, the *Commercial* featured an article written by Jack McClintock headlined "From Drug Addict to Committed Christian." The story was one that Cash had told from the late 1960s onward: with the help of June and the Lord, Cash kicked his drug habit. Despite what Cash said, he probably never gobbled upwards of a hundred pills a day, nor had he gotten drugs out of his system before the birth of John Carter. But the story generally was true to Cash. The problem was, by the late 1970s, neither Cash's music nor his personal story seemed fresh.[93]

Cash's show in Pine Bluff might have been more professional than inspired, but he was a man who seemed—at least in public—on the quiet end of a previously troubled life. His artistic struggles were not merely the result of shifting musical trends and tastes, but the result of bad choices. Cash initially turned down "The Gambler," a song written by Don Schlitz that became a career-making hit for Kenny Rogers after its release in November 1978. Rogers wasn't the first one to record the Schlitz song (Bobby Bare had a few years before), nor was Rogers new to the country music game. But Rogers's version of "The Gambler" proved definitive—and for him, highly lucrative: the album it titled sold millions of copies.[94]

Cash had cut his own version of the song before Rogers did, and he released it only a month after Rogers's, on Cash's *Gone Girl* album. Had Cash released the song earlier, though, it likely would not have mattered. "The Gambler" became Rogers's signature tune. Quite simply, Rogers did a better job with the song, and the timing was right for him to connect with a mass audience. Cash's version is capable, but Rogers's—sung slower and with more conviction—is a classic. It was one of those times when Cash could not turn another writer's song into one that seemed unquestionably his.

Despite the fact that there was a "New Johnny Cash" to reckon with in the 1970s, by 1978, the Johnny Cash Show was entering a dark period. On October 23, Mother Maybelle died. She was only sixty-nine but had suffered poor health for several years. Johnny, June, and the rest of the family saw a vital link broken between early country and its present-day incarnation. Mother Maybelle was buried in Hendersonville next to her husband Ezra, who had died three years before. Her contribution to country music and American guitar playing was enormous. While she was a side performer with the Johnny Cash Show, her presence was the kind that kept Cash rooted. Cash loved history, and Mother Maybelle was the embodiment of early country music.

The Cash family suffered other losses, too, though one was of Johnny's own doing. In 1980, Johnny fired Marshall Grant, who had been his bass player from the beginning of his career. Grant eventually sued Cash over money owed him (the case was settled out of court).[95] Grant obviously felt that Cash had not taken care of him financially in a way that was appropriate for their longtime relationship, especially given Grant's work as a road manager.

By then, many in the Cash family had come and gone. Luther Perkins and Glen Sherley were dead. Carl Perkins had left to pursue his own projects. And now, Marshall was on his own. The last album he played on with Johnny was *Silver*, the 1979 record that signified the twenty-fifth anniversary of Cash's music career. The album reached number 28 on the country charts, another mediocre performance for a new Johnny Cash album. *Silver* was formulaic, featuring the usual duet (this time with George Jones), a Jack Clement tune, and a train song.

The album, however, had one stand-out track: "(Ghost) Riders in the Sky," a 1948 song written by actor and musician Stan Jones. It was a rare song for Cash in that it featured horns, but it turned out to be one of his classics. It sold well, peaking at number 2 on the country charts. Cash did what he did best by turning the song into an epic—this time, one spun from the imagery of the Wild West. *The All Music Guide* snidely said that "Ghost Riders" was a song "hard to ruin," but Cash recorded what may be the definitive version of it.[96] The horns gave the track drama seldom captured on record since his "Ring of Fire" period. Backed by Bob Wootton's effective guitar work, Cash sang lyrics that mixed heaven, hell, and cowboys. Cash even lent solemnity to the "yippy-yi-ooh yippy-yi-ay" chorus.

Cash produced a number of memorable songs in the 1970s. Some were political, such as "Man in Black," "What Is Truth," and "Singin' in Viet Nam Talkin' Blues." Others, such as "One Piece at Time" were less weighty. "(Ghost) Riders in the Sky" was more somber, but it highlighted what had made Cash great for decades—a thumping beat, a convincing vocal, and ghosts of the past haunting the modern American landscape. Cash was right when he had told Arthur Smith that he still had a "few kicks" left in him.

A New Johnny Cash?

Over the course of the decade, the United States had experienced severe trials. But how much had Cash changed? He rode his 1968 comeback into a great success in the 1970s. By 1971, he was sober and the star of a successful variety show. He played for the president, and as a born-again Christian, allied himself with Billy Graham, America's most influential and respected preacher. As the decade wore on, however, Cash lapsed into familiar bad habits. Despite the fact that he and June were a super-couple in country music, their relationship was often tumultuous. Musically, by the mid-seventies, most of Cash's best work was behind him. When he did have a hit song, it was because the public responded to a musical formula relying on the boom-chicka-boom signature Cash sound, not something new. Even Cash's much vaunted religious deepening was nothing radical. Cash simply hoped to regain what he felt he had lost. Despite what Paul Conn wrote, a truly "new" Cash would have gone in a radical direction in the 1970s. Instead, Cash turned inward—as he always had—for inspiration. More often than not, it made for uninspired—albeit well-made and professional—music.

Cash's sound aged well because he stayed close to his roots. It also meant the music industry was passing him by in the 1970s, a decade that saw everything from progressive and glam rock, and experimentation with synthesizers, to the emergence of punk, New Wave, and heavy metal. None of these had much to do with what was going on in Nashville. The result was that Cash drifted closer to the softer pop country taking over the industry in the mid-to-late 1970s than the Outlaws. In the late sixties, Cash had rocker Carl Perkins start his shows. And in the 1970s, Cash could still rock hard when he had Perkins play with him on a song like "Blistered."

But later that decade, Cash was supported by the white gospel Oak Ridge Boys in Las Vegas.[97] The rock and roll days of Memphis seemed long past.

By the late 1970s, Cash was searching in vain for the kind of success and excitement he had felt when the decade began. Even so, he was a much-respected figure in country and American pop culture. As historian Dan Carter discovered when writing about George Wallace, the Alabama governor and segregationist symbolized the "Americanization of Dixie" and the "Southernization of America."[98] Johnny Cash, did, too. He was a Southerner and Arkansan, but he embodied America. Cash might have not taken advantage of the changing rock scene in the 1970s, but he would correct that mistake years later, during his final comeback, on the appropriately titled American Recordings label.

7

American

The 1980s were not a good time for Johnny Cash. His struggles with drugs continued. He also began having serious medical problems, including a heart condition that landed him in the hospital for major surgery. As was true in the late 1970s, Cash tried to remain artistically relevant and grounded in a decade that saw many of the greatest 1960s acts losing their way amid the pop- and synth-drenched landscape. As he always had, Cash took his music seriously, remained an earnest Christian, and made occasional visits to Arkansas to touch his roots again. He veered from project to project. Some were forgettable, while others, such as his tours and recordings with country supergroup the Highwaymen, were successful. Cash survived the 1980s and kicked off his last great comeback in the mid-1990s.

Jamaica

Often, though, it seemed the eighties would finish Cash. Sometimes he was self-destructive; at others, his wealth and fame worked against him. This was never truer than during a harrowing 1981 robbery in Jamaica. In the 1970s, the Cash family bought an eighteenth-century plantation house named Cinnamon Hill from John Rollins, a multimillionaire who had grown up poor in northern Georgia. Rollins made a fortune in the stock market, a success that led him to enter politics, first by becoming the lieutenant governor of Delaware (he ran for governor in 1960 and lost). A Republican, Rollins donated huge sums to the Grand Old Party. Rollins, like Cash, never forgot where he had come from—recall how Rosanne Cash wrote about her father and Rollins sitting around trying to "out-poor" each other with tales of their impoverished youth.[1]

Cinnamon Hill gleamed. It was also bizarre. It had an unsettling energy for those who knew Jamaica's colonial history and Cinnamon Hill's strange past. In the best of times, the property served as a place of contemplation and relaxation for Cash. "There was something about the bright evening sky," biographer Robert Hilburn has written of Cinnamon Hill, "that reminded him of the stars at night in Dyess on his walks to town when he was a boy."[2] The Cashes had a benign though paternalistic attitude toward the area. They were known for their philanthropy, but one must also acknowledge that they were millionaires living in a mansion sold to them by a millionaire. As a place built to house masters of African Americans who lived and worked in the slaughterhouse that was Caribbean slavery, Cinnamon Hill's beauty was offset by a darker side. Rosanne has claimed the place is haunted, a "fact freely acknowledged by skeptics and believers alike."[3] Whether or not the place was haunted (ghosts seem to gravitate toward mansions owned by rich white people), Cash was a sucker for local lore. And whenever he was in a place for a long period, he began writing songs.

On his 1973 album *Any Old Wind That Blows*, Cash included an original number, "The Ballad of Annie Palmer," about the mistress of a plantation in colonial Jamaica. The plantation, "Rose Hall," was located not far from Cinnamon Hill. The arrangement for "The Ballad of Annie Palmer" is lighthearted, striving as it does for a laid-back, Caribbean sound. The story and lyrics, however, are sinister. The song recounts the Palmer legend. Known as the "White Witch of Rose Hall," Palmer supposedly killed three husbands while she was alive and was a terror to slaves (5,000 Black workers in Cash's telling) on her sugar plantation. According to legend, she also had many African American lovers, but was killed during a slave insurrection in the 1830s. Cash's song only hints at the cruelty Annie Palmer showed toward her slaves or the possibility she murdered her husbands.

In 1929, Jamaican journalist and author Herbert George de Lisser published a novel about Palmer, *The White Witch of Rose Hall*. The fact that Palmer had been born in Haiti, famous for its voodoo, only added to the myth surrounding the plantation. Whatever Cash knew of the legend, it was based more on fiction than fact. "The perseverance of the legend," one scholar has written, "is particularly interesting given that it is thoroughly fabricated"—the product of the tale's "imperial agenda."[4] Cash did not have sinister motives in singing about Annie Palmer. For him it was just another folk tale. He sanitized "The Ballad of Annie Palmer," choosing not to get below the surface of the story and place that inspired him. Had Cash followed his genius, he might have had made an interesting concept album about Jamaica. Instead, on "The Ballad of Annie Palmer," he comes across as an amiable tour guide. To be fair, though, Jamaica is not America, and it was America that Cash knew.

Americans have a temptation to describe any place with beaches and palm trees as "paradise," but Jamaica, at least in economic terms and crime, is far from it. Today's tourists often spend their vacations at resorts heavily protected by walls and security guards. As was true of so many places by the early 1980s, Jamaica was seeing historically high crime rates. In 1962, Jamaica had one of the lowest murder rates in the world. The following decades, however, saw an alarming rise in crime. In 2009, there were 1,680 murders in a country of roughly three million people—a murder rate far higher than that of present-day New York City.[5] By the 1980s, the dangers of life in Jamaica were obvious to visitors. Mark Stielper, Cash's friend and family historian, visited the house several times. He remembered the drive from the airport to the house was "terrifying," with numerous memorials, bullet holes, and a strong police presence. Cash told him not to stop for anyone or anything until he arrived at the front gate of the house.[6]

Crime can hit anywhere at any time, but the home invasion at Cinnamon Hill was the worst criminal incident the family ever experienced. The violent reality of life in Jamaica hit the Cash family hard on a terrifying December night in 1981 when three armed men entered the house and demanded money. The criminals held the Cash family hostage for hours. Cash remained calm during the ordeal, even when one of the robbers put a gun to John Carter Cash's head. Luckily, no one in the family was harmed. The men eventually left after trashing the house and taking money and jewelry.[7]

According to the Cashes, the robbers themselves met with a violent end at the hands of Jamaican authorities.[8] The incident might have filled him with vengeance, but Cash managed to look at the criminals with empathetic eyes. "I grieve for desperate young men and the societies that produce and suffer so many of them, and I felt that I knew those boys," Cash wrote in his second autobiography.[9] He knew Jamaica was a poor country, and the thieves were men like those he encountered at Folsom, Cummins, or any of the hundreds of small towns and cities where he performed over the years. To his credit, Cash kept returning to Jamaica, and he tried to help the community. He gave money to SOS Village, a home for orphans and abandoned children. He also played concerts for the locals. Cash made a great impression on Jamaican musician Abdel Wright, who met him at an SOS show. Seeing Cash playing and singing, he said in 2006, made him think, "I want to do that one day."[10]

Even so, the home invasion at Cinnamon Hill was traumatizing. June wrote a detailed account of it in her second memoir *From the Heart.* "I have never in my life been more truly frightened," June wrote. "Being scared didn't surprise me, being angry did. For I was angry at these men who came into my house, threatened those I loved most, and wanted to steal or break things that were rightfully mine. The fear faded, but the anger is still there."[11] During the robbery, June had worried that her husband would do something rash. "He is a quiet and gentle man," she said of Johnny, "but he is a terror beyond words when he is mad. A gun in his belt would have definitely been a mistake that day of our lives—a big mistake. Guns kill people."[12] The fact the family survived might have owed as much to luck as anything else. Similar stories, whether in the United States or elsewhere, have not ended so well. Cash himself didn't like to talk about the incident. In his second autobiography, he said he instead wanted to talk about "the flip side of violence, tragedy, addiction, and all the other many trials and tribulations this world has to offer. So right at the beginning here, I'm going to take stock of my blessings and tell you what I'm thankful for. It always puts things in perspective."[13] Cash usually was not at a loss for words. But there were some things in his life—his divorce, harassment by hate groups, and the Jamaica home invasion—he didn't like to talk about. Still, Cash made sure Cinnamon Hill was well guarded after that particular trip to Jamaica, during which the family had been lax about security.

The crime was well publicized. The prime minister of Jamaica himself got involved.[14] Though the perpetrators received a type of justice, Cash took no pleasure in their fate. For him it was the kind of result that had no winner or loser. June still loved Jamaica and its people. "The island is warm, beautiful, and peaceful," she wrote, "but maybe there's no such place."[15] For Johnny, Cinnamon Hill remained a place of escape and a refuge from life's worries. For June, it seemed to symbolize the way tragedy and sadness invaded every aspect of her life.

The home invasion foreshadowed Cash's troubled 1980s. He had fired Marshall Grant. His marriage was often rocky. And as the decade opened, Cash had backslid into drug addiction.

The Fordyce Festival

Cash was not alone among famous 1960s artists who struggled in the eighties. Some didn't make it to the eighties at all. The Who lost drummer Keith Moon to a drug overdose in 1978 and then limped along for several years before taking a long break from touring. Led Zeppelin lost its drummer, John Bonham, in 1980 after he drank himself to death, a senseless loss that effectively split up the band for good. Superstar songwriters such as Bob Dylan and Neil Young also floundered. "Like everything else," *Rolling Stone* has written, "Dylan sucked in the '80s. He locked into a game of chicken with Neil Young, battling to see who could release more bad albums before the decade was out. (Dylan won, eight to seven)."[16] And on the night of December 8, 1980, John Lennon was murdered outside his New York City home by a deranged young fan. Over the 1980s, the spirit of the 1960s was dimmed by time, tragedy, and changes in popular music tastes.

For Cash, a return home was always a good way for him to stay grounded. Jamaica might have been a getaway, but in Arkansas, he always found "his people." In the spring of 1982, Cash played in Fordyce, in Dallas County, about a ten-minute drive from Kingsland. The April 24 show, a Saturday, was at the second annual Cotton Belt Festival. If the festival's name were not enough to certify the town's "country" credentials, there was the high school mascot, the red bug—an insect known as a cotton-stainer because of the yellow-brown stains the pests leave on cotton plants after feeding on them.

Fordyce, as is true of Kingsland, began as a railroad town in the late 1800s. Its most famous resident is Paul William "Bear" Bryant, the checkered-hat-wearing football coach at Alabama who obtained godlike status for his success in the blood sport that is the Southeastern Conference. Bryant coached at "Bama" for twenty-four years, during which time he won six national championships. Fordyce also had an odd and comical connection to the rock and roll world. In July 1975, police there arrested Keith Richards and fellow Rolling Stones guitarist Ron Wood for drug possession. The Stones—who could have been in serious trouble had the police searched their trunk—were held briefly. Their lawyer, Arkansas native Bill Carter, got them released, but only after a circus-like courtroom hearing, presided over by a drunken judge who had been hastily called away from the golf course.[17]

Things were quieter when Cash arrived for the Cotton Belt Festival. The town recognized him as a man of honor, though the event was more humble than the one surrounding Cash's visit to Kingsland six years before. Even so, it was a big deal for southern Arkansas. Cash had heard about the festival from Marie Cash, his first cousin, who still lived in the area and worked as a teacher. As an organizer for the event, Marie Cash got so many calls about the show that she lamented, "I'm about to lose my mind." People were excited about the concert, but she said some locals had more selfish reasons for calling her. Some wanted Johnny to come over to "eat fish or help them get a recording contract. I don't know what to do." Marie had not seen Johnny in years, but she was able to get in touch with him through Johnny's father, Ray, who contacted Johnny's agent in California, Lou Robin, about Fordyce. When Cash agreed to come, Marie was surprised. She didn't think Johnny would visit such a small place.[18] Fordyce, however, had more people than Kingsland and Dyess combined.

The weekend festival featured an arts and crafts show and quilting contest. The day before Cash appeared, "Steam Train" Maury, the "King of the Hoboes" made hobo stew and told stories. That same evening, locals held a square dance and listened to the Sparkman String Band (named after the tiny nearby town of Sparkman). Cash appeared on Saturday morning in a parade where he, June, and John Carter Cash were pulled around in a horse-drawn wagon. The man holding the reins was Joe Bill Meador, the festival's organizer. The parade was followed by a chess tournament, tobacco-spitting competition, and fiddle and harmonica music as well as the National Guard Band. The opening acts for Cash's show were Bucksnort (a Fordyce group) and the Ramblin' Rebel Band (a Hot Springs outfit). Tickets to see Cash were $8.[19]

Cash played his show on Saturday night at the high school. The concert was supposed to happen at the football field, but was moved to the gym because of rain. Cash gave the money from the concert to support

Cash, June, and John Carter take a ride through the streets of Fordyce for the 1982 Cotton Belt Festival. Cash was struggling as an artist at the time, but he still attracted large crowds, especially in his home state. Fordyce, located in Dallas County, neighbors Cash's birthplace of Cleveland County. While Cash was a big draw, Fordyce is best known for being the hometown of Bear Bryant, the legendary Alabama football coach who went to high school there. *Courtesy Dallas County Museum.*

the festival. Before the COVID pandemic, the festival had run every year since 1980 on the fourth weekend of April. Meador—the son of a prominent Fordyce business owner—later remembered Cash arriving in the "biggest, blackest, shiniest 18-wheeler truck I had ever seen." Meador noted, it was "solid black with 'Johnny Cash' in handwritten script on the side. I thought to myself, 'My goodness. Looky here, looky here.'" It was another Johnny Cash event that seemed to pull everyone from the community. When Meador drove Cash around town in the wagon, he said, "I'll never forget the adoration I saw in people's eyes as we went along that parade route." Meador remembered it "was like everyone had a kinship to Johnny and they felt like he was part of the family." Local residents and fans packed the gym. "We had people everywhere," he recalled, "in the bleachers, on the floor, standing in the doorways and even standing outside to hear the best they could. And Johnny had brought his full show—band, lights, video screen."[20]

Cash's own musical family had changed since he was last in Arkansas. Marshall Grant was gone, but Cash expanded his band into something called the "Great Eighties Eight." In addition to Wootton and Holland, Cash now had Earl Poole Ball on piano, Joe Allen on bass, Jerry Hensely on guitar, and Jack Hale Jr. and Bob Lewin on horns. Also in the mix was Mississippi native Marty Stuart—then only twenty-three years old—who played guitar with the band.

Stuart was a purist when it came to both country and rock and roll music. As was true of Wootton, he was a fan who became part of the band. He said one of the first albums he ever owned was *The Fabulous Johnny Cash*. A bass, mandolin, fiddle, and guitar player, Stuart was jamming with seasoned Nashville musicians by the time most kids entered high school. After he joined Cash's band, he found in Johnny "someone who would become my mentor, my lifelong chief, my band leader, my father-in-law for a time, my next-door neighbor, and one of the best friends I've ever had."[21] As was also true of Wootton, Stuart found himself becoming a literal member of the Cash family when he married Cindy Cash in 1983. The marriage, however, lasted only five years and produced no children.

Stuart tried to stay true to Cash's original boom-chicka-boom sound. He found the Great Eighties Eight a bloated project. Cash's act, he felt, had been so softened that it approached "Lawrence Welk" proportions.[22] Even so, Stuart enjoyed his time with Cash. He remembered traveling to Hendersonville Memory Gardens to visit the grave of Luther Perkins. At the plot, Cash told his old friend, "Love you Luther. I miss you." He would also leave gifts. After one visit, Stuart asked Cash about whether things were the same after Luther's death. "No, sir, it was never the same," he remembered Cash saying. Cash added that "it hurts because he didn't get to enjoy the big stuff."[23] It was left to Cash, Stuart, and the other members of his band to carry on in the 1980s.

Early on, Stuart realized the effect that Cash had on fans. He was at Cash's last prison show, played at Angola in 1980. There, in southern Louisiana, he remembered the mother of a death row inmate who proceeded to "get down on her hands and knees and lock her arms around

[Cash's] knees and beg him to call the governor to try to get some help for her son."[24] But neither Stuart's time in Cash's band nor his ties to the family would last. Two years after marrying Cindy, Stuart decided to pursue his own music career, during which he was more committed to Cash's original sound than Cash himself. Stuart did return to the Cash fold, however, during the American Recordings sessions.

The 1980s was not a great decade for Cash. Nor was it a good time for Fordyce and small towns like it. Fordyce peaked in 1980 at 5,175 residents, but over the next four decades, the town lost nearly a quarter of its population. Even so, the festival survived, organized and promoted by Joe Meador, who kept the wagon in which he drove Cash around on his twenty-nine-acre farm.[25]

Little Rock Roast

In the first week of August 1983, Cash again returned to Arkansas, this time for a roast in Little Rock to raise money for the Big Brothers charity. True to the format, Cash took punishment from the roasters, who chided him for his weight gain and singing abilities. Cash, who wore a tuxedo for the event, was compared to the rotund Penguin of the campy 1960s Batman TV show. Johnny was accused of not only singing off key but "talking off key" on his records. June took part in the fun, performing a song called "Will Ole Johnny Cash Be Unbroken." With her were several of the Cash/Carter children, including John Carter, Tara and Cindy Cash, and Rosey Nix—June's only daughter from her marriage to Edwin Nix. Celebrities in attendance included Minnie Pearl and Larry Gatlin.[26] The colorful governor of Arkansas, Republican Frank White, also attended. He knew how to tell jokes, but he didn't have much to say about Cash. One roaster, though, ably summed up Cash's appeal in his home state, saying Johnny was a man "who's been down as many times as he's been up. A man who carries his heart in his music. Here in Arkansas you speak our language."[27] Cash could always return to Arkansas to see "his people" and be reminded that he had legions of loyal and adoring fans.

As an artist, Cash struggled throughout the 1980s. As a person, he nearly found the decade fatal. Cash's drug addiction was about as bad as it ever had been. Gone were the days of hotel destruction and long nights in the desert alone. He never withered away physically as he had in the late 1960s,

Cash at the Little Rock roast in 1983 for the Big Brothers organization. *Courtesy Jon Kennedy Cartoon Collection, UA-Little Rock Center for Arkansas History and Culture.*

but his new struggles with addiction were quieter and in many ways sadder. His son John Carter saw firsthand the effect substance abuse had. The drugs often put his father into a senseless stupor. "Increasingly," John Carter remembered, "I would come home to find him in an almost trance-like state, as though he were asleep but somehow still functioning—but barely. Slurred, slow speech; bloodshot eyes; a head that drooped—those were the characteristics that told me that drugs had seized control of my dad."[28] The surgeries he had in the 1980s, combined with his continued drug use, relapse into smoking, continuously hard touring schedule, and lifelong bad eating habits, were putting his life in jeopardy.

On his records, Cash tried to maintain a balance between light and dark, serious songs and humor. In 1984, he released his infamous single "The Chicken in Black." The song has become a pet hate among some Cash fans, who see it as beneath the singer's dignity. "There are a couple of periods of Cash's career that many fans choose to ignore," says music writer C. Eric Banister. "One of the biggest entries in that category is his 1984 single 'Chicken in Black.'"[29] The song tells a convoluted story about Cash's brain being replaced by that of a chicken. The song might have annoyed purists, but it revealed Cash's ability to laugh at himself and has become something of a collector's item. It was another song in a long line of funny tunes, from "Rock Island Line" and "Everybody Loves a Nut" to "A Boy Named Sue," "One Piece at a Time," or any number of cuts off his mid-seventies children's album. Despite the song's ridiculous premise, it rose to number 45 on the country charts—not great, but still one of his better-performing songs in years. Some fans were appalled, while others with a more open mind have sought the song out for its kitsch value. Cash, however, regretted having recorded it.

Worse than "The Chicken in Black" was the fact that two years after its release, Columbia dropped Cash from its label, ending a thirty-year relationship. The only other label he had known was Sun. Columbia obviously was not impressed with Cash's recent output. Cash was still issuing respectable albums that remained true to his formula of mixing spiritual and more commercial country records. In 1986, Cash released a gospel record, *Believe in Him*, and *Heroes*, a Western-themed album he recorded with Waylon Jennings. It was a statement on Cash's earning potential in 1986 that when Columbia released a new compilation album—usually a surefire seller—it failed to chart.

As he did throughout his career, in the 1980s Cash balanced his reputation as a renegade with his devotion to Christianity. He finished work on *Man in White*, his only published novel, about the life of the apostle Paul, in 1986. For Cash, it was a labor of love. He had worked on the book for years between touring, recording, and family commitments. "I'm a traveling man," Cash reminded readers in the book's introduction, and the road had cut into his writing time.[30] In the 1970s, Cash had begun taking a scholarly approach to the Bible and telling his story about Christianity. He enrolled in a religious correspondence course on the Bible in 1974. He worked on *Man in White* for years, putting words on paper whenever he had the chance or inspiration. The publication of *Man in White* revealed, again, that Cash's religious life was a river running through his entire life and career—sometimes steady, sometimes dry, other times raging. "I'm a Christian," Cash said. "Don't put me in another box." As usual, he had the help of the faithful. June had given Cash notes on the manuscript, which she did "in her painfully honest way."[31]

Despite the book's obvious religious content, Cash essentially was still writing about prisoners and outlaws. St. Paul, according to the Bible, was a man who had persecuted Christians—like a malevolent guard at Cummins prison farm—only to suffer persecution himself. Paul was, as Cash summarized him, "beaten with rods, with the lash, with stones; he was insulted, attacked by mobs, and imprisoned; his own people hated him."[32] As Cash might have said, Jesus, the apostles, and the early saints were the original outlaws.

While not a huge seller (and few of his fans have probably read it; even his brother Tommy said he couldn't get through it), the book was well received.[33] It again revealed Cash's deep and earnest Christian beliefs while demonstrating his intellectual depth. *Man in White* was based on faith and research. Cash believed the Bible was the literal word of God, but he had no theological qualms about writing a book that was an imagined recreation of a major Christian figure. It was the kind of thing few men, let alone country-western singers, attempted with such conviction and skill. In 2006, the novel was reprinted with an introductory note by Billy Graham, who outlived Johnny and June by fifteen years.

Back in his home state, where there was no shortage of evangelical Christians, the *Arkansas Gazette* called *Man in White* "convincing," saying that Cash "masterfully paraphrases familiar Scriptures into thoughts and words." The *Gazette* thought the book "calls for a sequel,"[34] but Cash never published another work of fiction.

In the introduction to *Man in White*, Cash wrote about his mother in a way that sounded as if she had died. She had not, but Johnny did dedicate *Man in White* to his father Ray, who had died the previous year, two days before Christmas. Ray had been eighty-eight years old. Services were held for him at the First Baptist Church in Hendersonville, where he was buried. Ray apparently never went long without thinking of his days working in the cotton fields. Cash's secretary Irene Gibbs said Ray had a small plot of cotton near the Cash estate's offices. Gibbs said he did it, "just to keep his hand in."[35] Ray's grave marker was inscribed with the words, "Meet Me in Heaven," a shorter, more hopeful line than his son Jack's inscription: "Will You Meet Me in Heaven." Cash would write a song titled "Meet Me in Heaven" in 1996 for his *Unchained* album.

Johnny's dedication of the book to his father was characteristically stripped down. "This book is dedicated to my father, Ray Cash, 1897–1985, veteran of World War I. Discharge: Honorable. Conduct: Good." One might wonder why Johnny only mentioned the fact that his father served in the military. No reference was made to his qualities as a husband, father, or grandfather. But Cash would write about that later—and with far greater emotion.

Man in White was not about to reverse Johnny Cash's artistic or commercial woes in the 1980s. The dark mood within the Cash family later that decade was reflected in June Carter Cash's second memoir, *From the Heart*, published in 1987. Despite the reassuring title and the sunny, smiling picture of June on the hardcover edition, the book examines her life and career honestly, detailing the many problems that accompanied decades of celebrity. By the time the book came out, June had been married to Johnny for almost twenty years. It was not an easy marriage, complicated as it was by long stretches on the road, drug addiction, infidelity, and the trappings of fame.

June, no less than Johnny, was comfortable talking about the darker episodes of her life and career. The couple's relationship was often strained and at times came close to divorce. June nevertheless took her role as a loyal wife seriously and persevered. June initially wanted to call the memoir *Out of My Mind*, a title encapsulating the feelings of "hurt, confusion and despair" she felt at the time. And yet she chose a more positive title that honored the "'soaring' of the heart" she felt, and a faith in God that buoyed her spirits. The book came about when June was suffering through another one of Johnny's attempts at rehab, a time when June was "low, low, low."[36] The book begins with the December 1981 home invasion in Jamaica and recounts other dark chapters in the Cash family history, such as a would-be kidnapper who demanded a quarter-million dollars or else he would threaten the Cash children. Living a celebrity life was stressful, and June was frank about her reliance on painkillers, "I had to have a pill for pain every night—one for my back, one for my legs, and one for my head." June said the pills were "all aspirin," but more powerful prescription drugs became normal for her.[37]

From the Heart feels like a book written by a different person than *Among My Klediments*—a woman wearier and beaten down by life. Even so, she retained her humor and determination. Despite the highs and lows of celebrity, she used a family trip to Alaska as a chance to note "there's nothing like a little excitement to remind you that you're still married to Johnny Cash."[38] The book closes with a fitting meditation on the importance of home: Virginia. "All the world and all the places I have been," June wrote, "I've seen them hurt and seen sunshine faces, and yet I always stop and think of home."[39] Johnny might well have said the same thing about Arkansas.

The idea that the 1980s were a fallow time for Cash, ending only when he met Rick Rubin in the mid-1990s, is an oversimplification. Cash's records might have struggled to make much impact on 1980s country music. But he remained popular as an entertainer and collaborator. His most enduring work that decade was the music he recorded with the Highwaymen, a country supergroup consisting of Cash, Willie Nelson, Kris Kristofferson, and Waylon Jennings.

Cash was the only member of the group not from Texas. Nelson was from tiny Abbott (population 356), Jennings from Littlefield (population 6,372), and Kristofferson from Brownsville, a mid-sized city and one of the southernmost points in the United States. Kristofferson, as a child of a military father, moved around frequently growing up. He might not have been a true Texan, but as was the case with Waylon and Willie, he embodied the Outlaw spirit of Texas and the 1970s.

If "Chicken in Black" represented a creative low for Cash in the eyes of some fans and critics, he rebounded the next year with his first album with the Highwaymen, released in May 1985. *The Highwayman,* which just as well could have been called *The Outlaws,* contained no original songs by its four members. The quartet covered one of Cash's best songs, "Big River," but the most enduring tune was Jimmy Webb's 1979 composition "Highwayman," featuring all four members on vocals, narrating a story of highwaymen through history. Oddly for Cash, considering how much his music had drawn on American history rather than science fiction, he took vocals on the last portion of the song, concerning an outlaw from the future, who sings, "I'll fly a starship, across the universe divide." It might have been silly stuff, but the song was effective, and though recorded in the mid-eighties—a period of pop music known for overproduction—it holds up fairly well.

Supergroups seldom manage to be greater than the sum of their parts, and that was probably the case with the Highwaymen. Even so, few country fans were going to dismiss a group consisting of such legendary singers and songwriters. Those who saw the Highwaymen in concert, furthermore, got to see four living legends of American music. *The Highwayman* clocked in at a brisk 33:43, and with its solid song selection and A-list members, it reached number 1 on the country charts.

The Highwaymen convened for another record in 1989, *Highwayman 2*, released in February 1990. The group supported the album with another tour, bringing Cash back to Arkansas. As was typical of Cash, he returned not just as a performer but a man who took an interest in what was going on in his home state. Heavy rains had inundated Arkansas in the spring of 1990. The Highwaymen's two-month tour was supposed to start in Dallas. But in the wake of the Arkansas flooding, Cash persuaded the rest of the band to begin a day earlier in Little Rock to help publicize recovery efforts. "It's my pleasure to do something for Arkansas, because I love my home state," he told the *Arkansas Democrat*.[40] The flooding cost Arkansas an estimated $350 million in damage. Governor Clinton declared thirty-nine of Arkansas's seventy-five counties disaster areas. Farmers needed relief.[41]

In response, Cash organized the Arkansas Farm Flood Aid Concert. His efforts were similar to those of Willie Nelson, who—along with John Mellencamp and Neil Young—began Farm Aid in 1985, raising $9 million for struggling farmers that year. Cash's efforts in Arkansas were more modest. Even so, Cash and the Highwaymen managed to raise $196,437 for Arkansas farmers. The group pulled in $100,000 per show, but they gave all the proceeds from their Barton Coliseum performance on September 9 to farmers. Organizations in Arkansas, including the *Arkansas Democrat* (pitching in $50,000 on its own), the State Fair, and radio and TV stations covered other costs associated with the benefit show. Johnnie Holmes, manager of the Arkansas State Fair, had hoped to raise $200,000, and he came close to that figure. The crowd at the show numbered 6,530. Tickets were not cheap, ranging from $18.50 to $22.50. The high prices might have kept a few thousand people away who might otherwise have come. "I'm a little disappointed that we didn't fill [Barton Coliseum] up," said Lou Robin, Cash's manager. Perhaps Sunday wasn't the best choice for a concert in a town known for quiet Sunday nights. Robin, however, considered the show a success, saying it had brought attention to the disastrous flooding. "Just because it happened a while ago doesn't mean it went away," Robin added.[42]

The concert drew out some of the most powerful men in Little Rock. Mayor Floyd G. "Buddy" Villines gave Cash a key to the city at a news conference before the show. "When you come to Little Rock we kind of consider you a home boy," the mayor said. "I am," Cash responded.[43] Before the 7:30 performance, the conservative owner of the *Arkansas Democrat*, Walter Hussman, presented an oversized $50,000 check to Governor Clinton. Clinton was a country fan and a bit of a musician himself, who said he converted to country music in his twenties, "when Hank Williams and Patsy Cline reached down to me from heaven."[44] In the spirit of the event, Clinton appeared in a turquoise shirt and cowboy boots. A polarizing figure then as now, he was greeted with cheers and boos.[45]

The Highwaymen played thirty-two songs over two hours, including career highlights from individual band members. For Cash that meant "Folsom Prison Blues," "A Boy Named Sue," "Ragged Old Flag," and "Ring of Fire." Cash's concert funds might have only covered a mere fraction of the floods' financial toll, but his efforts were sincere and much appreciated. Also taking part in the recovery efforts was Feed the Children, which had set up food drops along the Highwaymen's tour route and was sending 160,000 pounds of food to the Pine Bluff area alone.[46]

Despite the success of the Highwaymen records and the joys of touring with his Outlaw buddies, Cash remained in an artistic rut. As usual, he found solace in his faith and stayed close to the church. He continued his work with Billy Graham. Graham and Cash were men who had espoused liberal principles in the past, but by the 1980s, many of their audience members were part of the conservative political wave of the Reagan period. Arkansas may have had a Democratic governor by 1989 in Bill Clinton, but the state was shifting to the Right along with the rest of the South. When Cash appeared before a crowd of 48,500 at War Memorial Stadium in Little Rock in September 1989, it was not Cash the rebel the people wanted to see but Cash the patriot and man of God. Cash's appearance capped an eight-day revival, part of one of Reverend Graham's Crusades.

A Bible Belt city, Little Rock was an ideal place to hold a crusade. Cash was once again among his people. During the event, he joked that "I'm kin to half the people here tonight, and I'm going to claim kin to the other half." Cash addressed his drug abuse during the crusade, but noted that in the face of addiction, the church had given him strength. Cash said he had confronted the issue of who would "deliver me from this body of death." For him, the answer was "living through the Lord Jesus Christ."[47]

The 1990s

As the Crusade showed, Cash remained a powerful and influential figure. He had recently finished recording a spoken-word version of the New Testament. Regardless of his album sales at any particular time, he drew crowds not only at theaters and arenas but anywhere he went. In July 1990, Cash was traveling through central Arkansas on vacation, taking time off between a date in Austin and an upcoming gig in Canada. Cash had a craving for some ice cream and stopped in the small town of Lonoke, just outside Little Rock. First Johnny and June visited a Walmart to do some shopping. June looked at clothes, while Johnny bought some marshmallows and went to the video section to grab a few Westerns. The store's manager said that news of Johnny's appearance at the store "spread like wildfire." Customers and employees were in awe at seeing a celebrity, and Johnny couldn't leave without signing the register tape for an employee. Nothing could have been "more Arkansas" at the time than Johnny Cash shopping in a Walmart. And the commotion continued across the street at the struggling Vicki's Ice Cream Churn. The daughter of the owner hoped Cash's visit would turn business around.[48]

On his way back to Nashville, Cash made a stop in Arkansas at his high school in Dyess for a fortieth-anniversary reunion. The papers eventually picked up the story, but Cash made sure there was no media present while it was happening. Harry Hall of North Little Rock, who graduated from the high school in 1951, was master of ceremonies for the reunion banquet. He said of Johnny, "We recognized him for his successes and gave him a plaque saying we hoped to see him at our 80th class reunion." Cash made a short speech noting the highs and lows of a long career. One of those highs was when a singing competition in Dyess back in the 1940s, when he performed "That Lucky Old Sun" for his classmates.[49]

Cash was always welcome in Arkansas, but he knew he would have to work for a real record label were he to remain viable and relevant. After leaving Columbia, Cash signed with Mercury. His work for the label was professional, but not exceptional. One 1988 album, *Classic Cash*, was simply a run through his greatest hits in the studio. In what was typical, self-deprecating hyperbole, Cash claimed Mercury only pressed five hundred copies of another record, *The Mystery of Life*.[50] Growing ever more desperate, Cash had plans to become a resident performer in Branson, Missouri, the Nashville (if one could make such a comparison) of the Midwest.

At least he would be close to home. Branson is near the Arkansas line, and while playing there, Cash liked to stay in the tiny town of Blue Eye, Arkansas, adjacent to Blue Eye, Missouri.[51] Blue Eye didn't even have enough people to fill a Greyhound bus, but Branson was becoming an attractive frontier for musicians and others who had fallen on hard times. As was true of any quasi-western area, it attracted scoundrels, such as the disgraced televangelist Jim Bakker, who spent five years in prison for fraud but set up a new ministry in Blue Eye, Missouri, where he has sold $150 water bottles, freeze-dried pizza, and quack medicinal cures.[52]

Cash was prepared to become a full-time performer in Branson at a new theater named for him. Thankfully for him, Cash put no money into the project. He found himself struggling to draw respectable, let alone sell-out, crowds. Plans for a Johnny Cash theater dissolved, but he still played dozens of dates at the Wayne Newton Theatre in 1993. The next year, with his theater deal crumbling and new opportunities opening, he played Branson only six times.[53]

The man who saved Cash from the dubious confines of Branson, and helped preserve his legacy as the greatest country artist of all time, was Rick Rubin. Though he looked like a stern, bearded prophet, Rubin was young. Born in 1963, he had cofounded the early hip-hop label Def Jam Records in New York City. He produced such "un-country" artists as the Beastie Boys, Run-DMC, and the Red Hot Chili Peppers. Rubin eventually decided he wanted to make a Johnny Cash album. As Marty Stuart said later, Rubin got Cash "out of the Nashville box and boiled him down beyond the myth to the essence of the boy from Arkansas with the God-given gifts that made him so special."[54]

That album became *American Recordings*, the most stripped-down record Cash had released up until that time. Not only did Cash not use a band, he didn't even use a pick. All the songs featured just Cash strumming on an acoustic guitar, along with two live cuts recorded at the Viper Room in Los Angeles. The Viper Room had gained notoriety as the place where actor River Phoenix overdosed in October 1993, not long before Cash's December 3 show. The atmosphere was fitting for Cash, and *American Recordings* introduced him to a new, younger audience.

Cash closed his Viper Room set with the five-minute, tragic-comic "Man Who Couldn't Cry." It was Loudon Wainwright III's song, but it sounded as if Cash could have written it, and most of the audience probably didn't know he hadn't. Cash once again made another artist's song his own, weaving together themes that he had sung about for decades. "The Man Who Couldn't Cry" approaches parody. He "lost an arm in a war, was laughed at by a whore," before being beaten and "bullied and buggered" in jail, while fed a diet of water and bread. Still, the man wouldn't cry, despite being attended by doctors, scientists, and theologians. The man eventually learns to cry again. The emotional trickle becomes a flood, however, and the man dies of dehydration. In heaven, he is reunited with his dog and his arm. The song was more over the top than anything Cash might have written, but it was funny. The crowd enjoyed it. Johnny Cash was back.

As was true of his 1968 resurgence, Cash's comeback coincided with a dramatic shift in American pop music. In September 1991, Nirvana released its major-label debut, *Nevermind*. The album sent the Seattle grunge scene into the stratosphere and became the yardstick by which alternative rock albums were measured. American youth had a new hero in Nirvana's tortured front man, the blonde-haired, blue-eyed Kurt Cobain. Nirvana sounded nothing like Johnny Cash. But the band had an aesthetic similar to that of Cash and the Tennessee Two: three guys making honest, straightforward, unpolished, groundbreaking music. Nirvana represented a break from the light synthpop and overproduced hair metal that dominated the 1980s airwaves. *Nevermind*, with its scorching guitar riffs and thundering drums, sold ten million copies and paved the way for Seattle bands such as Pearl Jam and Soundgarden.

Cobain's songs—epitomized by the four-chord riff on "Smells Like Teen Spirit"—represented yet another back-to-basics revolution in American music. Nirvana attracted fans through emotional lyrics and no-nonsense, punk-inspired playing. Had Johnny Cash been born not in 1932, but thirty years later in Seattle, he might have been one of the godfathers of grunge rather than Outlaw country.

Cash's resurgence coincided with Nirvana remaking the American soundscape. It also intersected with hip-hop, an adult-terrifying new sound that began in New York City in the 1970s and 1980s and spread to the West Coast. Groups as diverse as Public Enemy and the Beastie Boys rattled the cages of Reagan-era popular music. By the late 1980s, N.W.A., 2 Live Crew, and other groups were shocking parents and teachers in a way unseen since the early days of rock and roll. In the decade-long wake of disco, MTV-ready pop, and lovable but unthreatening Weird Al parodies, music was dangerous again.

As parents' groups and politicians sought to contain the latest explosion of youthful musical energy, Cash was an oldster finding a place in the new musical landscape. He was not alone. By the mid-nineties, Neil Young and Bob Dylan were producing some of their best music in years. As did Cash, they took a straightforward approach. Young's "Unknown Legend"—on his heavily acoustic *Harvest Moon*, released in late 1992—sounded like a cut from twenty years earlier. The same year, Dylan released *Good as I Been to You*. It featured no original material, but the album was the first in a creative outpouring. Dylan saved new his songs for *Time Out of Mind*, released in 1997. The double album was well received by critics and fans alike and won three Grammys. The Beatles also cashed in on the revival of 1960s music with their *Anthology* documentary and accompanying albums of outtakes and rarities.

The revival of Cash and other sixties musicians had a lot to do with the shift in sounds and tastes. It was also rooted in a technological shift, whereby compact discs provided a much better listening experience for music lovers than ever before. By the 1990s, vinyl records were literally being tossed into the dustbins of history. Vinyl lovers would have to hunt through stacks at flea markets, yard sales, and secondhand stores to find old copies of *At Folsom Prison*. Before the hipster-inspired vinyl revival made people shun digital music, compact discs represented a huge sound improvement over scratched or warped old records, not to mention clumsy cassettes. The digital nature of CDs would sow the seeds of their own demise later, but in the mid-nineties, everyone was too busy heading to Sam Goody or Tower Records to care much about the future of the music business. Music was more portable and cleaner sounding than it had ever been. Who cared if malls were charging $15–$20 for *Revolver,* or that a scratched CD was worse than a scratched record?

For Cash to find a new producer, a new label, and a new generation of fans amid a beneficial shift in technology was lucky for a man in his sixties. *American Recordings* proved artistically liberating for a number of reasons. Rubin gave Cash the freedom to record how and what he wanted, and Cash chose to cut an album of stark originals and covers that fit the dark mood of American music. Just a few weeks before the album's release, Kurt Cobain killed himself. With Nirvana fans and the grunge world reeling, the mood of Cash's new album matched that of many music fans.

American Recordings is indeed dark—and was an album Johnny had wanted to make for decades. In addition to Cash, there were offerings by such heavy-hearted songwriters as Kris Kristofferson, Nick Lowe, Tom Waits, and Leonard Cohen. Cash wrote four for the album. "Like a Soldier" was an extended metaphor for life's challenges and journeys. "Drive On" was about a Vietnam veteran concluding the only way to get through the horrors of war was to adopt the mantra "drive on. It don't mean nuthin'. Drive on. It don't mean a thing." "Let the Train Blow the Whistle" ruminates on death ("tell the gossipers and liars, I will see them in the fire"), while "Redemption" was darker still, telling the story of Jesus's redemptive suffering—Lucifer sought to "keep me in chains," but the singer wasn't fooled by "the tricks of six sixty-six."

Rubin and Cash's minimalist aesthetic resonated with an "alternative" crowd eager to find music that diverged from the mainstream. *American Recordings* sales did not come close to the mammoth success of Nirvana's *Nevermind* or the band's last studio album, *In Utero* (released September 1993). Sales of *American Recordings*, nevertheless—numbering 150,000 by the end of 1994—were the best Cash had seen since 1971.[55] Cash's choice of material covered the usual subjects of love, murder, and God. But Cash was again hip, even controversial. The video for *American Recordings*' opening track, "Delia's Gone," involved the murder of the singer's beloved Delia. Written by Karl Silbersdorf and Dick Toops, Cash had recorded "Delia's Gone" early in his career on his 1962 album *The Sound of Johnny Cash*. That version was done in his trademark boom-chicka-boom manner. On *American Recordings*, with just Cash on the guitar, "Delia's Gone" benefited from the bare-bones arrangement, making Cash sound like what he was—a depression-era troubadour. He also made significant lyrical changes—in the 1994 version, the narrator does not wind up serving hard time. Both versions, however, have a nihilism worthy of "Folsom Prison Blues."

The video for "Delia's Gone" included graphic footage of Cash shooting and burying Delia, played by model Kate Moss. Cash excised footage from the video to make it more palatable for television (for Cash, once an outlaw, always an outlaw).[56] Nevertheless, the song and video with its black-and-white photography—and, unfortunately, its overactive wind machine—were "gangsta" enough for Cash to win over the alt-music crowd.

The 1994 Kingsland Concert

As Cash was poised to reach a new generation of fans, he remained, as always, true to his roots. In March 1994—just before the release of *American Recordings*—Cash visited Arkansas for another homecoming concert. This time, Cash played in Kingsland, at the high school, to celebrate a new post office in Rison and to mark the US postal service releasing a Johnny Cash Pictorial Cancellation Stamp (available for a month in Kingsland).[57]

In contrast to his 1976 Rison show, Cash's Kingsland concert was more low-key. Cash was not the draw he once had been. It was, nevertheless, a major event for tiny, working-class Kingsland. People came out. Eighteen years before, the day threatened rain, but this time, on the last day of March, the weather was warm and sunny. Farmers in short sleeves, mesh baseball hats, and blue jeans milled around, waiting for Cash. Locals grabbed some food from the Assembly of God snack wagon and sipped cups of lemonade. High schoolers put on a decidedly modest fashion show. It was 1994 and still the era of big hair, loud sweaters, and oversized eighties clothes. In Kingsland, though, there was no shortage of cowboy hats. For some, the sight of a clown walking about Kingsland with balloons might have been as rare as seeing Johnny Cash in the flesh.[58]

Kingsland residents made the most of Cash's Thursday appearance—only his second in Cleveland County as a performer. At 10 a.m., the post office and several local businesses sponsored a Johnny Cash talent show with prizes for people who could lip-synch or sing a Cash tune. Prize money was offered, and participants were given the chance to perform before the Man in Black himself. Few people get to perform a world-famous singer's song in front of them, but Johnny Cash was the kind of musician who made that possible.

In preparation for Johnny's arrival, Kingsland had a town-wide clean up, and residents asked people to support the fire department, whose volunteers sold barbecue sandwiches for Cash fans. Townspeople also built a sidewalk at the post office site and tightened the local curfew. Kingsland City Council had the Cash memorial—unveiled in 1976—repainted. The man who helped do it was artist Emmett Hill, who had designed the cancellation stamp.[59]

It was as much Hill's day as it was Cash's. Hill had lived in Kingsland for twenty-four years. Originally from New Mexico, he moved to Kingsland in 1970 when his father retired. Hill had drawn since he was young, and relatives had urged him to stick with it. He taught art for disabled and elderly people in the area and donated his works to the Arkansas Children's Hospital in Little Rock. His views on art were likely similar to Johnny Cash's views on music. "Art is learning how to see," he told the *Cleveland County Herald*. "And it helps me escape. Your mind goes through an incubation period before you hatch an idea."[60] As was true of Cash back in the 1930s, Hill lived not far from the train tracks, which became a popular subject matter for him. Sylvia Reddin, the Kingsland postmaster, had given Hill the job to design the Cash cancellation stamp. Hill had the pleasure of presenting Cash with the drawing for the stamp on stage. He also signed envelopes after Johnny's brief concert.

To mark the stamp's debut, high school students had had a contest to see which classroom could make their doors look like envelopes. Many locals were in attendance as well as representatives from area businesses, the Pinnacle Stamp Club of Arkansas, the Assembly of God, the Church of Christ, and members of the National Guard. The winner of the Johnny Cash sing-alike contest was Bobby Joe Clements of New Edinburgh, Arkansas, a town of 130 people, located just to the south of Kingsland. Clements had convinced the *Herald*, "If you closed your eyes . . . you would have thought Johnny Cash was singing."[61] While not as large as the gathering in Cleveland County in 1976, the crowd at Kingsland that day, estimated at three thousand people, was larger than Kingsland and neighboring Rison combined.

Governor Tucker declared March 31 "Kingsland Post Office Day." The day involved not just Cash's concert but also an arts and crafts fair, historic photo exhibit, "Johnny Cash Mini Museum," stamp displays and exhibits, and refreshments. The festivities had a tent revival feel, and not just because Cash literally performed under a tent. According to the *Herald*, Kingsland "came alive like never before."[62] Before the gathering,

Mark Rivers, a cousin of Johnny's, read a passage from the Gospel of John, Chapter 15, concerning friends. As a further gesture of friendship, Kingslanders gave Johnny a homemade quilt.

By 1994, Cash seemed to be going it alone when it came to live performances. But he still liked to have his family with him. By now, Cash's father and mother were gone. Ray Cash had died in 1985, Carrie in 1991. Carrie Cash had been remembered as a "good neighbor, a family woman and a devout Christian." When she died, a neighbor in Dyess recalled her once hoeing cotton for them. "She was a fine lady, that's for sure."[63] Cash's parents were dead, but he took strength from his remaining family.

Dressed in trademark black, Cash did not bring his full band with him. Instead, he relied on a local group who backed him up on stage. June, wearing a beret and ruffled shirt under a heavy coat, joined Johnny with John Carter, Tommy, and Johnny's youngest sister, Joanne. Under a green-and-white tent, the audience sat on folding chairs and fanned themselves. The procession of acts was much longer than Cash's show. Before Cash took the stage, attendees saw a gospel group, were offered a not-so-brief history of Kingsland, and heard a blessing of the post office. As was true of his 1976 visit, Cash put his family at center stage. Johnny's brother Tommy—who had had his own success as a country singer—briefly took the stage to read a letter from the postmaster general honoring Cash.

Also on stage were a postal worker, a representative for Gov. James Guy Tucker Jr., and the middle-aged winner of the Johnny Cash sound-alike contest, who bore a resemblance to Arkansas politician Wilbur Mills (who was not there). An extended, operatic rendition of the national anthem was sung with bombast. Kingslanders were giving their all.

By 1994, the music landscape had changed dramatically from the time of Cash's 1976 show, but Kingsland hadn't shifted by much. Hometown fans were happy to see their most famous son. Cash was not one for long speeches, but he warmed up the crowd with humor, reminding the crowd that people often wondered how Kingsland was pronounced. "Kinslun! Kingslun!" Cash said to the laughing crowd. Turning more serious, Cash said he was back in Arkansas to "touch my roots again."[64] Such words would have been true for Cash at any time, but he was back where he had come from and less than a month away from one of his rootsiest albums, *American Recordings*.

In March 1994, Cash played in Cleveland County for the last time. He did not travel to Kingsland with his regular band, but with him as usual were June, John Carter, and his brother Tommy. The show happened just weeks before the release of Cash's *American Recordings* album—a collaboration with producer Rick Rubin that set off Cash's second major comeback. *Courtesy Stan Sadler.*

After a long wait, Cash obliged the crowd by playing several of his hits, including "Folsom Prison Blues" and "A Boy Named Sue." The small concert concluded with Cash and his family coming together for a rendition of "Will the Circle Be Unbroken?" As usual, Cash managed to bring together music, his family, community, and the faithful through one of his most well-worn songs.

American Recordings rebooted Cash's career, but he didn't let his new success go to his head. Talking to *Parade* magazine in 1995, he spoke yet again about his humbling addiction to amphetamines. He returned to other familiar topics: family and his fans. Whatever success he had, he credited to Ray and Carrie Cash. "I got a lot of really good stuff from my parents," he admitted, saying a "lot of my father is in my songs." Nearly twenty years after he had written it, Cash referenced "Ridin' on the Cotton Belt." It was never one of his popular songs, but it still had deep meaning for him. Cash then acknowledged his mother, from whom he said his voice came. "I got my presence and my height from her," he said. "Her values were like June Carter's, solid-rock values." Cash said he missed his parents every day.[65]

As Cash rode another comeback, his home state was becoming one of the most important in the nation, even if most people did not know it. Bill Clinton—born in Hope and raised in Hot Springs—was president. Walmart, headquartered in Bentonville in northwestern Arkansas, was growing into the biggest retailer in world history. But Arkansas continued to have a poor reputation in many respects, especially when it came to crime and the justice system. In 1994, HBO aired a show called *Bangin' in Little Rock*, documenting the city's rampant gang problem. Arkansas attracted further unwelcome headlines that August 4 when Governor Tucker executed three criminals in one day. Just before the executions, Johnny and June had sent the governor a telegram that said, "FOR GOD'S SAKE HAVE MERCY."[66] It did no good. Arkansas became the first state in thirty-two years to perform a triple execution in a twenty-four-hour period. The executions came not long after the conviction of the West Memphis Three: teenagers tried and convicted for the murder of three boys in that Arkansas city. They were eventually released, but it took more than a decade, and the men were never legally exonerated.

Not surprisingly, Damien Echols—the most outspoken of the West Memphis Three—listened to Johnny Cash while he was in prison at a supermax facility in Arkansas. He said Cash was among several artists that kept him going. Though he said Cash's music had a tendency to "fuck me up inside," Echols took solace from "what my parents listened to when I was growing up."[67] Many musicians took up the cause of the West Memphis Three, including Eddie Vedder of Pearl Jam and Rosanne Cash. Johnny, however, did not speak publicly about the controversy.

By the mid-1990s, Cash was receiving honors large and small. He had already been elected into the Rock and Roll and Country halls of fame. In 1996, Arkansas recognized him by putting him in the Arkansas Entertainers Hall of Fame, along with such stars as Glen Campbell and

Billy Bob Thornton. A few months after Arkansas recognized Cash's stellar career, he received a much bigger recognition. In December, President Clinton honored him at the Kennedy Center, an opera house and performing arts venue in Washington, DC. Cash was feted alongside Edward Albee, Jack Lemmon, jazz musician Benny Carter, and Native American ballerina Maria Tallchief. Clinton's remarks on Cash were heartfelt, but contained several factual errors. Cash did not grow up "chopping cotton in a small town in southeast Arkansas" (it was northeast Arkansas). Nor was Cash a "kid in the Army" when he wrote "Folsom Prison Blues"; it was instead the Air Force, and he likely wrote the song in Memphis after he left the service. Clinton also mentioned Cash's twenty-seven albums and fifty million records sold. In fact, his album output by 1996 was closer to fifty original records.[68]

Despite the mistakes in Clinton's speech, Cash was excited about receiving the award. He took the honor with accustomed humor, saying in his autobiography it was "exhausting and dangerous for my ego." He added it was "quite wonderful" to sit with the president and "the most powerful people in the world." As exciting as getting the award might have been for Cash, in noting the Kennedy honors, he recalled something that Ernest Tubb once told him: "Just remember this, son. The higher up the ladder you get, the brighter your ass shines." Tubb, who died in 1984, apparently had given Cash some sage advice. As big a star as he was, Cash was always close to a humbling moment. After the Kennedy Center Honors, his family took it as an opportunity to bring up some personal resentments. Cash remembered the "deep feelings they'd had for a very long time—told me things, that is, about the lives of girls whose daddy abandoned them for a drug. That was very hard."[69]

Cash took solace in his work. In 1996, he released the second of his American Recordings, *Unchained*. In contrast to its stark predecessor, *Unchained* paired Cash with rockers Tom Petty and the Heartbreakers. Petty was a legend in his own right, but recording with Cash clearly was a thrill for him. As was true of Cash, Petty was a southerner. In homage to their Dixie heritage, Cash sang "Southern Accents" on *Unchained*. "There's a southern accent, where I come from," the first line goes. "The young'uns call it country / The Yankees call it dumb." Rarely did Cash draw attention to his own southern-ness. The words were Petty's, but the line "that drunk tank in Atlanta's just a motel room to me" was one Cash could relate to.

Unchained combined Cash's ability to shift from country to rock and back again, as he always had. A listener can hear one of Cash's finest moments on the song "Rusty Cage," originally recorded by Soundgarden. It was a song well suited to Cash.[70] The lyrics spoke of the need of liberation from "bars and rusty chains." The song could have been about Cash leaving Arkansas, or struggling with his drug addiction, or his quest for spiritual liberation. The river is a metaphor in "Rusty Cage," one that Cash—as the author of "Big River"—must have appreciated. The song also benefited from dark imagery worthy of the Bible, speaking as it did of burning forest, "god's eyes in my headlights," dogs digging for bones, and "raining ice picks on your steel shore." By memorably covering a Seattle grunge band, Cash further ingratiated himself with the alternative rock crowd. And with Rick Rubin, Cash had found his most visionary producer since Sam Phillips. Rubin not only blended shades of light and dark with Cash's material, he took the listener from the early days of rockabilly to the present, where grunge reigned supreme.

In Cash's work with Rubin, the shadow of Arkansas fell long over the proceedings. On *Unchained*, Cash included an updated, more rocking version of "Country Boy," one of his earliest songs at Sun. This time, he performed with a full band. The song does not mention Arkansas, but "Mean Eyed Cat"—another one of the more rocking numbers—did. *Unchained*, ironically, also featured "I Never Picked Cotton," a 1970 song written by Bobby George and Charlie Williams and memorably recorded by Roy Clark of *Hee Haw* fame.

Clark was born in Virginia but he grew up in Staten Island and Washington, DC. "I Never Picked Cotton" might have been a line that rang true for Clark, but surely not for Johnny Cash. Rather, the song was about an Oklahoma man who refused to toil in the fields with his brothers and sisters. The narrator's father died in the coal mines, and the narrator sings of killing a "redneck" in Memphis who had told him to "go back to your cotton sack." The song ends with the man going to the gallows. It was another in a long line of tunes about outlaws, killers, and condemned men. Cash was a long way from the days of writing "Folsom Prison Blues." Still, one finds elements of his early career in "I Never Picked Cotton." Once again, Cash was exploring the South, the murder ballad, and the hard lives of field hands—the narrator says, as Cash did in real life, how much he hated such work.

Despite his newfound success and credibility with fans and critics, Cash continued to come to terms with his family and reflect on the mistakes he had made as a husband and father. In 1997, he wrote his second and last memoir, *Cash*, with Patrick Carr, an English music writer who grew up in the 1950s loving country music and later moved to New York City. Cash had already written and discussed his life many times before in song and in interviews. He had written his previous book, *Man in White*, by himself. Cash was a lifelong wordsmith, but *Cash* was something more like a transcribed oral history. He completed the book by giving lengthy interviews with Carr, who then formed Cash's words into straightforward and effective prose true to the voice of the Man in Black. According to Carr, many passages were hardly rewritten at all.[71]

The Cash of the mid-nineties was not the Cash of 1975's *Man in Black*. Unlike his previous autobiography, *Cash* was not a redemption story. In many ways, however, the singer's second autobiography was another tale of spiritual rebirth. In the twenty years between the books, Cash's life had followed many similar patterns: drug abuse, family problems, career lows and highs. It is a richer and more satisfying book than *Man in Black*. His first autobiography was honest about his drug problems and self-destructive behavior and *Cash* was just as dark. He wrote about his supposed suicide attempt in Nickajack Cave and the death of his brother. The most shocking new material in *Cash* was about Johnny's father, Ray—a self-described "evil man." Cash himself, in his letters from the 1950s, hinted at how much of a monster his father could be when drunk. But for many years, even long after his father's death and as recently as his 1995 interview with *Parade*, Cash had spoken well of his father.

What had changed? The autobiography was not *Parade* magazine. Carr was a seasoned rock critic. He was friends with New York City music writers such as the prickly and influential Robert Christgau of *The Village Voice*. Around Carr, Cash opened up as he had never before with any music writer. He apparently wanted to set the record straight about his father. During one afternoon with Carr, Cash chain-smoked cigarettes and told him some of the darkest secrets he had about his father. The specifics of Ray's abusiveness didn't make it into the book. A full chapter about his father was in the works, but Cash—concerned about family privacy and the possibility of discussing the issue endlessly in future interviews—chose at the last minute not to include it.[72]

Reviews of *Cash* were positive. In his home state, the *Arkansas Democrat-Gazette* said that the book featured a Cash who was "so unassuming and such a great storyteller it's hard to imagine anyone who likes music not enjoying these tales."[73] The book again showed Cash's ability to reach an audience beyond traditional country music. In the movie *High Fidelity*, about music and vinyl fanatics in Chicago, the main character, Rob, says his favorite book—despite the fact he had read *Love in the Time of Cholera* and *The Unbearable Lightness of Being*—was "Cash's autobiography *Cash* by Johnny Cash."

Cash's autobiography was published amid increasing medical problems. Cash stumbled bending over for a guitar pick at a show in Flint, Michigan, in October 1997. In November, he came down with a serious case of pneumonia. In June 1998, Cash took the stage in the Ryman Auditorium, where fans were first told [or where he first told fans] that his health problems were the result of Parkinson's disease. This diagnosis was later changed to Shy-Drager syndrome and then again to autonomic neuropathy. "People had prayer groups on the Internet for me," Cash said, referring to the new technology quickly revolutionizing information gathering, human interaction, and the music business. Cash believed "it was prayers that pulled me through," but he was no longer in any condition to tour. One of the greatest live acts in American history was effectively in retirement, at least when it came to live shows.[74]

Cash occasionally appeared on stage thereafter, though. In April 1999, he played at the Hammerstein Ballroom in New York at a show heavy with music celebrities. At the "All Star Tribute to Johnny Cash," Johnny played several of his signature songs, including "Folsom Prison Blues" and "I Walk the Line." All of Johnny's children were there, as were usual supporters such as Willie Nelson, Bob Dylan, Marty Stuart, and Kris Kristofferson. The show was organized not long after Cash had won a Lifetime Achievement Award at the Grammys ceremony.[75]

Despite his inability to tour, Cash continued to make music. He followed up *Unchained* with *Solitary Man*, released in 2000. He again collaborated with Tom Petty, who appeared on the album as a backing vocalist and organ player, along with Heartbreakers keyboardist Benmont Tench. Cash acknowledged Petty's influence by recording a version of "I Won't Back Down." He also dipped deep into his own personal music catalog, performing the 1949 song "That Lucky Old Sun," which high schooler Cash had sung for his classmates back in Dyess. Other Arkansas streams ran through the album, such as a new take on "Country Trash," originally released in 1973 on *Any Old Wind that Blows.*

Cash's career was coming full circle. "Solitary Man" was not just a title track (based on Cash's cover of a Neil Diamond song), but a statement of where he was as an artist. Cash, after all, was no longer touring or playing with his earlier bandmates. WS Holland and Bob Wootton were left to fend for themselves. Marshall Grant had long since departed. Cash was a beloved and world famous musician, who could get just about anybody to play with him. But he was in many ways on his own again. Rubin had cast Cash in the role of lone cowboy, searching the range for songs to record and interpret. It was a role Cash knew well. It essentially put Cash back in the Air Force barracks again, playing the songs he loved as a kid. The difference now was that he wasn't accompanied by drunken servicemen, but Tom Petty and Marty Stuart. The talent pool had improved, but as with any solo musical project, the American Recordings have a lonely feel.

But, Cash wasn't alone. American Recordings brought him to another generation of fans. And in the age of the internet, fans were more open than ever about his influence. In 1998, Teresa Ortega published an article that argued for Cash's importance as a lesbian icon. Her article quoted John Waters: "I used to hang out in this bar in Baltimore that was *really* heavy duty, I mean, where many of the women looked like Johnny Cash. And I met Johnny Cash this year and I . . . almost told him that."[76] It wouldn't be the last time Waters compared a Baltimore native to Cash. In his book *Role Models*, Waters wrote of a male cross-dressing stripper named Zorro who was "so butch, so scary, so Johnny Cash."[77] In her article, Ortega wrote of imitating Johnny Cash's voice, dress, and his guitar and harmonica playing. Ortega was drawn to Cash because of his support for "disenfranchised groups, from coal miners to Native Americans." She thought it fitting that "butch lesbians look to Cash."[78]

In 2002, Patrick Carr spoke again with Cash, who was, as always, honest about his health problems. By then his ailments included several bouts of pneumonia since he had last seen Carr. Cash nevertheless said he was "doing better" and "feeling great." He was having trouble putting down the vocals for his new record, but he had energy and was enthusiastic about his continued collaboration with Rubin. Cash said he was not suffering from Shy-Drager Syndrome but rather "autonomic neuropathy" and was not sure what the diagnosis meant. Based on what doctors told him, however, he said that had he actually been afflicted with Shy-Drager, he would have been dead already. Despite Cash's health problems, Carr noted "his intelligence is fierce" as well as "his life force." Given the fragile state of Cash's body, Carr asked him about death and what was "on the other side." Cash thought the afterlife would be "nice and peaceful." He didn't worry about dying. He thought of death in Christian terms, saying he would "be there with God in eternal bliss. Ecstasy." He told Carr he was "kind of disappointed" in knowing he was not going to die soon—continuing on meant "more of this pain!" Cash added that his health problems had not led him to doubt his faith or get angry at God.

His meditations on mortality were not lessened by the recent death of one of his friends and collaborators, Waylon Jennings, whose own life—full of near-death experiences—was a legend on par with Cash's. Jennings had died in Arizona in February 2002 from diabetes complications. As was true of Cash, Jennings had a long history of drug abuse, chain smoking, and ill health. Both men had undergone heart surgery. Not long before he died, doctors amputated one of Jennings's feet. Johnny and Waylon had a long history together. In what was a landlord's nightmare, they had roomed together briefly when Johnny was at the nadir of his drug addiction. They had also recorded together and made up one-half of the Highwaymen. Cash said he and Waylon had reconciled before Jennings died, and was happy to hear that Waylon had embraced Christianity toward the end of his life and supposedly "died with a smile."

Carr wondered: What were the three worst things that ever happened to Cash? Cash was evasive. Living with Ray Cash certainly was one. Others would have included the death of Jack, his divorce, run-ins with white supremacists over his wife's ethnicity, his profound embarrassment at losing his voice at the Carnegie Hall show, and getting arrested. Cash had many lows to go with his historic highs.[79]

A few months later, Cash released his fourth collaboration with Rick Rubin, *American IV: The Man Comes Around*. The album was the last he recorded, and it was more erratic than his earlier work with Rubin. It began with the terrific and apocalyptic title track. Accompanied by hard acoustic strumming, "The Man Comes Around" wove together lines about death and the Bible. It was Johnny Cash's last great original song, used to great effect in the 2004 remake of the zombie apocalypse classic *Dawn of the Dead*.

Cash's voice had become a mere croak, but he still gave power and pathos to "Hurt," a cover of a Nine Inch Nails song, and "I Hung My Head," about a cowboy accidentally shooting a man with his rifle. The latter song was written by Sting, but it felt like a song Cash might have written in 1965. Also perfectly fitted to Cash's sensibilities was his cover of Depeche Mode's "Personal Jesus." Other choices, however, were less fitting. Cash and Rubin overreached in their attempts to have Johnny cover "First Time Ever I Saw Your Face," "Bridge over Troubled Water," and "In My Life." The songs, thematically, were good choices. But musically, they did not suit Cash's singing style. "Bridge over Troubled Water" and "In My Life" were too iconic—and too far outside his vocal range—for Cash to have made his own.

Such was not the case with "Hurt," where Cash gave one of the best performances on the album. As is true of any great song, it had many meanings, especially for Cash. Most obviously, as a song about drug addiction, it appealed to Cash, a man in his seventies, who knew—despite what he might have told Patrick Carr in order to make himself or his fans feel better—that he was not in good physical shape. In fact, he was in agony. Starting in early 1990, Cash suffered from chronic, searing jaw pain that he sought to alleviate with pills. In addition to his physical problems, "Hurt" was a meditation on a lifetime of emotional pain. He probably had endured more hurt—and inflicted more—than most men his age.

The video Cash recorded in 2003 for "Hurt" also reached iconic status, containing as it did images from his life, including his visit to Dyess in the late 1960s for *The Man, His World, His Music*. In September of that year, the MTV Music Awards would honor it with a Best Cinematography award. The video also featured June, who, much to the shock of the family and the music world, died before Cash. June's marriage with Johnny was far from idyllic. As was true of Johnny, she had suffered from substance abuse problems, though hers were never as publicized as Johnny's. In May 2003, she entered a Nashville hospital for heart surgery. The operation seemed to have gone well at first and June was recovering. But one night she had a major heart attack and went into a coma. The heart attack cut off oxygen to her brain, leaving her in what would have been a permanent vegetative state. Johnny had to make the agonizing decision to turn off her life support. Then Cash and his family had to wait the three excruciating days it took for June to expire. On May 15, she died.[80]

June was as open in death as she had been in life. She did not want a private funeral. Instead, the ceremony was broadcast on local television. A crowd estimated at 1,800 people attended. Cash was there, though he was so feeble he had to sit in a wheelchair during the service. Among the Cashes, only Rosanne spoke. June was buried in the Hendersonville cemetery that was the final resting place of June's and Johnny's parents as well as Luther Perkins. Attendees at June's funeral included people as diverse as Robert Duvall and Sheryl Crow. The prime minister of Jamaica sent a message, saying June was a "philanthropist extraordinaire" who called Jamaica her "second home and loved and cared deeply for the people of her adopted country."[81]

Despite June's death and his own physical frailty, Cash had no desire to stop making music. He gave his last concert at Hiltons in western Virginia at the Carter Family Fold on July 7, 2003. Footage of the performance shows a Cash that looked twenty years older than he was. Not only did he have great difficulty moving, he could barely hold a guitar. But he managed to play some of his greatest hits, such as "Folsom Prison Blues" and "I Walk the Line." Cash had left the Tennessee Three behind long before, but now even June was gone. Cash not only looked old, he looked lonely—a solitary man, indeed.

Death and Remembrance

As was true of his hero Jimmie Rodgers, Cash kept working until he died. For Rodgers, death came in May 1933 as he was recording in New York; the ailing king of early country had long suffered from tuberculosis. Rodgers had a nurse with him in his final days, and he had to rest on a cot between takes to get enough energy for his next song. When Rodgers died, Cash was only a year old. Now, seventy years later, Cash and Rubin continued to record, even when Cash was too ill to get out of bed. Johnny died on September 12, 2003.

David Pryor, the former Arkansas governor and, in 2003, one of its senators, lauded Cash. Pryor had been in Rison for Cash's 1976 concert. "A poor child from Arkansas turned legend," he said, Cash "succeeded on the grandest scale, and taught us in the process that the dreams of a small boy on a small farm in a small town can be realized." In what was a true understatement, he added that Cash "will surely be missed." Tiny Cleveland County gave Cash a send-off appropriate to his legend. The *Herald* noted that Cash was an icon, but "folks in his native Cleveland County remember him as a simple, common man who never forgot his rural roots." Locals remembered Cash as "down to earth," a man, as Cash's second cousin Ricky Fore of Rison put it, who "wouldn't put on any aires [*sic*] at all." John Rivers Cash remembered seeing Cash in 1994 during his Kingsland concert. Cash was alone on a gravel road, he said, "kind of teary eyed." Cash said, "You know . . . sometimes I think I should have never left here." That of course, had not been Cash's decision to make back in 1935. By the time he returned to Cleveland County as an adult, moving back home must have seemed impossible, even had he wanted to. It's easy to dismiss such a sad lament. Perhaps it was just Cash being nostalgic. But nothing in his career suggests he pursued the limelight for its own sake. Cash was a country boy by nature, a country music icon by way of talent and luck and persistence. Other than being on stage, he was most at home in the outdoors with family—hunting and fishing in places like Cleveland County, where he could hear the birds and smell the pines.[82]

Throughout his life, Cash had managed to befriend Republicans and Democrats alike. He had played for Richard Nixon, and he counted Republican politician and millionaire John Rollins among his friends. Yet among those who spoke at Cash's funeral on September 15, 2003, was Bill Clinton's former vice president, Al Gore. Cash had helped Tex Ritter try to unseat Al Gore Sr. in the 1970 Senate primaries, but the younger Gore apparently held no grudge. A month later in *Rolling Stone*, Gore remembered Cash as a man who "felt a deep connection to the suffering of others. . . . He cared about social conditions and wanted laws and policies that would help the poor and disadvantaged."[83] Rosanne remembered her father as "a poet who worked in the dirt."[84] Cash himself had a sense of humor about the afterlife. "I don't think there'll be any banjos," he'd quipped in 1997.[85]

Fellow musicians were not hesitant with praise. "We both went through a lot of messes in the old days," said George Jones, "but ended up realizing what was important in life and changed our ways. Heaven is a better place with the death of Johnny Cash." Kris Kristofferson, who owed his career to Cash, said he "has always seemed larger than life to me. He's been my inspiration, my faithful friend, my champion. And he was damned funny, even in the darkest of times." Merle Kilgore, who had cowritten "Ring of Fire" with June, said Johnny was "raw and he was the truth." Kilgore went on to say that Cash, like other famous entertainers, had a way of "looking into your soul. . . . It was a strange feeling when Johnny Cash checked you out," Kilgore said.

The *Arkansas Gazette* said that Cash had written songs about "prison life, hardships, hobos and desperate loves, propelling the Arkansas native into one of the world's most admired and loved performers." The paper also noted his "Arkansas roots inspired many of his tunes." In a line worthy of Cash, the paper noted, "Cash strummed his family's blood and sweat across his guitar." To sum him up, the paper concluded with a quotation from Johnny himself. "I can sing of death," he said, "I've seen a lot of it. But I'm obsessed with life. I've been in that dark place. I fight the beast in me every day."[86]

It is fitting that the remembrances in Arkansas were more satisfying and focused than one written in Nashville and published nationwide. Peter Kilborn and Marta Aldrich's story on Nashville's reaction opened not with Cash's story but another's: a description of a 22-year-old music major, hot dog salesman, and self-professed songwriter struggling to make it in Music City. The obituary didn't really discuss Cash—"a 6-foot-2-inch man with crevices like hatchet marks through his cheeks who sold more than 50 million records"—until the fourth paragraph. Cash himself might have found it amusing that even in an obituary about the greatest country artist of all time, Nashville was more concerned with itself. It was fitting, though. Nashville never really knew what to do with Cash. As the obituary made clear, he was "country, he was rock, he was folk, he was rockabilly." The obituary praised Cash's music, but the piece underscored Nashville's self-consciousness over its authenticity problem. "Johnny Cash was original," one resident was quoted as saying. "When he opened his mouth to sing, you knew who he was. He knew who he was. Today's artists, it's pretty hard to tell them from one another." Such a claim had an element of truth, but likely what was true of Nashville in 2003—as is the case now, and probably always will be—is that Nashville records some of the best music as well as the worst.[87] But the city's remembrance of Cash reinforced the fact that he was never really a Nashville champion. "I always have felt on the outskirts of Nashville physically, spiritually, and emotionally," Cash told *Us Weekly* in 1997. "I never did totally conform."[88] Cash's bones might've been laid to rest in Tennessee, but his soul was in Arkansas.

Johnny had been devastated by June's death, but the final tracks he cut with Rick Rubin became the basis for two more American Recordings releases: *A Hundred Highways*, released in 2006; and *Ain't No Grave*, appearing in 2010, just a few days before what would have been Cash's seventy-eighth birthday. Both of the albums were well received commercially and critically. *A Hundred Highways* reached number 1 on both *Billboard*'s country chart and the *Billboard* 200. Both albums were true to Cash's life's work, mixing spiritual songs, train songs, and prison lamentations. Cash's sources were older (Hank Williams), newer (Bruce Springsteen), and everywhere in between (Larry Gatlin, Kris Kristofferson, and Gordon Lightfoot). The first two songs ("Help Me" and "God's Gonna Cut You Down") were religious but sung with Cash's usual edge. Cash had recorded "Help Me" on *The Gospel Road*, though it was then titled "Help." Rubin's production, with a tasteful use of cellos, gave the new version added power.

"God's Gonna Cut You Down" has a Delta feel, and the album as a whole has a bluesier atmosphere than most of Cash's records. As usual, Cash was bending the rules as he went along. On "Like the 309," he blended two huge musical influences: death and trains. Cash died only a few weeks after he recorded it. Everything Cash had experienced in Arkansas had followed him throughout this life. On his final recordings, he was still expressing what he had learned in the Delta so many years before.

Cash was buried in Hendersonville, in the same cemetery as June and his parents and Luther Perkins. He was a long way from Jack and other family members laid to rest in Arkansas. But a few years after his death, Arkansas would begin building a powerful legacy to its greatest entertainer. The work began in Dyess.

8

Home

In the year 2000, the members of the Arkansas Associated Press made a list of the ten most significant personalities in the state's twentieth-century history. Not surprisingly, Bill Clinton—who had not yet completed his second term as president—finished first. Clinton was not just the first president from Arkansas, he was, at the time, the second-longest-serving governor in Arkansas history, having held the office for ten years. In the top ten with Clinton were the late US senator J. William Fulbright; segregationist and longest-serving governor, Orval Faubus; retail giant Sam Walton; and African American civil rights leader Daisy Bates. Following Bates was Douglas MacArthur, who was born in Arkansas, lived there a mere six months, visited Arkansas only once, and never thought of it as his native state. After MacArthur were John McClellan, the longest-serving US Senator in Arkansas history, who died in 1977; University of Arkansas football coach Frank Broyles; and Don Tyson, the founder of Tyson Foods. In the second tier were the first female US senator, Hattie Caraway; colorful congressman and former head of the House Ways and Means Committee, Wilbur Mills; governor and senator David Pryor; Pulitzer Prize–winning journalist Harry Ashmore; Senator Joe T. Robinson; and Johnny Cash.[1]

One wonders where Cash would stand were the poll retaken. Cash has lost none of the popularity he enjoyed while he was alive. He arguably has become more popular since his death—three years after this poll—than he was at certain points in his career. Many Arkansans would be hard pressed to say who Wilbur Mills or Frank Broyles were. They are men much better known to scholars than anyone else. But Johnny Cash? Anyone who knows anything about music knows Johnny Cash. Indeed, people who know little about *anything* know who he is.

The world mourned one of its most legendary musicians in September 2003. It was also a deeply sad time for the Cash family. Throughout his career, Johnny Cash had made his family an integral part of his life and art. His passing represented a big break in the history of country music and signified a similarly unfortunate break in his family history. Johnny's sister died in April 2003. June Carter Cash passed that May. Johnny followed her a few months later. And on October 24, Rose Nix Adams, June Carter's troubled daughter, died from carbon monoxide poisoning inside a bus in Clarksville, Tennessee. With her in the bus was bluegrass fiddler Jimmy Campbell, who also died that day. Rosie was forty-five years old. Jimmy was forty.[2]

Walk the Line

Even before his passing, Cash was in talks with filmmakers about making a movie about his life. In the fall of 2005, he received the full Hollywood treatment in *Walk the Line,* directed by James Mangold, a New Yorker whose other credits included *Girl, Interrupted* and *3:10 to Yuma*. Cash biographer Robert Hilburn has called the film "fiction"—not a factual account but rather the story that June Carter Cash wanted the world to know. Johnny Cash himself worried the true story would not be told. They both had tried to get the movie made before they died. According to Rosanne, the script that became *Walk the Line* was sent to Cash, who suggested changes to make the story more accurate, only to see the studio reject his recommendations.[3]

The film had a long genesis, beginning as a collaboration between Cash and James Keach, a TV director and the brother of Stacy Keach. He was also the husband of Jane Seymour, star of the Wild West television show *Dr. Quinn, Medicine Woman*. Cash had appeared on the show, and he became friends with Keach, who eventually asked Cash to be godfather to his son John. James Keach wanted to direct a film about Cash, and he and Jane visited Hendersonville to talk with Johnny about it. Cash wanted the film to be an honest depiction of his life, revealing the "gnarly truth." Keach collaborated with screenwriter Gill Dennis to draft a script. With no studios interested in the project, Keach reached out to Mangold for help.[4]

Mangold thought the screenplay too deferential toward Johnny, calling it "very soft." He wanted more of June's story told. Johnny told Mangold that he thought the script lacked romance. Mangold countered by saying he couldn't inject romance until he understood the couple's real story. Mangold discussed his approach with Cash. "What's inside him?" Mangold wanted to know. "What makes him him? We pushed very hard to scratch deeper, and to fill the gaps of the stories."[5]

People close to Cash—such as Rosanne, Patrick Carr, and WS Holland—have stated their displeasure with how *Walk the Line* portrayed him. The film, despite its historical missteps, caught the spirit of Cash's early life and music. The depression-era scenes of Arkansas, for example, were actually shot in Dyess. The scene depicting Jack's death was filmed in the center of town.[6]

The relationship between Johnny and his father Ray contains a tension and pathos worthy of real life. Robert Patrick—the T-1000 cyborg in *Terminator 2*—played Ray Cash as a drunken lout. Ray is the villain of the piece, serving as a constant foil to Johnny's ambitions and happiness. After Jack's death, Ray shouts that his boy's death was the devil's work and that Satan "took the wrong son!" Later in the movie, when Ray is visiting Johnny's house for Thanksgiving, Ray is unimpressed. "Mister big shot, mister pill poppin' rock star," he snarls. "You ain't got nothin'. Big empty house. Nothin'. Children you don't see. Nothin'. Big ol' expensive tractor stuck in the mud. Nothin'."[7]

Those who criticize *Walk the Line* for its historical flaws are in a long line of critics frustrated with the inevitable changes that occur when Hollywood seizes a biographical subject. For one, star Joaquin Phoenix is not a native southerner, let alone from Arkansas. Johnny's real mother did not look at all like the glamorous singer Shelby Lynne. From a historical point of view, there is much to criticize. Johnny and June, for example, were not in a car together in the early stages of Cash's career, driving from gig to gig. In fact, years went by between their first meeting and June's decision to join the Johnny Cash Show. June certainly was not the person who inspired Cash to write "I Walk the Line" years before.

Neither Rosanne nor Kathy Cash liked the film. Kathy, in fact, refused to finish watching it. Rosanne Cash complained about the film's negative portrayal of her mother. In the film, Vivian dismisses Cash and the Tennessee Two as a band that could "barely play." As her daughters pointed out, Vivian was in fact supportive of Johnny when he started playing music in Memphis, and she was loyal to her husband long after she had good reason to divorce him. Rosanne summed up the film by saying it was "an egregious oversimplification of our family's private pain, writ large and Hollywood-style; and about the torment my sisters and I were suffering."[8] Overall, the movie portrayed June in the best possible light. June certainly deserved the Hollywood treatment, but the film took considerable liberties with her life story.

While it played loose with facts and history, *Walk the Line* was a critical and commercial success, grossing $186 million at the box office. The film was true to period details, even if it distorted many aspects of Cash's story. In addition to being a blockbuster, the film was well liked by the critics—it has an overwhelmingly fresh rating on Rotten Tomatoes—and received a handful of Academy Award nominations. Phoenix was nominated for Best Actor and Reese Witherspoon for Best Actress as June. Witherspoon won. The film holds up well, despite well-founded criticism of its inaccuracies and misrepresentations. *Walk the Line* featured inspired acting and crisp direction. It was entertaining. And perhaps most importantly, it brought Cash to a new audience.

Walk the Line ended in 1968, during the Folsom concert, when everything seemed about to go right for Johnny Cash. The historical reality was far different, but then again, there was only so much that Hollywood could pack into two hours. The movie, for example, never got to the "Hollywood" story of Bob Wootton joining the band—whereby the young Wootton was pulled on stage by Cash because his usual guitarist wasn't there.

But the Bob Wootton story was only one of many omissions made in the name of cinematic storytelling. On the heels of the Oscar nominations for *Walk the Line*, Robert Levine in the *New York Times* wrote of some viewers' disappointment in the film's secular nature. Rev. C. Clifton Black, a professor at the Princeton Theological Seminary, was "stunned" at the lack of spiritual content in *Walk the Line*. In the film's defense, it mostly dealt with a period when Cash did not put his Christianity at the forefront of his life and career. In the 1950s and 1960s, Cash recorded many religious songs, but he didn't act like much of a Christian. He cheated on his wife, ignored his children, gorged himself on drugs, and generally behaved with suicidal abandon. Director Mangold said he wanted to make a movie about Johnny, June, and the birth of rock and roll. He saw June as the true redemption figure in the film rather than Jesus. He said June was "beautiful in the way that God's light is beautiful." He also wanted to make a film that was economically viable. Johnny always thought of himself as a Christian, and he recorded piles of spiritual music, but his gospel and Christian-oriented songs never sold as well as the "outlaw" material, a fact that Cash and his fans well knew. Mangold and 20th Century Fox knew it, too. *Walk the Line* certainly portrays a secular Johnny, but it was the Johnny the public best knew and wanted to see. Mangold stopped the film's narrative around the time Johnny became more religious and open about his faith.[9]

New Johnny Cash songs kept coming out years after his death. Rick Rubin was shocked to hear of Cash's death in September 2003, as he had plans for more recording sessions. Cash's recordings were voluminous, however, and he left behind much unreleased material. In 2006, the same year Reese Witherspoon accepted her Oscar for best actress for playing June Carter Cash, Rubin released *A Hundred Highways*, which topped two *Billboard* charts. There was enough archival material to put out *Unearthed*—a box set of American Recordings songs—and *American VI: Ain't No Grave* in 2010, the last of the Cash–Rubin albums. True to Rubin's roots aesthetic, the cover of *Ain't No Grave* featured a picture of a young J. R. Cash, taken when he was a boy in Dyess.

Walk the Line took a major step in founding Johnny Cash's legacy. But in other areas, his legacy was not doing so well. As was the case with Luther Perkins in 1968, the culprit was a fire. In the spring of 2007, Cash's 13,880-square-foot house in Hendersonville, Tennessee, burned to the ground. Cash had been dead for four years, but those close to him, such as Marty Stuart, former husband of Cindy Cash, still lived in the area. The Hendersonville house was where "prominent things" happened and "prominent people in American history" visited, noted Stuart. There, one could find "everyone from Billy Graham to Bob Dylan."[10] Stuart said the house's architect, Braxton Dixon, was "the closest thing this part of the country had to Frank Lloyd Wright." He added that for Cash, the house was a "sanctuary and a fortress." Johnny had shot part of his legendary "Hurt" video there. It was also where a then-unknown Kris Kristofferson landed his helicopter to tout his demo and where Bob Wootton had first caught a glimpse of Bob Dylan (who was fishing at the time). Everyone from Shel Silverstein to Bono and Billy Bob Thornton had visited. But the fire's destruction was near complete.

At the time of the blaze, the owner of the house was Barry Gibb of the Bee Gees, who had bought the unusual mansion in January 2006 for $2.3 million.

Fire trucks arrived within a few minutes, but the place burned quickly. Richard Sterban of the Oak Ridge Boys—who had once toured with Cash—lived nearby. Sterban told a reporter that maybe it was "the good Lord's way to make sure that it was only Johnny's house."[11] One firefighter was injured in the tremendous blaze, which left only the chimneys standing.

Were one to interpret the catastrophe in a cosmic sense, it was yet another rejection of Cash by Nashville: fate was saying Cash's true legacy lay in Arkansas. Before Arkansas spent thousands of hours and a small fortune restoring his Dyess house, Cash's fans were preserving his legacy in small—yet no less determined—ways. In January 1998, the *Arkansas Democrat-Gazette* featured a story concerning Robert Williams, a native of Fayetteville, who was petitioning state leaders to recognize Cash's birthday as a holiday. Williams had heard about Cash's struggle with what was thought to be Parkinson's disease. He contacted the mayor of Kingsland, Charlie Crane, about honoring Cash. What appealed to Williams was Cash's place as "a man of the people."[12] Williams had wanted to promote Cash in his home state, but his disability prevented him, so he wrote hundreds of letters to over a hundred media outlets—mostly radio stations—to promote Cash's importance in Arkansas. Eventually he succeeded in getting Arkansas to recognize the occasion when Mike Huckabee signed the proclamation (HCR 1003) in 1999, which noted Cash was a "Native Arkansan and Great American."[13] Williams died in January 2012. Cash's music was played at his funeral.

At the time of the Hendersonville fire, the only historic Johnny Cash structure still standing in Arkansas was his house in Dyess. No one there seemed to have any serious interest in restoring it, or the money to do so. When Cash himself visited Dyess in the 1990s, he was saddened by what he saw. The house was "very far gone, falling slowly into the Delta mud, and the land all around it, as far as I could see, was just huge flat fields . . . probably owned by some big agricultural corporation. . . . I didn't remember the land being that flat." And by flat, Cash meant "the trees were all gone."[14]

By the 2000s, the population of Dyess had fallen to a few hundred—a fraction of what it was when Johnny Cash lived there. But the town's historic value remained. Over the years, people had visited the house, which, though crumbling and its famous resident long gone, still held interest. Sue Chambers, an area columnist known as "the Scribbler," had written in

2001 about the possibility of a museum being made from the depression-era Dyess Colony administration building at the center of town, noting that Cash should be invited to attend a dedication ceremony.[15] Chambers was something of a historian. A longtime contributor to the *Tri-City Tribune* and city council member in Lepanto, she had cofounded a museum in Lepanto in 1980 and had edited a history of the town.

Chambers visited the Cash house at a time when it was almost unrecognizable. It certainly had none of the simple charm of its mid-thirties design and construction. The house had been added to, but also looked as if it might fall over. Bars covered the windows. During her visit to the house, Chambers met people who claimed to have known Johnny personally. She encountered Beth McArthur Wallace, who remembered trudging through the "gumbo" soil and playing with the Cash family. "He wasn't called Johnny in those days," Wallace said. "He was called J. R."[16]

The Johnny Cash Boyhood Home

By the time Cash visited his old home for the 1969 film *The Man, His World, His Music*, the house was unoccupied. The Cashes had not lived there since the early 1950s, when the family moved closer to town. Dyess had fallen on hard times long before the restoration project began, but Cash's house was still there, and the 1930s structures at the center of town were still the most prominent in the community. As dilapidated as the Cash house had become, though, it was in private hands. Arkansas State University (ASU) wanted the house to become a project for its Arkansas Heritage program, which involved not only traditional coursework and graduate study but a series of restoration projects that had revived Lakeport Plantation, the only existing antebellum home in Arkansas on the Mississippi River. ASU had also restored the Hemingway House in Piggott, where the author wrote parts of *A Farewell to Arms*, and operated the Southern Tenant Farmers Museum in Tyronza.

In 2007, Gene Williams, a native of Dyess and a radio and television personality who had gone to high school around the same time as Cash—and who had spent years in the music business in West Memphis, Memphis, and Branson—gave money to help restore the Dyess administration building. With the help of Williams and a grant from the Arkansas Historic Preservation Program, the restoration of Dyess began.

Arkansas was ground zero for many early rock and roll acts, and it deserved recognition for it. Once-thriving clubs and historic music venues, however, were disappearing. By the 2010s, gone were such legendary spots as the Silver Moon in Newport, and in December 2010, the King of Clubs in Swifton, Arkansas (along historic Highway 67) burned down. The club had hosted such greats as Cash, Elvis, Conway Twitty, Jerry Lee Lewis, Carl Perkins, and Sonny Burgess, and had been planning a sixtieth-anniversary celebration before the fire.[17]

With Arkansas such a key player in the origins of rock and roll and rockabilly, clearly it was time to reclaim Johnny Cash for Arkansas. Preservationists and Cash fans were getting excited about efforts to restore the singer's home in Dyess. In May 2011, ASU acquired the Cash house. For some Arkansans, acknowledging Cash's historic place in Arkansas, the nation, and the world was long overdue. "Cash never forgot where he came from and never shied away from telling an audience about it," wrote one businessman and lifelong fan of Cash's music who was also sponsoring the Johnny Cash Music Festival in Jonesboro that year. "But we feel Arkansas has not done enough to honor this country music icon."[18] The restoration of Cash's house would be a cooperative effort among private and public funding sources as well as professional and grassroots organizers and workers.

People from northeast Arkansas were surprised at how Cash's home had not yet become a major tourist attraction. They saw what other states were doing with their musical heritage and wanted Arkansas to do the same. In 2008, Kirkley Thomas and Carmie Henry, managers at the Arkansas Electric Cooperative Corporation who were sponsoring Cash-related events in the state's northeast, drove to Dyess to meet with the mayor, Larry Sims. Thomas realized Dyess was missing an opportunity to attract visitors from around the world, people who might also want to see Dyess as part of a visit to Sun Studios or Graceland. Memphis was, after all, only fifty miles away. Mayor Sims, who had moved to the town in 1963 when he was ten, had already discussed plans to generate tourism in Dyess. In the early 2000s, he said, it "was kind of embarrassing" for tourists to visit the town. People didn't have anything to see beyond the dilapidated Cash house and the rundown historical buildings in the center of Dyess.[19]

In 2007, Dyess obtained the Dyess Colony administration building, which had been in private hands. Two years later, Thomas and Henry contacted Dr. Ruth Hawkins, who headed ASU's Heritage Sites Program, about a restoration project. Thomas, Henry, and Hawkins eventually met with Democratic state senator Steve Bryles of Blytheville to get funding for a Dyess restoration master plan. The plan was completed in March 2010 by John Milner Associates of Pennsylvania. Further funding arrived via a $337,888 Arkansas Natural and Cultural Resources grant to restore the administration building.[20]

In 2010, ASU made an offer to buy the Cash house from the present owner, but the offer was rejected. That fall, Ruth Hawkins attended a university alumni meeting, where she spoke with Bill Carter, the Arkansas lawyer who had managed to get the Rolling Stones out of trouble in Fordyce back in 1975. He hailed from Rector, a small town in Clay County in the state's northeastern corner, a few counties over from where Cash grew up. Carter was a man with a career as colorful as anything in the Cash story. And he showed that Johnny Cash had friends everywhere.[21]

With Carter's help, the Cash family became involved in the project. In May 2011, ASU, with help from the National Trust for Historic Preservation's Rural Heritage Development Initiative, acquired the Cash house from the reluctant owner. As preservationists worked to secure ownership, the mayor of Dyess was plain about what the project meant for his community. "It's really the only lifeline we've got, because we don't have any [colleges], don't have any businesses, factories, jobs, or anything." He added that the project would not be completed overnight. Rather, it was "a long drawn out plan but it's the only hope we've got." The restoration project hoped to get thirty thousand visitors to Dyess every year—a number far below the visitors to Graceland, roughly an hour away, but one that could provide an economic boost to an area that desperately needed it.[22]

The restoration, directed by Ruth Hawkins, was painstaking. Work began in January 2012. Contractors from Jonesboro began stripping the structure of anything not original to the house, including the additions to the porch and the doors. The 1,120-square-foot house was lifted off the ground so the highly unstable "gumbo" soil could be removed and sturdier soil put in. Workers also planned to put in a solid foundation and cover it with soil. The historic concrete piers would be put back in their original location.[23] The house was repositioned using GPS technology to assure that the house was in the exact place it was when first built.

To help raise money for the restoration, ASU began a Johnny Cash Music Festival in 2011. The concert had the immediate support of Rosanne, who thought the Dyess project "isn't about my dad," but instead "saving this town and creating opportunities for people."[24] Rather than spread out the performances, fans were treated to a long, four-hour concert with musicians such as Kris Kristofferson and George Jones, both of whom the *Arkansas Times* noted "might as well have been Cash's brothers."[25] Jones had time for only six songs, none of which were identified with Cash. Kristofferson—wearing cowboy boots that he said he bought back in 1968—played "Good Morning John," a song about Cash's recovery from drugs in the 1970s that had appeared on the 1985 Waylon Jennings album *Turn the Page*. Kristofferson was plain about Johnny's prominence in his memory. For him, Cash "was probably the most important human being in my life."[26]

One Arkansas reporter lauded the festival's decision to feature not academics or speakers, but "real salt-of-the earth musicians, family and friends." One might question whether the concert featured the musical "salt of the earth," considering how famous Kristofferson and Jones were. Nevertheless, the festival included Jonesboro musician Denny Strickland, who performed Cash's early hit, "Cry! Cry! Cry!"[27] Despite the star power on hand, playing his songs—as was so often the case with Johnny Cash's life, career, and legacy—became a family affair. John Carter, his then-wife Laura, and other members of the Cash family were there. John Carter acknowledged the role Dyess had played in his father's life. "He was a child of Arkansas. He put a lot of sweat and blood into that gumbo soil. Maybe now that's flowering fruits coming out." Cash went on to say the event wasn't about his father, but "the people, the soil and history that is yours and Arkansas'. . . . It's the history of my father's music, rebuilding and getting strength back to the community."[28]

Rosanne began the show with "Pickin' Time" and sang a duet with her ex-husband Rodney Crowell while Rosanne's husband John Leventhal accompanied them on guitar. They sang Crowell's song "No Memories Hanging Around," an ironic choice, considering the occasion. Obviously, memory played a central role in honoring Cash and his music. The restoration of his Dyess house was another way that Cash fans could remember him and the era in which he lived. For those who might not have known, the festival showed how deeply music ran in Cash's family. Chelsea Crowell, the daughter of Rosanne Cash and Rodney Crowell, sang "Give My Love to Rose." Tommy Cash played "I Walk the Line" and "Five Feet High and Rising," while Joanne sang "Come Home It's Supper Time." The festival was by all accounts a success. "It has been a long time since the state of Arkansas has witnessed a show of this magnitude," noted Charles Haymes from the *Cabot Star-Herald*.[29]

With seven thousand people in attendance, it was a sellout and raised $189,000 (including ticket and DVD sales) to aid in the restoration efforts.[30] The weekend, however, was not free of sadness. Before he could play a song at the concert, Marshall Grant fell ill and died at the age of eighty-three. He was the second member of the Tennessee Three to die.[31] Marshall was buried in Memphis, a city he had called home since the 1950s. The fact that he was laid to rest in Memphis and Cash and Luther were buried in Nashville was as symbolic as it was practical. Marshall refused to follow Cash and Luther to California in the band's early days. And he was the only member of the Tennessee Three who was ever fired. Now, in death, his separation from his bandmates was permanent.

Using Johnny Cash Music Festival proceeds, ASU paid $100,000 for the crumbling house, which was more than the home was worth. And yet, the owner (who used to charge Cash fans who had trekked to Dyess for taking pictures of the house) initially had refused to sell. ASU negotiated by threatening to build a replica house right next door to the administration building, which was being restored. Faced with the possibility of living in the dilapidated original near a meticulous reproduction two miles away, the owner reconsidered.[32]

The interior and exterior were restored to their original design and appearance. The exterior was painted white with green shutters. Interior walls were left unpainted, just as it had been when the Cashes arrived in 1935. Family artifacts were included, such as Carrie Cash's piano, a green enamel ice box, Ray's shaving kit and pocketknife, Carrie's handbag, and an afghan she made. A replica of a table Johnny built is in the house, with the original in the administration building in the center of town. Also in the administration building is a pillow that had belonged to Jack and was placed in the room he shared with his famous brother. Johnny had kept the pillow with him for years, eventually entrusting it to Vivian's care in 1967 after their divorce.

The effect of the restoration was complete. As Rosanne said upon visiting the house, "The strangest feeling overcame me—a sensation I imagine as close as I will ever get to actual time travel."[33] Arkansas State University hoped future visitors would have the same kind of experience.

The Cash project differed from ASU's earlier Lakeport Plantation restoration in many ways, but the most dramatic was the interior. Historians and restoration workers at Lakeport in the southern Arkansas Delta decided they would not fill the house with antebellum furniture and artifacts. Instead, they left the house empty, except for interpretative panels. But in Dyess, ASU restored the Cash kitchen, living room, and bedrooms as they would have looked during the depression and World War II. Thankfully, the university had the help of the people who had lived there: Tommy and Joanne Cash, the surviving Cash siblings.

The restoration project had support from Cash's family, historians, and fellow musicians. Maxine Brown, a native of Pine Bluff and singer in the group the Browns, said Cash "made such an impact and everybody loved him." Bobby Crawford, a drummer with Sonny Burgess and the Legendary Pacers, said Cash "never forgot he was from Arkansas." Crawford was a native of Cotton Plant, Arkansas, and he had toured with Cash in the late 1950s. He remembered how warm Cash was during a memorial show for Carl Perkins's brother. Cash talked to Crawford's mother and father backstage for a half hour about people they knew in Arkansas.[34]

Hundreds of people attended Cash's eightieth-birthday event in 2012, including Joanne and Rosanne Cash. For Rosanne, the occasion evoked bittersweet emotions. "He should've lived to 80," she remarked. "It's hard." But Rosanne added that it was "so uplifting to celebrate it this way, rather than going to a dark place about how sad it is he isn't still around."[35] Arkansas State University hosted the event, which kicked off a national fundraising campaign for the restoration. Rosanne, John Carter Cash, and Johnny's other daughters Tara, Cindy, and Kathy served on the National Advisory Council along with Tommy Cash. Willie Nelson and Kris Kristofferson also served as honorary council members. The Arkansas Steering Committee included Johnny's old high school friends A. J. Henson and J. E. Huff as honorary members.

At the birthday event, Rosanne and John Carter sang two songs, "Supper Time" and "No One Gets Out of Here Alive."[36] Ruth Hawkins said she was "working very hard to achieve authenticity in this restoration." The work included taking paint samples from the house and having them analyzed so the restoration workers could incorporate original colors.[37] Hawkins had help from the mayor of Dyess, who donated a piano that Carrie Cash had used in the house and now sits in the exact location it was in the 1940s. "I got such a joy out of playing that piano again today," said Joanne Cash. While the restoration included more than its fair share of celebrities, Joanne emphasized the Cash family's simple roots. "We were raised on cotton, popcorn, peanuts and Jesus," she noted, referencing one of her own songs. The Cash family unveiled a pillar with the words: "Established 1935—Reestablished 2012."[38]

The cost of restoring, furnishing, and landscaping the Cash house came to roughly $575,000. Three festival concerts in Jonesboro from 2011–2014 and private donations helped pay for the work.[39] ASU wanted to restore not only the house but the chicken coop, barn (to be used for educational programs and workshops), and the outhouse (the Cashes never had indoor plumbing). The university also wanted to restore the administration building in the center of town and the movie theater. Built in 1947, only the façade of the theater remained by 2012. A walking and cycling trail was planned to connect the buildings at the center of town with the Cash house, roughly two miles away. The trail would cross the Tyronza River bridge, where Cash liked to fish, and where he was the day his brother Jack died. As of this writing, however, the trail has not been built.

Money from the project was also allocated for a scholarship program for incoming ASU students, maintenance on the restored buildings, and an endowment for educational programs for secondary and college students. The project's planners believed heritage tourism could create 110 jobs and generate $9.8 million per year for local communities.[40]

Ten years after his death, the year 2013 was a good one for Cash. As the work in Dyess carried on, Nashville unveiled its Johnny Cash Museum, a for-profit venture featuring the largest amount of Cash memorabilia under one roof. Owned by Bill Miller, who knew Cash and worked in the "historical-documents business," visitors to the museum could see—among many other items—Johnny's acoustic guitar (complete with dollar bill), Luther's Fender, Fluke's drum set, and items from the famous Folsom concert. For those who couldn't visit Cash artifacts in Nashville, Sony issued a box set of all of Cash's Sun and Columbia material. John Carter Cash, furthermore, hinted at another album of American Recordings

In 2014, the Johnny Cash Boyhood Home was opened to the public. After many years of neglect (above), the house was restored in painstaking detail to its 1930s appearance (below). The project was the result of heroic efforts by Arkansas State University and various donors and other stakeholders to make Cash's house a virtual time machine. The university owns and operates the museum, part of a larger Dyess project that includes restored mid-twentieth-century buildings at the center of town. *Courtesy Johnny Cash Boyhood Home, Ken West photographer.*

material, noting, "I do believe there's enough to warrant a release he would be proud of."[41] By the time this was written, no such album has been released.

Nevertheless, in 2014, there appeared a new album of Cash material, *Out among the Stars.* Cash had recorded the initial tracks in his fallow 1980s period, but Columbia had never released them. At the time, the label was losing patience with Cash's lack of hits. The original producer was Billy Sherrill, in what proved a brief collaboration with Cash. The album featured two Cash originals and enough musicians—some featured on the original recordings; others, such as Marty Stuart, recruited by John Carter Cash in the 2010s for overdubs—to fill a tour bus. A Cash purist might wonder how authentic the recordings were. According to John Carter, some of the songs were unfinished when he found them.[42] *Out among the Stars* was decidedly rootsier in sound than the original masters must have been. The first song and title track features more dobro than any Cash tune since 1964's "Bad News." On the whole, the album covered the usual territory for Cash: a little gospel, blue collar songs, and duets with June. A departure from the Cash formula came courtesy of a humorous tune about infidelity featuring the briefest of cameos by Minnie Pearl. For those who thought of Cash as an Arkansan first and foremost, they might have been bothered by the inclusion of the song "Tennessee." The song, however, was written not by Cash but by Rick Scott, Nashville native and former member of the band Alabama.

The standout track on the record was "She Used to Love Me a Lot." While Cash originally recorded it in the early 1980s, the production is decidedly twenty-first century. The song sounds like the alt-country of the early 2000s and beyond, hinting at what Cash might have sounded like had he lived another ten or fifteen years. Would the Man in Black have approved of the production? Cash was always eager to hear new sounds. In one 1995 article, for example, Cash said he was listening to bands such as Palace, Lambchop, and Wilco.[43] By the 2000s, country had gone through another revival. Producers such as T. Bone Burnett and Jack White were giving country a rootsier, darker, and at times more rock-oriented sound. Some bands, such as Alabama outfit Drive-By Truckers, were combining country, rock, and punk with lyrics that did not shy away from politics and struck at the heart of the American class war. Burnett was producing everyone from Elton John to Gregg Allman and the Secret Sisters. On the Secret Sisters debut, Burnett made the Sisters sound as if they were right out of the late 1950s. On Allman's *Low Country Blues*, he employed a slow, swampy feel that was perfect for the blues-oriented Allman. Burnett also produced an odd but commercially and critically successful collaboration between Robert Plant and Alison Krauss. Rock and country were again cross-pollinating, with fruitful artistic results. No alt-country band, though, was selling records the way Cash did in his prime.

Even so, roots and hard rock country were cool again. Bands such as Drive-By Truckers had credibility among critics and serious music fans, as Cash always did, and they were addressing—as on the band's double LP *Southern Rock Opera*—major issues in southern and American history that no mainstream country artist would touch. The Truckers and other bands like them made country seem dangerous, energized, tuneful, and relevant again. But for those that liked quieter records, bluegrass was seeing a revival, too, helped enormously by the blockbuster soundtrack to the 2000 film *O Brother, Where Art Thou?*—another T. Bone Burnett creation.

Cash's death, sadly, came at a time when country was seeing another rise in popularity. Had he lived, it's likely he would have pursued projects much as he had done with Rick Rubin. Perhaps he would have cut a record with Jack White or T. Bone Burnett—maybe both. Another candidate might have been the Drive-By Truckers, who collaborated with Booker T. Jones in 2009.

The Fate of Northeastern Arkansas

Large music towns such as Nashville, New York, and Los Angeles will endure, and so will the music of Cash and other classic artists. Gone forever, however, is much of the Arkansas landscape that Cash once inhabited. The heroic efforts of Arkansas State University made Cash's boyhood home a landmark on par with Elvis's home in Tupelo. But some of the Arkansas towns associated with Cash have only just begun to recognize his importance. Dyess will see considerable tourist dollars and nationally publicized events concerning Cash's life and legacy. More challenged are towns such as Newport, where Cash, Elvis, and Sonny Burgess played in the 1950s. Newport—as was true of Dyess—laid the foundation for its own decline. In Newport, Arkansas historian Marvin Schwartz has noted, "the trees were everywhere," with forests "thick with massive hardwoods, stands of virgin timber in the river-bottom wetlands and on the dry flat prairies, ready to be claimed by whoever got to them first." When the forests were stripped bare, "only their names remained as signposts on the corners of downtown Newport streets."[44] Forests were destroyed to make way for farms, industry, and commerce. Newport became, like many Delta towns, a shell of its former self. The town's population today is not far from its peak in the 1980s, but the town is not the rocking hotspot it was in the 1950s, to be sure.

As of 2016, the largest employer in Newport was the prison system. The Department of Corrections has its Grimes and McPherson units located in the town, where 500 employees oversee a prison population of 1,900 inmates. Newport alone houses more inmates than the entire state of Arkansas did in 1969, when Cash played at Cummins. As one resident put it, "It's hard to be optimistic for small-town life. People still farm, but that doesn't employ many. These small towns are good places to live if you don't mind the solitude and isolation."[45] Farming still makes up a large portion of the Arkansas economy. By the twenty-first century, however, farmers had long shifted to mechanized harvesters and less labor intensive crops such as rice and soybeans. Cotton production has persisted, but the culture has changed. Newport mayor David Stewart once said, "When cotton went out, a lot of our economy went with it."[46] That did not mean that farmers couldn't make money from cotton. They could. Even so, farms got bigger. Agribusiness took over. As is true of economic stratification throughout the country, a smaller number of people in agriculture are responsible for a larger amount of the wealth being generated.[47]

Johnny Cash always had working class appeal. It wasn't just him, though. Several years before Johnny's death, the Tennessee Three faced the difficult reality of finding a way to pay their bills. The obvious choice was to continue playing music. WS Holland and Bob Wootton (who, as a singer, sounded eerily like Cash) managed to play together for a while and even recorded an album. For Bob Wootton, life after playing with Cash was especially hard. Bob had once been married to Anita Carter, but the marriage had not lasted long. In the mid-eighties, Bob married again. As country musicians do, Bob brought his family into the act, performing on stage with his wife and daughter. But life after the Tennessee Three was difficult. At one point, Bob took a job driving tour buses for other bands, such as the Smashing Pumpkins.[48] Later in his life, Bob was stricken with dementia. The "shy and idolatrous" Wootton died in April 2017.[49] Marshall Grant had proceeded him in death six years before. Bob was buried in Hendersonville Memory Gardens, the same cemetery as Johnny, June, Anita, Maybelle, and Luther. On Bob's tombstone, appropriately enough, is a guitar and a cross. His epitaph: "Keep it simple."

Johnny Cash was in many ways a man of a different time and place, someone who seemed to have one foot firmly in the nineteenth century. He was the kind of person everyone could like, not just for his music but also his attitude toward America and his native state, which has changed considerably since he left in 1950. The sharecroppers and cotton pickers are gone. But Arkansas still employs thousands of migrant workers every year, despite a conservative political culture that has made war on immigrants. Arkansas, as is true of the rest of the country, has seen a widening rift between the rural, conservative countryside and the urban, more progressive cities. Politically, Little Rock, where Cash had never spent much time, was becoming—like Austin or Atlanta—an island of blue in a sea of red.

Since his death, the country has been beset by rank partisan battles. Cash's politics were always "purple"—that is, he sought to bridge the gap between blue-state Democrats and red-state Republicans through his music, patriotism, and respect for human rights. He likely would have been angered, though not surprised, at the rise in rampant, public racism, sexism, and xenophobia that has emerged since the mid-2010s. His daughter Rosanne, as the most famous of Cash's descendants, has carried the political mantle for him.

The Man, His World, His Music

America continues to fight over symbols—the image of Johnny Cash among them. In June 2017, a deadly riot occurred in Charlottesville, Virginia, where heavily armed Nazis and other white supremacists convening for a "Unite the Right" rally marched in protest against the removal of a Robert E. Lee statue located in the fashionable and historic downtown. Among the crowd of white supremacists, one man was caught on camera wearing a Johnny Cash T-shirt. When the image of the protestor made the rounds on social media, Rosanne Cash responded in mid-August. In a sharply worded statement, she said white supremacists at Charlottesville represented everything her father stood against, saying that Johnny Cash was "a man whose heart beat with the rhythm of love and social justice." She added that he "would be horrified at even a causal use of his name or image for an idea or a cause founded in persecution and hatred." The family hoped that Johnny's name would be kept "far away from destructive and hateful ideology."[50]

Soon after, the Cash family realized that Cash's cover of the Tom Petty song "I Won't Back Down" was being used by Stormfront Radio, an outlet for white supremacists. In response, Universal Music Group sent a cease-and-desist letter to the radio station. In the face of such pressure, Stormfront, ironically, backed down. The station replaced Cash's cover song with "The South Shall Rise Again," by racist Louisiana country singer Johnny Rebel, known for such songs as "Nigger Hatin' Me" and "Kajun Ku Klux Klan." Stormfront, perhaps not surprisingly, blamed their troubles with UMG on "Jews."[51]

Johnny Cash appeals to just about every type of music fan, but at the beginning of the 2020s, his beloved United States seemed more divided and partisan than any time since the late 1960s. On a more positive note, from October 19 to 21, 2017, ASU held its first Johnny Cash Heritage Festival in Dyess. Visitors to the inaugural festival could tour the house, the visitor center, and the original administration building at the center of town. The visitor center, where lectures were held, was built on the spot where the Dyess movie theater once stood. The restored administration building now includes space for tourists, history panels, and lecture events.

The 2017 festival was a success, with thousands of visitors coming to enjoy the music and hear talks on Johnny Cash and depression-era Arkansas. The festival also benefited from mild October weather. On Friday night, visitors heard the surviving members of the Pacers—who had recently lost singer Sonny Burgess—outside the visitor center. On the morning of Saturday, October 21, Rosanne Cash gave a keynote address in the town community center. She talked about the government's role during the New Deal, saying officials during the Great Depression gave people not a "hand out, but a hand up."[52]

The festival, appropriately enough, included a cross-section of people from the Johnny Cash universe—everyone from his family members to locals, scholars, musicians, and bikers in recovery came together. During the Saturday afternoon main music event, attendees were treated to performances by Dyess native Buddy Jewell, Joanne Cash, Tommy Cash, Kris Kristofferson, and Rosanne. The musical acts performed under clear sunny skies on a large stage in a field next to the Cash house. Roy Cash, who cowrote the classic Johnny Cash song "I Still Miss Someone," also spoke. Since the inaugural event, other musicians have played at the Cash house, including Jamey Johnson, Alison Krauss, and Marty Stuart.

Dyess continued to host the Johnny Cash Festival. But as Cash made clear throughout his career, tragedy always rides alongside triumph. As of this writing, the COVID-19 epidemic is raging through the United States, taking with it hundreds of thousands of victims. As was true of so many museums and historic sites in the US, the Cash Festival in Dyess was cancelled in the fall of 2020. Cash's house in Bon Aqua, the Storytellers Museum and Hideaway Farm, where one can find the "One Piece at a Time" car, was also closed for an extended period. The deadly virus has done untold damage to the music industry. Pickers and singers usually don't sell many records, but they can survive on constant touring. During the pandemic, however, even the most seasoned and financially shrewd of bands faced hardship.

In 2020, Fluke Holland, the last surviving member of the Tennessee Three, died. Unlike Cash, Holland had never abused drugs or alcohol, though his love of race boats easily could have ended his life earlier than Cash's. After Cash stopped touring, Fluke didn't have royalties to fall back on, but he played into his eighties. When he performed in Little Rock in 2014, he not only played a great show, he loaded out his own drums at the end. In 2018, with guitarist Ron Haney, he published *Behind the Man in Black*, a short autobiography filled with the kind of stories Fluke liked to tell about life on the road. He had joked that were he to live to one hundred, he would do what he had never had done: smoke a cigarette and have a shot of whiskey. And he would always sign off interviews with the line, "Thank you for being my friend."

All of Cash's 1960s band has passed on, but many who knew Cash well are still alive. They have taken on the work of preserving Cash's legacy in print or through the creation of museums dedicated to Cash in Dyess or Nashville. They have also made efforts to establish more venues for country music. Cash's one-time son-in-law, Marty Stuart, has been working on his Congress of Country Music in his hometown of Philadelphia, Mississippi, a fifty-thousand-square-foot campus featuring a museum, classrooms, and theater. According to its website, the Congress will "embrace the roots of country music" and will include "internationally traveled memorabilia, photography, outsider/folk art and Native American crafts."[53] Perhaps Stuart can do for his hometown what Cash has done for Dyess.

Marty Stuart made a name for himself as a country traditionalist. Traditionalism is a form of preservation. Johnny Cash—like other great songwriters of his generation, such as the Kinks' Ray Davies—were preservationists. For Cash, preservation took on many forms, whether it was a love of folk and the Old West or delving deep into the history of his own United States. No musician in the 1960s was more American than Cash or as British as Ray Davies. But they both were obsessed with how the past could inform the present, while trying to use history to move their own music forward—to comment on new stories, new landscapes, and new people, while changing their music and hopefully the people who listened to it.[54]

Nearly twenty years after his death, Johnny Cash remains one of the most popular figures in American music. He doesn't sell as many records as he used to, but he continues to fascinate musicians and fans alike. The fact that Robert Hilburn's 2013 biography of Cash became a bestseller is evidence of the powerful hold Cash has on the public's imagination. His is a classic American story: a man who rises from poverty to obtain great wealth and fame, experiences enormous setbacks, marries the love of his life, finds Jesus again, and travels the world. In between triumphs were low times, where Cash battled addiction and personal demons. As an artist, he ended his life doing some of the best work of his career. Above all, Cash had an enormous drive and ability to reinvent himself, though each metamorphosis had its challenges.

Cash always stayed true to his roots. For him, it meant a close embrace of family, faith, history, and place. Perhaps more than all of these, a sense of place grounds us—for we cannot feel comfortable in anything until we are comfortable in our surroundings. For a man as restless as Cash, a sense of place was a mixed blessing. He was born and raised in rural Arkansas, and he returned to his home state often. But he knew it was not a place for an ambitious and talented young man. And yet, that's where his family was from, that's where his faith had begun. By committing to the life of the hardworking touring musician, Cash traded home for homelessness. As is true of so many musicians, he fell in love with what he sung about early in his career: the "Wide Open Road." Seemingly forever on the move, Cash, by drawing on his love of history and the American past, tried to stay grounded in the present and make sense of the enormous changes going on around him, especially in the 1960s, the decade when he made his most Americana- and folk-influenced records as well as his bestsellers.

Most of Johnny Cash's heroes were white country singers. But there was crossover between men of all races in the Delta and beyond, and Cash couldn't help but absorb the sounds that drifted along the Mississippi. Johnny's father, the boorish and abusive Ray Cash, certainly was no champion of the blues. And yet Johnny was much like Robert Johnson or Charlie Patton. He was in a long line of musicians who saw himself as a man and a guitar versus the world. Cash channeled the spirit of America—the whites, Blacks, and Native Americans who came before him—into his music. His voice was that of a born loner, who needed drugs, family, and his faith to save him from himself.

It is telling that Johnny Cash never played an electric guitar. Had he, Johnny might have been a lifelong rock and roller, but the acoustic guitar was the only instrument he really ever played. Kids in his neighborhood didn't play electric guitars, and the Cash house had no electricity anyway. Cash could have moved on from his acoustic guitar, but he never did. He could play the acoustic anywhere—in his house, on the porch, in a hotel room. It was what his musical heroes played. Despite his fame, fortune, and well-publicized concerts for prisoners, there is the enduring image of Cash standing alone—whether on stage or not—strumming his Martin. In the end, that's what the Johnny Cash mystique was: the enormous power of a man singing alone with an acoustic guitar. At its barest essentials, country music begins with a man and his guitar. Jimmie Rodgers knew it. Hank Williams knew it. The prisoners at Cummins and San Quentin knew it. Rick Rubin did too. The country musician's art stemmed from a man using his voice and guitar as a shield against suffering and heartbreak. It was the heart of the blues, and it was at the heart of American roots music. Johnny Cash was able to wrangle the ghosts of Williams, Patton, Johnson, and Rodgers to make dark and inspired music that will endure.

A scene in *The Man, His World, His Music* gets to the core of what Johnny Cash was. In the film, Cash visits his abandoned, decrepit home in Dyess. Accompanying himself on guitar, Cash sings "Busted." It's not a Cash original, and the Ray Charles version is better known. But there Cash is, strumming through a song about financial ruin in a crumbling, empty house built during the Great Depression. The song was written in the 1950s, but it is fitting for the 1930s, when Cash was born and moved to Dyess.

The scene might have been one inspiring dark reflection, but Cash instead lightens the surroundings with a song. In less than two minutes, Cash transforms a mundane, even depressing scene into an artistic statement. There he is: a man, his guitar, and a song. In that scene, you have Cash, his world, and his music.

Cash's legacy remains strong. In April 2019, the Arkansas legislature voted to remove its statues in the US Capitol. Cash was chosen as one of the new figures, along with civil rights leader Daisy Bates. Cash and Bates would replace the obscure Uriah M. Rose—a Confederate judge born in Kentucky—and the equally obscure senator and white supremacist governor James Paul Clarke, born in Mississippi. Rosanne and Joanne Cash were on hand as Republican governor Asa Hutchinson signed the bill for the privately funded Cash and Bates statues. Rosanne noted that Cash's statue being placed in the Capitol was made "even more special by the fact that he will be sharing this honor with Daisy Bates. She was a true humanitarian whose commitment to social justice, to civil rights is unparalleled."[55] Johnny Cash, the poor son of a cotton farmer, enshrined alongside a civil rights activist in the halls of the Capitol.

Not bad for a country boy from Mississippi County.

NOTES

Introduction

1. Peter Guralnick, *Lost Highway: Journeys & Arrivals of American Musicians* (Boston: Back Bay Books), 95.
2. Jesse W. Butler, "Cash Value: The Authenticity of Johnny Cash," in John Huss and David Werther, eds., *Johnny Cash and Philosophy: The Burning Ring of Truth* (Chicago: Open Court, 2011), 5.
3. Robert Hilburn, *Johnny Cash: The Life* (New York: Little, Brown, 2013), 177.
4. Only 2.1 percent of Arkansas's land area is covered by water. Using this metric, the state is much closer to Arizona (0.3 percent) than California (4.8 percent) and a far cry from watery Massachusetts (26.1 percent). Statistics available at the United States Geological Survey, "How Wet is Your State? The Water Area of Each State," accessed April 19, 2021, https://www.usgs.gov/special-topic/water-science-school/science/how-wet-your-state-water-area-each-state?qt-science_center_objects=0#qt-science_center_objects.
5. Arkansas was the fourth-largest producer of cotton in 2019. Texas was the first, with over six million bales. United States Department of Agriculture, "Crop Production," May 12, 2020, https://downloads.usda.library.cornell.edu/usda-esmis/files/tm70mv177/w0892x33f/c247fc69b/crop0520.pdf.
6. Michael Streissguth, *Always Been There: Rosanne Cash, The List, and the Spirit of Southern Music* (New York: Da Capo Press, 2009), 2.
7. Christopher Wren, *Winners Got Scars Too: The Life and Legends of Johnny Cash* (New York: Ballantine, 1971).
8. Michael Streissguth, *Johnny Cash: The Biography* (New York: Da Capo, 2007); Michael Streissguth, *Johnny Cash at Folsom Prison: The Making of a Masterpiece* (New York: Da Capo, 2004).
9. Leigh Edwards, *Johnny Cash and the Paradox of American Identity* (Bloomington: Indiana University Press, 2009); Huss and Werther, *Johnny Cash and Philosophy*.
10. Edwards, *Johnny Cash and the Paradox of American Identity*, 1.
11. Roy P. Basler, ed., *The Collected Works of Abraham Lincoln* (New Brunswick, NJ: Rutgers University Press, 1953), 1:108.
12. Nuci Memorial Foundation, *The Company We Keep: Drive-By Truckers' Homecoming and the Fan Community* (Athens, GA: Nuci's Space, 2019), 4.
13. Rosanne Cash, *Composed: A Memoir* (New York: Viking, 2010), 29.
14. Cash, *Composed*, 31.

15. Hilburn, *Johnny Cash*, 372–73.
16. Johnny Cash 1983 roast, DVD, courtesy of Ken King of Little Rock.

Chapter 1

1. *Cleveland County Herald*, April 6, 1994.
2. Margaret Robin, "Johnny Cash: Behind the Myth," *Hit Parader* (February 1970), 39.
3. In 2009, Glenrothes had the dubious distinction of being named the "most dismal town in Scotland." See *Daily Telegraph*, January 29, 2009, http://www.telegraph.co.uk/news/uknews/scotland/4386101/Glenrothes-named-most-dismal-town-in-Scotland.html.
4. Cindy Cash, *Cash Family Scrapbook* (New York: Crown, 1997), 154. For a more recent discussion of the Cash family's roots in Scotland, see Rosanne Cash, *Composed: A Memoir* (New York: Viking, 2010), 208–13.
5. Will of William Cash, signed February 16, 1708. The will was recorded in Westmoreland County in August 25, 1708. A copy of his will can be found among the data sheets kept by Marie Cash that are part of the Cash Family Papers in the possession of Wayne Cash of Maumelle, Arkansas (hereafter cited as Cash Family Papers).
6. John Cash affidavit, November [no day] 1832. A handwritten copy is in the Cash Family Papers. On a summary of Christie's Campaign, see Tom Hatley, *The Dividing Paths: Cherokees and South Carolinians through the Revolutionary Era* (New York: Oxford University Press, 1995), 194–97.
7. John Cash affidavit, November [no day] 1832, Cash Family Papers.
8. Annette Rawls, *Cleveland County, Arkansas: Our History and Heritage* (Rison, AR: Cleveland County Historical and Genealogical Society, 2006), 108.
9. 1820 United States Census (Free Schedule) for Moses Cash, Wards, Elbert, Georgia; 1830 United States Census (Free Schedule) for Moses Cash, Elbert, Georgia; 1840 United States Census (Free Schedule) for Moses Cash, District 199, Elbert, Georgia. All census information was accessed through Ancestry.com.
10. James Oakes, *The Ruling Race: A History of American Slaveholders* (New York: Alfred A. Knopf, 1982), ix–xix, 39–41.
11. Data sheet for Reuben Cash, Cash Family Papers.
12. A typed copy of Reuben's will can be found in Rawles, *Cleveland County, Arkansas*, 109. A handwritten copy is in the Cash Family Papers.
13. Christopher Wren, *Winners Got Scars Too: The Life and Legends of Johnny Cash* (New York: Ballantine, 1971), 25.
14. James L. Huston, *The Panic of 1857 and the Coming of the Civil War* (Baton Rouge: Louisiana State University Press, 1987), 53.

15. Don Thurman, *A Historical Review of the Timber Industry in Cleveland County, Arkansas* (Rison, AR: Cleveland County Historical Society, 2004), 4.
16. Antonio D'Ambrosio, *A Heartbeat and a Guitar: Johnny Cash and the Making of* Bitter Tears (New York: Nation Books, 2009).
17. Thurman, *Historical Review of the Timber Industry*, 2.
18. Thurman, *Historical Review of the Timber Industry*, 2.
19. Cleveland County Historical Society, *The Impact of Agriculture on Cleveland County, Arkansas, from 1830 to 1950* (n.p., 2006), 7.
20. 1860 United States Census (Slave Schedule), Joseph M. Meriwether, Smith Township, Bradley County, Arkansas.
21. Cleveland County (AR) Bicentennial Committee, *Cleveland County Potpourri: Recollections from History and Folklore* (self-published, 1976), 24.
22. Robert W. Fogel and Stanley M. Engerman, *Time on the Cross: The Economics of American Negro Slavery* (1974; reis., New York: W. W. Norton, 1995), 250.
23. 1850 United States Census (Agriculture Schedule), R. Cash, Elbert County, Georgia. Reuben does not appear in the Slave Schedules.
24. 1860 United States Census (Free Schedule), Reubin [*sic*] Cash, Smith Township, Bradley, Arkansas. "Reubin Cash" is not listed in the 1860 Slave Schedules. A "Reuben Cash" is listed in the Slave Schedules from Banks County, Georgia. Did this belong to our Reuben Cash? If they did, they numbered two slaves, hardly enough for a plantation.
25. James M. McPherson, *Battle Cry of Freedom: The Civil War Era* (New York: Oxford University Press, 1988), 615n.
26. Wren, *Winners Got Scars Too*, 25.
27. Johnny Cash, *Man in Black* (Grand Rapids, MI: Zondervan, 1975), 28.
28. Stephen Miller, *Johnny Cash: The Life of an American Icon* (New York: Omnibus, 2003), 5; Robert Hilburn, *Johnny Cash: The Life* (New York: Little, Brown, 2013), 5.
29. Clay Ouzts, "Elbert County," *New Georgia Encyclopedia*, last modified October 31, 2018, https://www.georgiaencyclopedia.org/articles/counties-cities-neighborhoods/elbert-county.
30. Janet B. Hewett, ed., *The Roster of Confederate Soldiers, 1861–1865, Volume III: Buff, Aaron, to Coirrier, E. F.* (Wilmington, NC: Broadfoot, 1995). This information is also available at the online Soldiers and Sailors database administered by the National Park Service. The Fourth Arkansas Cavalry included a Moses Cash in its ranks. But the Fourth was a Union force, and the Moses Cash in it was in his thirties. Reuben Cash is also not listed in the index to the *Roster of Confederate Soldiers of Georgia*. See Juanita S. Brightwell, Eunice S. Lee, and Elsie C. Fulghum, *Roster of the Confederate Soldiers of Georgia, 1861–1865: Index* (Spartanburg, SC: Reprint Company, 1982), 77.
31. James M. McPherson, *For Cause and Comrades: Why Men Fought in the Civil War* (New York: Oxford University Press, 1997), viii.

32. William L. Shaw, "The Confederate Conscription and Exemption Acts," *American Journal of Legal History* 6, no. 4 (October 1962): 376.
33. Mark K. Christ, *Civil War Arkansas, 1863: The Battle for a State* (Norman: University of Oklahoma Press, 2010).
34. Daniel Sutherland, *A Savage Conflict: The Decisive Role of Guerrillas in the American Civil War* (Chapel Hill: University of North Carolina Press, 2009), 210.
35. On George England, see Goodspeed, *Biographical and Historical Memoirs of Southern Arkansas,* 606.
36. Information on Gunn's wartime service can be found in the Cash Family Papers.
37. 1860 United States Census (Free Schedule), Elbert County, Georgia; Lilian Henderson, *Roster of the Confederate Soldiers of Georgia, Volume IV* (Hapeville, GA: Longina and Porter, 1959), 189. More detailed information on Seaborn J. Cash can be found at the History of the 38th Regiment Georgia Volunteer Infantry website, http://38thga.com/drupal/node/100 (accessed April 20, 2021).
38. David Hacker, "Census-Based Count of the Civil War Dead," *Civil War History* 57, no. 4 (December 2011): 306–47. Hacker has argued that the death toll is closer to 750,000 soldiers rather than the more commonly accepted figure of 620,000.
39. See Drew Gilpin Faust, *This Republic of Suffering: Death and the American Civil War* (New York: Vintage, 2008).
40. Data sheet for John S. Cash, Cash Family Papers.
41. *Cleveland County Herald*, July 14, 1898.
42. 1870 United States Census, Reuben Cash, Hurricane Township, Bradley, Arkansas.
43. *Pine Bluff Weekly Press*, December 30, 1880.
44. Will of Reuben Cash, November 8, 1880, Cash Family Papers.
45. *Cleveland County Herald*, January 27, 2012.
46. Helen Goggans, "Arkansas Sesquicentennial, 1836–1986: A History of Kingsland, Arkansas" (self-published, 1986), 8.
47. Johnny Cash and Patrick Carr, *Cash: The Autobiography* (New York: HarperCollins, 1997), 4.
48. 1880 United States Census, William H. Cash, Smith Township, Cleveland, Arkansas; 1900 United States Census, William H. Cash, Smith Township, Cleveland, Arkansas.
49. Doris Mitchell Lisemby, *Taproots in Fertile Soil* (Arkadelphia, AR: Autumn Years Ministries, 1993), 87.
50. George Carpozi Jr., *The Johnny Cash Story* (New York: Pyramid, 1970), 20. Tom Dearmore, an Arkansas journalist, also repeated the legend of Cash's Indian ancestry, saying that Cash had "the face and stature of his Cherokee

forebears." See Dearmore, "First Angry Man of Country Singers," *New York Times Magazine*, September 21, 1969, p. 42.

51. Hilburn, *Johnny Cash*, 165–66.
52. Cleveland County Bicentennial Committee, *Cleveland County Potpourri*, 1.
53. Entry for January 18, Tara Cash Schwoebel, ed., *Recollections by J. R. Cash* (Jonesboro: Arkansas State University, 2014). This useful volume, unfortunately, has no page numbers.
54. Entry for January 19, Schwoebel, *Recollections*. Schwoebel claimed that Edgar was an engineer, but the 1930 and 1940 censuses list him as working in a store, not for the railroad.
55. Goggans, "Arkansas Sesquicentennial," 4.
56. Goggans, "Arkansas Sesquicentennial," 5.
57. Cleveland County Historical Society, *The Impact of Agriculture*, 17.
58. Cleveland County Bicentennial Committee, *Cleveland County Potpourri*, 3.
59. *Cleveland County Herald*, March 30, 1932, quoted in Leland C. Ackerman, *Here and There: Weekly Columns from the* Cleveland County Herald (n.p., 2003), 7.
60. Goggans, "Arkansas Sesquicentennial," 10.
61. Wren, *Winners Got Scars Too*, 25–26.
62. Joe Hyams, *Bogie: The Biography of Humphrey Bogart* (New York: Signet, 1966), 33.
63. On the Second Arkansas Infantry, see "The Arkansas National Guard and Camp Pike in World War I," *Arkansas Military History Journal* 11, no. 3 (Summer 2017), esp. 5–31; Wren, *Winners Got Scars Too*, 27. Although Brest has more days of rain than what Ray might have been used to, the city gets less total rain annually than Pine Bluff, Arkansas, the closest city to where Ray Cash grew up.
64. Wren, *Winners Got Scars Too*, 28.
65. Garth Campbell, *Johnny Cash: He Walked the Line, 1932–2003* (London: John Blake, 2003), 2.
66. Thurman, *Historical Review of the Timber Industry*, 3.
67. Helen Beatrice Goggans and Harold Sadler, "Footprints on the Sand of Time," accessed April 21, 2021, http://www.argenweb.net/cleveland/footprints-in-the-sand.htm.
68. Thurman, *Historical Review of the Timber Industry*, 19.
69. Kathy Cash discusses the lynching story in Michael Streissguth, *Johnny Cash: The Biography* (New York: Da Capo, 2007), 4. Richard Buckelew's 1999 dissertation, "Racial Violence in Arkansas: Lynchings and Mob Rule, 1860–1930," lists no lynching in Cleveland County in the period that might have corresponded with the Cash family story. However, the lynching might have occurred in a neighboring county or might not have been reported at all. Lynching was so common in the late nineteenth and early

twentieth centuries that it did not always arouse local or state media attention. Participants, furthermore, while not worried about recriminations, were not interested in documenting such activity. For an insightful look at the difficulty one historian had in researching a mass lynching in early twentieth-century Arkansas, see Vince Vinikas, "Specters in the Past: The Saint Charles, Arkansas, Lynching of 1904 and the Limits of Historical Inquiry," *Journal of Southern History* 65, no. 3 (August 1999): 535–64.

70. *Pine Bluff Commercial*, June 18, 1959.
71. *Cleveland County Herald*, May 29, 1924.
72. Data sheet for Thomas William Davis Cash (always called Dave Kelly Cash), Cash Family Papers.
73. Donald Holley, "The Second Great Emancipation: The Rust Cotton Picker and How It Changed Arkansas," *Arkansas Historical Quarterly* 52, no. 1 (Spring 1993): 45.
74. Wren, *Winners Got Scars Too*, 30.
75. Goggans, "Arkansas Sesquicentennial, 1836–1986," 11.
76. On Marie Cash's life, see scrapbook in Series 1, Box 1, Folder 9, Life Interrupted Collection, UALR Center for Arkansas History and Culture, Little Rock. The quotation concerning her thoughts on her genealogy project can be found in a note underneath "The Reuben Cash Family: Native of Elbert County, Georgia," Cash Family Papers.
77. Jeannie Sakol, "The Grit and Grace of Johnny Cash," *McCall's* (July 1970), 111.
78. Carpozi, *The Johnny Cash Story*, 19. On the weather, see the *Cleveland County Herald*, February 26, 1932, which notes a high of 72 degrees in Little Rock and says "fair and warmer weather . . . prevails almost throughout the country, the only sections reporting rainfall were Washington and the South Atlantic coast."
79. *Arkansas Gazette*, September 28, 1969.
80. *Cleveland County Herald*, March 9, 1932.
81. John Carter Cash, *House of Cash: The Legacies of My Father, Johnny Cash* (San Rafael, CA: Insight Editions, 2011), 33.
82. *Cleveland County Herald*, March 30, 1932, quoted in Ackerman, *Here and There*, 7.
83. *Cleveland County Herald*, quoted in Ackerman, 7.
84. Wren, *Winners Got Scars Too*, 31–34.
85. Lisemby, *Taproots in Fertile Soil*, 94.
86. Lisemby, *Taproots in Fertile Soil*, 221–22.
87. Cash, *Recollections*, entries for July 27, July 28, January 21, January 16, January 17, and August 12, respectively.
88. Streissguth, *Johnny Cash*, 9.

Chapter 2

1. Johnny Cash, liner notes to *American Recordings*, Johnny Cash, American, 1994, p. 1.
2. Christopher Wren, *Winners Got Scars Too: The Life and Legends of Johnny Cash* (New York: Ballantine, 1971), 39.
3. Van Hawkins, A *New Deal in Dyess: The Depression Era Agricultural Resettlement Colony in Arkansas* (Jonesboro, AR: Writers Bloc, 2015), 10.
4. John Fante, *1933 Was a Bad Year* (Santa Barbara, CA: Black Sparrow Press, 1985).
5. Thomas E. Hall and J. David Ferguson, *The Great Depression: An International Disaster of Perverse Economic Policies* (Ann Arbor: University of Michigan Press, 1998), 141. By 1935, Arkansas's unemployment was actually below the national average.
6. Fred C. Smith, *Trouble in Goshen: Plain Folk, Roosevelt, Jesus, and Marx in the Great Depression South* (Jackson: University Press of Mississippi, 2014), 121.
7. Donald Holley, "Trouble in Paradise: Dyess Colony and Arkansas Politics," *Arkansas Historical Quarterly* 32, no. 3 (Autumn 1973): 203–16.
8. Dan W. Pittman, "The Founding of Dyess Colony," *Arkansas Historical Quarterly* 29, no. 4 (Winter 1970): 314.
9. Wren, *Winners Got Scars Too*, 44.
10. David Hayden, "A History of Dyess, Arkansas" (master's thesis, Southern Illinois University, 1970), 30.
11. Nancy Isenberg, *White Trash: The 400-Year History of Class in America* (New York: Penguin, 2016), 214, 215 (quoted).
12. Jeannie Whayne, *Delta Empire: Lee Wilson and the Transformation of Agriculture in the New South* (Baton Rouge: Louisiana State University Press, 2011), 174–75.
13. John Otto, *The Final Frontiers, 1880–1930: Settling the Southern Bottomlands* (Westport, CT: Greenwood, 1999), 37.
14. Emergency Relief Administration State of Arkansas [hereafter cited as ERA]. *Dyess Colony Agricultural Colonization Project* (Little Rock: ERA of Arkansas, 1934), 9.
15. Carr interview with Cash, *Journal of Country Music*, July 9, 2002.
16. Hayden, "A History of Dyess, Arkansas," 14.
17. ERA, *Dyess Colony Agricultural Project*, 3.
18. Entry for April 29, Tara Cash Schwoebel, ed., *Recollections by J. R. Cash* (Jonesboro: Arkansas State University, 2014). Ironically, in the 1960s, at the depths of his drug period, Cash set a wildfire in California at a national

park. The fire did serious damage, though no one was harmed by it. He later paid a hefty fine to the federal government to cover the damage.

19. Entry for April 21, Cash, *Recollections*.
20. Whayne, *Delta Empire*, 11.
21. Hayden, "A History of Dyess, Arkansas," 19.
22. See Sir Ronald Ross, *The Prevention of Malaria* (London: John Murray), 1911.
23. ERA, *Dyess Colony Agricultural Project*, 5.
24. Whayne, *Delta Empire*, 69.
25. Whayne, *Delta Empire*, 137, 163, 176 (quoted).
26. Whayne, *Delta Empire*, 61.
27. ERA, *Dyess Colony Agricultural Project*, 42.
28. ERA, *Dyess Colony Agricultural Project*, 25.
29. ERA, *Dyess Colony Agricultural Project*, 21.
30. Some farmers eventually obtained more than twenty acres. Historian Van Hawkins notes that a single, middling farmer could handle at most about thirty-four acres. See Hawkins, *A New Deal in Dyess*, 4.
31. Hayden, "A History of Dyess, Arkansas," 17.
32. ERA, *Dyess Colony Agricultural Project*, 8–9.
33. ERA, *Dyess Colony Agricultural Project*, 34.
34. Wren, *Winners Got Scars Too*, 51.
35. Wren, *Winners Got Scars Too*, 40.
36. ERA, *Dyess Colony Agricultural Project*, 1.
37. ERA, *Dyess Colony Agricultural Project*, a–d.
38. Whayne, *Delta Empire*, 34, 43, 113–14, 124–25.
39. In 2014, the Klan bought space on a billboard for a website hosting white pride radio programs. The ad featured a young girl holding a puppy.
40. Guy Lancaster, *Racial Cleansing in Arkansas, 1883–1924: Politics, Land, Labor, and Criminality* (Lanham, MD: Lexington Books, 2014).
41. On statistics for the 1890s, see the CSDE Lynching Database, http://lynching.csde.washington.edu/#/search (accessed April 22, 2021).
42. Whayne, *Delta Empire*, 131.
43. For example, the Delta town of Helena, south of Memphis, was home to Abraham H. Miller, a former slave. By the early twentieth century, he was regarded as the wealthiest Black man in Arkansas. His wife, Eliza, became the first woman in the state to own a movie theater.
44. Whayne, *Delta Empire*, 120.
45. ERA, *Dyess Colony Agricultural Project*, 36.
46. ERA, *Dyess Colony Agricultural Project*, 19.
47. ERA, *Dyess Colony Agricultural Project*, 50.
48. Hayden, "A History of Dyess, Arkansas," 47.
49. Hayden, "A History of Dyess, Arkansas," 34, 42–43.
50. Hayden, "A History of Dyess, Arkansas," 45.

51. "Mrs. Roosevelt Visited in Dyess," undated newspaper article, vertical files, Mississippi County Historical and Genealogical Society, Osceola.
52. ERA, *Dyess Colony Agricultural Project,* 55.
53. *Arkansas Democrat*, September 7, 1990.
54. David Welky, *The Thousand-Year Flood: The Ohio-Mississippi Disaster of 1937* (Chicago: University of Chicago Press, 2011), 177–81.
55. Wren, *Winners Got Scars Too*, 47–51.
56. Hayden, "A History of Dyess, Arkansas," 53.
57. Hayden, "A History of Dyess, Arkansas," 61.
58. United States Department of Commerce, *Cotton Production and Distribution, Bulletin 201, Year Ending July 31, 1964* (Washington, DC: Government Printing Office, 1965), 21. Arkansas is still a major cotton-producing state today, and the United States is the third-largest producer of cotton in the world. The United States, furthermore, is the world's leading exporter of cotton.
59. In 1937, prices were 8.13 cents per pound. In 1936, they had been 12.16 cents per pound. These prices come from Hayden, "A History of Dyess, Arkansas," 59. To put Great Depression cotton prices in perspective, when the Civil War broke out, the South, where cotton was king, produced four million bales, with the price of cotton being about 13.5 cents per pound.
60. In some parts of Arkansas, handpicking of cotton persisted into the 1960s, especially at the notorious prison farms. But people who were picking by hand by then were an exception.
61. Cash and Carr, *Cash*, 25–26.
62. Cash and Carr, *Cash*, 25.
63. Entry for June 19, Cash, *Recollections.*
64. Rosanne Cash, *Composed: A Memoir* (New York: Viking, 2010), 35.
65. Wren, *Winners Got Scars Too*, 70.
66. Finch quoted in Memphis *Press-Scimitar*, April 21, 1938, in Hayden, "A History of Dyess, Arkansas," 68.
67. Pittman, "The Founding of Dyess Colony," 320.
68. Hayden, "A History of Dyess, Arkansas," 72–85.
69. Undated advertisement, vertical files, Mississippi County Genealogical and Historical Society, Osceola, Arkansas.
70. *Walk the Line,* directed by James Mangold, written by Gill Dennis and James Mangold (Century City, CA: 20th Century Fox, 2005), Bonus Features DVD, disc 2.
71. Entry for October 7–8, Cash, *Recollections.*
72. Entry for August 15, Cash, *Recollections.*
73. Entry for October 22 and 26, Cash, *Recollections.*
74. Miller, *Johnny Cash*, 36.
75. Pittman, "The Founding of Dyess Colony," 325.

76. Entry for January 25, Cash, *Recollections.*
77. Alan Brinkley, *Voices of Protest: Huey Long, Father Coughlin, and the Great Depression* (New York: Alfred A. Knopf, 1982).
78. Donald Grubbs, *Cry from the Cotton: The Southern Tenant Farmers' Union and the New Deal* (Chapel Hill: University of North Carolina Press, 1971), 71. See also James D. Ross Jr., *The Rise and Fall of the Sothern Tenant Farmers Union* (Knoxville: University of Tennessee Press, 2018).
79. H. L. Mitchell, "The Founding and Early History of the Southern Tenant Farmers Union," *Arkansas Historical Quarterly* 32, no. 4 (Winter 1973): 365.
80. Entry for May 7, Cash, *Recollections.*
81. Hayden, "A History of Dyess, Arkansas," 46.
82. Entry for April 12, Cash, *Recollections.*
83. Entry for December 1, Cash, *Recollections.* This translation is from the King James Bible.
84. Entry for December 20, Cash, *Recollections.*
85. Entry for December 23, Cash, *Recollections.*
86. Entry for December 26, Cash, *Recollections.*
87. Hayden, "A History of Dyess, Arkansas," 22.
88. Entry for May 31, Cash, *Recollections.*
89. Entry for February 23, Cash, *Recollections.*
90. Entry for March 1, Cash, *Recollections.*
91. Wren, *Winners Got Scars Too*, 73.
92. Entry for June 25, Cash, *Recollections.*
93. Nan Snider, "Tommy Cash Visits Dyess," *Poinsett County Democrat Tribune*, April 27, 2006, www.democrattribune.com/story/1370718.html.
94. Entry for October 20, Cash, *Recollections.*
95. Entry for January 30, Cash, *Recollections.*
96. Michael Streissguth, *Johnny Cash: The Biography* (New York: Da Capo, 2007), 3.
97. Johnny Cash to Vivian Cash, January 3, 1952; Vivian Cash, *I Walked the Line: My Life with Johnny Cash* (New York: Scribner, 2007), 49.
98. Rosanne Cash, "Goin' Back to Dyess," *United Hemispheres Magazine*, November 1, 2015.
99. Wren, *Winners Got Scars Too*, 60. On "Ray," see entry for February 27, Cash, *Recollections.*
100. Cash and Carr, *Cash*, 321.
101. Cash and Carr, *Cash*, 273.
102. Cash and Carr, *Cash*, 68. He also mentioned her in his first autobiography, *Man in Black* (Grand Rapids, MI: Zondervan, 1975), 82.
103. Gayle F. Wald, *Shout, Sister, Shout!: The Untold Story of Rock-and-Roll Trailblazer Sister Rosetta Tharpe* (Boston: Beacon Press, 2007), 42.

104. Cash, *Man in Black*, 102; Wald, *Shout, Sister, Shout!*, 70; Cash's 1992 induction speech can be found at https://www.rockhall.com/inductees/johnny-cash (accessed April 24, 2021).
105. Olivia Carter Mather, "Race in Country Music," in *The Oxford Handbook of Country Music*, ed. Travis D. Stimeling (New York: Oxford University Press, 2017), 345.
106. On Broonzy's Arkansas roots, see Bob Riesman, *I Feel So Good: The Life and Times of Big Bill Broonzy* (Chicago: University of Chicago Press, 2011).
107. Diane Pecknold, ed., *Hidden in the Mix: The African American Presence in Country Music* (Durham, NC: Duke University Press, 2013); Charles Edward Smith, "Big Bill Broonzy Sings Folk Songs," in liner notes to *Big Bill Broonzy Sings Folk Songs*, Folkway Records, 1962 (quoted).
108. The New York rap group De La Soul sampled Cash's "Five Feet High and Rising" on their 1989 debut album, *3 Feet High and Rising.* Ice-T said there have been few lines more "gangsta" than Cash saying he shot a man in Reno just to watch him die. And Snoop Dogg, who has recorded with Willie Nelson, has called Cash "my main man" and a "real American gangsta."
109. Wren, *Winners Got Scars Too*, 63.
110. Johnny Cash, "You Have to Call Me the Way You See Me," *Southern Cultures* 21, no. 3 (Fall 2015), 9.
111. Entry for May 17, Cash, *Recollections*.
112. Wren, *Winners Got Scars Too*, 67.
113. Hayden, "A History of Dyess, Arkansas," 101.
114. Cash, *Man in Black*, 40–48; Cash and Carr, *Cash*, 31–36; Wren, *Winners Got Scars Too*, 64–66.
115. John Hayes, "'Big River': Johnny Cash and the Currents of History," in *Gods of the Mississippi,* ed. Michael Pasquier (Bloomington: Indiana University Press, 2013), 186.
116. Ray Cash data sheet, Cash Family Papers.
117. Johnny to Vivian Cash, June 13, 1952, Cash, *I Walked the Line*, 71.
118. Cash, *I Walked the Line*, 288.
119. Johnny to Vivian Cash, July 1, 1952, Cash, *I Walked the Line*, 77–78.
120. Cash, *Composed*, 133.
121. Entries for October 30, December 28, and December 3, Cash, *Recollections*.
122. Entry for January 28, Cash, *Recollections*.
123. Johnny to Vivian Cash, June 13, 1952, Cash, *I Walked the Line*, 72.
124. Entry for April 17, Cash, *Recollections*.
125. Entry for October 14, Cash, *Recollections*.
126. Entry for August 5, Cash, *Recollections*.
127. Entry for August 18, Cash, *Recollections*.
128. Entry for January 29, Cash, *Recollections*.

129. Entry for November 29 and February 10, Cash, *Recollections.*
130. Hayden, "A History of Dyess, Arkansas," 62. Cash said as much in his daughter's book of his recollections. See entry for November 28, Cash, *Recollections.*
131. Entry for March 21 and March 23, Cash, *Recollections*; Hayden, "A History of Dyess, Arkansas," 59.
132. Entries for June 9 and June 11, Cash, *Recollections.*
133. Entry for April 3, Cash, *Recollections.*
134. Entry for February 9, Cash, *Recollections.*
135. Wren, *Winners Got Scars Too*, 73.
136. In late 2020, the Cash estate released an album of the Royal Philharmonic backing Cash. The album was recorded recently, not done in Cash's lifetime. One wonders what Cash would have thought of the idea had he still been alive.
137. On Cash's love for the Chuck Wagon Gang, see entry for May 11, Cash, *Recollections.*
138. Entry for August 3, Cash, *Recollections.*
139. *Arkansas Democrat*, September 7, 1990.
140. Entry for February 22, Cash, *Recollections.*
141. Entry for August 28, Cash, *Recollections.*
142. Entry for May 23, Cash, *Recollections.*
143. Entry for February 23, Cash, *Recollections.*
144. Cash and Carr, *Cash*, 37–38.
145. Robert Hilburn, *Johnny Cash: The Life* (New York: Little, Brown, 2013), 33. Hilburn, unfortunately, provides no citation for this information. The story apparently was told by Cash in a private interview to someone in the late 1990s.
146. Entry for March 13, Cash, *Recollections.*
147. Entry for March 19, Cash, *Recollections.*
148. Wren, *Winners Got Scars Too*, 75–76.
149. Entry for February 17, Cash, *Recollections.*
150. Entry for August 1, Cash, *Recollections.*
151. Hayden, "A History of Dyess, Arkansas," 109.
152. Christopher Wren, "The Restless Ballad of Johnny Cash," *Look*, April 29, 1969, p. 72.
153. Wren, "The Restless Ballad," 68.

Chapter 3

1. Marvin Schwartz, *We Wanna Boogie: The Rockabilly Roots of Sonny Burgess and the Pacers* (Little Rock, AR: Butler Center Books, 2014), 107.
2. Lester Bangs, *Psychotic Reactions and Carburetor Dung* (New York: Anchor, 2003), 327.

3. Johnny Cash, "I Walk the Line" (Disc 1, Track 7), *Live around the World: Bootleg, Volume III*, Columbia, 2011.
4. *New York Times*, September 21, 1969.
5. Johnny to Vivian Cash, September 22, 1951, Vivian Cash, *I Walked the Line: My Life with Johnny Cash* (New York: Scribner, 2007), 28.
6. Johnny to Vivian Cash, July 19, 1952, Cash, *I Walked the Line*, 84.
7. Johnny Cash to Thomas and Irene Liberto, February 27, 1953, Cash, *I Walked the Line*, 117.
8. Johnny to Vivian Cash, January 25, 1952, Cash, *I Walked the Line*, 52.
9. Johnny to Vivian Cash, May 4, 1953, Cash, *I Walked the Line*, 140.
10. Johnny to Vivian Cash, June 21, 1952, Cash, *I Walked the Line*, 73.
11. Johnny to Vivian Cash, January 25, 1952, Cash, *I Walked the Line*, 53.
12. Johnny Cash, liner notes (page 4) to *American Recordings*, Johnny Cash, American, 1994.
13. Gordon Cotton, "Reid Cummins' Guitar Changed Country Music Forever," *Vicksburg Daily News*, September 22, 2019, https://www.vicksburgnews.com/reid-cummins-guitar-changed-country-music-forever/.
14. Christopher Wren, *Winners Got Scars Too: The Life and Legends of Johnny Cash* (New York: Ballantine, 1971), 80.
15. Johnny to Vivian Cash, January 28, 1952, Cash, *I Walked the Line*, 54.
16. Johnny to Vivian Cash, December 1, 1952, Cash, *I Walked the Line*, 102.
17. Johnny to Vivian Cash, July 11, 1952, Cash, *I Walked the Line*, 81.
18. Johnny to Vivian Cash, April 23, 1953, Cash, *I Walked the Line*, 131–34.
19. Johnny to Vivian Cash, April 24, 1953, Cash, *I Walked the Line*, 135.
20. Johnny to Vivian Cash, May 3, 1953, Cash, *I Walked the Line*, 138.
21. Johnny Cash and Patrick Carr, *Cash: The Autobiography* (New York: HarperCollins, 1997), 82; Donald A. Carter, *Forging the Shield: The U.S. Army in Europe, 1951–1962* (Washington, DC: Center for Military History, 2015), 111–113.
22. Cash and Carr, *Cash*, 82.
23. Robert Hilburn, *Johnny Cash: The Life* (New York: Little, Brown, 2013), 47.
24. Michael Foley, *Citizen Cash: The Political Life and Times of Johnny Cash* (New York: Basic, 2021), 119.
25. The date is given in Steve Turner, *The Man Called Cash: The Life, Love, and Faith of an American Legend* (Nashville: W Publishing Group, 2004), 251.
26. Johnny to Vivian Cash, January 2, 1954, Cash, *I Walked the Line*, 226.
27. Johnny to Vivian Cash, July 13, 1953, Cash, *I Walked the Line*, 154.
28. Johnny to Vivian Cash, January 2, 1954, Cash, *I Walked the Line*, 226.
29. Johnny to Vivian Cash, November 26, 1953, Cash, *I Walked the Line*, 211.
30. Johnny to Vivian Cash, December 19, 1953, Cash, *I Walked the Line*, 216–17.
31. Johnny to Vivian Cash, November 12, 1953, Cash, *I Walked the Line*, 203.
32. Johnny to Vivian Cash, November 21, 1953, Cash, *I Walked the Line*, 209.

33. Schwartz, *We Wanna Boogie*, 265.
34. Johnny to Vivian Cash, December 3, 1953, Cash, *I Walked the Line*, 213.
35. Johnny to Vivian Cash, November 23, 1953, Cash, *I Walked the Line*, 210.
36. Johnny to Vivian Cash, February 6, 1954, Cash, *I Walked the Line*, 234.
37. Johnny to Vivian Cash, February 6, 1954, Cash, *I Walked the Line*, 234.
38. Johnny to Vivian Cash, October 8, 1953, Cash, *I Walked the Line*, 197.
39. Johnny to Vivian Cash, March 12, 1952, Cash, *I Walked the Line*, 59–60.
40. Johnny to Vivian Cash, August 18, 1953, Cash, *I Walked the Line*, 183.
41. Johnny to Vivian Cash, December 15, 1953, Cash, *I Walked the Line*, 216; Johnny to Vivian Cash, October 27, 1951, *I Walked the Line*, 37.
42. Cash discusses multiple attempts to remove cysts. See Johnny to Vivian Cash, February 5, 1953, 109–10, and February 21, 1953, pp. 114–15, both in Cash, *I Walked the Line*.
43. Cash, *I Walked the Line*, 272.
44. Cash, *I Walked the Line*, 269.
45. Johnny to Vivian Cash, November 26, 1953, Cash, *I Walked the Line*, 211.
46. C. Stuart Chapman, *Shelby Foote: A Writer's Life* (Oxford: University Press of Mississippi, 2003), passim; Peter Goddard and Ronnie Hawkins, *Ronnie Hawkins: Last of the Good Ol' Boys* (Toronto: Stoddard, 1989), 83.
47. Entry for November 12, Tara Cash Schwoebel, ed., *Recollections by J. R. Cash* (Jonesboro: Arkansas State University, 2014).
48. Schwartz, *We Wanna Boogie*, 264.
49. Allen R. Coggins, *Tennessee Tragedies: Natural, Technical, and Societal Disasters in the Volunteer State* (Knoxville: University of Tennessee Press, 2011), 216–17.
50. Chapman, *Shelby Foote*, 149, 180.
51. Bobby Lovett, *The Civil Rights Movement in Tennessee: A Narrative History* (Knoxville: University of Tennessee Press, 2005), 269–78, 289.
52. Wren, "The Restless Ballad of Johnny Cash," *Look*, April 29, 1969, p. 74.
53. Cash, *I Walked the Line*, 275; Terry Gross, "Johnny Cash: In His Own Words," *Fresh Air*, November 4, 1997, accessed April 29, 2020, https://freshairarchive.org/segments/johnny-cash-his-own-words.
54. The place to begin reading about Sam Phillips is in Peter Guralnick's biography, *Sam Phillips: The Man Who Invented Rock 'n' Roll* (New York: Little, Brown, 2015).
55. Guralnick, *Sam Phillips*, 536–38.
56. Guralnick, *Sam Phillips*, 73–185.
57. Ben Wynne, *In Tune: Charlie Patton, Jimmie Rodgers and the Roots of American Music* (Baton Rouge: Louisiana State University Press, 2014), 175.
58. Entry for July 8, Cash, *Recollections*.
59. Entry for August 25, Cash, *Recollections*.

60. Guralnick, *Sam Phillips*, 207–12.
61. Guralnick, *Sam Phillips*, 204.
62. Sleepy LaBeef, another Arkansan, issued records on the Sun label in the 1970s, but Sam Phillips had sold the company in 1969.
63. Peter Cooper, *Johnny's Cash and Charley's Pride: Lasting Legends and Untold Adventures in Country Music* (Nashville: Spring House, 2017), 14.
64. Cooper, *Johnny's Cash and Charley's Pride*, 20.
65. Schwartz, *We Wanna Boogie*, 128.
66. Jim Marshall, *Johnny Cash at Folsom & San Quentin* (London: Reel Art Press, 2018), 13.
67. Stephen Miller, *Johnny Cash: The Life of an American Icon* (New York: Omnibus, 2003), 47.
68. For details on Luther circa January 1946, see World War II Draft Cards Young Men, 1940–1947, "Luther Monroe Perkins, Jr.," available at Ancestry.com.
69. Rich Kienzle, "The Primitive Genius: Luther Perkins," *Vintage Guitar* (July 2008), 120.
70. Cash, *I Walked the Line*, 277.
71. Marshall Grant, *I Was There When It Happened: My Life with Johnny Cash* (Nashville: Cumberland House, 2006), 27.
72. Grant, *I Was There When It Happened*, 32.
73. Cooper, *Johnny's Cash and Charley's Pride*, 39.
74. Jonathan Silverman, *Nine Choices: Johnny Cash and American Culture* (Amherst: University of Massachusetts Press, 2010), 4–18; Michael Hinds and Jonathan Silverman, *Johnny Cash International: How and Why Fans Love the Man in Black* (Iowa City: University of Iowa Press, 2020), 21; Hilburn, *Johnny Cash*, 639; Greg Laurie, *Johnny Cash: The Redemption of an American Icon* (Washington, DC: Salem, 2019), 210.
75. Robert Christgau, "King Crimson, *In the Court of the Crimson King*," accessed April 30, 2021, https://www.robertchristgau.com/get_artist.php?name=King+Crimson.
76. Robert Christgau, "Darkest America," accessed April 30, 2021, https://www.robertchristgau.com/xg/bn/2012-08.php; on Tom Waits, see Robert Christgau, "Effective but Defective," accessed April 30, 2021, https://www.robertchristgau.com/xg/rock/waits-02.php; on Hendrix, see Robert Christgau, "Anatomy of a Love Festival," accessed April 30, 2021, https://www.robertchristgau.com/xg/music/monterey-69.php. The phrase "psychedelic Uncle Tom" was used in reference to Hendrix's performance at the Monterey International Pop Festival of 1967. Christgau's editors at *Esquire* changed the phrase to the not-necessarily-less-offensive "just another Uncle Tom," but in November 2002 Christgau said he preferred the original phrasing. On Christgau's obsession with Black authenticity, see Noah Berlatsky,

"Robert Christgau and Blackface," *Splice Today*, accessed April 30, 2021, https://www.splicetoday.com/pop-culture/robert-christgau-and-blackface.

77. Hugh Barker and Yuval Taylor, *Faking It: The Quest for Authenticity in Popular Music* (New York: W. W. Norton, 2007), 331–32.
78. Keith Richards with James Fox, *Life* (New York: Little, Brown, 2010), 105.
79. Schwartz, *We Wanna Boogie*, 13.
80. Cash, *I Walked the Line*, 281.
81. *Davenport (Iowa) Daily Republican*, March 21, 1901.
82. Carl Perkins and David McGee, *Go, Cat, Go! The Life and Times of Carl Perkins, the King of Rockabilly* (New York: Hyperion, 1996), 17.
83. Perkins and McGee, *Go, Cat, Go!*, 36–37.
84. It didn't stop in the 1960s. On his terrific *Run, Devil, Run* album in the late 1990s, Paul McCartney covered "Movie Magg."
85. Schwartz, *We Wanna Boogie*, 119.
86. Grant, *I Was There When It Happened*, 50.
87. Perkins and McGee, *Go Cat, Go!*, 212.
88. Perkins and McGee, *Go Cat, Go!*, 120.
89. *Billboard*, May 23, 1970, C-3.
90. Cash, *I Walked the Line*, 274.
91. Cash, *I Walked the Line*, 276–77.
92. Ralph LaRossa, *Of War and Men: World War II in the Lives of Fathers and Their Families* (Chicago: University of Chicago Press, 2011), 32.
93. Cash, *I Walked the Line*, 278.
94. Cash, *I Walked the Line*, 276.
95. Turner, *The Man Called Cash*, 250.
96. Peter Lewry, *I've Been Everywhere: A Johnny Cash Chronicle* (London: Helter Skelter, 2001), 18.
97. Editors of *Rolling Stone*, *The* Rolling Stone *Interviews* (New York: St. Martin's, 1981), 275.
98. Grant, *I Was There When It Happened*, 44.
99. Cash, *I Walked the Line*, 276.
100. Cash, *I Walked the Line*, 277–83.
101. Johnny to Vivian Cash, October 13, 1951, Cash, *I Walked the Line*, 30.
102. *Arkansas Gazette*, August 3, 1955.
103. *Forrest City Daily Times-Herald*, September 1, 1955, and September 5, 1955.
104. *Crowley Ridge Chronicle*, September 8, 1955.
105. *Texarkana Daily News*, November 17, 1955.
106. Michael Streissguth, ed., *Ring of Fire: The Johnny Cash Reader* (Cambridge, MA: Da Capo, 2003), 46.
107. Schwartz, *We Wanna Boogie*, 241.

108. Schwartz, *We Wanna Boogie*, 252.
109. Schwartz, *We Wanna Boogie*, 270.
110. Schwartz, *We Wanna Boogie*, 268–69.
111. Schwartz, *We Wanna Boogie*, 268.
112. Schwartz, *We Wanna Boogie*, 289.
113. *Arkansas Democrat-Gazette*, April 29, 2012.
114. Schwartz, *We Wanna Boogie*, 66–67.
115. Schwartz, *We Wanna Boogie*, 35–44, 118.
116. Schwartz, *We Wanna Boogie*, 279.
117. *Arkansas Gazette*, April 16, 1972.
118. According to Schwartz, Porky—perhaps knowing Clayton was a man who could not control himself—supposedly gave the money back to Carl when the games ended. See Schwartz, *We Wanna Boogie*, 295.
119. Schwartz, *We Wanna Boogie*, 173.
120. Johnny Cash, *Man in Black* (Grand Rapids, MI: Zondervan, 1975), 87.
121. Editors of *Rolling Stone*, "100 Greatest Country Songs of All Time," *Rolling Stone*, June 1, 2014, https://www.rollingstone.com/music/music-lists/100-greatest-country-songs-of-all-time-11200/1-johnny-cash-i-walk-the-line-1956-11876/.
122. *Arkansas Gazette*, May 27, 1956.
123. Guralnick, *Sam Phillips*, 300–301.
124. Cash, *I Walked the Line*, 282.
125. *Eagle Democrat* (Warren, AR), May 23, 1957, and May 30, 1957 (quoted).
126. Robert Cochran, "Ride It Like You're Flyin': The Story of 'The Rock Island Line,'" *Arkansas Historical Quarterly* 56, no. 2 (Summer 1997), 205–6.
127. Robert Christgau, *Christgau's Record Guide: The '80s* (New York: Pantheon), 85.
128. Guralnick, *Sam Phillips*, 380.
129. Guralnick, *Sam Phillips*, 547.

Chapter 4

1. Rich Kienzle, liner notes to *Town Hall Party: Johnny Cash and the Tennessee Two, Live! 1958*, Johnny Cash, Sundazed 5170. LP. 2003.
2. It is listed as "Frankie and Johnny" on the original album.
3. Thomas Bailey Jr., "Roy Cash Sings Praises of Statue Memorializing Uncle Johnny," Memphis *Commercial Appeal*, December 22, 2015, http://archive.commercialappeal.com/entertainment/music/roy-cash-sings-praises-of-statue-memorializing-uncle-johnny-27801bb1-b953–24c7-e053–0100007fd6da-363308151.html/.

4. Kim Williams, "Al Bell and Buddy Jewell to Be Inducted into the Arkansas Entertainers Hall of Fame," updated July 2015, https://www.arkansas.com/articles/al-bell-and-buddy-jewell-be-inducted-arkansas-entertainers-hall-fame.
5. Richard Kienzle, "Bob Wootton: 'Boom-Chicka' and the Man in Black," *Vintage Guitar* 22, no. 9 (July 2008): 32–33.
6. John Einarson, Ian Tyson, and Sylvia Tyson, *Four Strong Winds* (Toronto: McClelland and Stewart, 2011), 214.
7. Michael Streissguth, ed., *Ring of Fire: The Johnny Cash Reader* (Cambridge, MA: Da Capo, 2003), 51–53.
8. *Arkansas Democrat*, May 10, 1959.
9. *Arkansas Democrat*, May 13, 1959.
10. *Arkansas Gazette*, May 14, 1959.
11. *Arkansas Gazette*, May 16, 1959.
12. *Arkansas Gazette*, May 17, 1959.
13. Kenneth Stampp, *The Peculiar Institution: Slavery in the Ante-Bellum South* (New York: Knopf, 1956); Stanley Elkins, *Slavery: A Problem in Institutional and American Life* (Chicago: University of Chicago Press, 1959).
14. Hardin is called "Little Arkansas" in John Wesley Hardin, *The Life of John Wesley Hardin* (Winchester, Ohio: Badgley, 2011), 43, 52. The nickname might have been a reference to the Little Arkansas River, where Hardin was active in Kansas. See Leon Metz, *John Wesley Hardin: Dark Angel of Texas* (Norman: University of Oklahoma Press, 1998), 44.
15. Michael Scott Cain, *The Americana Revolution: From Country and Blues Roots to the Avett Brothers, Mumford & Sons, and Beyond* (New York: Rowan and Littlefield, 2017), ix.
16. Vivian Cash, *I Walked the Line: My Life with Johnny Cash* (New York: Scribner, 2007), 286–87.
17. Robert Hilburn, *Johnny Cash: The Life* (New York: Little, Brown, 2013), 185–86.
18. Cash, *I Walked the Line*, 284.
19. *Cleveland County Herald*, May 20, 1959.
20. "Cane River Bait Company featured in APHN Tri-Centennial Exhibit," *Beauregard Daily News*, June 13, 2014, https://www.beauregarddailynews.net/article/20140613/NEWS/140619871.
21. The two later became lovers, though Cash was not yet prepared to destroy his marriage or family by leaving them for another woman with deep connections to the music industry. See Hilburn, *Johnny Cash*, 185, 190–91.
22. Marvin Schwartz, *We Wanna Boogie: The Rockabilly Roots of Sonny Burgess and the Pacers* (Little Rock, AR: Butler Center Books, 2014), 120.
23. Carl Perkins and David McGee, *Go, Cat, Go! The Life and Times of Carl Perkins, the King of Rockabilly* (New York: Hyperion, 1996), 177–78.

24. *Cleveland County Herald*, June 24, 1959. The *Pine Bluff Commercial* reported on June 18 that Dave had died the day before. See https://www.findagrave.com/memorial/25072472/dave-kelly-cash.
25. Hilburn, *Johnny Cash*, 190.
26. WS Holland and Ron Haney, *Behind the Man in Black: The WS Holland Story* (Jackson, TN: Drum Cat, 2018), 3.
27. Perkins and McGee, *Go, Cat, Go!*, 70.
28. Schwartz, *We Wanna Boogie*, 305.
29. June Carter Cash, *Among My Klediments* (Grand Rapids, MI: Zondervan), 15.
30. Cash, *Among My Klediments*, 39.
31. Cash, *Among My Klediments*, 34.
32. Mark Zwonitzer and Charles Hirshberg, *Will You Miss Me When I'm Gone?: The Carter Family and Their Legacy in American Music* (New York: Simon & Schuster, 2002), 313.
33. *Los Angeles Times*, "June Carter, 73," *Chicago Tribune*, May 16, 2003, https://www.chicagotribune.com/news/ct-xpm-2003-05-16-0305160086-story.html.
34. Zwonitzer and Hirshberg, *Will You Miss Me When I'm Gone?*, 347–49.
35. June Carter Cash, *From the Heart* (New York: Prentice Hall, 1987), 108–9.
36. Saul Holiff to Johnny Cash, June 12, 1961, Saul Holiff Collection, University of Victoria Special Collections.
37. Cash, *I Walked the Line*, 292.
38. Saul to Barbara Holiff, July 11, 1963, Saul Holiff Collection, University of Victoria Special Collections.
39. Saul Holiff to Johnny Cash, December 27, 1961, Saul Holiff Collection, University of Victoria Special Collections.
40. Johnny Western to Saul Holiff, July 1, 1961, Saul Holiff Collection, University of Victoria Special Collections.
41. Entry for November 26, Tara Cash Schwoebel, ed., *Recollections by J. R. Cash* (Jonesboro: Arkansas State University, 2014).
42. Rosanne Cash, *Composed: A Memoir* (New York: Viking, 2010), 159.
43. Julie Chadwick, *The Man Who Carried Cash: Saul Holiff, Johnny Cash, and the Making of an American Icon* (Toronto: Dundurn, 2017), 265.
44. Gene Beley, "Folsom Prison Blues," *Virginia Quarterly Review* 81, no. 1 (Winter 2005), 219.
45. Cash, *I Walked the Line*, 293.
46. Cash, *Composed*, 13.
47. Chadwick, *The Man Who Carried Cash*, 158.
48. Johnny Cash, *Man in Black* (Grand Rapids, MI: Zondervan, 1975), 106–13.
49. Hilburn, *Johnny Cash*, 226–31.
50. Cash, *I Walked the Line*, 294.
51. Jonathan Silverman, *Nine Choices: Johnny Cash and American Culture* (Amherst: University of Massachusetts Press, 2010), 66.

52. Scott Reynolds Nelson, *Steel Drivin' Man: John Henry, the Untold Story of an American Legend* (New York: Oxford University Press, 2008).
53. Johnny Cash, "A Letter from Johnny Cash," *Broadside*, March 10, 1964, 10, https://singout.org/downloads/broadside/b041.pdf.
54. Johnny to Vivian Cash, February 26, 1952, Cash, *I Walked the Line*, 57.
55. *Billboard*, May 23, 1970, C-10.
56. Cash, *From the Heart*, 46.
57. Antonio D'Ambrosio, *A Heartbeat and a Guitar: Johnny Cash and the Making of* Bitter Tears (New York: Nation Books, 2009), 14–15.
58. Stephen Miller, *Johnny Cash: The Life of an American Icon* (New York: Omnibus, 2003), 109.
59. *Billboard*, August 22, 1964, p. 31.
60. Chadwick, *The Man Who Carried Cash*, 179.
61. *Osceola Times*, August 12, 1965.
62. *Arkansas Gazette,* August 1, 1965.
63. Johnny Cash to Saul Holiff, July 14, 1965, Saul Holiff Collection, University of Victoria Special Collections.
64. C. Eric Banister, *Johnny Cash FAQ: All That's Left to Know about the Man in Black* (Milwaukee: Backbeat Books, 2014), 106.
65. *The Thunderbolt* article can be found at https://blackhistorycollection.files.wordpress.com/2018/04/thunderbolt5.jpg; on the Council, see *New York Post*, October 6, 1966.
66. Cash, *I Walked the Line*, 303.
67. Chadwick, *The Man Who Carried Cash*, 222.
68. Johnny Cash, *Forever Words: The Unknown Poems* (New York: Blue Rider Press, 2016), 37–39.
69. The number is probably closer to 100,000 per night—still an impressive figure. For specifics, see Jerry M. Hay, *Tennessee River Guidebook: Charts and Details from Beginning to End* (Floyds Knob, IN: Indiana Waterways, 2010), 84.
70. Jeffrey Ostler, *Surviving Genocide: Native Nations and the United States from the American Revolution to Bleeding Kansas* (New Haven: Yale University Press, 2019), 116.
71. Johnny Cash and Patrick Carr, *Cash: The Autobiography* (New York: HarperCollins, 1997), 232.
72. Johnny Cash, Billy Zeoli, and Al Hartley, *Hello, I'm Johnny Cash* (Old Tappan, NJ: Fleming H. Revell Company, 1976).
73. Peter Guralnick and Johnny Cash, *Johnny Cash: The Last Interview and Other Conversations* (New York: Melville House, 2020), 64–65; Cash and Carr, *Cash*, 230–32.
74. Hilburn, *Johnny Cash*, 321; Chadwick, *The Man Who Carried Cash*, 221.
75. Streissguth, *Johnny Cash*, 137.

76. Larry E. Matthews, *Caves of Chattanooga* (Huntsville, AL.: National Speleological Society, 2007), 102.
77. Charles Paul Conn, *The New Johnny Cash* (Old Tappan, NJ: Fleming H. Revell, 1973), 31.
78. Miller, *Johnny Cash*, 151–152.
79. *Arkansas Gazette*, February 2, 1968.

Chapter 5

1. *Osceola Times*, February 1, 1968, and February 8, 1968.
2. *Osceola Times*, February 1, 1968.
3. *Osceola Times*, February 1, 1968.
4. *Arkansas Gazette*, February 2, 1968.
5. *Arkansas Gazette*, February 2, 1968.
6. *Arkansas Gazette*, February 5, 1968.
7. Yes, Tomato. It is a small unincorporated town in Mississippi County, and it has had the distinction of having the second smallest post office in the country.
8. *Arkansas Gazette*, February 5, 1968.
9. Carl Perkins and David McGee, *Go, Cat, Go! The Life and Times of Carl Perkins, the King of Rockabilly* (New York: Hyperion, 1996), 310.
10. *Arkansas Gazette*, February 5, 1968.
11. *Arkansas Gazette*, February 5, 1968.
12. *Osceola Times*, February 8, 1968.
13. *Arkansas Gazette*, February 5, 1968.
14. Cathy Urwin, *Agenda for Reform: Winthrop Rockefeller as Governor of Arkansas* (Fayetteville: University of Arkansas Press, 1991), 22, 54–55, 109, 177, 181.
15. Urwin, *Agenda for Reform*; 198; John Ward, *Arkansas Rockefeller* (Baton Rouge: Louisiana State University Press, 1978), 166.
16. Christopher Wren, *Winners Got Scars Too: The Life and Legends of Johnny Cash* (New York: Ballantine, 1971), 224.
17. "Inaugural Address Delivered by the 37th Elected Governor of Arkansas, The Honorable Winthrop Rockefeller, Tuesday, January 10, 1967," Record Group 3, Box 35, Folder 2a, Winthrop Rockefeller Collection, University of Arkansas at Little Rock (hereafter cited as UALR).
18. Ward, *Arkansas Rockefeller*, 87–113.
19. Arkansas State Police Criminal Investigation Division, *Tucker Prison Farm Investigation Report, 1966* (Little Rock: The Division, 1967?), esp. 2, 11–12, 14–15, 17–19, 25–26, 29, 38, 41–43, 45, 49, 51, 57.
20. Jeannette Rockefeller interview, June 20, 1985, Oral History Collection, UALR.

21. Arkansas State Police, *Tucker Prison Farm Investigation Report*, 14–15, 18, 24, 38.
22. On the need for vocational training, see Thomas O. Murton and Joe Hyams, *Accomplices to the Crime* (New York: Grove Press, 1969), 30.
23. Murton and Hyams, *Accomplices to the Crime*, 56–57.
24. James Phelan, "The Prison Scandal that Won't Stay Buried," *True: The Man's Magazine*, October 1968, p. 85.
25. Arkansas Penitentiary Study Commission, *Report of the Arkansas Penitentiary Study Commission* (Little Rock: Arkansas Penitentiary Study Commission, 1968), 6.07–6.08.
26. Murton and Hyams, *Accomplices to the Crime*, 63.
27. Murton and Hyams, *Accomplices to the Crime*, 183.
28. See *The Times* (London, England), January 29, 1968; *Corpus Christi Times*, February 1, 1968; *New York Times*, February 4, 1968; *Los Angeles Times*, February 4, 1968; *New York Post*, February 6, 1968; *Evening Bulletin* (Philadelphia, PA), March 28, 1968; *Economist* (London, England), March 30, 1968; *Bunte* (Munich, Germany), February 21, 1968; *Confidential* (New York, NY), June 1968.
29. Memphis *Commercial Appeal*, February 13, 1968.
30. Johnny Cash, "Folsom Prison Blues," (1968); liner notes to *At Folsom Prison* (CD). New York: Columbia Music.
31. Peter Lewry, *I've Been Everywhere: A Johnny Cash Chronicle* (London: Helter Skelter, 2001), 64–65.
32. *Foreman Sun*, August 22, 1968.
33. *WR '68 Campaigner* 2, no. 3 (September 27, 1968), Winthrop Rockefeller Collection, UALR Center for Arkansas History and Culture.
34. Johnny Cash to Vivian Cash, November 30, 1953, Vivian Cash, *I Walked the Line: My Life with Johnny Cash* (New York: Scribner, 2007), 212.
35. Winthrop Rockefeller Collection, Record Group 7, Reel-to-Reel 758–761, UALR.
36. *Arkansas Traveler*, September 18, 1968.
37. Rich Kienzle, "Bob Wootton: 'Boom-Chicka' and the Man in Black," *Vintage Guitar* 22, no. 9 (July 2008), 32–33.
38. Kienzle, "Bob Wootton," 33.
39. Kienzle, "Bob Wootton," 33.
40. Kienzle, "Bob Wootton," 120.
41. As a testament to his singing, after Johnny Cash's death, Wootton performed Cash songs on his own and with WS Holland.
42. Wootton quoted in Julie Chadwick, *The Man Who Carried Cash: Saul Holiff, Johnny Cash, and the Making of an American Icon* (Toronto: Dundurn, 2017), 213.
43. Kienzle, "Bob Wootton," 120.

44. Audio from September 17, 1968 show, Winthrop Rockefeller Collection, RG 7, Reel-to-Reel 758–761, UALR.
45. Johnny Cash, *Man in Black* (Grand Rapids, MI: Zondervan, 1975), 166.
46. Audio from September 17, 1968 show, Winthrop Rockefeller Collection, RG 7, Reel-to-Reel 758–761, UALR.
47. Marshall Grant, *I Was There When It Happened: My Life with Johnny Cash* (Nashville: Cumberland House, 2006), 164.
48. Kienzle, "Bob Wootton," 120.
49. *Northwest Arkansas Times*, September 20, 1968.
50. *Harrison Daily Times*, September 20, 1968.
51. Lewry, *I've Been Everywhere*, 65–66.
52. Grant, *I Was There When It Happened*, 163–164.
53. Cash, *Man in Black*, 168.
54. Cash, *Man in Black*, 167.
55. Speech of October 1, 1968, Record Group 7, Reel 771, Winthrop Rockefeller Collection, UALR.
56. *The Advance-Monticellonian*, October 3, 1968.
57. *Hot Springs New Era*, October 18, 1968.
58. Urwin, *Agenda for Reform*, 111.
59. Cash's letter is inserted in page 116 in John Carter Cash, *House of Cash: The Legacies of My Father, Johnny Cash* (San Rafael, CA: Insight Editions, 2012).
60. Cash apparently never recorded "When I Get Out of Cummins" in the studio. It seems the Cummins concert was the only time he played it. A complete, official sound recording of the performance was never released to the public. A transcription of the song can be found in Tom Dearmore's article in the *Arkansas Gazette*, September 28, 1969. However, Dearmore apparently did not have access to a sound recording of the song. The tune as Cash sang it differs slightly from Dearmore's transcription. A clip of Cash's song can be found in Record Group 7, Audio Reel 1324, Winthrop Rockefeller Collection, UALR. I've tried to write the song as Cash sang it.
61. *Arkansas Gazette*, September 28, 1969.
62. Leigh Edwards, *Johnny Cash and the Paradox of American Identity* (Bloomington: Indiana University Press, 2009), 20.
63. Edward L. Ayers, *Vengeance and Justice: Crime and Punishment in the 19th Century South* (New York: Oxford University Press, 1984), 188.
64. Lamar House, "Memories of a Slave Prison: A True Story," 157. House's memoir can be found in Box 10, Folder 13, Arkansas Small Manuscripts Collection, UALR.
65. Calvin R. Ledbetter Jr., "The Long Struggle to End Convict Leasing in Arkansas," *Arkansas Historical Quarterly* 52, no. 1 (Spring 1993), 22, 26–27.
66. *Arkansas Gazette*, June 30, 1976; *Los Angeles Times*, January 6, 2002.
67. *Pea Pickers Picayune*, March 1, 1969.

68. *Arkansas Gazette*, April 11, 1969.
69. David Ragan, *The Great Johnny Cash* (New York: MacFadden-Bartell, 1970), 28–31.
70. Entry for December 5, Tara Cash Schwoebel, ed., *Recollections by J. R. Cash* (Jonesboro: Arkansas State University, 2014).
71. Urwin, *Agenda for Reform*, 152–53. For a partial transcript of the testimony, see C. Fred Williams, et al., *A Documentary History of Arkansas* (Fayetteville: University of Arkansas Press, 1984), 253–60.
72. Rockefeller can be heard on the edited broadcast of the concert, which was produced by KATV of Little Rock. I was able to view "Johnny Cash at Cummins" courtesy of Ken King of Little Rock, who owns a copy.
73. *Arkansas Gazette*, September 28, 1969. On the origins of the *Picayune*, see *Arkansas Democrat*, November 17, 1968.
74. *Pea Pickers Picayune*, April 10, 1969.
75. *Pea Pickers Picayune*, April 18, 1969.
76. *Arkansas Gazette*, September 28, 1969.
77. Ragan, *The Great Johnny Cash*, 31.
78. *Arkansas Gazette*, November 28, 1969. Cash apparently donated $5,000 to both the Tucker and Cummins chapel projects in 1970. Commissioner Sarver reported that half of the $5,000 donation went to purchase ice machines for the kitchen and that the prisoners themselves would decide how to spend the rest of the money. See C. Robert Sarver, *Arkansas Department of Correction Annual Report to the Governor and the General Assembly Covering Period March 1, 1968 to September 30, 1970* (Little Rock: n.p., 1970), 12.
79. Evie Blad, "Water Again Seen Sacred at Repaired Prison Chapel," *Arkansas Democrat-Gazette*, May 14, 2011, http://www.arkansasonline.com/news/2011/may/14/water-again-seen-sacred-repaired-prison-c-20110514/.
80. *Arkansas Democrat*, April 16, 1969; *Arkansas Gazette*, April 17, 1969.
81. Huckabee was elected to two terms but also served the last two years of James Guy Tucker Jr.'s governorship after Tucker resigned in the wake of the his conviction following the Whitewater investigation.
82. *Arkansas Gazette*, January 30, 1977.
83. For a full text of the *Holt v. Sarver* decision, see www.leagle.com/decision/1970671309FSupp362_1597 (accessed May 20, 2021).
84. "Recent Cases, Constitutional Law. Cruel and Unusual Punishment. Arkansas State Penitentiary System Violates the Eighth Amendment, *Holt v. Sarver*, 209 F Supp. 362 (E. D. Ark. 1970)," *Harvard Law Review* 84, no. 2 (December 1970), 459.
85. For a timeline of events, see Tom Wicker, *A Time to Die* (New York: Quadrangle, 1975), 311–14.
86. *Hearings before the Subcommittee on National Penitentiaries of the*

Committee on the Judiciary (Washington, DC: US Government Printing Office, 1972), 71–88.

87. Robert Hilburn, *Johnny Cash: The Life* (New York: Little, Brown, 2013), 438–39.
88. Michael Streissguth, ed., *Ring of Fire: The Johnny Cash Reader* (Cambridge, MA: Da Capo, 2003), 186–87.
89. Bill Clinton to Hugh B. Patterson Jr., October 15, 1985, Box 63, Folder 5, Hugh B. Patterson, Jr., Papers, UALR.
90. Suzi Parker, "Blood Money," *Salon*, December 24, 1998.
91. *Arkansas Democrat-Gazette*, December 12, 2002.
92. Pew Trusts, "Consensus Report of the Arkansas Working Group on Sentencing and Corrections," January 1, 2011, https://www.pewtrusts.org/en/research-and-analysis/issue-briefs/2011/01/01/consensus-report-of-the-arkansas-working-group-on-sentencing-and-corrections.

Chapter 6

1. Marshall Grant, *I Was There When It Happened: My Life with Johnny Cash* (Nashville: Cumberland House, 2006) 183.
2. Johnny to Vivian Cash, May 23, 1953, Vivian Cash, *I Walked the Line: My Life with Johnny Cash* (New York: Scribner, 2007), 146.
3. *Billboard*, May 23, 1970, C-6.
4. Stephen Miller, *Johnny Cash: The Life of an American Icon* (New York: Omnibus, 2003), 127–128.
5. *Arkansas Gazette*, May 1, 1970.
6. *Berkshire Eagle*, December 19, 1969, p. 15.
7. National Archives, "Vietnam War U.S. Military Fatal Casualty Statistics," accessed May 20, 2021, https://www.archives.gov/research/military/vietnam-war/casualty-statistics.
8. Johnny Cash, *Live around the World: Bootleg, Vol. III* (Disc 1), Columbia, 2011.
9. Johnny Cash, *Man in Black* (Grand Rapids, MI: Zondervan, 1975), 178–179.
10. *New York Times*, April 18, 1970.
11. Johnny Cash, "Introduction: President Richard Nixon," *Live around the World: Bootleg, Vol. III*, Columbia, 2011.
12. *Washington Post*, reprinted in the *Delta Democrat-Times* (Greenville, MI), December 5, 1969.
13. *ReMastered: Tricky Dick and the Man in Black*, directed by Barbara Kopple, 2018, Netflix.
14. Christopher Wren, *Winners Got Scars Too: The Life and Legends of Johnny Cash* (New York: Ballantine, 1971), 16.
15. Streissguth, *Outlaw: Waylon, Willie, Kris, and the Renegades of Nashville* (New York: HarperCollins, 2013), 6.

16. Streissguth, *Outlaw*, 64.
17. Rosanne Cash, *Composed: A Memoir* (New York: Viking, 2010), 201.
18. Robert Hilburn, *Johnny Cash: The Life* (New York: Little, Brown, 2013), 310–11.
19. Greg Laurie, *Johnny Cash: The Redemption of an American Icon* (Washington, DC: Salem, 2019), 221.
20. Charles B. Thorne, "The Watering Spas of Middle Tennessee," *Tennessee Historical Quarterly* 29, no. 4 (Winter 1970–1971), 351. As of this writing, the farm is called the Storytellers Hideaway Farm and Museum, where one can see not only the farm but Cash's "One Piece at a Time" car, too.
21. *Playboy* (November 1970), 139–40, 148, 209–14.
22. *Osceola Times*, September 24, 1970.
23. *Osceola Times*, September 24, 1970.
24. *Cleveland County Herald*, October 14, 1970.
25. Charles Paul Conn, *The New Johnny Cash* (Old Tappan, NJ: Fleming H. Revell, 1973), 54.
26. Russell Chandler, *The Overcomers: Outstanding Christians Share the Secrets of Successful Living* (Old Tappan, NJ: Fleming H. Revell, 1978), 131.
27. Chandler, *The Overcomers,* 133.
28. Chandler, *The Overcomers,* 135.
29. Cash, *Man in Black*, 89–99.
30. Chandler, *The Overcomers*, 135.
31. Conn, *The New Johnny Cash*, 11.
32. Nick Tosches, *Country: The Twisted Roots of Rock and Roll* (New York: Dell, 1977), 135–36.
33. Rodney Clapp, *Johnny Cash and the Great American Contradiction: Christianity and the Battle of the Soul of the Nation* (Louisville, KY: Westminster John Knox Press, 2008), 43, 140n.
34. Julie Chadwick, *The Man Who Carried Cash: Saul Holiff, Johnny Cash, and the Making of an American Icon* (Toronto: Dundurn, 2017), 254–55.
35. *Arkansas Democrat*, September 12, 1971.
36. *Arkansas Gazette*, October 4, 1971.
37. *Arkansas Gazette*, January 27, 1972.
38. Jimmy Carter did not coin the phrase "national malaise," though his well-known speech of July 15, 1979, where he discussed America's "moral and spiritual crisis," became identified with the idea.
39. Donald Holley, "The Second Great Emancipation: The Rust Cotton Picker and How It Changed Arkansas," *Arkansas Historical Quarterly* 52, no. 1 (Spring 1993): 71.
40. Conn, *The New Johnny Cash*, 72–74.
41. Memorandum of April 2, 1970, from Murray Chotiner to H. R. Haldeman,

Nixon Library, accessed May 25, 2021, https://www.nixonlibrary.gov/virtual library/documents/donated/040270_chotiner.pdf; Ogden Standard *Examiner*, April 21, 1970.

42. Eric M. Uslaner and Thomas Zittel, "Comparative Legislative Behavior," *The Oxford Handbook of Political Science*, ed. Robert E. Goodin (New York: Oxford University Press, 2009), 401.
43. *Arkansas Gazette*, July 27, 1972.
44. Robert Hilburn, *Cornflakes with John Lennon: And Other Tales from a Rock 'n' Roll Life* (New York: Rodale, 2009), 24.
45. Editors of *Rolling Stone*, *The* Rolling Stone *Interviews* (New York: St. Martin's, 1981), 277.
46. Editors of *Rolling Stone*, *The* Rolling Stone *Interviews,* 274–76.
47. *New York Times*, December 13, 1973.
48. *New York Times*, December 13, 1973.
49. *Osceola Times*, February 21, 1974.
50. Conn, *The New Johnny Cash*, 16.
51. Steven P. Miller, *Billy Graham and the Rise of the Republican South* (Philadelphia: University of Pennsylvania Press, 2009), 28, 104. In 1958, one of Graham's associates wrote to Martin Luther King Jr., saying that Graham "has never engaged in politics on one side or the other." See Grady Wilson to King, July 28, 1958, in *The Papers of Martin Luther King, Jr., Volume VI,* ed. Clayborne Carson (Berkeley: University of California Press, 2000), 458.
52. Hilburn, *Johnny Cash*, 375.
53. By 1971, far fewer men were dying each week in Vietnam than in previous years, but the number was still significant. In 1970, 6,173 servicemen—119 per week—were killed in Vietnam. This was roughly half the 1969 number. "Man in Black" was released in March 1970. When one considers that Cash was writing the song based on what he knew about the war over the entirety of 1970, his was an accurate figure. On casualty figures, see National Archives, "Vietnam War," accessed May 25, 2021.
54. Conn, *The New Johnny Cash*, 30.
55. Bill C. Malone, ed., *The New Encyclopedia of Southern Culture, Volume 12* (Chapel Hill: University of North Carolina Press, 2014), 201.
56. Cash, *Man in Black*, 13 (first quotation), 9 (second quotation).
57. Mark Zwonitzer and Charles Hirshberg, *Will You Miss Me When I'm Gone?: The Carter Family and Their Legacy in American Music* (New York: Simon & Schuster, 2002), 335–73.
58. Johnny Cash to Saul Holiff, March 5, 1974, Saul Holiff Collection, University of Victoria Special Collections.
59. Johnny Cash to Saul Holiff, April 28, 1974, Saul Holiff Collection, University of Victoria Special Collections.

60. Saul Holiff to Johnny Cash, December 2, 1974, Saul Holiff Collection, University of Victoria Special Collections.
61. Larry Linderman, Johnny Cash interview, *Penthouse* (November 1975), 66.
62. Linderman, 108.
63. Linderman, 108–110.
64. Hilburn, *Johnny Cash*, 372–73.
65. *Cleveland County Herald*, March 17, 1976.
66. *Arkansas Gazette*, March 19, 1976.
67. *Arkansas Gazette*, January 8, 1976.
68. *Arkansas Democrat*, March 21, 1976.
69. *Arkansas Democrat*, March 21, 1976.
70. *Arkansas Gazette*, March 3, 1976.
71. *Arkansas Democrat*, March 21, 1976; *Cleveland County Herald*, March 24, 1976.
72. *Arkansas Democrat*, March 21, 1976.
73. *Arkansas Gazette*, March 21, 1976.
74. *Arkansas Democrat*, March 21, 1976.
75. *Arkansas Gazette,* March 21, 1976.
76. *Cleveland County Herald*, March 24, 1976.
77. *Cleveland County Herald*, March 17, 1976.
78. *Cleveland County Herald*, March 20, 1976.
79. *Arkansas Gazette*, March 21, 1976.
80. *Arkansas Democrat*, March 21, 1976.
81. *Arkansas Gazette*, March 21, 1976.
82. *Arkansas Gazette,* March 21, 1976.
83. *Arkansas Gazette*, March 21, 1976.
84. *Arkansas Gazette*, March 21, 1976.
85. *Cleveland County Herald*, March 17, 1976.
86. *Cleveland County Herald*, March 24, 1976.
87. Cash was inducted into the Country Hall of Fame (which was opened in 1964) in 1980, and the Rock and Roll Hall of Fame in 1992. He joined the Gospel Music Hall of Fame in 2010.
88. The long version is available on the compilation album accompanying the book by John Carter Cash, *House of Cash*.
89. "Johnny Cash—Ridin' on the Cotton-belt (The [Arthur] Smith Show in '77), July 2, 2017, video, 8:27, https://www.youtube.com/watch?v=Lv-CowKNSQQ.
90. Streissguth, *Outlaw*, 50.
91. Nadine Hubbs, *Rednecks, Queers and Country Music* (Berkeley: University of California Press, 2014), 153.
92. *Pine Bluff Commercial*, January 16, 1978.
93. *Pine Bluff Commercial*, January 16, 1978.

94. According to *Billboard*, by October 1980, the album had sold four million copies, and by 1997, five million. See *Billboard*, October 18, 1980, and September 13, 1997.
95. Marshall Grant, *I Was There When It Happened: My Life with Johnny Cash* (Nashville: Cumberland House, 2006), 324–25.
96. Ritchie Unterberger, "*Silver*," *AllMusic*, accessed June 14, 2021, https://www.allmusic.com/album/silver-mw0000227637.
97. *People*, May 28, 1979.
98. Dan Carter, *The Politics of Rage: George Wallace, The Origins of the New Conservatism, and the Transformation of American Politics* (New York: Simon & Schuster, 1995), 14.

Chapter 7

1. Rosanne Cash, *Composed: A Memoir* (New York: Viking, 2010), 35.
2. Robert Hilburn, *Johnny Cash: The Life* (New York: Little, Brown, 2013), 436.
3. Cash, *Composed*, 33.
4. Laura Lomas, "Mystifying Mystery: Inscriptions of the Oral in the Legend of Rose Hall," *Journal of West Indian Literature* 6, no. 2 (May 1994): 72.
5. Don Robotham, "Crime and Crisis in Jamaica," FOCAL: Canadian Foundation for the Americas, accessed May 29, 2021, http://www.focal.ca/en/publications/focalpoint/307-september-2010-don-robotham; United Kingdom Home Office, "Country Policy and Information Note Jamaica: Fear of Organised Criminal Groups," August 2019, https://assets.publishing.service.gov.uk/government/uploads/system/uploads/attachment_data/file/824431/Jamaica-Org-Crim-Groups-CPIN-v3.0-August_2019.pdf.
6. Greg Laurie, *Johnny Cash: The Redemption of an American Icon* (Washington, DC: Salem, 2019), 239.
7. June Carter Cash, *From the Heart* (New York: Prentice Hall, 1987), 135–45.
8. Johnny Cash and Patrick Carr, *Cash: The Autobiography* (New York: HarperCollins, 1997), 55; Cash, *From the Heart*, 143.
9. Cash and Carr, *Cash*, 56.
10. *Jamaica Tourist*, issue 3 (2006), 20, https://ufdcimages.uflib.ufl.edu/UF/00/09/40/94/00003/Issue%2003.pdf.
11. Cash, *From the Heart*, 135.
12. Cash, *From the Heart*, 136.
13. Cash and Carr, *Cash*, 10–11.
14. Glenne Currie, "Cash's Christmas," UPI Archives, December 26, 1981, https://www.upi.com/Archives/1981/12/26/CASHS-CHRISTMAS/3925378190800/.
15. Cash, *From the Heart*, 1.

16. Dave Marsh with John Swenson, eds., *The* Rolling Stone *Album Guide* (New York: Fireside, 2004), 265.
17. Bill Carter and Judi Turner, *Get Carter: Backstage in History from JFK's Assassination to the Rolling Stones* (Nashville: Fine's Creek, 2006), 150–51.
18. *Arkansas Gazette*, April 23, 1982.
19. *Arkansas Democrat*, April 23, 1982.
20. Rex Nelson, "Fordyce on the Cotton Belt," *Rex Nelson's Southern Fried* (blog), April 19, 2011, http://www.rexnelsonsouthernfried.com/?p=2323.
21. Jim Marshall, *Johnny Cash at Folsom & San Quentin* (London: Reel Art Press, 2018), 11.
22. Hilburn, *Johnny Cash*, 479.
23. Marshall, *Johnny Cash at Folsom and San Quentin*, 15.
24. *Billboard*, March 30, 2002, p. 95.
25. Zoie Clift, "Meet Joe Meador: Founder of the Fordyce on the Cotton Belt Festival," updated February 2016, https://www.arkansas.com/articles/meet-joe-bill-meador-founder-fordyce-cotton-belt-festival.
26. *Arkansas Gazette*, August 5, 1983.
27. Digital copy of televised roast in possession of Ken King of Little Rock.
28. John Carter Cash, *Anchored in Love: An Intimate Portrait of June Carter Cash* (Nashville, TN: Thomas Nelson), 92.
29. C. Eric Banister, *Johnny Cash FAQ: All That's Left to Know about the Man in Black* (Milwaukee, WI: Backbeat Books, 2014), 240.
30. Johnny Cash, *Man in White: A Novel about the Apostle Paul* (Nashville: WestBow Press, 2007 [1986]), xii.
31. Cash, *Man in White*, xxii–xxiii.
32. Cash, *Man in White*, xvi.
33. Miller, *Johnny Cash*, 285.
34. *Arkansas Gazette*, September 14, 1986.
35. *South Florida Sun-Sentinel*, December 26, 1985.
36. Cash, *From the Heart*, ix.
37. Cash, *From the Heart*, 11.
38. Cash, *From the Heart*, 163.
39. Cash, *From the Heart*, 197.
40. *Arkansas Democrat*, September 7, 1990.
41. *Arkansas Democrat*, September 9, 1990.
42. *Arkansas Gazette*, September 10, 1990.
43. *Arkansas Democrat*, September 10, 1990.
44. Bill Clinton, *My Life* (New York: Alfred A. Knopf, 2004), 55.
45. *Arkansas Gazette*, September 10, 1990.
46. *Arkansas Democrat*, September 10, 1990.
47. *Arkansas Gazette*, September 25, 1989.
48. *Arkansas Gazette*, July 7, 1990.

49. *Arkansas Gazette*, July 7, 1990.
50. Cash and Carr, *Cash*, 342. The album apparently made as little impact on Cash's memory as it did on his fans. The album is referred to as *The Meaning of Life* in his autobiography.
51. Michael Streissguth, *Johnny Cash: The Biography* (New York: Da Capo, 2007), 236.
52. Kansas City *Star*, May 5, 2018, August 22, 2017, April 23, 2020.
53. Lewry, *I've Been Everywhere: A Johnny Cash Chronicle* (London: Helter Skelter, 2001), 223.
54. Will Hodge, "Johnny Cash's 'Unchained' at 20: Inside the Making of a Masterpiece," *Rolling Stone*, November 4, 2016, https://www.rollingstone.com/music/music-country/johnny-cashs-unchained-at-20-inside-the-making-of-a-masterpiece-108557/.
55. Hilburn, *Johnny Cash*, 554.
56. Stephen Miller, *Johnny Cash: The Life of an American Icon* (New York: Omnibus, 2003), 338.
57. In 2013, Cash would be honored with a first-class Forever Stamp that featured a likeness of him from his early years.
58. Video of concert day courtesy of Ken King of Little Rock.
59. *Cleveland County Herald*, March 2, 1994.
60. *Cleveland County Herald*, March 9, 1994.
61. *Cleveland County Herald*, April 6, 1994.
62. *Cleveland County Herald*, April 6, 1994.
63. *Arkansas Gazette,* March 13, 1991.
64. *Cleveland County Herald*, April 6, 1994.
65. *Parade*, June 11, 1995.
66. James Guy Tucker Jr., Papers, UALR-CAHC; *New York Times*, August 5, 1994.
67. Phoebe Reilly, "West Memphis Three's Damien Echols on the Music Gave Him 'Life after Death,'" *Spin*, August 13, 2012, http://www.spin.com/2012/08/west-memphis-threes-damien-echols-on-the-music-gave-him-life-after-death/.
68. United States Government Printing Office, *William J. Clinton, 1996 (In Two Books), Book II—July 1 to December 31, 1996* (Washington, DC, 1998), 2179.
69. Cash and Carr, *Cash*, 162–63.
70. The song was written by Chris Cornell, who struggled with depression and substance abuse before hanging himself in a hotel room in 2017.
71. Author interview with Patrick Carr, October 12, 2017.
72. Patrick Carr to author, April 4, 2021.
73. *Arkansas Democrat-Gazette*, December 28, 1997.
74. *Arkansas Democrat-Gazette*, June 26, 1998.
75. *Arkansas Gazette*, April 18, 1999.
76. Teresa Ortega, "'My Name Is Sue: How Do You Do?': Johnny Cash as Lesbian

Icon," in *Reading Country Music: Steel Guitars, Opry Stars, and Honky Tonk Bars*, ed. Cecilia Tichi (Durham, NC: Duke University Press, 1998), 222.
77. John Waters, *Role Models* (New York: Farrar, Straus and Giroux, 2010), 132.
78. Ortega, "'My Name Is Sue: How Do You Do?'" 232.
79. *Journal of Country Music*, July 9, 2002.
80. Hilburn, *Johnny Cash*, 611–14.
81. *Baptist Press*, May 19, 2003.
82. *Cleveland County Herald*, September 17, 2003.
83. Matt Diehl, "Remembering Johnny," *Rolling Stone*, October 16, 2003, https://www.rollingstone.com/music/music-news/remembering-johnny-186961/.
84. Cash, *Composed*, 167.
85. *Us Weekly*, February 1997, http://www.maryellenmark.com/text/magazines/us%20weekly_new/925B-000-012.html (accessed May 31, 2021).
86. *Arkansas Democrat-Gazette*, September 13, 2003.
87. *Lexington Herald-Leader* (*New York Times* News Service), September 14, 2003.
88. *Us Weekly*, February 1997, http://www.maryellenmark.com/text/magazines/us%20weekly_new/925B-000-012.html (accessed April 4, 2021).

Chapter 8

1. "News and Notices," *Arkansas Historical Quarterly* 49, no. 1 (Spring 2000), 121–22.
2. "June Carter Cash's Daughter Found Dead," *Chicago Tribune*, October 26, 2003, https://www.chicagotribune.com/news/ct-xpm-2003-10-26-0310260488-story.html.
3. Sharon Waxman, "The Secrets That Lie Beyond the Ring of Fire," *New York Times*, October 16, 2005, https://www.nytimes.com/2005/10/16/movies/the-secrets-that-lie-beyond-the-ring-of-fire.html.
4. Waxman, "The Secrets."
5. Waxman, "The Secrets."
6. Ruth Hawkins to author, January 6, 2020.
7. *Walk the Line,* directed by James Mangold, written by Gill Dennis and James Mangold (Century City, CA: 20th Century Fox, 2005).
8. "Johnny Cash's Daughter Angry over Biopic," *NME*, November 11, 2005, https://www.nme.com/news/music/johnny-cash-41-1365332; Rosanne quoted in Rosanne Cash, *Composed: A Memoir* (New York: Viking, 2010), 188.
9. Robert Levine, "Cash Film's Missing Ingredient: Religion," *New York Times*, March 4, 2006, https://www.nytimes.com/2006/03/04/movies/MoviesFeatures/cash-films-missing-ingredient-religion.html.
10. "Famous Lakeside Home of Johnny and June Cash Burns Down," *Seattle Times*, April 10, 2007, https://www.seattletimes.com/entertainment/famous-lakeside-home-of-johnny-and-june-cash-burns-down/.

11. Party Ben, "Johnny Cash's House Burns Down," *Mother Jones*, April 11, 2007, https://www.motherjones.com/politics/2007/04/johnny-cashs-house-burns-down/ (accessed June 1, 2021).
12. *Arkansas Democrat-Gazette*, January 30, 1998.
13. Phyllis Williams to author, 2014 (no date). The legislature's resolution can be found at http://www.arkleg.state.ar.us/assembly/1999/R/Bills/HCR1003.pdf (accessed June 1, 2020).
14. Johnny Cash and Patrick Carr, *Cash: The Autobiography* (New York: HarperCollins, 1997), 387–88.
15. *Poinsett County Democrat Tribune*, July 12, 2001.
16. Undated article, vertical files, Mississippi County Historical and Genealogical Society, Osceola.
17. Keith Boles, "King of Clubs Burns in Swifton," *KAIT 8*, updated December 14, 2010, https://www.kait8.com/story/13666525/king-of-clubs-burns-in-swifton/.
18. *Rural Arkansas Living* (July 2011), 24.
19. Sheila Yount, "Walking the Line in Dyess," *Rural Arkansas Living*, July 2011, p. 12.
20. Yount, "Walking the Line in Dyess."
21. Arkansas State University, "Arkansas Bestows Awards on Bill Carter for Work with Entertainers and Johnny Cash Boyhood Home Project," March 12, 2013, http://www.astate.edu/news/arkansas-bestows-awards-on-bill-carter-for-work-with-entertainers-and-johnny-cash-boyhood-home-project.
22. Gwendolyn Purdom, "Arkansas State University to Restore Johnny Cash's Boyhood Home," *Preservation*, April 27, 2011. Her article notes that twenty thousand visitors were expected every year, but Ruth Hawkins has said projections were closer to thirty thousand, which have proven accurate.
23. *Arkansas Democrat-Gazette*, February 26, 2012.
24. Purdom, "Arkansas State University to Restore."
25. *Arkansas Times*, August 10, 2011.
26. *Jonesboro Sun*, August 4, 2011.
27. *Cabot Star-Herald*, August 10, 2011.
28. *Jonesboro Sun*, August 4, 2011.
29. *Jonesboro Sun*, August 4, 2011.
30. Figures come from Ruth Hawkins in message to author.
31. *Arkansas Times*, August 10, 2011.
32. Ruth Hawkins to author, April 16, 2019.
33. Rosanne Cash, "Goin' Back to Dyess," *Hemispheres Magazine*, November 1, 2015.
34. *Arkansas Democrat-Gazette*, February 26, 2012.
35. Patrick Doyle, "Johnny Cash's Family Kicks Off Blowout Celebration of Country Icon's 80th," *Rolling Stone*, March 1, 2012 http://www.rollingstone

.com/music/news/johnny-cashs-family-kicks-off-blowout-celebration-of-country-icons-80th-20120224.

36. *Jonesboro Sun*, February 27, 2012.

37. Seth Rogovoy, "Restoration of Johnny Cash's Boyhood Home to Mark 80th Birthday of Late Music Icon," *The Rogovoy Report*, February 7, 2012, http://rogovoyreport.com/2012/02/07/johnny-cash-boyhood-home/ (accessed June 2, 2021).

38. *Jonesboro Sun*, February 27, 2012.

39. The festival concerts raised a total of $429,866. This and the $575,000 figure come from Ruth Hawkins.

40. *Jonesboro Sun*, March 4, 2012.

41. Doyle, "Johnny Cash's Family."

42. Phil Hebblethwaite, "How Johnny Cash Became an Even Bigger Star after His Death," *The Guardian*, March 27, 2014, https://www.theguardian.com/music/2014/mar/27/johnny-cash-out-among-the-stars-again.

43. Paul Gorman, "Johnny Cash," *Music Week*, 1995, https://www.rocksbackpages.com/Library/Article/johnny-cash.

44. Marvin Schwartz, *We Wanna Boogie: The Rockabilly Roots of Sonny Burgess and the Pacers* (Little Rock, AR: Butler Center Books, 2014), 307.

45. Arkansas Economic Development Commission, "Largest Employers for Jackson County," accessed June 2, 2021, https://www.arkansasedc.com/docs/default-source/compare-arkansas/employers-by-county/jackson-county.pdf?sfvrsn=891e19d0_2.

46. Schwartz, *We Wanna Boogie*, 317.

47. James M. MacDonald and Robert A. Hoppe, "Large Family Farms Continue to Dominate U.S. Agricultural Production," *Amber Waves* (blog), US Department of Agriculture Economic Research Service, March 6, 2017, https://www.ers.usda.gov/amber-waves/2017/march/large-family-farms-continue-to-dominate-us-agricultural-production/.

48. Richard Kienzle, "Bob Wootton: 'Boom-Chicka' and the Man in Black," *Vintage Guitar* 22, no. 9 (July 2008), 124.

49. Shaun Braun, "Good Ole Boy," *Playboy* (November 1970), 140.

50. Andy Cush, "Johnny Cash's Kids to Neo-Nazi Wearing His T-Shirt: Our Dad Would Be 'Horrified' by You," *Spin*, August 17, 2017, https://www.spin.com/2017/08/johnny-cash-rosanne-statement-white-nationalists-horrified/.

51. Anastasia Tsioulcas, "After Labels Object, White Nationalist Stormfront Radio Stops Using Johnny Cash," *The Record*, NPR, September 14, 2017, https://www.npr.org/sections/therecord/2017/09/14/550989052/white-nationalist-stormfront-radio-no-longer-using-johnny-cash-s-music.

52. Notes taken by author at event, October 21, 2017.

53. "About: Future Home to the Largest Private Collection of Country Music

Artifacts in the World," Marty Stuart's Congress of Country Music, accessed November 5, 2021, https://congressofcountrymusic.org/about.

54. For a look at Davies in a historical context, see Mark Doyle, *Songs of the Semi-Detached* (London: Reaktion, 2020).

55. Sean Clancy, "Statues of Bates, Cash Approved for U.S. Display," *Arkansas Democrat-Gazette*, April 12, 2019, https://www.arkansasonline.com/news/2019/apr/12/statues-of-bates-cash-approved-for-u-s-/?news-politics (accessed June 2, 2021).

SELECTED BIBLIOGRAPHY

Manuscript Collections

Cash Family Papers.
Private Collection, in possession of Wayne Cash, Maumelle, Arkansas.
UALR Center for Arkansas History and Culture, Little Rock.
Arkansas Small Manuscripts Collection.
Gov. James Guy Tucker Jr. Papers.
Hugh B. Patterson Papers.
Oral History Collection.
Winthrop Rockefeller Collection.
University of Victoria Special Collections, Victoria, British Columbia.
Saul Holiff Collection.

Published Sources

Ackerman, Leland C. *Here and There: Weekly Columns from the* Cleveland County Herald. N.p., 2003.

Arkansas Penitentiary Study Commission. *Report of the Arkansas Penitentiary Study Commission*. Little Rock: Arkansas Penitentiary Study Commission, 1968.

Arkansas State Police Criminal Investigation Division. *Tucker Prison Farm Investigation Report, 1966*. Little Rock: The Division, 1967?

Ayers, Edward L. *Vengeance and Justice: Crime and Punishment in the 19th Century South*. New York: Oxford University Press, 1984.

Bangs, Lester. *Psychotic Reactions and Carburetor Dung*. New York: Anchor, 2003.

Banister, C. Eric. *Johnny Cash FAQ: All That's Left to Know about the Man in Black*. Milwaukee: Backbeat Books, 2014.

Beley, Gene. "Folsom Prison Blues." *Virginia Quarterly Review* 81, no. 1 (Winter 2005): 218–27.

Braun, Shaun. "Good Ole Boy." *Playboy* (November 1970), 138–40, 148, 209–14.

Brightwell, Juanita S., Eunice S. Lee, and Elsie C. Fulghum. *Roster of the Confederate Soldiers of Georgia, 1861–1865: Index*. Spartanburg, SC: Reprint Company, 1982.

Campbell, Garth. *Johnny Cash: He Walked the Line, 1932–2003*. London: John Blake, 2003.

Carpenter, Heath. *The Philosopher King: T-Bone Burnett and the Ethic of a Southern Cultural Renaissance*. Athens: University of Georgia Press, 2019.

Carpozi, George Jr. *The Johnny Cash Story*. New York: Pyramid, 1970.

Carter, Bill, and Judi Turner. *Get Carter: Backstage in History from JFK's Assassination to the Rolling Stones*. Nashville, TN: Fine's Creek, 2006.

Cash, Cindy. *Cash Family Scrapbook*: New York: Crown, 1997.

Cash, John Carter. *Anchored in Love: An Intimate Portrait of June Carter Cash*. Nashville, TN: Thomas Nelson, 2007.

———. *House of Cash: The Legacies of My Father, Johnny Cash*. San Rafael, CA: Insight Editions, 2012.

Cash, Johnny. *Forever Words: The Unknown Poems*. New York: Blue Rider Press, 2016.

———. *Man in Black*. Grand Rapid, MI: Zondervan, 1975.

———. *Man in White: A Novel about the Apostle Paul*. Nashville, TN: WestBow Press, 2007.

———. "You Have to Call Me the Way You See Me," *Southern Cultures* 21, no. 3 (Fall 2015): 5–17.

Cash, Johnny, and Patrick Carr. *Cash: The Autobiography*. New York: HarperCollins, 1997.

Cash, Johnny, Billy Zeoli, and Al Hartley. *Hello, I'm Johnny Cash*. Old Tappan, NJ: Fleming H. Revell Company, 1976.

Cash, June Carter. *Among My Klediments*. Grand Rapids, MI: Zondervan, 1979.

———. *From the Heart*. New York: Prentice Hall, 1987.

Cash, Rosanne. *Composed: A Memoir*. New York: Viking, 2010.

Cash, Vivian. *I Walked the Line: My Life with Johnny Cash*. New York: Scribner, 2007.

Chadwick, Julie. *The Man Who Carried Cash: Saul Holiff, Johnny Cash, and the Making of an American Icon*. Toronto: Dundurn, 2017.

Chandler, Russell. *The Overcomers: Outstanding Christians Share the Secrets of Successful Living*. Old Tappan, NJ: Fleming H. Revell, 1978.

Chapman, C. Stuart. *Shelby Foote: A Writer's Life*. Oxford: University Press of Mississippi, 2003.

Clapp, Rodney. *Johnny Cash and the Great American Contradiction: Christianity and the Battle for the Soul of a Nation*. Louisville, KY: Westminster John Knox Press, 2008.

Cleveland County Historical Society. *The Impact of Agriculture on Cleveland County, Arkansas, from 1830 to 1950*. Rison, AR: Cleveland County Historical and Genealogical Society, 2006.

Cochran, Robert. "Ride It Like You're Flyin': The Story of 'The Rock Island Line,'" *Arkansas Historical Quarterly* 56, no. 2 (Summer 1997): 201–29.

Conn, Charles Paul. *The New Johnny Cash*. Old Tappan, NJ: Fleming H. Revell, 1973.

Cooper, Peter. *Johnny's Cash and Charley's Pride: Lasting Legends and Untold Adventures in Country Music*. Nashville, TN: Spring House, 2017.

D'Ambrosio, Antonio. *A Heartbeat and a Guitar: Johnny Cash and the Making of* Bitter Tears. New York: Nation Books, 2009.

Dolan, Sean. *Johnny Cash*. New York: Chelsea House, 1995.

Editors of *Rolling Stone*. *The* Rolling Stone *Interviews*. New York: St. Martin's, 1981.

Edwards, Leigh H. *Johnny Cash and the Paradox of American Identity*. Bloomington: Indiana University Press, 2009.

Emergency Relief Administration State of Arkansas. *Dyess Colony Agricultural Colonization Project*. Little Rock: ERA of Arkansas, 1934.

Foley, Michael Stewart. "A Politics of Empathy: Johnny Cash, the Vietnam War, and the 'Walking Contradiction' Myth Dismantled," *Popular Music and Society* 37, no. 3 (July 2014): 338–59.

———. *Citizen Cash: The Political Life and Times of Johnny Cash*. New York: Basic, 2021.

Goddard, Peter, and Ronnie Hawkins. *Ronnie Hawkins: Last of the Good Ol' Boys*. Toronto: Stoddard, 1989.

Goggans, Helen. "Arkansas Sesquicentennial, 1836–1986: A History of Kingsland, Arkansas." Self-published, 1986.

Goodspeed. *Biographical and Historical Memoirs of Southern Arkansas*. Chicago: Goodspeed, 1890.

Grant, Marshall. *I Was There When It Happened: My Life with Johnny Cash*. Nashville, TN: Cumberland House, 2006.

Guralnick, Peter: *Sam Phillips: The Man Who Invented Rock 'n' Roll*. New York: Little, Brown, 2015.

Guralnick, Peter and Johnny Cash. *The Last Interview and Other Conversations*. New York: Melville House, 2020.

Hatley, Tom. *The Dividing Paths: Cherokees and South Carolinians through the Revolutionary Era*. New York: Oxford University Press, 1995.

Hawkins, Van. *A New Deal in Dyess: The Great Depression Era Agricultural Resettlement Colony in Arkansas*. Jonesboro, AR: Writers Bloc, 2015.

Hayden, David. "A History of Dyess, Arkansas." Master's thesis, Southern Illinois University, 1970.

Hewett, Janet B., ed. *The Roster of Confederate Soldiers, 1861–1865, Volume III: Buff, Aaron, to Coirrier, E. F.* Wilmington, NC: Broadfoot, 1995.

Hilburn, Robert. *Johnny Cash: The Life*. New York: Little, Brown, 2013.

Hinds, Michael, and Jonathan Silverman. *Johnny Cash International: How and Why Fans Love the Man in Black*. Iowa City: University of Iowa Press, 2020.

Holland, WS, and Ron Haney. *Behind the Man in Black: The WS Holland Story*. Jackson, TN: Drum Cat, 2018.

Holley, Donald. "The Second Great Emancipation: The Rust Cotton Picker and

How It Changed Arkansas." *Arkansas Historical Quarterly* 52, no. 1 (Spring 1993): 44–77.

———. "Trouble in Paradise: Dyess Colony and Arkansas Politics." *Arkansas Historical Quarterly* 32, no. 3 (Autumn 1973): 203–16.

Huss, John, and David Werther, eds. *Johnny Cash and Philosophy: The Burning Ring of Truth*. Chicago: Open Court, 2008.

Huston, James L. *The Panic of 1857 and the Coming of the Civil War*. Baton Rouge: Louisiana State University Press, 1987.

Isenberg, Nancy. *White Trash: The 400-Year Untold History of Class in America*. New York: Penguin, 2017.

Kienzle, Richard. "Bob Wootton: 'Boom-Chicka' and the Man in Black." *Vintage Guitar* 22, no. 9 (July 2008): 32–33, 120.

———. "The Primitive Genius: Luther Perkins," *Vintage Guitar* 22, no. 9 (July 2008): 120.

Laurie, Greg, and Marshal Terrill. *Johnny Cash: The Redemption of an American Icon*. Washington, DC: Salem Books, 2019.

Ledbetter, Calvin R. Jr. "The Long Struggle to End Convict Leasing in Arkansas," *Arkansas Historical Quarterly* 52, no. 1 (Spring 1993): 1–27.

Lewry, Peter. *I've Been Everywhere: A Johnny Cash Chronicle*. London: Helter Skelter, 2001.

Light, Alan. *Johnny Cash: The Life and Legacy of the Man in Black*. Washington, DC: Smithsonian Books, 2018.

Linderman, Larry. "Johnny Cash." *Penthouse*, November 1975, 64–66, 108–10.

Lisemby, Doris Mitchell. *Taproots in Fertile Soil*. Arkadelphia, AR: Autumn Years Ministries, 1993.

Marshall, Jim. *Johnny Cash at Folsom & San Quentin*. London: Reel Art Press, 2018.

McPherson, James. *Battle Cry of Freedom*. New York: Oxford University Press, 1988.

———. *For Cause and Comrades: Why Men Fought in the Civil War*. New York: Oxford University Press, 1997.

Miller, Stephen. *Johnny Cash: The Life of an American Icon*. New York: Omnibus, 2003.

Murton, Thomas O., and Joe Hyams, *Accomplices to the Crime*. New York: Grove Press, 1969.

Neimark, Anne E. *Johnny Cash: A Twentieth-Century Life*. New York: Viking, 2007.

Nelson, Scott Reynolds. *Steel Drivin' Man: John Henry, the Untold Story of an American Legend*. New York: Oxford University Press, 2008.

Pecknold, Diane, ed. *Hidden in the Mix: The African American Presence in Country Music*. Durham, NC: Duke University Press, 2013.

Perkins, Carl, and David McGee. *Go, Cat, Go! The Life and Times of Carl Perkins, the King of Rockabilly*. New York: Hyperion, 1996.

Pittman, Dan W. "The Founding of the Dyess Colony." *Arkansas Historical Quarterly* 29, no. 4 (Winter 1970), 313–26.

Ragan, David. *The Great Johnny Cash.* New York: MacFadden-Bartell, 1970.

Rawls, Annette. *Cleveland County, Arkansas: Our History Our Heritage.* Marcelline, MO: Walsworth, 2006.

Robin, Margaret. "Johnny Cash: Behind the Myth." *Hit Parader* (February 1970), 37–42.

Sakol, Jannie. "The Grit and Grace of Johnny Cash." *McCalls* (July 1970), 29, 110–11.

Schultz, James Willard, and George Varian. *Lone Bull's Mistake: A Lodge Pole Chief Story.* New York: Houghton Mifflin, 1918.

Schwartz, Marvin. *We Wanna Boogie: The Rockabilly Roots of Sonny Burgess and the Pacers.* Little Rock, AR: Butler Center Books, 2014.

Schwoebel, Tara Cash, ed. *Recollections by J. R. Cash.* Jonesboro: Arkansas State University, 2014.

Silverman, Jonathan. *Nine Choices: Johnny Cash and American Culture.* Amherst, MA: University of Massachusetts Press, 2010.

Smith, Fred C. *Trouble in Goshen: Plain Folk, Roosevelt, Jesus, and Marx in the Great Depression South.* Jackson: University Press of Mississippi, 2014.

Stimeling, Travis D., ed. *The Oxford Handbook of Country Music.* Oxford University Press, 2017.

Streissguth, Michael. *Always Been There: Rosanne Cash, the List, and the Spirit of Southern Music.* Cambridge, MA: Da Capo, 2009.

———. *Johnny Cash at Folsom Prison: The Making of Masterpiece.* Cambridge, MA: Da Capo, 2004.

———. *Johnny Cash: The Biography.* Cambridge, MA: Da Capo, 2006.

———. *Outlaw: Waylon, Willie, Kris, and the Renegades of Nashville.* New York: HarperCollins, 2013.

———, ed. *Ring of Fire: The Johnny Cash Reader.* Cambridge, MA: Da Capo, 2003.

Thomson, Graeme. *The Resurrection of Johnny Cash: Hurt, Redemption, and* American Recordings. London: Jawbone, 2011.

Thurman, Don. *A Historical Review of the Timber Industry in Cleveland County, Arkansas.* Rison, AR: Cleveland County Historical Society, 2004.

Tosches, Nick. *Country: The Twisted Roots of Rock and Roll.* New York: Dell, 1977.

Turner, Steve. *The Man Called Cash: The Life, Love, and Faith of an American Legend.* Nashville, TN: W Publishing Group, 2004.

Urwin, Cathy. *Agenda for Reform: Winthrop Rockefeller as Governor of Arkansas, 1967–1971.* Fayetteville: University of Arkansas Press, 1991.

Ward, John. *Arkansas Rockefeller.* Baton Rouge: Louisiana State University Press, 1978.

Welky, David. *The Thousand-Year Flood: The Ohio-Mississippi Disaster of 1937.* Chicago: University of Chicago Press, 2011.

Whayne, Jeannie. *Delta Empire: Lee Wilson and the Transformation of Agriculture in the New South*. Baton Rouge: Louisiana State University Press, 2011.

Williams, C. Fred, et al. *A Documentary History of Arkansas*. Fayetteville: University of Arkansas Press, 1984.

Woodward, Colin. "'There's a Lot of Things that Need Changin': Johnny Cash, Winthrop Rockefeller, and Prison Reform in Arkansas." *Arkansas Historical Quarterly* 79 (Spring 2020): 40–58.

Wren, Christopher. "The Restless Ballad of Johnny Cash," *Look*, April 29, 1969, 68–75.

———. *Winners Got Scars Too: The Life and Legends of Johnny Cash*. New York: Ballantine, 1971.

Wynne, Ben. *In Tune: Charlie Patton, Jimmie Rodgers and the Roots of American Music*. Baton Rouge: Louisiana State University Press, 2014.

INDEX